THE MOTOWN® STORY

THE MOTOWN® STORY

DON WALLER

CHARLES SCRIBNER'S SONS   **New York**

This book is not an authorized history of the Motown Record Corporation and should not be construed as having their endorsement.

Copyright © 1985 Don Waller

Library of Congress Cataloging in Publication Data

Waller, Don
The Motown story.

Includes index.
1. Sound recording industry—United States.
2. Motown Record Corporation. I. Title.
ML3790.W29   *1985   338.7'6789912455'00977434*   85-2110
ISBN 0-684-18293-9
ISBN 0-684-18347-1 (pbk.)

This book published simultaneously in the
United States of America and in Canada—
Copyright under the Berne Convention.

1 3 5 7 9 11 13 15 17 19 H/C 20 18 16 14 12 10 8 6 4 2

1 3 5 7 9 11 13 15 17 19 H/P 20 18 16 14 12 10 8 6 4 2

Printed in the United States of America.

Packaged by Rapid Transcript, a division of March Tenth, Inc.
Composition by Folio Graphics Co., Inc.
Designed by Chic Ago

To
Papa Zita
and
Igor

CREDITS

Researched and written	November 1982–November 1984, Los Angeles
Edited	Michael Pietsch, Charles Scribner's Sons, New York, 1984
Guest vocalists	Billie Jean Brown, Esq. (Chapter 4); Melvin Franklin of the Temptations (Chapter 6); Lamont Dozier (Chapter 8); and Earl Van Dyke (Chapter 9)
Photography	Billie Jean Brown, Esq.; Tom DePierro/ Airwave International; Michael Ochs Archives; James Kriegsman, Sr.; Chuck Krall; Gary Leonard; Earl Van Dyke; and the Cultural Warehouse
Special thanks	to my wife, Barbara, for her patience; to my parents, Roy and Kitty, and my brother, Jim, just because . . .
V.S.O.P. thanks	to Ken Barnes and Richard Cromelin, two of the best editors a friend could have; to Doug Moody, for most of the information in Chapter 2; to Tom DePierro, for much of the Discography; and to Diana Price, "Agent Double-O-Soul" herself, for the belief
Tea and sympathy	Roger Zumwalt, Jay Allen, Irving S. Feffer, Esq., Jeff Gold, Gary Stewart, Steve Propes, Gail Mitchell, Mark Shipper, Thom Gardner, Phast Phreddie, Marcia Berger, Richard Agata, Sean Ross, Brendan Mullen, Mike Dowd, Laura Stewart, Joel Whitburn, Georginna Challis, Don Snowden, George and Moira Waddell, Gladys Knight and the Pips, Nick Ashford and Valerie Simpson, Junior Walker, and George Clinton
Book production	Rapid Transcript

Contents

Chapter One
FUNCTION AT THE JUNCTION   11

Chapter Two
MONEY   24

Chapter Three
HITSVILLE, U.S.A.   43

Chapter Four
REFLECTIONS   59

Chapter Five
THE MOTORTOWN REVUE   70

Chapter Six
MEET THE TEMPTATIONS   105

Chapter Seven
I SECOND THAT EMOTION   124

Chapter Eight
THE SOUND OF YOUNG AMERICA   136

Chapter Nine
THE FUNK BROTHERS   154

Chapter Ten
DON'T LEAVE ME THIS WAY   168

DISCOGRAPHY   204

ANSWERS TO TRIVIA QUESTIONS   249

INDEX   251

Chapter One

FUNCTION AT THE JUNCTION

Blam blam-blam splash
Doot-doot-doot-WOW!
Say yeah yeah yeah
Say yeah yeah yeah

Any Motown story should have a great intro. All the best Motown records do. If you're any kind of pop music fan—or if you have a real feel for nonsense—you probably recognized the above-quoted gibberish as the opening bars to Marvin Gaye's 1962 butt-kicker "Stubborn Kind of Fellow." If so, you probably also know that The Motown Story goes something like this:

In 1959 Berry Gordy, Jr., borrowed $800 from his family's savings account to make a master recording. By 1961 Gordy had scored his first million-seller on his own (Tamla) label, the Miracles' "Shop Around." By the end of the decade Gordy's Detroit-based company had racked up twenty-two number one pop hits, forty-eight number one R&B hits, and was the largest black-owned business in America.

"Hitsville, U.S.A.," read the sign on the two-story frame house at 2648 West Grand Boulevard, in Detroit, and, for once, the slogan wasn't far from fact. At its peak, in 1966, an astonishing *75 percent* of the company's releases made the charts. The industry average was, and is, about 10 percent.

Gordy moved his empire from Detroit to Los Angeles in 1972 and spent much of the past decade involved in various film projects, notably *Lady Sings the Blues*, for which ex-Supreme Diana Ross earned a Best Actress Academy Award nomination. The record label, meanwhile, weathered the

changes in the marketplace by virtue of its superstar talent roster (Ross, former Miracles mainman Smokey Robinson, Stevie Wonder, Marvin Gaye, and the Jackson 5) and its incomparable catalog of sixties classics.

Every time you hear a Motown song played on the radio or every time, say, Linda Ronstadt rerecords an old Martha and the Vandellas tune, Motown is getting its (literal) two cents' worth through its music publishing arm, Jobete. Think about it.

Though no longer the hit factory that it was in the mid-sixties, Motown is still in business, still getting its fair share of hits. While Motown recently signed a distribution agreement with MCA, it remains one of the few major independent labels left in the States. (A&M and Arista are the other major independents. Both are distributed by RCA. All other U.S. labels of note are handled through the Big Six distributors: MCA, RCA, PolyGram, CBS, WEA, and Capitol-EMI, all of which are part of even larger conglomerates.)

Today, Motown's artist roster ranges from the mainstream pop balladry of Lionel Richie to the glitzy, bad-boy funk of Rick James. Smokey and especially Stevie are solid sellers, and with an occasional left-field smash such as the Dazz Band's "Let It Whip" (1982), not to mention that Jobete catalog, the label will easily survive another twenty-five years.

That, in the proverbial nutshell, is The Motown Story. So WHY ARE YOU READING THIS? I mean, I'd rather *listen* to music than read about it. Remember way back on page one? "Stubborn Kind of Fellow"? There's no way that reading a bunch of nonsense syllables can give you the simultaneous feeling of tension and exhilaration you get from listening to those ten seconds of music. Which is why the majority of limp-noodled English majors masquerading as rock writers focus on such sophomoric matters as lyrics or hairstyles.

Let's try this academic approach to Junior Walker, an *auteur* if there ever was one, and his *magnum opus* from 1965, "Shotgun." Notebooks ready? (*Shotgun blast. A tenor sax screeches.*)

> *I said, "Shotgun!!!"*
> *Shoot him 'fore he runs now*
> *Do the Jerk, baby . . .*

Even someone as hopelessly square as a TV preacher knows what's missing. It's the beat, the Beat, the BEAT! That's what rock 'n' roll, rhythm 'n' blues, soul, funk, Motown, and any other pop music that's worth more than the quarter it takes to zone out on a video game has always had going for it. It's the heartbeat, the very pulse of life itself, the old in-out, in-out, as little Alex so fondly put it.

Don't get me wrong. A song filled with clever turns of phrases—say, Smokey Robinson's composition for the Marvelettes, "The Hunter Gets Captured by the Game" (1967)—is infinitely preferable to one saddled with shopworn or stupid lyrics, but a brilliantly constructed melody line and a sharp hook can elevate the most common expression into greatness. Consider the Four Tops' 1966 chartbuster, "Reach out, I'll Be There." What makes this song great?

1. It has a melodic, propulsive bass line playing off a drummer who sounds like he's imitating a can press.

2. Lead vocalist Levi Stubbs sings another instantly memorable melody as if he's about to burst into flames at any moment.

3. The production is flawless, from the flutes that introduce a third melody (which reappear on the choruses) and the exotic percussion that adds a third rhythmic dimension, to the highest-of-highs and lowest-of-lows mix and the wailing harmonies that seem to echo from the cold distance of the Void itself.

4. About two-thirds of the way through, Levi Stubbs yells, "Just look over your *shoulder*!" and in that split second of total abandon, the whole Eddie Holland–Lamont Dozier–Brian Holland construction crystallizes and explodes. H-bomb. Wipeout. All she wrote.

That's what you remember and *that's* what makes "Reach Out, I'll Be There" a great record. Motown only cut a couple hundred of 'em.

At least that's how I hear it. Truthfully, a song either makes you feel something or it doesn't, and what's mesmerizing to one is monotonous to another. Now, I could sling adjectives all night, raving about the shimmering guitar line running through the Spinners' "It's a Shame" (1970) or the crazed drumming that powers Stevie Wonder's "Uptight" (1966), but if you've never heard those particular records, it's doubtful you'd believe me.

So don't just sit there. Get up. Go over to your turntable or tape deck and throw on one of your favorite Motor City mamajamas. And if by some wild chance you don't own any Motown records, that's no excuse. You can walk into the lamest record store in Snake's Navel, Kansas, and pick up a copy of the Supremes' *Greatest Hits, Volumes 1–2*.

As a matter of fact, if you're looking for classic Motown tracks, you can choose from any one of 10 double- or triple-

1. Who was the female member of the Miracles?
2. What is Stevie Wonder's real name?
3. Which Motown recording group has been together for thirty years without a personnel change?

album anthologies, 18 more LPs in the "Superstars" series, 26 individual greatest hits albums, a five-record "Motown Story" boxed set, 4 more various artists' compilation LPs, and 208 double-sided hit singles. All of which are currently (February 1985) in print.

The simple availability of these records is proof of Motown's pervasive influence. They sold 'em by the millions then and they're still selling 'em today. And it's not some camp interest, fueled by the latest generation of bohemians ravaging the thrift stores for the flotsam and jetsam of consumerism twenty years past. Hell, no. Motown stays right there in your face.

Not a week goes by you don't hear at least one vintage Motown masterpiece on the radio. Not to mention the recent remakes. The first time I typed this sentence (January 1983), Phil Collins' version of the Supremes' 1966 hit "You Can't Hurry Love" was racing up the charts, followed by Luther Vandross doing the Temptations' 1965 smoothie, "Since I Lost My Baby," and somebody named Wolf's Vocoder-workout on "Papa Was a Rolling Stone," a chart-topper for the Temptations back in 1972.

Prominent Motown covers of 1982 included Sister Sledge's "My Guy" (Mary Wells, 1964), the Rolling Stones' "Going to a Go-Go" (the Miracles, 1966), A Taste of Honey's "I'll Try Something New" (the Miracles, 1962), Carl Carlton's "Baby I Need Your Loving" (the Four Tops, 1964), and Van Halen's "Dancing in the Street" (Martha and the Vandellas, 1964). Then there was Bananarama's "He Was Really Sayin' Somethin' " (the Velvelettes, 1965), the Jam's "War" (Edwin Starr, 1970), and Tina Turner/B.E.F.'s "Ball of Confusion" (the Temptations, 1970). Enough said.

Not only the songs but the stars of Motown are still around. Switching labels to Columbia, Marvin Gaye came out of exile in 1982 with "Sexual Healing," his biggest hit since 1977's "Got to Give It Up." Diana Ross left Motown for RCA in 1981. Her string of Top 10 hits, which goes back to Bernard Edwards and Nile Rodgers' tongue-in-Chic 1980 productions "Upside Down" and "I'm Coming Out," continues.

Then there's the Jacksons (5), who severed ties with Motown in 1975. The group hasn't looked back since. Especially Michael Jackson, whose solo career skyrocketed with the meteoric success of 1979's quadruple-platinum *Off the Wall* LP. His 1982 follow-up, *Thriller*, has done slightly better: 35 million copies sold.

Several peripheral Motown acts are also now chart perennials. The Isley Brothers had already enjoyed a pair of monster hits with "Shout" (RCA, 1959) and "Twist and Shout"

(Wand, 1962) when they linked up with Motown for their 1966 blockbuster, "This Old Heart of Mine." Two years later the group was gone, surfacing again in 1969 with "It's Your Thing" on their own label, T-Neck. They've averaged about a hit a year since.

Nick Ashford and Valerie Simpson were among Motown's top songwriting and production teams, responsible for such sophisticated soul classics as "Ain't Nothing Like the Real Thing" (Marvin Gaye and Tammi Terrell, 1968) and "Ain't No Mountain High Enough," the latter a hit for Marvin and Tammi in 1967 and again for Diana Ross in 1970, when they decided to become a performing unit. Ashford and Simpson jumped to Warner Bros. in 1973. Within five years the duo's discs were a cinch to make the R&B Top 10. They now record for Capitol, where they've been equally successful to date.

Meanwhile, back at Motown, the Temptations returned from artistic limbo with an assist from Rick James, who fashioned "Standing on the Top," the group's first major hit in seven years. Smokey Robinson checked in with his latest in a recent string of hits ("Tell Me Tomorrow"), and onetime child prodigy Stevie Wonder knocked out his usual pair of smashes ("That Girl" and "Do I Do").

Finally, the *style* created by the singers, songwriters, producers, and musicians of Motown has been a constant source of inspiration to two decades' worth of musicians, black and white. Stevie Wonder, of course, is the prime mover. Wonder's percussive keyboards, rich textures, and penchant for synthesized bass lines have been swallowed up whole. Records such as Yarbrough and Peoples' "Don't Stop the Music" (1981), Junior's "Mama Used to Say" (1982), the Culture Club's "Church of the Poison Mind" (1983)—a direct lift of "Uptight"—and Chaka Khan's "I Feel for You" (1984)—a record that features snippets of "Fingertips, Pt. 2"—are only the most obvious examples of Stevie's enormous influence.

Wait a minute. Recapping all this recent history is bringing us closer to Dullsville than Hitsville. The most important thing about Motown is that people still care about its music. And it's not just knee-deep.

It's Miami Steve Van Zandt, former guitarist for Bruce Springsteen and the E Street Band and leader of Little Steven and the Disciples of Soul, sitting up nights, playing Miracles albums 'til the grooves turn gray, just to get Marv Tarplin's guitar parts *right*.

It's ABC, a young British group with all of four U.K. hits under their collective belts, going on in interviews about how they aspire to be the next Holland-Dozier-Holland rather than the next Beatles.

4. When they first signed with Motown, how many members did the Supremes number?

5. Motown's music publishing company, Jobete, is world-famous. How did Berry Gordy come up with the name?

6. What was the first Motown record with the now-famous map on the label?

It's Kool and the Gang lead vocalist James Taylor's self-compliment on his falsetto skills—"Just like Marvin [Gaye]," he says—during the fade of 1981's "Take My Heart."

It's all this and more. It's also the reason I'm writing this book. This isn't just the black version of the old Horatio Alger myth. If Berry Gordy had made his millions manufacturing hair-straightening products, how many people would want to know about it?

As proof that old folkies are good for something, I shall now quote from the works of that esteemed philosopher John Sebastian: "The magic's in the music and the music's in me" ("Do You Believe in Magic," 1965).

That's right. The magic's in the music and that's what this book is all about—the magic of Motown.

The point is, this book is not a dull slab of freeze-dried nostalgia. Sure, the sixties were Motown's finest hour, and I love that music. I also go aper than ape over Wilson Pickett, Otis Redding, Sam and Dave and the southern soul sounds of Stax-Volt, and whenever I hear a fabulous soul one-shot like the Ideals' "You Lost and I Won" (Satellite, 1965) or Roger Collins' "She's Looking Good" (Galaxy, 1966) or McKinley Mitchell's "The Town I Live In" (One-der-ful, 1962), I break out—in a *coooold* sweat.

Soul music might be almost my favorite, but I don't spend all my waking hours listening to it. I'd rather be diggin' the latest Roxy Music or X or Prince or Blasters LPs. The Small Faces mean as much to me as the Talking Heads do, as do the Fleshtones, as does Little Junior Parker, who—if he were alive—would probably be wondering what his picture sleeve for "Driving Wheel" is doing next to the one for the Raspberries' "Let's Pretend" on my living room wall.

I'll never understand what people think was so wonderful about the sixties. Black people rode at the back of the bus, a single reefer could get you ten years in the slammer, women had to travel to Tijuana or Sweden for abortions, and oral sex with your spouse was against the law. Myself, I'd rather live in the present tense.

This isn't a book on black history, either. By Berry Gordy's own calculations, when a Motown record sold a million, an estimated 70 percent of those copies were bought by whites. Motown is pop music, because it was *popular*, and as such, belongs to anyone who wants it.

One more thing. I'm not here to dish the dirt. If you want to know about A, B, C, and Mr. X and Y, then come to Los Angeles and start hanging out at Martoni's with all the national promotion directors, who, of course, know all about those kinds of things. You'd have to build a Hilton to house *all* the Motown rumors.

The true facts are these: The Annual Upper Midwest Convention of Feed Grain Salesmen parties harder than the record business, which—despite the aura of glamour with which it likes to surround itself—is a business just like any other. Sales managers drink too much and stick too many white powders up their noses; secretaries sleep with their bosses; accountants and lawyers steal the company blind; and when something goes right, everybody takes the credit for it. Sound like any place you've ever worked?

Knowing that anyone is capable of anything, I figure that people's personal lives have less to do with their music than is often imagined, which, as I keep repeating, double-beating, is what we're concerned with here.

I'm also assuming you already know something about Motown, even if it's only a passing familiarity with the hits. That's cool, because getting hit records *is* what The Motown Story is all about.

Plus, everybody knows the hits, so when I describe the marvelous way Contours lead singer Billy Gordon's voice *s t r e t c h e s   t h e   n o t e s   o u t* on their 1962 brain eraser "Do You Love Me," you know exactly what I'm talking about. That way, when we venture into the uncharted realm of Motown obscurities, you can decide for yourself if I'm jivin' or jammin'.

But I know you aren't reading this just to scope my verbal pyrotechnics, gratuitous scatology, sarcasm, insults, high-school flashbacks, and occasional flights of pure fantasy on a pile of records you've probably played 5,283 times by now. No, you want to know something *more*.

Most people want to know about the stars, the ones who sang their favorite songs (but with a different meaning since you've been gone). Others want to know about the songwriters and producers; the events surrounding a certain recording session or those that inspired a particular tune.

A few of you want to know something about those unsung heroes, Motown's house band, and given that the *real* magic in Motown's music often takes place in that tiny space between the beat and the accent the drummer *actually played*, wouldn't you say those cats down in Studio A were equally responsible for the company's success? What time is it?

Time to turn over that Supremes album you bought several pages back and turn this mother out. I don't know how much you'll learn from reading this, but if you like to play games, there are one hundred Motown trivia questions scattered

throughout the margins of this book. The answers can all be found somewhere in the text (and on page 249). Have fun.

Because having fun, getting loose and fulla vital juices, being willing to make a fool of yourself, is what rock, soul, pop, and Motown—call it what you will, you cannot enslave a fool—are all about. If reading this book doesn't make you want to throw the sucker across the room, dash over to your box, and start dancing to your Motown records, then remind me not to invite you to the Function at the Junction.

Now dig who's gonna be there: Long Ding Dong from Burma, Be-Bop A-Lula from *terra firma,* Agent Double-O-Soul, Diana Price, and she's bringin' all the ice from "Miami Vice." And we're gonna have *food.* Double chiliburgers and *cordon bleu,* pepperoni pizza and greazy snoots. And what're we gonna do? We gonna tear it up, burn it down, we goin' 'round 'n' 'round, down at the Function at the Junction.

Yeah, I know these aren't the real words, but that's OK, 'cause you know who else is gonna make it? All the bad muthas, monkey-huggers, major dudes in party moods, foxy chicks with foxy eyes (in mini-skirts up to their thighs), Doctor John and Jolé Blon, Mr. Jones, Daddy Rollin' Stone, Sam the Sham from Birmingham and Hollywood Fats from Where It's At. Heart-stoppin', silk-stocking pleasers, all. I mean some finger-poppin', future-shockin' seizures, y'all. AND YOU'RE GONNA MISS IT!

You're gonna miss it because *the only way you're going to get anything worthwhile out of this book is by playing a stack of your favorite Motown wax while you read it.* Hey, I haven't been listening to these records for six solid months without learning something from 'em. Namely, find a hook and wear it out.

If the feeling you get from those grooves isn't proof positive that Motown cut some of the best pop records ever, textbook examples really, then you've probably frosted your last mirror.

So how did they do it?

Well, as my stockbroker neighbor keeps telling me, "The scenery only changes for the lead dog." Too zen for you? Try this:

MOTOWN MAGIC MOMENT #1

Standing before his key songwriters, producers, and executives at the company's weekly music meeting, Berry Gordy asks, "Would you buy this record for a dollar or would you buy a sandwich?"

Born in Detroit on November 28, 1929, Berry Gordy, Jr., claimed to have learned about business "through osmosis." His parents had migrated to the Motor City from Milledgeville, Georgia, seven years earlier. They were not auto assembly-line workers. Berry Gordy, Sr.—whom we'll refer to by his later nickname, "Pops"—was a plastering contractor. His wife, Bertha, was a combination real estate and insurance agent. With the help of their eight children, four boys (Robert, George, Fuller, and Berry, Jr.) and four girls (Esther, Loucye, Anna, and Gwen), they also ran a neighborhood grocery store and a print shop, living in a flat above the family businesses.

Prior to founding Motown, Berry Gordy had been a professional featherweight boxer, fighting four- and six-round preliminary bouts for $150 purses. He decided to quit the fight game about the time the Army drafted him in 1951. An eleventh-grade high-school dropout who passed his equivalency exam during his stint with Uncle Sam, Gordy came out of the service in 1953 with plans to open a record store.

By 1955 his 3-D Record Mart had gone under, and Gordy found himself working as a trimmer on a Ford assembly line. He nailed down upholstery, fastened knobs on dashboards, and attached chrome strips to the outside of cars. Sixty-four cars an hour, eight hours a day, five days a week. Take-home pay: $79.88.

Gordy had married Thelma Coleman shortly after his discharge. By 1956 the couple had three children (Hazel Joy, Berry Gordy IV, and Terry) and Thelma had filed for a divorce. For a man with a wife and three toddlers, eighty bucks a week clearly wasn't enough. Gordy quit his job at Ford in 1957 and began to concentrate on songwriting, cutting a demo with an old buddy from his boxing days, Jackie Wilson.

The song, "Reet Petite," cowritten by Berry Gordy and local musician Tyran Carlo, was a mid-sized hit for Brunswick Records that year. It lauched Wilson's solo career and marked Berry Gordy's entry into the record business, netting him $1,000 for his efforts. (Tyran Carlo, by the way, is a pseudonym for writer-producer Billy—sometimes known as Roquel—Davis. Our paths will cross again.)

Over the next two years Berry Gordy would cowrite several more hits for Wilson, including the magnificent "Lonely Teardrops" (Brunswick, 1958). Unhappy with the way his songs were being recorded, Gordy decided to produce them himself and got successful all over again. Marv Johnson's "You Got What It Takes" (United Artists, 1960) was Gordy's first production to crack the pop Top 10. (We'll go into these early days in greater detail in the next chapter.)

7. What is the only Motown song to hit number one on the *Billboard* pop charts twice, the second time by a non-Motown artist?

8. Which Motown artist recorded the original version of "Devil with the Blue Dress On?"

9. The Temptations once recorded a single for Motown under what false name?

In addition to his extraordinary business sense, Gordy had developed into a songwriter and producer to be reckoned with. If you have talent yourself, it's not hard to spot it in others, which explains how Gordy was able to assemble the finest group of staff songwriters and producers this side of the Brill Building: Smokey Robinson, Holland-Dozier-Holland, Norman Whitfield and Barrett Strong, Mickey Stevenson and Ivy Jo Hunter, Johnny Bristol and Harvey Fuqua, and a host of others, some of whom never saw a single one of their records released.

Gordy was demanding; he rejected the first one hundred songs Smokey Robinson wrote. The woman who coauthored "You've Made Me So Very Happy," a midchart success for her in 1967 and a huge hit for Blood, Sweat and Tears two years later, elaborates on Gordy's songwriting philosophy:

MOTOWN
MAGIC
MOMENT #2

"Berry told us, 'Write a song like it's happening right then, so people who are listening can associate with it.' "
—BRENDA HOLLOWAY

Along the way, Gordy discovered another bedrock 'n' roll truth. No matter how good the lyric or the arrangement, a record doesn't have a snowball's chance in hell if the singer stinks up the room. Once Motown had a rhythm track recorded, artist after artist would be called in to take a shot at it, each knowing that only one version would be released as a single. The others would wind up as album cuts, maybe. Was competition tough? Is the Pope Polish?

Getting the picture? Motown had the *singers*, the *songs*, the *producers*, and the *musicians*, the last of whom Gordy signed to long-term contracts that made them salaried employees and prevented them from recording for any other company. It was these four elements, coupled with Berry Gordy's drive, foresight, ability to motivate people, and his unholy passion for quality control, that made Motown.

But that's not The Motown Story. For one thing, none of this happened in a vacuum. Timing had a lot to do with it. For instance, at the same time "Reet Petite" was moving up the 1957 charts, Arkansas Governor Orville Faubus was ordering the State National Guard to block black students from entering Central High School in Little Rock. Suddenly, Gordy's decision to keep Mary Wells' and the Marvelettes' photographs off their early sixties album covers so that white southern record store owners would be more willing to stock the records, seems more shrewd than paranoid.

You got what it takes. A portrait of the artist as a young executive: Berry Gordy.

10. What Motown artist scored her first hit on her first record with a song she had written for Jackie Wilson?

11. What famous comedian recorded for Motown as a member of Bobby Taylor and the Vancouvers?

12. Which Motown artist cowrote and recorded the original version of the 1969 Blood, Sweat and Tears hit "You've Made Me So Very Happy"?

Similarly, I don't think it's entirely coincidence that 1964, the year the Federal Civil Rights Act was passed and Sidney Poitier became the first black actor to win an Academy Award, was the year the Supremes began a string of *five* consecutive number one pop hits.

I could be wrong. But I'm not. Without the accompanying change in race relations, Motown would have had a much tougher time getting white program directors to play its records.

At any rate, 1964 is an unusual year. The music trade magazine *Billboard* (whose weekly best-seller lists serve as the basis for all the chart positions quoted in this book) published no R&B charts that year. Some say that there wasn't enough difference between what white kids and black kids were buying to make the distinction. That may be, but if so, out of the twenty-three records to reach the coveted number one position that year, how come only five of these were by black artists? (Incidentally, Motown scored three of them: Mary Wells' "My Guy" and the Supremes' "Baby Love" and "Where Did Our Love Go." The others were the Dixie Cups' "Chapel of Love" and—believe it or not, *I* sure don't—Louis Armstrong's "Hello Dolly.")

Motown's success must be examined in the light of the revolution within the record industry as well. The Beatlemania of 1964 sent sales figures through the ceiling, and the disc business started a fifteen-year growth period that continued until 1978, when a sagging economy and the policies of the past finally caught up with it. Meanwhile, a concurrent technological revolution led to the twenty-four-track recording studio, the rise of FM stereo radio, the Moog synthesizer, and (even earlier) the electric bass, to name but a few developments.

Black music went through its own peculiar changes. Once the white audience embraced R&B, the black music of the fifties, in the form of white cover versions, the black audience's response was to create something they could call their own. So R&B gave way to the more rhythmically adventurous soul, which itself later became funk.

Even more important, once black artists saw white acts fighting for (and getting) greater artistic freedom, they demanded the same privileges. Finally, as the white-owned major labels realized the sales potential in black music, they established their own Black Music Departments, now staffed and run by black execs.

These last two developments cannot be underestimated when it comes to explaining Motown's declining share of the market through the seventies and into the eighties. The Motown phenomenon was as much a product of the times as were the company's records. Which brings us right back to where we began this tale.

That's okay, The Motown Story is a series of concentric circles, like the grooves on a 45 spinning 'round and 'round. In motion they're invisible; playing the record is the only way to bring those stories to life. Either way, the only thing you can read is the label.

And—as Jackie Wilson once sang—*that's why* this book is constructed like a classic Motown single. Think of the raw facts as the rhythm track, the interviews as the background vocalists, the anecdotes (those Motown Magic Moments) as the horn parts, and the trivia questions as the strings, added for sweetening.

The pictures, of course, speak a thousand words each, which makes them the lead vocalists, and the element of total abandon belongs to that Stubborn Kinda Fella—me—and everybody else down at the Function at the Junction, so you better come on, right now. . . .

Chapter Two
MONEY

> "I always figured I was ultra-hip as a kid, you know, let's listen to some jazz. I didn't know what R&B was until I started in the record shop. But when I started writing tunes, I found out I didn't really feel the jazz. My feeling was what I'd heard in church and the beats. Whenever I found myself playing, I really had the funky beat."
> —**BERRY GORDY,** *Detroit Free Press*, 1969

The Motown Story begins in 1957, when Berry Gordy coauthors his first hit (Jackie Wilson's "Reet Petite") and immediately decides to start producing records himself. Gordy's first production effort, which he also wrote, was the Five Stars' "Ooh Shucks," issued on George Goldner's Mark-X label later that year.

You say you've never heard of, let alone heard, this record? Neither did too many people back in 1957, when you could've bought a copy for ninety-eight cents. Today, it'd cost you fifteen bucks.

I'm not making this up. Truth is always stranger than fiction, especially in the world of record collecting, where a mint-condition, original copy of "Ooh Shucks" is considered very rare. So are a lot of the other discs mentioned in this chapter. That doesn't necessarily mean they're good records, although some of them are as sharp as the crease in a pimp's slacks.

"Ooh Shucks" is quite forgettable but of historical interest mostly because of Gordy's involvement and because the Five Stars' lineup includes Walter Gaines and C. P. Spencer, founding members of the late sixties Motown recording group the Originals.

At a Detroit talent show in 1958 Gordy discovers the Miracles, then consisting of Claudette Rogers, Ronnie White,

COURTESY MICHAEL OCHS ARCHIVES

Warren "Pete" Moore, Bobby Rogers, and William "Smokey" Robinson. The quintet is young and "from the suave part of the slums," as leader Smokey, who already loves a contradiction, will later recall, and the Miracles' white-chocolate sound, as sweet as it is soulful, reflects these qualities perfectly. No wonder Gordy got excited.

The doo-wop sound—so named for its practice of reducing background vocal lines to utter nonsense—is hotter than a two-dollar pistol, and the Silhouettes' "Get a Job," a true rocking Tower of Babble and rolling boil of social comment, is the number one record in the country. Gordy and the Miracles waste little time cutting an answer record—"Got a Job," released on another of New Yorker George Goldner's independent labels, End. The Miracles' first recording gets a few spins and dies a quick death.

A few months later the Miracles will issue a second record on End, the hideously rare "I Cry." Both of these early tracks are noteworthy for their (relatively) clean sound, obvious attention to detail, and Smokey's unmistakable falsetto. This

You really got a hold on me. The former Claudette Rogers (left) and William "Smokey" Robinson (second from right) had been high-school sweethearts, but when Mrs. Smokey Robinson decided motherhood and membership in the Miracles didn't mix, hubby and the rest of the group—(from left) Ronnie White, Warren "Pete" Moore, and Bobby Rogers—continued as a quartet.

wasn't some idiot bastard son of Sammy Glick rounding up five *shwartzes* off the nearest street corner and trying to ensure a hit by putting "teenage" somewhere in the title.

However, "Everyone Was There," sung by Berry's brother Robert Gordy under the pseudonym Robert Kayli and a good-sized pop hit for New York indy Carlton Records in 1958, sounds almost that bad. The only thing this record proves is that Berry Gordy spent a lot of time studying the charts—his lyrics are little more than a collection of then-popular song titles, which seems prophetic in that Robert Gordy will go on to greater things as Jobete's publishing director. (In 1961, still using the fake name, he'll also become the first member of the Gordy family to record as a Motown solo artist with "Small Sad Sam," issued on Tamla as an answer to Jimmy Dean's chart-topping novelty "Big Bad John.")

During 1958 Berry Gordy will cowrite two more hits for Jackie Wilson: "To Be Loved" and the fabulous "Lonely Teardrops," the latter Gordy's first R&B number one and his first tune to go Top 10 on the pop charts. Along the way Gordy

Workout, Stevie, workout. Little Stevie Wonder (left) and late R&B great Jackie Wilson provide music to aerobicize by.

uncovers his second major songwriting talent, Eddie Holland, who at the time is more concerned with a singing career.

Listening to Eddie's first recording, a Berry Gordy production entitled "You," it's not hard to hear what attracted Gordy to Holland—namely, his "Is-it-Jackie-Wilson-or-is-it-Memorex?" vocal style. Actually, this particular track owes as much to Platters lead singer Tony Williams as it does to Jackie, which no doubt explains why Chicago-based major Mercury Records, which then had the Platters under contract, was inspired to issue the disc in the first place.

The single's B-side, "Little Miss Ruby," is more mysterious. It's a cornpone-flavored number credited on the label as having been "taken from the film soundtrack *Country Music Holiday.*" Efforts to locate the soundtrack LP or even anyone who remembers having seen the film have so far proved about as successful as the Moody Blues' search for the Lost Chord.

Meanwhile, back in Detroit, Kudo Records, a small, mostly gospel label, will issue four more Gordy 1958 productions. Two are of significance: Marv Johnson's first recording, "My Baby-O," and Brian Holland's (Eddie's brother) only known solo vocal performance, "Shock."

Marv Johnson had been Berry Gordy's partner in the ill-fated 3-D Record Mart. He, too, appears to have been bitten by the Jackie Wilson bug and "My Baby-O" sounds like "Lonely Teardrops" sideways, right down to the percussive, vaguely Latinized groove.

Brian Holland's disc is bluesy, with a nifty "You give me *shock!*" intro, but his vocal control is shaky. It's a great record to own, although not necessarily to listen to.

Berry Gordy's other pair of Kudo releases was "Cry Baby Heart," a pure pop number, cowritten by Berry and Janie Bradford and sung by the dubiously talented Nancy Peters, and a rough version of the Falcon's "This Heart of Mine," which this Detroit group would later record in a more polished format on Berry's sister Gwen Gordy's independent Anna label. Gwen and Billy (Roquel) Davis, aka Tyran Carlo, also briefly ran Check-Mate Records, a Detroit-based subsidiary of the Chicago independent R&B giant Chess Records.

Anna Records was established in 1958, surviving until 1961, when Gordy began his first round of buying up the local competition. At least one of Anna's 1958 releases is vital to the development of The Motown Story. "Hope and Pray" b/w "Oops, I'm Sorry" by the Voice Masters not only features the vocal stylings of Originals-to-be Walter Gaines, C. P. Spencer, and lead singer Ty Hunter, but a later edition of the group would include Lamont Dozier *and*—making his first vinyl appearance—Mr. David Ruffin, a future Temptation. These

13. Which Motown artist produced a pair of hits for Motown recording group the Originals?
14. Which Motown recording group did Richard Street leave to join the Temptations?
15. What was the name of Motown's first white recording group?

Voice Masters' sides are something less than the sum of the talent involved; evidently no one remembered to bring anything resembling an original song to the session.

Nevertheless, four years down the road, Lamont Dozier will join forces with the Holland brothers. The partnership will become the most successful songwriting team in history, writing more number one hits than any other nonperforming songwriters. Lamont also swears it's Eddie singing on "Shock," using his brother's name to beat a contract. *Hmm* . . . .

The Anna label was then distributed by George Goldner, whom Berry Gordy linked up with for another 1958 production, Malcom Dodds and Tunedrops' "Can't You See (I'm in Love with You)," issued on End. Gordy cowrote the number with sister Gwen, who, with Tyran Carlo, made up the brain trust that was responsible for most of the Jackie Wilson hits. 'Nuff said about *that* one.

The next wave in Motown's development comes from a combination boutique–beauty parlor–candy store known as the House of Beauty. It's a popular women's hangout; Raynoma Liles, whom Berry Gordy will marry next year once his divorce from Thelma becomes final, gets her hair done there. All of a sudden, the store's owner, Carla Murphy, wants to front the money for a record label, to be called (naturally, although natural hairstyles won't be hip for another nine years) H.O.B. Records.

The initial H.O.B. release, Herman Griffin's "I Need You," 1958, is something of a milestone. It's the first disc to give label credit to the Rayber Voices, a loose-knit collection of background singers named after Raynoma and Berry. It's also the *very first* song to be published by Gordy's new music publishing company—Jobete—which he's named after his three children: Hazel *Jo*y, *Be*rry IV, and *Te*rry.

"I Need You" is also a pretty funky record, one whose gospel roots are showing. Bass-heavy, with an organ lurking somewhere in the murk, it could pass for a Falcons track, minus the harsh lead.

Vocalist Herman Griffin provides his own footnote. He not only recorded as a solo artist for both Motown and Tamla in the early sixties but also married Mary Wells and reportedly persuaded her to exit Motown for 20th Century-Fox Records when Wells turned twenty-one.

Berry Gordy's interest in H.O.B. was scarcely permanent, ending after this one release. H.O.B. Records, however, continued as part of local singer-entrepreneur Mike Hanks' family of labels (D-Town, Wheelsville, and MRC, among others).

Perhaps if Carla Murphy had been a better businesswoman, you might be reading The H.O.B. Story. She certainly had the cash flow needed to fund such a venture. A more likely explanation for Gordy's change of heart would be that Berry Gordy knew he needed, shall we say, *complete control* of his operation. In 1959 he would finally get it.

Right now, I imagine a third of the people reading this chapter have had it up to their hat racks with labels and artists and all these records no one's ever heard of. Another third are screaming, "This is *in*-credible stuff. I wanna *hear* these records!" The rest of you are probably mumbling something about what all this means. Sure, we can trace these people's names and everything, but . . .

But my ass. It means there was an awful lot of raw talent in Detroit, which at the time had the fourth largest black population of any American city, trailing (in order) New York, Chicago, and Philadelphia, yet had no major recording company to exploit this situation.

It means that Berry Gordy had the best ears since Dumbo; he was associated with three of his chief lieutenants— Smokey Robinson and the Holland brothers—almost from day one. And that he spent a fair amount of time learning his trade. (My definition of an overnight success is someone you wouldn't want to eat breakfast with the next morning.) Not only as a songwriter and producer but as a hustler, Jack. How many records has he been on? How many deals has he cut? And all that you've just heard happened in slightly over *one year.*

It also means that Gordy was paying close attention to everything on the charts: doo-wop records, pop records, answer records, gimmicks-a-go-go. And every trend bubbling under as well: especially uptown R&B (what producers got when they set a gospel-style vocalist against an orchestra) and its traveling companion, the pure gospel, rib tips 'n' grits movement, which will soon transform R&B into soul.

So with his heart in the charts and his feet on the street, Berry Gordy founds Tamla Records in January 1959. Gordy originally wants to call it Tammie Records, after the then-popular Debbie Reynolds film of that title, but the name has already been taken. Tamla is located at 1719 Gladstone Street, Detroit 6—the address is printed on the label—and the first release is Marv Johnson's "Come to Me" (Tamla 101).

"Come to Me" sounds like another page from the Jackie Wilson songbook with the flute from Bobby Day's 1958 ornithology-rock classic, "Rockin' Robin," thrown in for good luck. The master is swiftly sold to New York–based United

Come to me. Formerly Berry Gordy's partner in the 3-D Record Mart, Marv Johnson made the very first record issued on the Tamla label.

COURTESY TOM DEPIERRO/AIRWAVE INTERNATIONAL

Artists Records, which presses the tune on its own label, distributes it, promotes it, and picks up a mid-sized hit. UA also picks up Marv Johnson's services as a recording artist.

Eddie Holland's "Merry Go Round" is the second Tamla release (Tamla 102). It, too, is sold to UA, where despite an almost-clever lyric, the record bombs. This doesn't stop UA from inking Holland to an exclusive recording contract; however, they don't bother signing him to a similar songwriting agreement. Holland will cut another three or four undistinguished discs from UA before returning to Motown in late '61.

Although it wasn't issued on Tamla, Gordy placed a third record with UA in 1959; Wyatt "Big Boy" Sheppard's "Need Your Lovin', Part 4." Published by Jobete and written and produced by Berry and Anna Gordy, the song is simply a thinly disguised runaround on Larry Williams' 1957 anorexia-rock classic, "Bony Moronie." Next victim.

"Bad Girl," the Miracles' third release, is, in a manner of speaking, the first Motown record. No copies were made available to the public, but at least *two* separate sets of test pressings, numbered G-1 or (more rarely) TLX 2207, were manufactured.

Getting technical for a second, I'll try to explain this irregularity. A "test pressing" is a vinyl—back then they were styrene—record. Usually, only a few copies are made. They're most often used to check the quality of the record before commercial copies are made available for sale to the public. The lack of commercial copies of "Bad Girl" indicates that Berry Gordy was most likely using the test pressings as demos, which are basically sales tools designed to stir up interest in the song or performance.

In the case of "Bad Girl," it's known that Gordy was negotiating with Cameo-Parkway Records in Philadelphia and Chess Records in Chicago over the rights to issue the track. Chess won out and the Miracles' "Bad Girl" (Chess 1734) nicked the charts in September 1959.

For once, this lack of success is surprising. "Bad Girl" is a superfine record with a beautiful melody, witty lyrics, and—even more surprising—flute embellishments that don't get in the way of the dovetailing vocal lines. It's great. What more can I say?

I could say that Berry Gordy may be a lot of things, but lazy isn't one of them. If the Tamla label seems a little slow getting off the ground floor, keep in mind that all through 1959, Gordy is forced to divide his time writing and producing Marv Johnson and Eddie Holland records for United Artists, and writing—which means producing demos, too—for Jackie Wilson at Brunswick. Gordy will cowrite three more Top 10 R&B hits ("That's Why," "I'll Be Satisfied," and "Talk That Talk") for Wilson in 1959, after which their professional relationship ends.

Marv Johnson, meanwhile, will get the chance to wrap his vocal cords around what will be Berry Gordy's biggest record yet, a punchy paean to the pleasures of the flesh, 1959's "You Got What It Takes." Gordy's writing and production efforts will keep Johnson on the charts for another two years, but it's the out-of-the-blue success of "You Got What It Takes" that brings Gordy the bucks he needs to put Tamla into the black. (Like Eddie Holland, Johnson will rejoin the Motown family when his UA contract is up. He'll manage three singles on Gordy Records between 1965 and '68, only one of which will so much as dent the charts.)

Now it gets confusing. In March 1959 Gordy decides to change Tamla's numbering system to a five-digit series, which will remain in effect until 1982. The first record in this series is a typical fifties honking sax instrumental, the Swingin' Tigers' "Snake Walk, Pts. 1 and 2" (Tamla 54024). Gordy neither wrote nor produced this rarity. From the sound of the record I'd say somebody came in the door with a tape under his arm and Gordy gave it a shot. Weird.

What's even weirder is that the very next record on Tamla

16. What is Junior Walker's real name?
17. Prior to her arrival at Motown, Tammi Terrell made records under her real name. What is it?
18. What Motown recording artist won first prize on the "Ted Mack Amateur Hour" while still in grade school?

(Chico Leverett's "Solid Sender" b/w "I'll Never Love Again") is assigned the exact same catalog number—Tamla 54024. "Solid Sender" is a nice slice of bragging, uptempo R&B with a seamless lead-to-bass vocal interchange in the break. The flip is a rather plain ballad, although Leverett's warm vocals are distinctive enough to give it some character. But why the same number?

Actually, duplicated numbers are not uncommon in the world of R&B labels; there are several instances at Motown alone. (We'll get to the others when they come up.) Sloppy record-keeping is the usual culprit.

Similarly, it's not unusual to find R&B labels with numbering systems that begin elsewhere than at the logical starting point: 1000 or 101 or whatever. Some label owners were superstitious (711 is a common first number), others wanted to give distributors the impression they'd been in business for longer than one record, and others picked a number they'd hit that week, their girlfriend's birthday or—as with Berry Gordy—the number of their first hit. Jackie Wilson's "Reet Petite" was numbered Brunswick *55024*. As for the thousand-digit difference, Gordy was never one to do things *exactly* the same way twice. Case closed.

There is another Tamla numerical oddity. In December 1959 the label created a four-digit numbering series that only lasted for one record, Nick and the Jaguars' "Ich-I-Bon #1" (Tamla 5501). Talk about wild. This record wasn't released, it escaped. Again, it's an instrumental that Gordy must've found on his doorstep one morning, but it sounds like a three-way bar-fight between the Rock-A-Teens' "Woo-Hoo," Dick Dale and His Del-Tones' "Miserlou," and the Chantays' "Pipeline." The only thing is, the last two records won't exist for at least another couple years.

Tamla's second release—now that they've got their famous five-digit numbering system together—is only slightly less spacey. It's the tender tale of a young boy who befriends a strange creature only to see it die (aw . . .). Everything's cool by the third verse, though, when the critter phones the kid's home to let him know it's all right.

Sound familiar? You've got "It"—that's the title—recorded by the dynamic duo of Ron and Bill in May 1959. Ron and Bill being none other than two-fifths of the Miracles, Ronnie White and William "Smokey" Robinson. Gordy leased this cupcake to Argo Records, a subsidiary of Chess, which is undoubtedly where Steven Spielberg first heard of "It." (Incidentally, this is Smokey's only non-Miracles recording prior to his leaving the group in 1972.)

Speaking of subsidiary labels, the short-lived Rayber is

COURTESY THE CULTURAL WAREHOUSE

"It" takes two. Miracles members Ronnie White (left) and William "Smokey" Robinson as their 1959 alter egos, Ron and Bill.

COURTESY THE CULTURAL WAREHOUSE

Goin' to the hop. The Satintones—(from left) Vernon Williams, Sonny Sanders, James Ellis, Sammy Mack, and Robert Bateman—were the first act to record on the Motown label.

Tamla's first, predating Motown Records by at least two months. Wade Jones' "I Can't Concentrate" (Rayber 101), written by Berry and Smokey, is not only the sole Rayber release, it's also the only Wade Jones recording known to man or beast. All we know for certain about Wade is that he sure sounded an awful lot like Sam Cooke.

In 1959 Gordy signs Tamla's first vocal group, the Satintones. (Other than those curious test pressings, none of the Miracles' records have been issued on a Gordy-owned label.) "Motor City" b/w "Going to the Hop" is the Satintones' first—and only Tamla—release; their next five discs will all appear on the Motown label, which the group will also debut.

As their name implies, smooth harmony was the Satintones' specialty, even on a fast track such as "Motor City," in which we learn lead singer James Ellis' fondness for the car capital stems from his having met his love there. It's just ho-hum, while the flip, in which we find James attempting to reach his destination in his "raggedy jalop" is just plain dumb.

At this point Tamla's output has been less than earth-shattering. One good riff will change all this. How did it happen? Let's ask someone who was there . . . .

"We were just a small company then and most of the employees were musically inclined, so we all got together in the studio. I was playing the piano and the idea just sort of came around and Berry and Janie [Bradford] got together and did the lyrics on it."
—**BARRETT STRONG**

MOTOWN MAGIC MOMENT #3

There you have it. The secrets of the universe revealed. "The idea just sort of came around." What'd you expect? Some sort of detailed dissertation on blue notes, melismata, and polyrhythms? This is "Money" (Barrett Strong, 1960) we're talking about. You know the one that goes: "The best things in life are free. Blam! Blam! But you can give'em to the birds and bees. I need MUH-HUH-UN-NY!"

I mean, it's real simple. They took some old blues lick that's been here since dirt *and* John Lee Hooker, looked around, and said, "What do we need? We need *money*."

It's like John Lennon said, "I came out of the sticks to take over the world." And he oughta know, 'cause he cut the tune himself. Cut it to the bone. Blew Barrett Strong, the Kingsmen, the Rolling Stones, and all the garage bands, bar bands, punk bands, and, yes, even all the Art bands back to Detroit, Portland, the London School of Economics, and whatever inky nowheresville void the Flying Lizards came from. Look, if there's any doubt that "Money" isn't one of the greatest rock 'n' roll songs ever written, then how come it's the only nonoriginal song ever officially issued by both the Beatles and the Rolling Stones?

"Money" was first pressed on Tamla, then quickly leased to Anna Records, which had more clout thanks to its distribution agreement with Chess Records. (Berry Gordy knew he had a hit and didn't want to get beat out of it by bootleggers or a cover version.) It was the first hit in the Tamla 54000 series, and if Motown likes to think of it as their starting point, you can certainly understand why.

Now, it's a long way from a single leased hit to that Supremes 1964–65 string of five consecutive pop number ones, and right now (1960) the Supremes aren't even the Supremes—they're the Primettes, and there are four of them: *Diane* Ross, Mary Wilson, Florence Ballard, and Barbara Martin. The quartet is still in high school, but they are ambitious.

The Primettes audition for Berry Gordy, who tells 'em to come back when they finish school. Unruffled, they promptly go out and make their first—and only—record for one of Gordy's competitors. The Primettes' "Tears of Sorrow" (Lupine) is a crudely produced affair, but you can hear a very young Diane Ross getting her patented breathy style together.

Other future Motown stars on the 1960 horizon are the Distants, three-fifths of whom will become the Temptations, and Lamont Anthony—as Lamont Dozier is now calling himself—whose bluesy solo disc "Let's Talk It Over" (Anna) will undergo a few small changes before it becomes "Darling Baby," a 1966 smash for the Elgins.

Love is here and now you're gone.
When the Supremes first joined Motown, they were known as the Primettes, and they were a quartette. (Clockwise, from top) Diana Ross, Flo Ballard, Mary Wilson, and Barbara Martin.

19. Which Motown recording group released the first version of "Papa Was a Rolling Stone?"

20. What year did Motown move its offices from Detroit to Los Angeles?

21. Holland-Dozier-Holland were Motown's hottest songwriting-production team. What are their first names?

"Let's Talk It Over" was actually the B-side. The flip was originally titled "Popeye" and, according to Lamont, started to make some noise in Detroit. When King Features, who owned the rights to the cartoon character, found out about this, this Negro nonsense, they ordered the disc withdrawn. Anna obligingly recut the vocal track and reissued the record as "Benny the Skinny Man," but it somehow wasn't the same. (As for the Distants, these and other early recordings will be covered in Chapter 6.)

Independent of Motown, a subtle revolution is taking place. Spurred by the success of two 1959 vocal group records (the Drifters' "There Goes My Baby" and the Skyliners' "Since I Don't Have You"), both of which feature string sections more prominently than ever before, R&B record producers all over the country erupt in an outbreak of violins.

Gordy is down on this trend in a hot minute, and in 1960, the *very first* record to be issued on the Motown Records label, the Satintones' "My Beloved," is called back and rereleased after strings have been added. Both versions are given the same catalog number: Motown 1000. The only difference to the eye is the master number, otherwise known as those funny little scratchings you find on the space between the label and the record's grooves. The Satintones' earlier release is marked MT 12345; the one with strings, MT 1000 G3. Either way, it's got a good beat.

The Miracles' first Tamla release ("The Feeling Is So Fine," 1960) is likewise swiftly withdrawn, to be replaced by a completely different song, "Way over There." Again, both bear the same catalog number: Tamla 54028. Still not content, Gordy calls this tune (master number H55501) back so strings can be added (master number H5501 T-3).

Gordy's instincts were right. The second version of "Way over There" was the first Tamla release to benefit from national distribution and went on to sell sixty thousand copies, though it failed to chart nationally. To further complicate matters, the second "Way over There" was rereleased as Tamla 54069 in 1962, when it did make the lower reaches of the pop charts.

Musically, there's virtually no difference between the first and second versions of "Way over There," except, of course, that the strings have been added. They both rock with the same liquid, rhumba-gospel drive, and the vocals are as propulsive as they are cushy, which is—depending on how you look at it—why the strings either enhance or detract from the record's deliberately distant, other-worldly mood. (Kinda like Van Morrison's *Astral Weeks* LP.)

On the other hand, if there's such a thing as the Great Lost Miracles Record, "The Feeling Is So Fine" has got to be it. This one feels like raw silk. The groove is similar to "Way over There," but faster and jerkier, bottom-heavy with fat baritone sax, and Smokey's quicksilver vocals darting in and out of the harmonies, constantly punishing the beat. Unfortunately, only four copies are known to exist and they go for about $350.

Less extraordinary—and also far less rare—is the Miracles' second Chess single, "I Need a Change." When Gordy leased "Bad Girl" to Chess, the Chicago label demanded the rights to a follow-up as part of the deal, so Gordy handed them this rather colorless track, which went nowhere upon its release in the spring of 1960.

The Miracles' "Shop Around" (Tamla 54034) will also get the once-over twice. The original recording (master number H55518-A2) is a little slower, the saxes a little louder, and the ice-blue guitar accompaniment more pronounced. The second version (master number H55518 L13) was approved in December. Eight weeks later it would be the number 2 record in the country, and Tamla's first R&B number one.

When he isn't spending his time ordering the Miracles back into the studio, Gordy is cruising for new talent. After all, he has his new Motown Records label to think about. Seventeen-year-old Mary Wells is his most successful find.

Wells comes to Gordy with a song she has written for Jackie Wilson. (Gordy must've gotten this one all the time.) He asks her to sing it for him a cappella. She does. And the next thing Wells remembers, Gordy is in the studio, driving her through twenty-two takes of her song, "Bye Bye Baby" (1960). Wells is a virgin to vinyl and her performance is . . . *volcanic.*

"Bye Bye Baby" was the first Top 10 R&B hit on the Motown label, but Mary Wells was not the first female artist Berry Gordy signed. Wells was the first woman signed to Motown Records, true. However, Mable John's initial Tamla Records release ("Who Wouldn't Love a Man Like That"), an easygoing finger-snapper conceived as the woman's answer to "You Got What It Takes," beat Wells to the punch by a couple of months. (Wells did get the first hit, so we'll let her keep the bragging rights.)

Gordy had three good reasons for setting up Motown, his second major label. One was radio airplay. It was too easy for program directors to say, "We're sorry. We can only play one of your company's records." But if you had two companies . . .

The second was record distributors. By giving one label's

Danger heartbreak dead ahead.
Having begun as a quintette, the Marvelettes—(from left) Gladys Horton, Georgeanna Dobbins, Wanda Young, and Katherine Anderson—spent less than a year as a foursome before stabilizing as the trio who posed for a more famous publicity photo wearing the same outfits.

COURTESY THE CULTURAL WAREHOUSE

distribution rights to one pirate and the other's to the shark across the street, you could be more sure that each record you released would get someone's undivided attention.

The third reason for even more basic. Gordy knew that only by keeping his employees constantly competing against one another could he get them to extend themselves in ways they hadn't thought possible. (Some people call this survival of the fittest; others call it capitalism.)

The Supremes, Marvin Gaye, the Temptations, the Contours, and Jimmy Ruffin all made their first records for Gordy in 1961. None of these was a hit. Instead, first-hit honors went to the Marvelettes, whose debut recording of "Please Mr. Postman," on Tamla, brought Berry Gordy his first number one pop record. (The disc also topped the R&B charts, making it Gordy's first double number one.)

In the meantime Gordy has established a third label, Miracle, which dissolves into the Gordy Records label by 1962. Supposedly there were twelve releases on Miracle, but collectors have only located nine discs, of which three are whitebread pop gross-outs and two more are by the Temptations.

The remaining four are Jimmy Ruffin's first recording; the Valadiers' original version of the Monitors' 1966 hit, "Greetings (This is Uncle Sam)"; future Originals member Freddie Gorman's only Motown solo effort; and a dazzling performance by an obscure vocal group, the Equadors, who, based on this piece of aural evidence, were tossed into the trunk of a Kandy Orient Purple '57 T-Bird and exiled to another galaxy for daring to make a record so good that one listen to it caused human beings to glow radium-green in the dark. Either that or they got discouraged and went back to driving forklifts on the swing shift at Chrysler. We just don't know.

What we do know is that the Equadors' "Someone to Call My Own" has an excellent, fast, quasi-Latin groove that lands somewhere between a kicked-in-the-ass Drifters and Maurice Williams and the Zodiacs' uptown cousins. The flip, a classy ballad titled "You're My Desire," is almost as hip.

Jimmy Ruffin's "Don't Feel Sorry for Me," a showcase for his considerable falsetto skills, was the initial Miracle label release. Jimmy, whose younger brother, David, will join the Temptations in 1964, was drafted shortly after the record's release, putting his recording career on ice for the next three years.

The thought of induction strikes terror into many a young man's heart, as evidenced by the Valadiers' black comic vision, "Greetings (This Is Uncle Sam)," which didn't seem half as funny when the Monitors recorded it at the height of the Vietnam conflict. The Valadiers, incidentally, were Motown's first white group.

As for Freddie Gorman's solo flight ("The Day Will Come"), it's good uptown R&B, spotlighting Freddie's ability to do Ben E. King's—or maybe Brook Benton's—thing.

The practice of cutting answer records—otherwise known as trying to cash in on someone else's hit—is as old as the record business, and Gordy tried this avenue to revenue more than once. (He even released an answer to one of his own company's hits: Debbie Dean's "Don't Let Him Shop Around.")

In 1961 one of Gordy's answer records gets him in trouble. The Shirelles are bulleting up the charts, asking the eternal question, "Will You Still Love Me Tomorrow." The Satintones

COURTESY THE CULTURAL WAREHOUSE

White but still all right. Signed on the strength of no less than Jackie Wilson's recommendation, the Valadiers were Motown's first white recording group.

reply with a quick "Tomorrow and Always" (Motown 1006). Unconvinced, Gordy orders them to say it again, so he can hear it (master number H625; previously H55596). Unamused, the publishers of "Will You Still Love Me Tomorrow" howl "copyright infringement," and the courts order the Satintones to shut up.

Never one to waste a catalog number, Gordy replaces the Satintones' response with a backdated fifties-style ballad, "Angel." It nose-dives, and the saga of Motown 1006 sinks slowly into the sunset. Two more stiffs and the Satintones, whose shifting lineup included James Ellis, Chico Leverett, Robert Bateman, Sonny Sanders, Joe Charles, Vernon Williams, and Sammy Mack, will follow that sun. Especially James, whose wanderlust has already been well documented in these pages.

Bateman, Sanders, and Charles don't exactly fade away and radiate. Bateman, who had brought Mary Wells and the Marvelettes to Gordy's attention, became a Motown recording engineer, copping cowriter's credits for his work on the Marvelettes' "Please Mr. Postman" and "Playboy." Sanders went on to produce and arrange a number of mid-sixties soul hits for Detroit indies Ric-Tic and Golden World, later taking his talents to Brunswick and Chess. Charles turned up as half of the male-female duo Lo and Joe, whose "Little Ol' Boy, Little Ol' Girl" will be issued on the Harvey label in 1962.

Harvey Records was the second of two Detroit-based indies founded by ex-Moonglows lead singer Harvey Fuqua and his entrepreneurial wife, Gwen Gordy. Harvey and Gwen's first venture was Tri-Phi Records, where the Spinners, who would sing backups on that Lo and Joe duet, made their 1961 recording debut.

"That's What Girls Are Made For," the Spinners' first disc, went Top 10 R&B and Top 30 pop. Their second, "Love I'm So Glad I Found You," spent a week at number 91 and failed to chart R&B. (*Billboard*'s R&B chart listed only thirty titles back then.) Both tunes are polished performances, with harmonies so glossy the quintet must've been able to see their own reflections in 'em.

The Spinners, wailing sax-fiend Junior Walker, party-disc specialist Shorty Long, and triple-threat (songwriter-producer-vocalist) Johnny Bristol would all be welcomed into the Motown family when Berry Gordy purchased the Tri-Phi and Harvey labels in 1963.

Fuqua, a talented writer-producer in his own right, would also prove a valuable addition, but the most successful artist to benefit from the Motown-Fuqua connection was someone who not only had never recorded for Tri-Phi or Harvey but actually became part of *the* family—Marvin Gaye, who married Anna Gordy.

Gaye had been a member of the Moonglows during the latter part of their career, even singing lead on the group's 1959 recording, "Mama Loocie" (Chess). When the Moonglows disbanded, Gaye followed Fuqua to Detroit, where Berry Gordy spotted him and signed him—originally as a session drummer—in 1961. (Gaye's first Tamla effort as well as the Supremes' and the Contours' debuts are covered in Chapter 5.)

The pivotal year in The Motown Story is 1962. Berry Gordy's company is far from the hit factory it will become, and America's leading business magazine, *Fortune*, won't get around to doing a feature on Motown until 1967, but by the end of 1962, Gordy's cash-flow problems are ancient history.

Take a look at Motown's '62 track record: eleven Top 10 R&B hits, four of 'em R&B number ones. All four (Mary Wells' "Two Lovers" and "You Beat Me to the Punch," the Contours' "Do You Love Me," and the Miracles' "You Really Got a Hold on Me"), plus the Marvelettes' "Playboy" and a third Wells performance ("The One Who Really Loves You"), would be Top 10 pop hits as well.

You or I might be tempted to *PARRR-TY!* Gordy's reaction was to hustle harder. Free of his outside production commitments, he established two more subsidiary labels, Mel-O-Dy and Gordy.

Bearing a favorite B.G. slogan ("It's what's in the grooves that counts"), Gordy Records would join Tamla and Motown as the company's three primary labels. Mel-O-Dy was soon discontinued, although the Mel-O-Dy name would be revived in the seventies as a short-lived Motown country music subsidiary. Which makes some sense, since most of the initial Mel-O-Dy's releases were horrible pop and country noises in the first place.

However, four of the earlier Mel-O-Dy recordings are noteworthy. Male vocal group the Creations checked in with "This Is Our Night," a greasy but charming rip-off of a similarly titled Shirelles' tune; "Mind over Matter," credited to the Pirates, is actually the Temptations working under a pseudonym; while the Vells—whose members included latter-day Vandellas Roslyn Ashford and Annette Sterling—contributed "There He Is (at My Door)," a slightly better than average girl group number.

The fourth of these 1962 Mel-O-Dy releases is the most significant. "Dearest One" is not only Lamont Dozier's first recording for Gordy, it's also the first Holland-Dozier-Holland collaboration. There's nothing spectacular about the tune. In

22. What female Motown group also recorded a single for the company under the name the Darnells?
23. How did Martha and the Vandellas come up with the group's name?
24. What Motown recording artist married songwriter-producer-label exec William "Mickey" Stevenson?

fact, "I Didn't Know," an uptown R&B effort Dozier had recorded under the name Lamont Anthony for Check-Mate Records earlier that year, is probably a better disc. But "Dearest One" was H-D-H's first. And that means it's the beginning of the end of the beginning.

Oh, I know I should mention that 1962 was the year Smokey Robinson began producing hit records and that '62 was the year producer Mickey Stevenson started getting *his* hits and meanwhile the Four Tops—who've been around since 1954 without a single personnel change—are cutting strained versions of "Pennies from Heaven" on the tiny Riverside label and won't get to Motown until 1964.

Why 1962? After all, the Holland-Dozier-Holland team didn't write or produce a single hit 'til '63. And even throughout 1963, when by year's end Motown could announce gross sales of $4.5 million, *everybody's* hits were sporadic. It wasn't 'til '64 that they got the machine in high gear.

I should also mention that '62 was the year Martha and the Vandellas and Little Stevie Wonder made their vinyl appearances and that the former cut two singles for Check-Mate under the name the Dell-Fi's with Gloria Williams—who sang lead on that Vells' track I was talking about a few paragraphs back—as the lead singer, but damn, baby, how much of this trivia does it take to make you see that there are ten different versions of The Motown Story in this book?

And if reading this chapter hasn't made you wanna "clap your hands, kick your feet and, as a matter of fact, tear you up," as those *batos locos* from East El Lay, the Blendells, promised on the intro to their gloriously besotted, burrito-breathed 1964 version of Little Stevie Wonder's 1962 non-hit, "La La La La La," then I suggest you try this version of Berry Gordy's history, from the February 8, 1960, issue of *Time* magazine:

> SO MUCH (Jackie Wilson; Brunswick, mono and stereo) Singer Wilson, who bears a startling physical resemblance to Sammy Davis, Jr., is presented to his fans as "Mr. Excitement." The excitement consists of a bludgeoning Neanderthal style, and the package should be labeled "For Unregenerate Rock and Rollers Only."

Or you could read on . . .

Chapter Three
HITSVILLE, U.S.A.

 Oh, we have a very swinging company
Working hard from day to day. . . .
—from Motown's official company song

Motown had fewer than one hundred employees prior to 1965, so it wasn't hard to call them all together for monthly meetings, which always began with the official company song. *Everybody* had to sing it. Not everyone wanted to, but Berry Gordy would scan his flock for those less-spirited souls and make them lead the congregation if he didn't feel their efforts were genuine.

The rest of the meeting was devoted to recitations of recent accomplishments by each department head and the inevitable Berry Gordy pep talk. Awards for the producer, songwriter, and singer of the month were handed out, and all the neat and clean employees of Hitsville, U.S.A., went back to pleasing the world with songs the DJs were glad to play.

Sounds corny, but it worked. Consider this endorsement from Parliament-Funkadelic leader George Clinton, who was a Motown songwriter for several years in the early sixties:

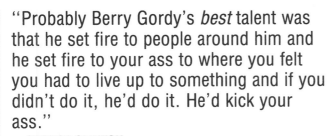 "Probably Berry Gordy's *best* talent was that he set fire to people around him and he set fire to your ass to where you felt you had to live up to something and if you didn't do it, he'd do it. He'd kick your ass."
—GEORGE CLINTON

 MOTOWN MAGIC MOMENT #4

Now consider some statistical evidence: From 1960 to 1970 Motown released 535 singles, of which 357—or 67 percent—were chart hits. Motown scored 21 double number ones (number one R&B and number one pop), six others topped the pop charts but missed the top R&B spot, and another 29 were number one R&B hits. That's 56 number one records. And that doesn't begin to tell The Motown Story.

One reason for Motown's decade of chart dominance—174 Top 10 R&B hits, 94 Top 10 pop numbers—is obvious. Motown cloned itself. The old "if they liked it once, they'll like it again (and again)" theory was never more applicable. Once Holland-Dozier-Holland cooked up a "Reach out, I'll Be There," it was no sweat to knock off a "Standing in the Shadows of Love" and even less to whip up a "Bernadette." One idea, three hits, no errors.

H-D-H might've been the masters of the practice, cutting their teeth on Martha and the Vandellas' "Heat Wave," "Quicksand," and "Live Wire" trilogy and sprouting fangs on the Supremes' "Where Did Our Love Go," "Baby Love," and "Come See about Me" series, but every producer on the label used this new, improved approach to house-cloning.

These three-stage follow-ups made good business sense. For openers, they guaranteed a healthy cash flow. If you knew even the third version of the hit would sell at least 150,000 copies—or ten times your break-even point—wouldn't you take it?

By cloning yourself you also kept the competition from muscling in on your turf. This didn't stop people from trying; there were at last count 5,283 Motown imitations recorded during the sixties. Some of these, such as Edwin Starr's "Stop Her on Sight" (Ric-Tic, 1966) or the Poets' "She Blew a Good Thing" (Symbol, also 1966), are every bit as good as the Motown originals that inspired them. Those particular records were hits. Most of the other imitations weren't, aced out by the steady stream of soundalikes that rolled like clockwork off what Motown's own ad copy boasted as being "Detroit's *other* world-famous assembly line."

"I earned 367 million dollars in sixteen years. I must be doing something right."
—BERRY GORDY

It wasn't just Berry Gordy's willingness to wring every last dollar out of an idea that made Motown. Nor was he the first black American to own a successful record company. Tickle the ivories, Professor Longhair, I feel a historical digression comin' on. . . .

MOTOWN
MAGIC
MOMENT #5

Bobby Robinson, who owned the record store next door to New York's legendary Apollo Theater, set up Red Robin, later Robin Records, and started getting hits from local doo-wop group the Vocaleers as far back as 1953. Over the next ten years Robinson would front a variety of labels (notably Everlast, Enjoy, Fire, and Fury), which despite producing several national hits—and such undeniably great records as Wilbert Harrison's "Kansas City," Lee Dorsey's "Ya-Ya," King Curtis' "Soul Twist," and future Motown stars Gladys Knight and the Pips' first hit, "Every Beat of My Heart"—were never more than minor independent labels. Robinson still keeps his hand in, cutting gospel LPs and the occasional disco 12-inch.

Peacock Records began even earlier (1949), founded by Don Robey, who owned Houston's most popular black nitespot, the Golden Peacock. Robey acquired Duke Records four years later, and on the strength of such R&B chart perennials as Little Junior Parker and Bobby "Blue" Bland as well as gospel superstars the Dixie Hummingbirds and the Five Blind Boys of Mississippi, remained in business until 1973, when the sale of his empire to ABC Records reportedly netted him a very cool million. Robey died of a heart attack in 1975.

There were also several minor black-owned operations. In 1957 New Yorker Juggy Murray formed Sue Records, which introduced Ike and Tina Turner to an unsuspecting world. Vocalist extraordinaire Sam Cooke and his manager, J. W. Alexander, ran Hollywood-based Sar Records from 1960 to '62, uncovering such talents as Lou Rawls, Johnnie Taylor, and the Valentinos, the last of which featured brothers Bobby and Cecil Womack.

Meanwhile, way down the Mississippi down to New Orleans, a group of black session musicians organized the short-lived A.F.O. (All for One) cooperative label; and black-owned Minit Records, aided by the formidable talents of songwriter-producer Allen Toussaint, racked up a number of national hits, including Jessie Hill's "Ooh Poo Pah Doo," Ernie K-Doe's "Mother-in-Law," and the all-time greatest rock 'n' roll song about rock 'n' roll—the Showmen's "It Will Stand." Again, commercially speaking, this was strictly the minor leagues.

Motown's only real black-owned rival was a Chicago label, Vee-Jay Records, established by Vivian Carter and James Bracken in 1953. Vee-Jay began cutting local gospel groups, moving swiftly into blues (Jimmy Reed, John Lee Hooker, Elmore James) and doo-wop (the Spaniels, the El Dorados, the Dells). By the early sixties the company had expanded into soul (Jerry Butler, Betty Everett, Gene Chandler) and white rock (the Four Seasons). Vee-Jay was also the first U.S. record company to issue a John, Paul, George, and Ringo record,

25. What is Edwin Starr's real name?
26. Which Motown-published song has been recorded by more than two hundred artists?
27. Back in the sixties, Motown signed a rock group whose members included Rick James and Neil Young. What was this group's name?

"From Me to You," which spent three weeks at number 116 in 1963.

The label failed to acquire exclusive rights to the Beatles, however, and when subsequent Capitol releases shot to the top of the charts, all Vee-Jay could do was issue the album's worth of material they'd been sitting on for the past year. After twelve years of hits, a combination of (ahem) irregular business practices and what can only be described as a distinct lack of foresight crippled the company. By 1965 Vee-Jay was bankrupt. Incidentally, former Vee-Jay president Ewart Abner later became president of Motown Records; he now serves as Stevie Wonder's business adviser. The current president of Motown Records, Jay Lasker, was formerly executive VP at Vee-Jay.

All these black-owned labels had one thing in common. Like 99 percent of their white-owned competitors (Atlantic Records being the notable exception), they thought small, which is why they're all out of serious business and Berry Gordy isn't.

What it all comes down to is details. At Motown, Berry Gordy had the last word on everything. While everyone but Phil Spector was operating under ye olde "throw ten records against the wall and hope one sticks" philosophy, *Gordy was releasing less than 10 percent of what Motown was recording.*

Motown's weekly music meetings, where songwriters, producers, and executives would argue the merits of the company's prospective releases, are the stuff of legend. Once, this committee sat down and listened to sixty-eight finished tracks—they chose *one* (the Supremes' "Love Child") to be the next single. Ever wonder what the other sixty-seven sounded like? Don't bother. I'll bet they sucked. Can I get a witness?

MOTOWN
MAGIC
MOMENT #6

"They wanted every song that we put out to be a hit. Not just a song to listen to. When people heard a Motown record, they were supposed to go out and buy it, a million copies. That's what we were aiming for."
—BRENDA HOLLOWAY

At Motown the thinking started before you went into the studio.

"I remember us working on 'I Want You Back' for three weeks. Just rehearsing it and rehearsing it and rehearsing it. The Corporation—Berry Gordy, Fonce Mizell, Deke Richards, and Freddie Perren—wrote it and they wanted the song a certain way. When we got it right, then we recorded it."
—JERMAINE JACKSON

Experimentation was encouraged, however.

"You did what you had to do in order to get that part of it. If it took foot stomps—that's me, the Originals, the cat that swept the floor and everybody else walking on a wooden board in the middle of the floor in 'Twenty-five Miles,' getting that effect—that's what you did."
—EDWIN STARR

As much as Motown relished the assembly-line, hit-factory comparisons, Gordy's corporate image-polishing extended to the paper sleeves in which Motown singles were sold. "Hitsville, U.S.A.," was only one side of the Motown image. The others were upward mobility ("Another one going places") and good, clean, wholesome fun ("The sound of young America").

Gordy and company were staunch integrationists. Although Gordy recruited clerical help from a nearby black business school, several key Motown staffers were white record biz veterans whom Gordy knew from his days as an independent producer. Barney Ales headed the sales department, responsible for getting Motown records to distributors and record stores; Phil Jones handled promotion, which in the record business means getting radio stations to play your company's discs; and Al Abrams oversaw Motown's early publicity efforts.

There was a certain innocence to Motown's desire for acceptance. How else can you explain the Supremes posing for pictures introducing their very own brand of *white* bread? Or that the Supremes made an appearance on the mid-sixties "Tarzan" TV series, playing (what else?) a trio of nuns? Or

"Detroit's other world-famous assembly line." Standing in front of the original Motown headquarters, founder Berry Gordy's and VP/ Sales Barney Ales' sons (from left) Berry Gordy IV and Steve Ales; pitch hot wax and add another couple coats of image polish.

that long before Berry Gordy decided to become a movie mogul, Motown artists would make their silver screen debuts in such hard-hitting, slice-of-life docudramas as *Beach Ball* (the Supremes, 1965), *Muscle Beach Party* and *Bikini Beach* (Little Stevie Wonder, in a pair of 1964 Frankie Avalon–Annette Funicello vehicles)?

Motown was not completely without a black consciousness. Gordy released a single of Rev. Martin Luther King, Jr.'s "I Have a Dream" speech in 1963, a year before the Federal Civil Rights Bill was passed. (Gordy reissued the single in 1968, shortly after King was assassinated; Motown still keeps three of the Nobel Peace Prize winner's spoken-word albums in print.)

Perhaps a more accurate indicator of Gordy's political leanings can be found closer to his heart. Berry Gordy divorced Raynoma, who bore him a third son (Kerry), in 1962 and although he never married his next companion (Margaret Norton), he acknowledges his fourth son, whom the couple named Kennedy. Both boys grew up to be Motown recording artists. Kerry leads funk-rock group Kagny and the Dirty Rats, while Kennedy, using the stage name Rockwell, proved you can never be too rich, too thin, or too paranoid with Winston Smith's favorite R&B/pop smash of 1984, "Somebody's Watching Me."

Which brings us to the fourth and most important facet of the Motown image: the famous "family atmosphere." It wasn't hard to think of Motown as a family business. By the mid-sixties, a third of the payroll were Gordys. Berry himself played Papa Lord God and everybody else—relatives or not—took on the roles of eager-to-please children. Witnesses?

"At the time we were all children and if a group of grown-ups are over a bunch of teenagers, they're going to become like a family if they're around each other all day. If the Miracles got a hit record, we just all got excited about it."
—MARY WELLS

MOTOWN MAGIC MOMENT #9

Well, okay, Wells was an impressionable teenager. But ask any vintage Motown artist about this period and a hypnotic, splattered mist drifts over their eyes.

"In those days the company was really a family, and it was just really a lot of fun and a learning experience to be around it. And everybody involved was tryin' to help you get a hit. It was a beautiful experience, and I wouldn't trade it for anything."
—FREDDIE GORMAN, the Originals

MOTOWN MAGIC MOMENT #10

Wow, that mist is filling the whole room.

"When I got to Motown, it was like I was in a dream world. I looked at Motown as being my husband, because you had to be loyal to the Motown family. You had to keep yourself up in your trade—your voice had to be up to par—and you didn't even *think* about going to another label."
—BRENDA HOLLOWAY

MOTOWN MAGIC MOMENT #11

COURTESY THE CULTURAL WAREHOUSE

Somebody's watching me. Rockwell (born Kennedy Gordy), Berry's fourth son, wasn't the first member of the Gordy family to record for Motown, but he was the first to get a hit. Don't think Papa wasn't proud.

Obviously, you don't inspire that kind of loyalty simply by making your employees all stand up and sing some silly sisboom-bah fight song, even if it was written by Smokey Robinson. Motown laid a fatherly hand on every aspect of its artists' careers. When acts weren't in the studio or rehearsing material for an upcoming recording session, they were busy getting a hot wax and another couple coats of image-polish from what Motown called its "Artist Development Department."

Here, Motown artists took lessons in voice and choreography, the latter courtesy of the great Cholly Atkins, who with his former partner Honi Coles had been one of America's top black dance teams. (Some of their most spectacular routines have been preserved on celluloid; the duo appeared in several black musicals of the thirties and forties.) Prior to Motown's hiring him, Atkins had been putting most of New York City's doo-wop groups through their synchro-mesh paces. Rock 'n' roll owes a lot to Cholly Atkins.

Artistic Development also functioned as what can only be described as a charm school. Motown artists were taught grooming, table manners, how to sit, walk, talk, even how to smoke a cigarette with grace and elegance. In short, how to act just like Mr. and Mrs. Elmer Honkhauser, recently arrived in the Big Apple from Omaha and celebrating their twentyfifty wedding anniversary at the Copacabana.

If the sight of Marvin Gaye—prior to his funky space reincarnation—in top hat 'n' tails working out on traditional tap routines now seems like a living definition of the word *absurd*, back then the Motown acts certainly took this schooling seriously.

Can't forget the Motor City. Standing on the front porch of Motown's original Detroit offices at 2648 West Grand Boulevard are (from left) Rebecca Jiles, the late "Pops" Gordy (Berry Gordy's father), and Faye Hale. Both women are more than twenty-year veterans of the label, and, even more impressive, both are still with the company.

COURTESY BILLIE JEAN BROWN, ESQ.

COURTESY TOM DePIERRO/AIRWAVE INTERNATIONAL

You've made me so very happy. Yacht to know better than to wear your heart on your wrist, Brenda, even aboard the **Hitsville II.**

© 1976 CHUCK KRALL

Dancing machine. A former star of stage and screen as half of the legendary Coles and Atkins dance team, Cholly Atkins was Motown's staff choreographer.

MOTOWN MAGIC MOMENT #12

"We would work with Cholly Atkins sometimes for hours. I mean, you wouldn't feel like fooling with anybody else, because by the time Cholly got through beatin' it into you, you were *done*, you know? But every artist had to attend these classes, so when we went out, we went out as a finished product."
—**KATHERINE ANDERSON, the Marvelettes**

Some artists thrived on the experience.

MOTOWN MAGIC MOMENT #13

"What Motown left with me was fond memories of discipline, the almighty force of discipline, especially in performance. Motown was the forerunner of fifteen hours in front of the mirror and make sure that the steps are right. They made me, personally, see the need for discipline in showmanship."
—**EDWIN STARR**

A few weren't so enchanted.

MOTOWN MAGIC MOMENT #14

"Yeah, we went to Finishing School. Once. And the guys said all Cholly could teach us was the proper way of coming onstage and the proper way of exiting the stage. As far as choreography—our routines came from each member of the group, basically [lead singer] Billy Gordon—Cholly couldn't teach us our own choreography. We were the only ones."
—**JOE BILLINGSLEA, the Contours**

Motown looked after its artists in other ways, mostly via International Talent Management, Inc., affectionately known as ITMI. This particular division of Motown not only provided you (the artist) with personal management but served as your booking agent for live performances, made sure your mortgage or child-support obligations were met, and paid your taxes, too. All this conflict of interest cost you a flat 10 percent.

That's not as bad as it sounds. Financially, Motown's acts could've done worse. Nowadays, you (the artist) will pay *at least* 10 percent to your personal manager and *at least* another 10 percent to your booking agent.

At the time, Motown's contracts were no worse than any other operation's, although there were a couple of rather interesting clauses. For one, there was no guarantee an artist would have even a single record released while under contract to Motown.

For two, the label was keen on signing artists to a different contract for each service it performed, which no doubt explains why they all expired at different times, right? And if you believe that, try getting a new record deal with your former record company still serving as your manager.

ITMI was also responsible for putting together the famous "Motortown Revues." These were package tours where a half dozen of the label's top acts would all perform on the same bill, further reinforcing the Motown image of unity and group strength.

The Motortown Revues were one of Berry Gordy's many better ideas. To send each act out individually would've been a logistical nightmare and most likely financial suicide. This way, not only was the label top-billed over the artists, but the entire program remained under the company's control. Which was good. While other acts struggled with pickup bands who barely knew the performer's songs, Motown supplied its troupe with a well-drilled band of riffslingers drawn from the label's seemingly bottomless pool of session hit men.

The first Motortown Revue began in 1962 with forty-five people traveling in five cars and a bus. A typical early sixties tour might include the Miracles, the Supremes, the Temptations, Little Stevie Wonder, Martha and the Vandellas, and the Marvelettes, playing anywhere from two to four shows a day for thirty to forty-five consecutive dates.

Most of the Motown artists remember these days as some kind of fun, stressing the fellowship of the road, the pranks, and the "friendly competition." However, they all say the long bus rides were a drag, especially in the Deep South, where hotels willing to admit blacks were scarce, and often the only place to wash up would be a bus terminal.

Finding a restaurant could also be tough; many meals had to be carried out the back door and eaten on the bus. Sometimes even stopping to use the rest room could be a problem, as gun-toting service station owners were not above telling you to just keep right on driving, boah.

Another one going places. Berry's sister, Esther Gordy Edwards, who headed the company's International Talent Management, Inc. (ITMI) division, married a Michigan state legislator.

Don't mess with bills. Berry's sister, the late Loucye Gordy Wakefield. Universally acclaimed by Motown staffers as the hardest-working employee the company ever had, Loucye's job was collecting the money from distributors. When her eternal reward came all too soon, Motown established a memorial scholarship in her honor.

Too hip for the room. A good show starts in the dressing room and works its way to the stage. Among those caught between sets circa 1963 are (from left) Ronnie Spector of the Ronettes, Muhammad Ali, Dionne Warwick, Little Stevie Wonder, Dionne's sister Dee Dee Warwick, and Mary Wells.

COURTESY TOM DEPIERRO/AIRWAVE INTERNATIONAL

ITMI did its best to schedule around these situations and—since Motown road managers were picking up everyone's box office receipts in cash—tried to keep the lowest profile possible.

MOTOWN
MAGIC
MOMENT #15

"The first time we went out, Berry Gordy had all the guys sit in the back of the bus and all the girl acts sit in the front and everyone was chaperoned. A lot of the Motown brass would chaperone women and we had chaperones, too. We were grown men with chaperones."
—**JOE BILLINGSLEA, the Contours**

It wasn't easy to relax.

MOTOWN
MAGIC
MOMENT #16

"At that time in the South you'd have to do one show for the blacks and one show for the whites, and you'd go in there and some of them would yock it up and really have a good time with you. Then you'd go back out and wonder who's going to have to pull the gun first because of getting the bus overturned or something like that."
—**KATHERINE ANDERSON, the Marvelettes**

The crowds themselves could get pretty wild.

"One time in Kansas City a guy jumped onstage firing a pistol, yelling, "Play that 'Shotgun' *one more time*."
—JUNIOR WALKER

Berry Gordy might have literally put Motown on the map when he changed the Motown Records label design in late 1961. But by 1964, when Beatlemania swept America and every British rock group from the Animals to the Zombies cleaned up, forty-two of the sixty records released on the Motown family of labels hit the pop charts, and Gordy's "The sound of young America" slogan began to seem like a self-fulfilling prophecy.

Hey, you gotta believe. And Motown believed in the three R's: Recording, Rehearsing, and Roadwork. The coordination all this required would've tied an octopus in knots, but Gordy and company managed to keep all the balls in the air.

Motown was hotter than stolen kisses, so Gordy added a pair of subsidiary labels—Soul and V.I.P. Records. Soul was the first out of the chute, in March 1964, with Shorty Long's magnificent slow-grind "Devil with a Blue Dress." V.I.P. came nine months later with the Serenaders' "I'll Cry Tomorrow," promotional copies of which had originally appeared on the Motown Records label, as its debut. (See discography for logo design changes on the V.I.P., Soul, Tamla, and Gordy labels.)

In 1965 Gordy decided turnabout was fair play and invaded England. The initial Motown U.K. tour was timed to coincide with the launch of Motown's own British label (Tamla Motown Records) and spotlighted the talents of the Supremes, the Four Tops, and Little Stevie Wonder. (Prior to this, Motown's U.K. records had been issued on the Fontana, Oriole, and Stateside labels.)

There were one hundred acts under Motown contracts by 1966, and the two-story house on West Grand Boulevard had mushroomed into six such buildings, all clustered around the original headquarters. Eventually, the hassle of having to run across a fairly busy street every time you wanted to talk to someone in Artist Development got to be a throbbing purple pain, and in 1968, Gordy moved the whole operation to a ten-story office building at 2547 Woodward Avenue in downtown Detroit.

Also in 1968 Gordy bought out his biggest local competitor, the Golden World and Ric-Tic family of labels, headed by Janet Jackson and Eddie Wingate. Although these labels had

A reputation of being gentle but bold. Agent Double-O-Soul himself, Edwin Starr.

COURTESY TOM DEPIERRO/AIRWAVE INTERNATIONAL

produced several hits and boasted a strong talent roster, only for Edwin Starr would the hits continue. Gordy also got a new recording studio out of the deal, which may have been his main reason for the purchase. He certainly didn't need any more talent.

So who were those one hundred acts? Well, you probably know half of them, either by their string of smashes or their one big hit. The others you probably don't wanna know, but a few names are real head-slappers. Try this one on your friends:

Did you know that sixties TV stars Soupy Sales, Paul Petersen of "The Donna Reed Show," and Irene Ryan, who played Granny on "Beverly Hillbillies," were all once Motown artists? And so were such veteran mainstream black entertainers as Billy Eckstine, Barbara McNair, Diahann Carroll and Leslie Uggams. Not forgetting character actor Scatman Crothers, comic genius Richard Pryor, and ventriloquist Willie Tyler (and Lester).

And did you know Motown released records by such white mid-sixties garage-rock bands as the Merced Blue Notes, who

COURTESY TOM DePIERRO/AIRWAVE INTERNATIONAL

Love's gone bad. Among the best of Motown's white garage bands was this pack of Grosse Pointe, Michigan, semilegends, the Underdogs.

really were from that particular Northern California suburb, and the Underdogs, from Grosse Pointe, Michigan, who cut a tough version of H-D-H's "Love's Gone Bad" that should've been a hit but wasn't?

Motown had another interesting rock group in the Mynah Birds, whose lineup consisted of such future movers and shakers as Steppenwolf's Goldie McJohn, Buffalo Springfield's Bruce Palmer and Neil Young—yes, *that* Neil Young—and none other than Mr. "Superfreak" himself: Rick James(!). Motown recorded several songs by the group, but nothing was ever released. Don't hold your breath waiting.

The company's best-known venture into the white "progressive rock" market was Rare Earth Records, established in 1968. Along with the Rare Earth group, who thumped out a trio of ham-fisted pop hits, the label's biggest success came with white staff songwriter R. Dean Taylor's gawdawful "Indiana Wants Me" (1970), an "I'm on the lam, but I ain't no sheep" saga that would've fit right in on Bruce Springsteen's 1982 *Nebraska* LP.

But did you know that the Rare Earth label issued albums

from Australia's Easybeats and England's Love Sculpture? And that the former's ranks included those true pop wizards/ cult heroes, the writing-production team of (Harry) Vanda and (George) Young? And that the latter group featured the flying fingers of guitarist Dave Edmunds, whose flashy fret-grinding and rare good taste have made him a cult hero in his own right?

Probably not. Mainly because the records weren't hits. Neither were any of the releases on Motown's gospel (Divinity), jazz (Workshop), or spoken-word (Black Forum) labels. Some hit factory. That sound you hear is another myth biting the dust.

Sure, Motown cranked out hit after hit after hit. Motown also experimented nonstop. Not only by recording so many different kinds of music but by trying everything they could think of to create those hit formulas in the first place.

Sure, Motown was tough. So are the odds against success. Motown was also flexible.

Everybody was a talent scout. The Miracles' Ronnie White brought Stevie Wonder to the label, and Gordy recording artist Bobby Taylor discovered the Jackson 5.

Everybody sang background on each other's sessions. That's the Supremes answering Marvin Gaye on "Can I Get a Witness," and there are up to ten extra voices on certain Four Tops tracks.

Personal growth was both encouraged and expected. Martha Reeves of Martha and the Vandellas fame began her Motown career as a secretary in the company's Artists & Repertoire Department, and performers were assigned a producer's code when they joined the label on the theory they might grow into the role.

Of course, these new producers were still under exclusive contract to Motown, which only underscores the difference between simple myth and complex reality. Hitsville, U.S.A., was no more a time and place than Arthur's Camelot.

As Berry Gordy told Robin Seymour, local DJ and host of Detroit's own "Teen Town" TV show, which devoted an entire hour-long program to Motown back in 1965, "In the amount of time we have here, it's impossible to really get to the bottom of our organization, as to how it really is inside and who is really responsible. It's not a one-man organization, but it's in the tradition of teamwork. It's so many people that we can't even mention here—the unseen heroes, so to speak. People like Esther Edwards, Ralph Seltzer and . . ."

Chapter Four
REFLECTIONS

 "Billie Jean's not in yet!"
—**LOIS ATKINS,** Billie Jean Brown's secretary, 1965–75

"**T**hat's how a typical day at Motown usually started," Billie Jean Brown laughs. Billie Jean, who spent most of her nineteen years at Motown as head of the Quality Control Department, quickly adds that while she didn't always have to be there at nine, she'd usually be in the office "no later than about nine-thirty."

When Berry Gordy needed someone to write Miracles press releases, he asked Cass Technical to send over some likely prospects. Billie Jean, editing the school paper at the time, won the competition and began hanging around the offices after school, answering fan mail and playing a lot of darts.

Back in 1960 space was limited, so Billie Jean worked out of Gordy's office, a converted bedroom with dart boards on the back of its doors. Gordy, being fond of a gentlemanly wager, liked to lure unsuspecting visitors into sporting propositions with taunts of "I'll bet you can't even beat this girl here." Right.

By 1961 Billie Jean had graduated from Cass Technical and into a full-time job at Motown. Offered a choice between receptionist and tape librarian, she took the former, only to be given the latter. Six months later Motown's tape library was organized, which explains why there are no duplicated release numbers after 1960.

What it doesn't explain is how a $22-a-week tape librarian becomes responsible for quality control. Billie Jean does:

"I could always be counted on to give my honest opinion. When a producer would bring a track into Mr. Gordy's office and there'd be some disagreement, he'd always say, 'Let's ask the kid.'

"See, I wasn't personally involved in it," Billie Jean elaborates. "And I don't care who you are. When you're real close to something, you can't be totally objective. Also I was young and I didn't understand some of the role-playing, the political

COURTESY BILLIE JEAN BROWN, ESQ.

Can I get a witness? Billie Jean Brown, age nineteen. This is a lawyer?

things going on around maybe a certain track. I'd always been brought up to speak my mind. So I did."

Apparently, this was one of those rare historical instances where an employee's honest opinion was rewarded. By 1963 Billie Jean had her own office (next to Gordy's), her own secretary, and her own department, which she would oversee for the next sixteen years. "Of course," she hastens to add, "the final decision was always Mr. Gordy's. After all, it was his money."

In 1979 Billie Jean decided to switch careers, said good-bye to Motown, and enrolled in law school. She currently lives in Los Angeles, and as of this writing, anxiously awaits the results of her bar exam.

In my innocence I asked her to re-create a typical day in the life of Hitsville, U.S.A., but that's impossible. Not only because such a place never existed but because people don't work that way. What's the average day at your job like? "Oh, the same-old, same-old." Exactly.

So think of the following anecdotes, philosophy, and remembrances of things past as snapshots from a family album, like the sepia-tinted wedding picture of Smokey and Claudette Robinson tucked into the corner of your family's mounted photo collage, which, along with the framed December 28, 1968, *Billboard* chart that shows Motown holding down five of the week's Top 10 records, is the only visible clue of how you spent nineteen years of your working life, and the view from inside the picture starts to sound like this:

"I'd go in and read the memos that were waiting for me. Check the first mail—we had interoffice mail deliveries, usually about 10 a.m. You'd check your memorandums and get 'em answered if you needed to answer anything right away.

"Some of 'em didn't need answering. You'd get memos from the Sales Department, reminding you of deadline dates for certain releases that had been set. The date you had to have your master sent off [to the pressing plant] or approved. You'd get something from the Production Department saying they need label copy—we used to do label copy out of our department—by a certain day. You'd get notification of somebody having a meeting [*chuckles*] and I'd start listening to records. I spent most—I would say easily half—of every week listening to records.

"Mostly ours. Of course, I did listen to outside, aside from listening to the radio, being on top of things. We all had radios. Along with turntables, there were a couple of radios and usually a piano in every office. I had a little tin radio that had been built for me that was designed to simulate the sound of a car radio. After you got a mix that was absolutely everything you thought you wanted it to be, using normal systems, then you'd listen to it on there. The theory being that fully half of the people hear a record for the first time on a car radio."

Note: A "mix" determines the relationship between the various sounds you hear on a record. The same basic tracks (vocals, drums, strings, etc.) can be made softer or louder as the situation demands.

Motown used a car radio to test mixes because they knew a radio station's broadcast signal cuts off at a certain point on each end of the sound spectrum and therefore exaggerates the midrange. Motown countered this by making sure they got as much high and low end as possible into their recordings so that the overall effect would not be lost when you heard them on the radio. Nowadays, this is common practice. In the early sixties it was practically revolutionary.

Berry Gordy was big on technology. He employed a resident electronics genius, Michael McLain, who built Motown one of the first eight-track recording facilities in the country.

While almost all independent and even most major record companies were still using two-track or four-track tape recorders—basically, the number of tracks determine the number of instruments you can record separately—Gordy was getting cleaner recordings than just about anyone. Gordy's records were more acceptable to white radio stations because, unlike most R&B discs, they didn't sound like they were recorded at the bottom of the La Brea tar pits. They also were harder for competing record companies to duplicate, imitate, or "improve" on.

Along with building Billie Jean's "little tin radio," McLain equipped Berry Gordy's office with a tape recorder, a second two-track tape recorder that was used for mixdowns, and, best of all, a system by which Gordy could listen to playbacks direct from the recording studio downstairs. Quality control, indeed.

"Then the routine got to be where a lot of music wasn't listened to during the day," Billie Jean continues. "It got so bad with producers and songwriters and artists and everybody interrupting me, 'When you gonna play my song? When you gonna play my song?' that I finally put a picture of an ear on my door with a note saying, 'If you want to hear your song, place your ear here.' But you know Stevie Wonder never paid attention [*chuckles*].

"So it got to be I'd come in late and five-thirty or six, when everybody was preparing to go home, I would spend a good

28. On what label did the Commodores make their Motown recording debut?
29. Several of the Jackson 5's early hits are credited as having been written by "The Corporation." Who were the four people that made up this writing team?
30. When Lionel Richie was a member of the Commodores, what instrument did he play?

couple of hours evaluating things. No phones to be bothered with. Most of the people would be gone. You got a lot more done that way.

"When you get into listening to a mix—especially a comparison of mixes—it takes total concentration when you're getting down to the finite evaluation of one mix over the other.

"And *you can't evaluate records from a tape*, which is something we took a long time trying to convince people. You cannot sit there and say, 'This is a terrific mix,' playing a tape. It might not go on the grooves. Some of 'em just don't cut. They sound hot, but they will not cut without skipping. Or you've got to lower it so low that you lose the edge. So everything was reduced to a disc."

By 1963 Motown had its own disc-cutting operation, located in the basement of the third building. Bob Dennis and, later, Larry Miles were responsible for transferring the sound on a tape onto what was originally a blank plastic disc by means of a stylus. (The same way your record player works, only in reverse. Instead of "reading" the grooves in the record, the disc-cutting machine puts them in the plastic.)

"In many cases it would take longer to get the mix than to write the song and record it. I remember 'Your Precious Love' with Marvin and Tammi. If you listen to the record, at the very end of the fade, she falls off the microphone. She falls back and there's almost a word loss. And there was a lot of time spent trying to duplicate that mix, bring that spot up. There must've been tons of mixes. At least forty. They never quite had that little something—I don't know what it was— there was something about that particular mix that nothing else came up to it. So I put it out. Got a phone call about it, too [*laughs*].

"You start out with your one mix. You listen to the tape and you say, 'I like that, but I want to change one thing.' So you do another mix and you change that one thing and ten mixes later, you think you've got what you want. But—because you changed one something each time—you've gotten so far away from what you started with that there's no real relationship between that first mix and the last one.

"I don't think Mr. Gordy ever came out of his office without having twelve mixes that he really liked and he'd want discs cut on all twelve. Or maybe he'd say, 'Just cut the last four.' And I'd get those cut immediately and I'd get what we call rundowns [acetate disc versions] cut on the other ones.

"And on more than one occasion—I had to do it with him and I had to do it with Brian [Holland]—just about the time the look of total disappointment would cross their faces, I'd

COURTESY BILLIE JEAN BROWN, ESQ.

produce the rundown of the second mix that was done, and *that* would be the closest to what they wanted. They'd say, 'Where'd this come from?' and I'd smile and say, 'You just did it, but you didn't hear it' [*chuckles*]. It's like when you see a child every day, you don't notice that it's growing."

When Billie Jean wasn't comparing mixes or evaluating freshly recorded material, it seemed she was in a meeting: "1963–1964–1966, that was the era of meetings."

Monday morning was A&R. In attendance were Berry Gordy, Billie Jean Brown, and producers Brian Holland, Lamont Dozier, Eddie Holland, Smokey Robinson, Hank Cosby, Ivy Jo Hunter, Clarence Paul, Norman Whitfield, various songwriters, and department head/producer Mickey Stevenson. Topics discussed usually centered around who needs to release an LP and do we have enough usable tracks in the can? What new songs have been written over the past week? And who needs a single out right away?

Management meetings took place on Tuesday mornings. These were the province of ITMI topkick Esther Gordy Edwards and were mostly devoted to deciding who the support acts would be on the Motortown Revues and in what order these acts would appear. In general, this was determined by who had the hottest record or—in the case of some acts—who had a record released.

Sales meetings were Thursday mornings, under the direction of Motown VP/Sales Barney Ales, who operated out of the second building. Along with a look at the week's sales figures, these meetings involved setting up a schedule that would guarantee x number of records would be released and that these would sell x number of records so the company could be sure its monthly billings would cover its overhead.

"We have a very swinging company. . . . " Motown creative staff meeting, Las Vegas, 1969. (Seated, from left): producer-songwriter Frank Wilson, former Miracles member Claudette Robinson, current Motown Productions president Suzanne de Passe, sales honcho Barney Ales, Berry Gordy, Billie Jean Brown, company troubleshooter Ralph Seltzer, and Robert Bullock. (First row, from left): unidentified, secretary Rebecca Jiles, engineer Calvin Harris, unidentified, salesman Tom Noonan, A&R person Betty Ocha, ex-Rayber Voice Raynoma Singleton, Jobete's Mike Ossman, Iris Gordy-Bristol, and tape librarian Fran Heard-Maclin. (Top row, from left): Tony Jones, unidentified, unidentified, promo majordomo Phil Jones, Larry Maxwell, sales director Al Klein, Pat Cosby, and husband/producer Hank Cosby. Others unidentified.

All this is standard stuff. The real action took place at the quality control meetings every Friday morning in Berry Gordy's office. Billie Jean Brown, Esther Gordy Edwards, Mickey Stevenson, Smokey Robinson, Barney Ales, Faye Hale, Taylor Cox, Irv Biegel—basically all the department heads, their subordinates, and the full flower of Motown's producers and songwriters—gathered for listening sessions that often stretched on for up to eight hours. Generally, between twenty and forty finished recordings were played and their merits discussed. Ah, to have been a fly on the wall.

Berry Gordy solicited everyone's opinion, even the cat who ran the tape recorder, but he had no use for technical mumbo jumbo. Whenever somebody started banging on about a record's EQ or some such jargon, Gordy quickly cut them off. As far as Berry Gordy was concerned, there were only two kinds of records: "fantastic" or "garbage"—hits or flops.

Ever the diplomat, Billie Jean glosses over what undoubtedly must have been some, shall we say, heated conversations, preferring to emphasize "the cooperation factor."

If you produced a song on the Four Tops and you lost out to H-D-H (surprise, surprise), you didn't get too frosted. After all, you knew everyone was equal coming out of the chute the next time around. And if you did win out, Brian Holland would even go into the studio and help you remix the record if Gordy decided that's what was needed. No hard feelings, no.

There was also a tie-breaking system. All things being even, the producer who'd cut the last hit record on the act automatically won out. No hard feelings, no.

Like most of us, Billie Jean's memory improves when it comes to recounting her own corporate victories:

"The Tempts and I grew up together and they were always around. And I went to record hops with them and I watched their rehearsals and we always got along real good. But they got real upset with me when I was gonna put out this record. They were just furious. And I got called into Mr. Gordy's office and there were all the Tempts. They were really upset because they thought I'd made the wrong choice—that the record I'd chosen to put out was not going to be a hit.

"So Mr. Gordy asked me to bring it to him and asked me to bring this other record they wanted out. And we played the both of 'em and the record I wanted went out. It was 'Beauty's Only Skin Deep' [laughs]. I mean, if you're gonna be that wrong.

"Another time was with [Brenda Holloway's] 'Every Little Bit Hurts.' Mr. Gordy didn't want to put that out. He said it was a waltz and waltzes don't sell and the tempo was too slow and anyway it wasn't going to be a hit. And everything he said, I hit him with his own phrases.

"Anyway, it was late and my car was in the shop, so I asked Mr. Gordy if he could give me a ride home. All the way we sat on opposite sides of the back seat—just as far apart as you could get—both of us staring out our own window. Finally, Mr. Gordy looked over and he said to me, 'You know, you've gotta lotta nerve.'"

The cooperation factor also meant that everybody did a little bit of everything:

"I remember one time myself, the engineer, Mr. Gordy, and his secretary were all crammed into the studio control room. And it was small. Mr. Gordy was producing and we sat through fifty-seven takes of I don't even remember what song until Mr. Gordy was satisfied he'd got what he wanted. He asked the engineer to play it back and the engineer had forgotten to turn on the tape. That's when I decided to learn the technical end of it.

"You hung around. I played ashtray on a lotta records. Tap it with a drumstick. We used to take mallets like you play a vibraphone with and beat on the top of a grand piano because you'd get the sound of the piano strings vibrating along with the percussion. People used to play our records and try to figure out how we did some of the things—you wouldn't believe some of the sounds you can get shaking black-eyed peas in a jar [laughs].

"Sometimes you were called on. You'd go into the studio and somebody would say, 'Ooh, I don't like that line.' Again, it's real difficult for the person who wrote the song to think of another line and change it, because they wrote it. They obviously like that line, so they can't get away from it. But someone else can come in, and I used to be able to do it—couldn't write a song, couldn't come up with an original idea to save my life [chuckles]—and because you're outside of it, it's easy to come up with three or four words [laughs]."

Billie Jean's most famous songwriting credit is as the cowriter of Shorty Long's "Here Comes the Judge."

"That one was different. That one I did a lot of work on [laughs]. The idea was mine. And I actually produced that record with Shorty Long. See, Sammy Davis, Jr., had been doing the routine on 'Laugh-In' for weeks. We thought it was cute at first and, of course, he kept coming back with it. I was sitting in Mr. Gordy's office and I said, "You know, that's a lot of publicity. It's too bad we don't have a record like that.'

"Mr. Gordy said, 'You're right. Who can we get to do it?' Again, it's one of those 'who needs a record out right now?' things.

31. Who sang lead on the Spinners' "It's a Shame?"
32. Which member of Motown recording group the Originals was the coauthor of the 1964 Reflections hit "Just Like Romeo and Juliet"?
33. What Motown group scored the original hit version of Bonnie Pointer's "Heaven Must've Sent You"?

COURTESY TOM DEPIERRO/AIRWAVE INTERNATIONAL

" **. . . and thirty days for the African twist.**" The court's in session. The Honorable Frederick "Shorty" Long now presiding.

"Shorty Long needed a record out. So I got with him and gave him the idea—'cause Mr. Gordy and I were leaving, going to New York to critique Sammy Davis, Jr.'s revamped *Golden Boy*—and I said, 'When we get back in a couple of days, have the music laid out and we'll get it together.'

"When I came back, the track had been cut. Shorty and I got together, got the lyrics and the story together, and finished it up. I got it mixed and got it out. I think there were about eight or ten renditions of it and ours was the most successful."

According to Billie Jean, most of the unusual songwriting collaborations found on Motown records stemmed from this free-flowing atmosphere:

"Janie Bradford began as Motown's receptionist. After she grew and she didn't have to be a receptionist any longer, Janie worked in the publishing company. And the nice part about working for a record company is that you can write lyrics in between time and nobody's gonna scream and holler at you while you're on the job.

"You've also got people who live on the fringe of things, right? Someone like Ivy Hunter, who lives on the fringe, had friends and acquaintances, who were like maybe heavy into gambling or alcohol or drugs. And some of these people might come through and they'd come down looking for him with a song. And these people were creative or had been at some point in time. They weren't interested in a royalty six months down the line. You need a fix, you need a fix now. You cannot wait six months. So nobody wanted to wait. Gimme a couple hundred bucks now. Yeah, it's yours. I won't say it happened a lot, but it did happen.

"A lot of things weren't planned. 'Ain't No Mountain High Enough' was originally to be done on Tammi Terrell, and I said, 'Boy, that'd sure be great on Marvin. You know, Marvin needs a hit record.' 'Cause Marvin was in a little lull at that point in his record success. So, since Tammi already knew about the record—we'd already sent her a demo—we decided to make a duet out of it."

What about some of the things that were planned, such as getting the Motown acts off the chitlin circuit and into the Copacabana?

"I went to Chicago with the Miracles once and they were on a bill with Shep and the Limelights, Gladys Knight and the Pips, Moms Mabley, Chuck Jackson, and headlining the show were the Shirelles. If you can imagine each of 'em coming off, pouring sweat—no applause.

"It was like there was a freeze. What do you *do* to please these, this audience? They paid *two dollars* to get in and see all this talent. And everybody's working' their buns off tryin' to please these people. Three and four shows a day during the week! Last show starts at midnight or some off-the-wall thing.

"And the money was not that much. How much money could there be with that number of acts and two bucks a head? Real dumps, boy. If I were an act, I'd have been thrilled to get to the Copacabana.

"The other thing was—and it's still the same—the gamble is on the company. The company is the one that spends the money. The artist isn't risking anything. You go in, they give you a shot, let you record, and whatever recording costs are, if it doesn't happen, you can walk away.

"If they release you or you get out of your contract, you can go out, walk outside the building, and find a million dollars on the street and you get to keep it. You're not required to pay back that company a penny of the money they spent on you. That's the nature of the business.

"I'm not with Motown right now. I don't depend on them for a paycheck, so I'm free to say what I want to say. It sounds real tired and kinda clichéd, but it's true: There are a lotta talented people in the world and you can't afford to have an attitude problem. No one is irreplaceable.

"There were times—and I understand where some of the artists were coming from—but then again, they weren't seeing the whole picture. Like some people are always saying in interviews about how they used to have to sweep the floors at Motown."

Note: She's talking about the Spinners, who also worked in the stockroom and chauffered other Motown artists—the group wasn't exactly riding a string of hits.

"*They got paid for it!* The business is exciting, but you need the stability of a certain income coming in every week. You can't expect to be paid just to be an artist." (Wouldn't you just love to have this woman working for you?)

"Yeah, sometimes people would get real upset. But it's like family. You get in a fight with your old lady or old man or your kid, there may be some things that you're gonna say that you don't really mean on a particular occasion.

"I don't like to knock anybody, but I'd have to say, for example, Mary Wells. Now, you will never realize it if you don't really listen to it, but Mary Wells was Smokey with a different voice, okay? The work that was put into every cut she sang. Not just the demos. He started with her at the piano. Hours and hours and hours.

"Sure, she had a unique voice and her voice was so totally different from his that you couldn't hear that it was all Smokey. If it was [Spinners lead singer] G. C. Cameron, you'd hear that it was Smokey, because G.C. could mimic the

sound. Mary couldn't mimic the sound but she brought something of her own to it.

"However, the amount of work put in getting each cut—she knew it, I knew it, everybody else knew it, and her husband, who was as far as I'm concerned the cause of her forgetting what was going on and leaving because we weren't treating her properly—he knew it.

"And all those rumors about Motown making such a big effort to keep her down. Bullshit. We didn't have enough money to keep anybody else down when we were too busy spending what we had to try to bring our own up.

"Like Smokey always used to say, 'If you want to find out who the *real* singers are, take them into the studio and drop all the tracks but the voice [chuckles].'"

Billie Jean is rolling now.

"Then there was what I call the 'memo era.' Everything had to be in writing, in triplicate. Minutes from every meeting. Remix forms. You kept a card file on all the artists, and everything they recorded was put on there. We were more like a paper factory than a hit factory for a while there [laughs].

"I remember one time I needed a new coat. I'm hard on coats. I always wear 'em out at the sleeve. Now, all the other department heads could give their people raises. But I worked for Mr. Gordy. So I decided to play innocent.

"So I put on my coat inside out, and I went into Mr. Gordy's office. He looked at me and said, 'What's wrong with your coat?'

"I told him, 'Nothing's wrong with my coat.'

"He said, 'Go do a memo giving yourself a raise.'"

Billie Jean goes on to say how she was paid very well—the raises might've been a little late in coming, but they were substantial. ("I had no right to be making the kind of money I was making at that age.")

Sitting in an apartment full of books, Billie Jean confesses that her car—a mid-seventies Mercedes sedan—is "my only status symbol."

"Now, I have another car. An old station wagon that I use to haul things. And a couple times a week I'd drive it into work, just so it wouldn't sit. 'Cause what do I care.

"One night I was one of the last ones there and Diana had to be at the studio. She was recording. So I had to drive her.

"Diana decides she needs some brandy for her throat. Now, if you know rich people, they never carry any money and I didn't have any money 'cause I was just going into work. So I drop her off at the studio and I'm driving around trying to find a place where I can buy liquor with a credit card.

34. Michael and Jermaine Jackson were the second pair of brothers to record as Motown solo artists. Who were the first?

35. Joe Stubbs, brother of Four Tops lead vocalist Levi Stubbs, sang lead with two different Motown groups. What are their names?

36. What is current Motown recording artist Rockwell's real name?

"So I go into a Thrifty drugstore and all they have is two kinds of brandy. Now, I don't drink and the only brandy I know is Courvoisier and you know Thrifty's isn't gonna have that. They had Hiram Walker and they had something called Napoleon brandy. So I figured Napoleon, he's French, it has to be good.

"I went back to the studio and poured it in a cup and sent it down to Diana. They were all standing around taking a break. She took one sip and screamed, 'Who went back to the Detroit projects to get this?' "

Billie Jean laughs, lights another Salem, and stares out her second-floor living room window. Low clouds. It's getting dark. You can barely make out the Hollywood sign. She glances at the half inch of cold tea remaining in her Mabel John promotional coffee cup.

My shadow's getting too long for the room. I tell her thanks and good-bye, and assure her that if there's any poetic justice in this world, the person who cowrote "Here Comes the Judge" should have no problem passing the bar exam. She manages a dry chuckle.

Driving home, it starts to rain. I punch on my radio and Diana Ross is singing the opening lines of "Reflections."

It was too perfect. . . .

Chapter Five

THE MOTORTOWN REVUE

"We were like carrying a banner for Detroit. Every time we'd go to New York, Chicago, different places, they would have the Motortown Revue and the so-and-so revue—wherever we were at—and it was like a duel. And so we brought the banners back home. We set *fire*."

—COUNCIL GAY, the Contours

In 1951 there was a local talent show at Detroit's Paradise Theater. The winners were Hank Ballard and the Midnighters (minus Hank Ballard and then known as the Royals), Little Willie John, and, in third place, Jackie Wilson. All three became what would now be called "R&B superstars" and they all had to leave Detroit to do it.

Record companies had been pulling talent out of Detroit for years. The great jazz/blues songstress Dinah Washington, blues giant John Lee Hooker, and alto sax man Paul Williams were among the first, back in the forties. By the end of the next decade, you could add Della Reese, Johnny Ray, LaVern Baker, and bandleaders Willie Bryant and Todd Rhodes to the Motor City cavalcade of stars.

Then there were the rock 'n' rollers: happy organist Dave "Baby" Cortez and wildman Andre Williams, whose greasy instrumentals and caustic humor have made him a minor cult hero among connoisseurs of the bizarre. Detroit also produced a pair of exceptional vocal groups in Nolan Strong and the Diablos, led by Barrett's cousin, and the Falcons, whose ranks included future soul stars Wilson Pickett, Eddie Floyd, and Joe Stubbs, Levi's brother.

Not forgetting the Queen of Soul, Aretha Franklin, her singing sisters, Erma and Carolyn, and her father, the Reverend C. L. Franklin, who recorded several albums' worth of sermons for Chess Records. It's still hard to believe that with all this talent knocking around, Detroit had no major recording company prior to Motown.

Berry Gordy didn't exactly step into a vacuum. Several local R&B labels predated Tamla, notably Fortune and Anna Records. Dozens of others sprang up in the wake of Gordy's success. Thelma Gordy herself formed a pair of flyweight labels, Thelma and GeGe Records.

Although Motown's competitors cut an awful lot of good records, from artists such as J. J. Barnes, the Dynamics, the Detroit Emeralds, the Fantastic Four, Lee Rogers, the Volumes, the Reflections, Jay Wiggins, the Dramatics, the Parliaments, and Edwin Starr, most of these had little impact beyond the city limits.

They might have been great soul records, but Berry Gordy

COURTESY BILLIE JEAN BROWN, ESQ.

Superfreak. Shown here in his "Wine-Head Willie" character, this funnyman emceed most of the Motortown Revues before hitting the bigtime with **Ghostbusters.**

wasn't interested in making great soul records—Motown is a pop label, remember? That's why Berry Gordy not only didn't sign anyone who couldn't sing but signed only those artists who he thought could make the transition into the wider, whiter pop market. He had no use for a Wilson Pickett.

Nine times out of ten, Gordy was right. With a very few exceptions Motown's artists were from Detroit. Judging from the track record, they were the cream of the crop. And since the competition within Motown itself was so fierce, the most talented artists on the roster were the ones who rose to the top.

Of course, this survival-of-the-fittest scenario seems a little too pat, considering that acts like the Spinners, Gladys Knight and the Pips, the Isley Brothers, and even the Jacksons sold more records after they left Motown than while they were there. Nor does it take into account the obvious differences an artist's, shall we say, attitude can make in determining one's success. Talent will ultimately win out unless it self-destructs first, which brings us right back to the survival of the fittest again.

But right now it's star time, ladies and gentlemen, star time! So without further ado, I now present to you those stars of stage, screen, and rhythm 'n' blues, the MOTORTOWN REVUE!!!

THE CONTOURS

A truly fantabulous rock 'n' roll band, these proud Detroiters represented Motown at its R&B raunchiest. "Do You Love Me" (1962) remains their undying claim to fame, with its great fake fade-out two-thirds of the way through (works every time) and this immortal introduction, which houses just about all the Contours' philosophical tenets:

> *You broke my heart 'cause I couldn't dance*
> *You didn't even want me around*
> *And now I'm back to let you know*
> *I can really shake 'em down. . . .*

And you know that's right.

Billy Gordon, Sylvester Potts, Billy Hoggs, Hubert Johnson, and Joe Billingslea were the original Contours. Guitarist Hugh Davis joined in 1962. Several members exited over the next five years, to be replaced by Council Gay, Jerry Green, Temptation-to-be Dennis Edwards, and former Falcon Joe Stubbs, the last of whom sang lead on "Just a Little Misunderstanding" (1966), a fine, fine, superfine record that was a bigger hit in Britain than in the United States.

Of course, the Limeys were a little late catching on. Pick up on this 1962 U.K. review of the Contours' then-current LP:

"If you like weirdie vocal group sounds this disc is for you. This five-singers, one-guitarist group produces some wild, shouting vocals, with a different sound or two instrumentally as well. In this way, it's exciting but not everyone's meat."

Berry Gordy wasn't all that impressed on first audition, either. It was only when Hubert Johnson's cousin Jackie Wilson pulled B.G.'s coat and hipped him to the group that Gordy came across with a seven-year contract. "Whole Lotta Woman" b/w "Come on and Be Mine" (Motown 1008, 1961) was the Contours' first disc, notable chiefly for its nonalbum B-side. Their second, "Funny" b/w "The Stretch," is significant only in that it's the first Motown record with the now-famous map on the label.

After "Do You Love Me," the group's first release on Gordy Records and that label's first hit, the Contours cut loose with a

"Watch me now . . . " They could Mashed Potato, they could do the Twist. The Contours (from left): Hugh Davis, Hubert Johnson, Billy Gordon, Billy Hoggs, Joe Billingslea, and Sylvester Potts.

COURTESY MICHAEL OCHS ARCHIVES

string of similar jive-bombs: "Shake Sherrie" (1963) featured a bug-eyed, sloppy-drunk groove that made it almost a standard among Merseybeat combos, while 1964's "Can You Do It"—complete with E-Z eight-step instructions, "it" being a dance—was revived by producer Frank Zappa as a vehicle for Grand Funk back in 1976.

Best of all these minor hits was Smokey Robinson's tender tale of romance and finance, "First I Look at the Purse" (1965), in which lead Contour Billy Gordon proclaims that his need for a "one-button suit" is so great that he doesn't care if the woman's covered with a rash, long as she's got the cash to spring for it.

Audiences apparently agreed with the Contours' tongue-in-chic approach. Then-member Council Gay recalls that "women threw purses on stage" when the song was performed.

"See, we were not only a singing group, we were an entertaining group," Council continues. "We danced, did all kinds of gymnastics and little skits, you know? Just like Broadway, we tried to give the people what they paid for—a show. We did it all."

"We used to have fun," adds Joe Billingslea, "because—not braggin', but anyone back in the sixties can tell you—we were the most dynamic group that Motown had. We used to have competitions against the Temptations. They would have beautiful harmony, nice routines—we couldn't sing as well as they could but we'd kill 'em on stage. The Miracles the same way. It was friendly competition—we were friends—but on stage it was a job."

Of course, the Temptations remember these days a little differently. Who's right? I don't know, but the last act I'd want to follow—besides Huey "Piano" Smith and the Clowns, because you never know what a band that admits to being clowns is liable to do—is one that inspires women to throw their purses on stage. I mean, isn't *that* what rock 'n' roll is all about?

THE ELGINS

Best known for "Darling Baby" and "Heaven Must've Sent You," both of which cracked the R&B Top 10 in 1966, this three-man, one-woman group has an unusual history.

Sandra Edwards, who sang lead, began her Motown career under the name Sandra Mallett. Backed by the Vandellas, she recorded "It's Gonna Be Hard Times" for the Tamla label in 1962. It's good, especially Sandra's vocal. It's likewise very rare.

Meanwhile, the guys in the group (Johnny Dawson, Cleo

37. Who is the male voice singing on the Supremes' hit "Someday We'll Be Together"?
38. What Motown song is the only tune ever to be officially issued by the Beatles and the Rolling Stones?
39. Which member of Holland-Dozier-Holland never recorded as a Motown solo artist?

COURTESY TOM DEPIERRO/AIRWAVE INTERNATIONAL

"Duke" Miller, and Robert Fleming) were also recording for Tamla under a different name. As the Downbeats, they cut a smooth, almost supper-club ballad entitled "Your Baby's Back" that bought a one-way ticket to Nowheresville upon its release in '62.

When the two acts merged and resurfaced on the V.I.P. label in 1966, early copies of "Darling Baby" were credited on the label as being sung by the Downbeats. Motown swiftly slapped an Elgins sticker over the copies and corrected the "mistake" on subsequent pressings.

There's no mistaking the greatness of Sandra's performance, though. Her phrasing on "let's talk it over, baby, baby, baby, baby, let's talk it over *one more time*" makes for ten of the most yearning seconds in Motown's history.

As for "Heaven Must've Sent You," let's just say that when you go to look up the meaning of the word "irresistible" in future dictionaries, you'll get a recording of this song. Credit writers-producers H-D-H and give the drummer (Benny Benjamin) some.

THE FOUR TOPS

Together since 1954 without a personnel change, the Four Tops (Levi Stubbs, Lawrence Payton, Abdul "Duke" Fakir, and Renaldo "Obie" Benson) began their career as the Four Aims. They made one record, singing backup vocals on some off-the-wall Detroit label. They changed their name to the

Four Tops in 1956, when they cut their second disc ("Kiss Me Baby"), this time for Chess Records.

Over the next six years the group leaned more toward a supper-club style, working the Miami–Las Vegas–Catskills resort circuit and recording a third single ("Ain't That Love") for Columbia Records in 1961. (This Columbia track was reissued in 1965 in an attempt to cash in on the Four Tops' newfound success. Berry Gordy asked Columbia not to release it, but the label persisted. Motown stopped getting its records pressed at Columbia facilities shortly thereafter . . .)

Upon their arrival at Motown in 1963 the Four Tops were groomed for more of this same "two weeks in the lounge" action, cutting an album's worth of material for Motown's jazz subsidiary, Workshop Records. Any plans to release this LP were scrapped soon after H-D-H ran down to the local club the group was working and hauled them into the studio at 3 a.m. to record a song the trio had just written.

The tune was "Baby I Need Your Loving" and it climbed to number 11 nationally in a year (1964) when *Billboard* published no R&B charts. It's also a classic. And dig how much mileage lead singer Levi Stubbs gets out of this one simple accent: "Baby, I need your lovin'/*Got* to have all your lovin'." Hear it and know the meaning of soul.

"Just look over your shoulder! . . ."
The Four Tops in action.

COURTESY TOM DePIERRO/AIRWAVE INTERNATIONAL.

"My real style of singing is just a natural thing," Levi explains. "What I mean by that is I don't consider myself as being a heckuva singer, man. I'm more of a stylist, if you will."

And what style! Whatever Levi's raw, rough-edged voice lacked in range, it more than made up for in emotional weight. Take 1965's double number one, "I Can't Help Myself." Little kids might've played jump rope to these lyrics, but even they never doubted for a second the weakness of the man in love who sang them.

Other than the moody "Ask the Lonely" (Mickey Stevenson and Ivy Jo Hunter, 1965) and the magnificent "Loving You Is Sweeter Than Ever" (Hunter and Stevie Wonder, 1966), the best Four Tops tunes came from the pens of Holland-Dozier-Holland, of which "Reach Out, I'll Be There" (1966) and "Standing in the Shadows of Love" (1967) were the real mindbusts.

When H-D-H left Motown in 1969, the Four Tops' career took a dive. Actually, the decline began a year earlier with ill-conceived versions of the Left Banke's "Walk Away Renee" and Tim Hardin's "If I Were a Carpenter." (Although if you've gotta hear anyone sing those songs, it might as well be Levi Stubbs.)

COURTESY TOM DEPIERRO/AIRWAVE INTERNATIONAL

Pop tops. As seen on the sheet music for their first pop number one hit, Four Tops members (clockwise, from upper right) Abdul "Duke" Fakir, Renaldo "Obie" Benson, Lawrence Payton, and Levi Stubbs each had his own view of success.

Later discs such as Smokey Robinson's rambling "Still Water (Love)" and a slick remake of Tommy Edwards' "It's All in the Game" (both 1970) were fine performances, but most of the tunes from this period had all the impact of soggy cereal. Realizing something was missing, the Four Tops exited Motown for Dunhill Records in 1972.

Things looked up during the first couple of years at Dunhill, and 1973's huge hit, "Ain't No Woman (Like the One I've Got)," was particularly good. But the problem of finding material custom-tailored for Stubb's highly individual style eventually caught up with the group and they went through some lean years in the late seventies before returning to the top of the R&B charts with "When She Was My Girl" (Casablanca, 1981).

Cynics can sneer that the song was a complete throwback, but when Levi screams, "The big-legged girl is gone," there's no argument that—after thirty years—the Four Tops are still good for a spin.

MARVIN GAYE

A notoriously stage-shy performer, Marvin Gaye was nevertheless Motown's most versatile voice. The son of a Washington, D.C., minister, Gaye began singing in church. He soon graduated to a local doo-wop group known as the Rainbows, whose other members reportedly included future soul giants Billy Stewart and Don Covay. None of the above sang lead, however, and after two records on the Red Robin label, the group evaporated.

Marvin went into the Air Force. When his hitch was up, he formed the Marquees, who recorded unsuccessfully for OKeh Records in 1958. A year later, he joined Harvey and the Moonglows.

Despite his background as a doo-wopper, Marvin had eyes for a career as a jazz singer, and his first Tamla effort, "Let Your Conscience Be Your Guide" (1961), was in a jazz-blues bag. After two more flops, he suddenly exploded with the tough "Stubborn Kind of Fellow" (1962), on which the Vandellas provided the gospel chorus. "Can I Get a Witness" (1963), featuring the Supremes—uncredited—in the Vandellas' role, was cut from the same shroud, as was "Pride and Joy" from earlier that year.

"Hitch Hike"—also from '63—was tougher yet, with a *bomp-bomp-ba-bomp* (pause) *ba-bomp-bomp-bomp* guitar intro that the Velvet Underground nicked for their own "There She Goes Again" (1967). Other than 1965's "How Sweet It Is," which was more in a finger-snapping, Sam Cooke

COURTESY BILLIE JEAN BROWN, ESQ.

Come and get these memories.
Fresh from the "Stubborn Kind of
Fellow" recording session, Marvin
Gaye and the Vandellas (from left),
Rosalind Ashford, Martha Reeves,
and Annette Beard.

groove, Marvin's best mid-sixties discs were almost hard-rock numbers.

"Baby Don't You Do It" (1964) rode a modified Bo Diddley lick, "I'll Be Doggone" (1965) spotlighted a Byrds-like, folk-rock guitar line, and both "One More Heartache" (1966) and "Ain't That Peculiar" (1965) were built around fast, shifty guitar patterns, courtesy Miracles guitarist Marv Tarplin, who cowrote the last three tunes.

However, Marvin's best sixties record was in a completely different mold. Even though the song had been a hit for Gladys Knight and the Pips the year before, no one had ever heard anything like it. Listening to Marvin's version of "I Heard It through the Grapevine" (1968) was like overhearing a murder being plotted and gradually realizing the "victim" they're talking about is *you*. "Voodoo music," the late guitarist Mike Bloomfield once called it, and that was back when Mike's opinion still meant something.

Marvin's ability to handle this wide range of styles, including the underrated "Too Busy Thinking about My Baby"

(1969), a full-blown uptown R&B number that's as sunny as "Grapevine" is dark, made him the natural choice when one of Motown's female stars needed a partner for a boy-girl duet. Mary Wells was up first ("Once upon a Time" b/w "What's the Matter with You Baby," 1964), followed by Kim Weston ("It Takes Two," 1967) and Tammi Terrell, with whom the combination yielded four Top 10 pop hits in two years. (For more on these discs see each woman's entry.)

The association with Tammi Terrell ended on a painful note. In 1967 she collapsed onstage in Marvin's arms. Three years and eight operations later, she died from complications brought on by a brain tumor. It would be four years before Marvin resumed live performances.

By this time, Marvin's versatility had taken him to new heights. Beginning in 1971 with *What's Going On*, Marvin started singing, writing, producing, and playing most of the instruments on his recordings. But we're getting ahead of ourselves. (We'll cover most Motown performers' seventies careers in Chapter 10.)

BRENDA HOLLOWAY

If good looks could kill, Brenda Holloway would've put half the male population of her native Los Angeles on the critical list. Voluptuous, and with a voice to match, it's not hard to see why she's what you might call a cult figure.

Seriously, the woman could *sing*. Brenda says she developed her steel-belted vocal cords early on. "Everybody says I'm loud," claims Brenda. "It was bein' raised in Watts [*laughs*]. They don't have any mikes in Watts. They get stolen from the church."

When Motown first opened its West Coast office back in the mid-sixties, Brenda was the major discovery. She'd recorded previously for the L.A. indy label Donna, but her 1964 Tamla debut ("Every Little Bit Hurts") became her biggest hit. A big, beautiful, bluesy ballad, the song is a surefire showstopper and, as such, has become a standard of its type.

The lilting "When I'm Gone" (1965) is even better. Brenda's vocal sounds *so* confident; we'll let her tell the story:

"Mary Wells left Motown and she was gone," Brenda giggles. "And Smokey was without an artist, and if you ever see Smokey without an artist, it's like a day without sunshine. So he needed someone to fill that space and I was available and, uh, I tried to sound like Mary Wells."

So much for the confidence theory. After scoring a minor hit with the original version of "You've Made Me So Very Happy" (1967), mostly because the tune's odd tempo changes

COURTESY MICHAEL OCHS ARCHIVES

Every little bit hurts. Brenda Holloway shows why she's known as a cult figure.

work at cross-purposes to her throaty, lounge-soul delivery—check out those fabulous open-air choruses, though—Brenda got tired of waiting for Motown to make her a superstar.

Nowadays, she only sings in church, where she *still* doesn't have a microphone and probably doesn't need one.

THE ISLEY BROTHERS

Ronald, Rudolph, and O'Kelly Isley had already racked up a pair of monster hits ("Shout" and "Twist and Shout") before coming to Motown. "This Old Heart of Mine" (Tamla, 1966) was the Isleys' only real hit during their three-year stay at the label, but it too was a certified monster.

Everything about this record is just the hippest, from the pulsating bass line to the glittering string arrangement that keeps breaking away from the vocalists and actually increases the energy level. Sophisticates will also notice how the disc's cyclical, rolling feel—the snowball effect—is due to the continual up-then-down motion of the chord progression. Simple but effective.

Several of the Isleys' other Tamla recordings are nearly as good: "Behind a Painted Smile," "Just Ain't Enough Love," and a percussive workout on "Take Me in Your Arms (Rock Me a Little While)" that beats Kim Weston's 1965 hit version

COURTESY MICHAEL OCHS ARCHIVES

Family atmosphere. Successful before, during, and after their stay at Motown, the Isley Brothers (from left), O'Kelly, Ronnie, and Rudolph Isley. They're now into their fourth decade of hits.

like a red-haired stepchild. As for the Doobie Brothers' 1975 remake, it only hurts when you laugh.

After these nonhits and a 1968 British tour where they became reacquainted with their onetime backup guitarist, a certain Mr. Jimi Hendrix, the Isleys decided to make a few changes. They left Motown, added two more brothers (Ernie and Marvin) and a cousin (Chris Jasper) to the act and fired up the funk with "It's Your Thing" (1969), their first hit for the group's own T-Neck label. They're now into their *fourth decade* of hits.

GLADYS KNIGHT AND THE PIPS

Gladys had won first prize of $2,000 on the 1952 Ted Mack National Radio Contest at age eight. Five years later she and

If I were your woman. Having won first prize in the 1952 National Radio Amateur Contest, eight-year-old Gladys Knight curtsies for the judges.

COURTESY MICHAEL OCHS ARCHIVES

"Perfection in performance."
That's what Gladys Knight and the Pips—(from left) Edward Patten, William Guest, Gladys, and Merald "Bubba" Knight—liked to say the name "Pips" stood for. As if anyone who wore fishnet stockings with a plastic dress wasn't capable of a put-on.

the Pips (brother Merald "Bubba" Knight and cousins Edward Patten and William Guest) made a one-off single for Brunswick Records that's so obscure even *they've* probably forgotten about it. Their first hit came in 1961 with "Every Beat of My Heart," a song that appeared on three different labels. Here's how it happened:

The Pips first cut the tune—a hit for the Royals (remember them?) ten years earlier—for the tiny Atlanta indy Huntom Records, which sold the rights to Vee-Jay Records, which issued it nationally. Meanwhile, Bobby Robinson had already heard the Huntom recording, signed the group to his own Fury Records and had them rerecord the song exactly the way they'd done it the first time. Vee-Jay got the bigger pop hit, Fury the bigger R&B number. Of course, this doesn't have much to do with The Motown Story, but it's interesting to note how all these names intersect, no?

After a second hit for Fury ("Letter Full of Tears," 1961) and a couple of years at Maxx Records, Gladys and the guys came to Motown, where they racked up eleven Top 10 R&B hits in six years.

"I Heard It through the Grapevine" (Soul, 1967) was the funkiest, playing off the tension created by the Pips' tight harmonies, which threatened to box the volatile Gladys in at every turn. Pure call-and-response, me-and-you, the natural truth.

By the turn of the decade the group had moved from down-home gospel fire to lush, equally soulful ballads. "I Don't Want to Do Wrong" and "If I Were Your Woman" (both 1971) and, especially, 1973's "Neither One of Us (Wants to Be the First to Say Goodbye)" feature not only the longest song titles this side of Dave Mason but also some of the steamiest lead vocals in all of pop music. You really don't appreciate these records until you've heard a half dozen of Merv's or Mike's or Sammy's guests take a crack at 'em. Pretty scary stuff.

The mildly humorous "Daddy Could Swear, I Declare" (1973) was Gladys Knight and the Pips' last Motown smash. That year they switched to Buddah Records, where they continued to crank out the hits, of which "Midnight Train to Georgia" (also 1973) was the first, the biggest, and probably the best. One reason for the move was the promise of a film career, and Gladys did star in 1976's *Pipe Dreams*, in which she played the wife of a construction worker who follows him to Alaska in his search for a job on the then-current oil pipeline project. Her real-life husband, Barry Hamlinson, played the male lead, while the Pips did the soundtrack for this celluloid disappearing act. Maybe if they would've sung "I Heard It through the Pipeline" . . .

After that, the group went through a dry spell—when contract hassles forced Gladys to take off on a solo career that didn't—but they reunited and now record for the Columbia label, where they recently scored a huge comeback hit with "Save the Overtime for Me."

SHORTY LONG

There's not much to say about Shorty (born Frederick) Long that hasn't been covered earlier. He came to Motown as part of the Anna/Harvey/Tri-Phi contingent, kicked off the Soul subsidiary with "Devil with the Blue Dress" in 1964 and died at age twenty-nine. (He drowned while fishing in the Detroit River.)

"Here Comes the Judge" (1968) was his biggest hit—Top 10 pop and R&B—and is noteworthy for the priceless couplet in which Shorty claims he would rather be lost in the jungles of

Brazil than to face that morning's judge knowin' how the magistrate feels.

That Shorty. What a card. Motown apparently thought so, too. Along with hipping everybody to the "Function at the Junction" (1966), Shorty emceed many a Motortown Revue.

MARTHA AND THE VANDELLAS

The group was originally known as the Dell-Fi's and there were four members: Martha Reeves, Rosalind Ashford, Annette Sterling (née Beard), and then-lead singer Gloria Williams. They got their first label credit singing backups on budding soul star J. J. Barnes' "Won't You Let Me Know" (Kable, 1960). The quartet recorded a couple of singles on Check-Mate under their own name as well.

When these discs didn't exactly burn a hole in the charts, Martha, who had already done some solo singing as Martha Lavaille, decided to resume her solo career. She auditioned for Motown and was offered a job as a secretary to A&R chief Mickey Stevenson. It was $35 a week and a chance to learn the business, so she took it.

COURTESY TOM DEPIERRO/AIRWAVE INTERNATIONAL

Love makes me do foolish things.
Martha and the Vandellas (from left), Betty Kelly, Martha Reeves, and Rosalind Ashford. Gowns by Carpeteria.

In 1962. when Mary Wells failed to show for a session, Martha recommended her old group be used as a replacement. To avoid contractual difficulties, the Del-Fi's changed their name to the Vells, and the tune that Mary Wells missed out on—"There He Is (at My Door)"—was issued on Motown's short-lived Mel-O-Dy subsidiary. It flopped, and Gloria Williams quit the business for good.

Rechristened the Vandellas—a name Martha reportedly derived from local landmarks *Van* Dyke Avenue and *Della* Reese—the trio became Mickey Stevenson's favorite backup vocalists. Sometimes they were given label credit, as on the Marvin Gaye and Sandra Mallett sides previously mentioned, and sometimes they weren't, as on Marvin's "Hitch Hike" and "Pride and Joy."

So when Mary Wells missed yet another session, guess who was in line for a break? "I'll Have to Let Him Go" (Gordy, 1962) was the group's first under the name Martha and the Vandellas and, in Martha's words, "Didn't sell but about three copies and I think we bought all three of 'em."

Their second ("Come and Get These Memories," 1963) did better, hitting the R&B Top 10, and the group's star was on the rise. The explosive "Heat Wave" (also '63)—recorded in the middle of winter and held for a July release—the festive "Dancing in the Street" (1964) and the claustrophobic "Nowhere to Run" (1965) were their classics from this period. Martha came on like a maniac wielding a blowtorch, and the combination of her fiery vocals with some of Motown's hottest rhythm tracks sent all three tunes straight into the pop Top 10.

Martha, Rosalind, and former Velvelette Betty Kelly, who joined in 1963, kicked out another half dozen hits, but after 1968 the winds of fortune shifted and Martha Reeves and the Vandellas—as they were known from 1967's "Honey Chile" on—never hit the Top 40 again.

This fall from grace was anything but smooth. Martha's sister Lois Reeves took over for Betty Kelly in 1968. Two years later Sandra Tilley, also a former Velvelette, replaced Rosalind Ashford. By 1971 the group called it quits.

Martha went solo, to widespread indifference. Through it all she managed to keep her sense of humor. When asked by an interviewer if the "Jimmy Mack" celebrated in 1967 song was, in fact, a real person, Martha replied, "Well, I met about six Jimmy Macks after we recorded it."

THE MARVELETTES

From the booming metropolis of Inkster, Michigan—located about thirty miles outside Detroit—came five school-

40. Who wrote Motown's company song?

41. Motown's staff choreographer had been a featured dancer—with his partner—in several forties musicals. What is his name?

42. What was the first record officially issued on the Motown label?

girls (Gladys Horton, Katherine Anderson, Georgeanna Dobbins, Juanita Cowart, and Wanda Young) who called themselves the Casingettes, because they all agreed they can't-sing-yet.

Despite the group's modest view of their own talents, the first time they walked into a recording studio, they walked out with a number one pop record—"Please Mr. Postman" (Tamla, 1961). Also a new name, the Marvelettes.

Personnel started changing almost immediately. Juanita exited before their second release, titled (what else?) "Twistin' Postman."

The Marvelettes remained a quartet for about a year, during which they pulled down two more huge hits: "Beechwood 4-5789" and "Playboy," the latter cowritten by lead singer Gladys Horton.

When they all graduated from high school, Georgeanna Dobbins, who had written the basics of "Please Mr. Postman" overnight, chose life as a Motown secretary over life as a Marvelette and the group carried on as the trio we all know and love. Anne Bogan replaced Gladys Horton in 1969, but after 1968 the Marvelettes' career was a dead issue.

The Marvelettes' hits, however, will live forever. "Please Mr. Postman" might have Motown's all-time greatest intro ("Wait!" the girls scream in unison), while "I'll Keep Holding On" (1965) uses ever-ascending key changes to create a subtle sense of rising tension that's rivaled only by the Kinks' 1964 chord-crusher, "You Really Got Me," a record that employs the same device, known in musical circles as "modulation."

Then there's the slinky "Don't Mess with Bill" (1966), featuring Wanda Young in the lead vocal spotlight, and "Danger Heartbreak Dead Ahead" (1965) with its great, dopey "Who knows what evil lurks in the hearts of men?" intro. ("It's vanity, insanity," the girls answer.)

Equally deep are "Too Many Fish in the Sea" (1964), in which the girls take turns advising us that there are short ones and tall ones, fine ones and kind ones, and "The Hunter Gets Captured by the Game" (1967), which sports some of the songwriter Smokey Robinson's cleverest metaphors.

Sassy, trashy, and classy. At their peak the Marvelettes could dish it out, pick it up, and put it on with the best of 'em. As for that mysterious, bargain-basement Crystals imitation "Too Hurt to Cry," issued under the name the Darnells on Gordy Records in 1963—hey, our lips are sealed.

THE MIRACLES

One of Berry Gordy's earliest finds, the Miracles (William "Smokey" Robinson, Ronnie White, Bobby Rogers, Warren

"Gather 'round, swingers and friends. . . . " The Miracles: live from Bob Uecker's seats.

"Pete" Moore, and Claudette Rogers) began their recording career back in 1958. By 1964, when Claudette—now Mrs. Smokey Robinson—decided motherhood and membership in the Miracles didn't mix, the group had already waxed such classic tracks as "Shop Around" (Tamla, 1961) and "You Really Got a Hold on Me" (1962).

Blessed with the warmest falsetto in all of pop, lead singer Smokey proved you don't have to scream to be soulful. Lung-pumping ballads such as "The Tracks of My Tears" and "Ooh Baby Baby" (both 1965) were Smokey's specialty, but the Miracles cut their share of uptempo chartbusters as well.

"Mickey's Monkey" (1963), "Going to a Go-Go" (1966), and "The Tears of a Clown" (1970) all rock as hard as anything in the Motown catalog, while "I Gotta Dance to Keep from Crying" (1964), with its superb "Gather 'round swingers and friends" intro, makes for sound advice that can be taken to heart as well as feet.

The post-Claudette quartet racked up nearly two dozen hits in the eight years between 1964 and 1972, of which 1967's shimmering "The Love I Saw in You Was Just a Mirage" stands as the Miracles' minor masterpiece. Stately acoustic guitar lines, breathless vocals, and an absolutely gorgeous melody combine with some of Smokey's thorniest lyrics ("Now all that's left is lipstick traces of kisses you only pretended to feel") to produce an aura of unreality that you could eat with a spoon. The sequence in *American Gigolo* where Richard Gere sings the tune along with Smokey on the stereo while trying to decide which $700 suit to wear is every bit as ice as Mick Jagger's more famous rendition of "Memo From Turner" in *Performance*.

After 1972 Smokey took a three year sabbitical to spend some time with his family. As a performer-songwriter-producer of undeniable talent, he'd been working his booty to the bone for the last fourteen years. Although the group was billed as Smokey Robinson and the Miracles from 1967 on, it should be noted that the Miracles were never a one-man show. Many of their songs were group collaborations, and with the addition of a new lead singer (Billy Griffin) the Miracles kept going well into the seventies. (Both Smokey's and the Miracles' stories continue in Chapter 10.)

THE MONITORS

Another three-man, one-woman group, the Monitors (Sandra and John "Maurice" Fagin, Warren Harris, and Richard Street), is chiefly remembered for its 1966 remake of "Greetings (This Is Uncle Sam)," a song originally recorded by white vocal group the Valadiers for the Motown subsidiary label Miracle five years earlier.

The Monitors' version released on V.I.P. is a slicker recording and the rap by the "drill sergeant" in the middle is a little different, but other than that, the two records are almost identical. Same cascading, recruiting-poster "I need you" background vocals, same "you're in the army now" break followed by a blood-curdling falsetto screech, same . . . Yeah, real laff-a-minute stuff.

THE ORIGINALS

This Detroit quartet's name was particularly appropriate. Half the group, Walter Gaines and C. P. Spencer, had been making records for Berry Gordy as far back as 1957, when they were two of the Five Stars. A third Original, Freddie Gorman, had recorded as a solo artist for Gordy's Miracle label back in 1961. Only the fourth member, Hank Dixon, had no previous Motown-related experience. (Note: The *original* Originals were a quintet, with Joe Stubbs, fresh from his stint with the Contours, as the fifth member. When, despite his earthy lead vocal, the floor-shaking "Need Your Loving (Want It Back)" flopped upon its 1966 release as the B-side of "Good Night, Irene"—huh?—Joe split to join 100 Proof Aged in Soul.)

From 1965 to 1969 the Originals were Motown's first-string male background vocalists, singing on hits by Marvin Gaye, Stevie Wonder, Jimmy Ruffin, Shorty Long, and, as Hank

43. Who was the first member of the Gordy family to record for the company?
44. Which recording group left Motown to form their own record label, which they've maintained since 1969?
45. The man who sang Motown's first major hit later became one of the company's top songwriters. What is his name?

The original Originals. Although best known as a quartet, the Originals—(from left), Walter Gaines, C. P. Spencer, Hank Dixon, and Freddie Gorman—began as a quintet with ex-Contour Joe Stubbs as the fifth member.

Dixon recalls with a wry chuckle, "even some of the girl groups."

Marvin Gaye was responsible for bringing the Originals out of the session shadows and into the spotlight when he cowrote and produced "Baby I'm for Real" (Soul, 1969), a lovely flashback to the days when Marvin himself doo-wooped his way through many a street-corner standard. The Originals responded by singing the sap out of the sucker, and the result was a number one R&B hit.

"The Bells" (1970), also cowritten and produced by Marvin, found the Originals on similar turf and was almost as big a hit. Again, the group's harmonies were as fine as their vines, but then any doo-wop tune with the word "bells" in its title is bound to be good.

The Originals hung tough for another six years but were unable to duplicate their previous successes. Some things you just can't put into words. Doo-wop, shoo-bop.

JIMMY RUFFIN

Drafted shortly after he cut his first record for the Miracle label in 1961, Jimmy Ruffin was forced to put his career on hold for three years. Upon his return, Jimmy—whose younger brother, David, was then a member of the Temptations—became part of the Soul label's roster.

"What Becomes of the Brokenhearted" (1966), a widescreen ballad of epic sweep and grandeur, was Jimmy's only Top 10 pop record. It also set the pattern for most of his later recordings: all sudsy, melodramatic choruses and orchestrations thick as a Russian novel.

Several of these sonic soufflés saw R&B chart action, and he did even better in England, where he scored three Top 10 hits

I'VE PASSED THIS WAY BEFORE

Ruffin tuff. David's older brother, Jimmy, looking just as smooth as he sang.

in 1970 alone, but despite his considerable vocal talents, Jimmy was always at the mercy of his material. Most of the time he ended up pushing more soap than Procter and Gamble (or Gamble and Huff).

Disenchanted, Jimmy left the label in 1974. His light, pure tone and cloud-scraping falsetto have brought him only occasional success since.

THE SPINNERS

Like Diana Ross, Smokey Robinson, and the Jacksons, the Spinners have been awarded a star on Hollywood Boulevard's Walk of Fame. Unlike those artists, the Spinners (Henry Fambrough, Billy Henderson, Pervis Jackson, Bobbie Smith, and George W. Dixon) weren't honored for their string

COURTESY TOM DEPIERRO/AIRWAVE INTERNATIONAL

It's a shame. That song and the one featured on this particular piece of sheet music were the only Motown hits for the Spinners (from left), Henry Fambrough, Bobbie Smith, Billy Henderson, Chico Edwards, and Pervis Johnson.

of Motown successes. Those you could count on one finger, which pretty much summed up the quintet's feelings toward the label when they, too, exited in 1974.

The Spinners had already racked up a Top 10 R&B—and Top 30 pop—hit with "That's What Girls Are Made For" (Tri-Phi, 1961), three years before they came to Motown. During their seven years with the company, the group managed only two hits: the gently propulsive "I'll Always Love You" (Motown, 1965) and the sizzling "It's a Shame" (V.I.P., 1970), which was their sole pop success.

Along with a jangling guitar line that could drive a truck, "It's a Shame" featured a glass-shattering lead vocal from G. C. Cameron, who was the latest in a parade of fifth members. C. P. Spencer—who certainly got around town—was first, followed by Chico Edwards, George Dixon, G. C. Cameron, the late Phillippe Wynne, and, currently, John Edwards.

This constant turnover might explain some of the Spinners' lack of success. However, the group is widely remembered as being among Motown's hardest-working employees. They used to hang around the Artist Development Department, waiting for other acts to cancel, so they could cop the extra rehearsal time.

All this dedication paid off when the group moved to Atlantic Records. There, with Phillippe Wynne on lead vocals and producer Thom Bell feeding them the properly pearlescent material, the Spinners churned out *six* million-selling singles in four years, of which the glistening "I'll Be Around" (1972) was the most monumental.

G. C. Cameron, who was then romantically involved with Gwen Gordy, chose to remain at Motown as a solo artist. The decision didn't do much for G.C.'s career. Meanwhile, the Spinners—as you might expect from a group that took their name from a then-popular style of hubcap—keep rolling along.

EDWIN STARR

A vocalist of hog-calling power, Edwin Starr (born Charles Hatcher) was also no stranger to success: Along with cowriting the 1966 pop smash "Oh How Happy" for the Shades of Blue (Impact Records), he'd recorded a pair of Top 10 R&B hits for another local Detroit label (Ric-Tic) prior to his arrival at Motown in 1967.

Both 1965's "Agent Double-O-Soul" and 1966's "Stop Her on Sight (S.O.S.)" are excellent discs, the former being the funniest—and therefore the hippest—undercover lover routine ever committed to wax (possible exception: Jamo Thomas' crazed "I Spy (for the F.B.I.)," recorded a year later), while the latter is simply one of the best non-Motown Motown records ever made.

Berry Gordy wasn't about to let Edwin Starr or Ric-Tic kingpin Eddie Wingate get away with this form of flattery too often; he bought out Wingate's masters, artists, and studio within the year.

The investment paid off two years later when Edwin stomped out "Twenty-five Miles" (Gordy, 1969), a tune he proudly refers to as having "the greatest vamp in the world. You can keep ah-ah-ing from now till next year."

After 1970's number one pop hit "War," in which he asked the musical question "War . . . What is it good for?" and answered it himself—"Absolutely *nuthin'!*"—Edwin's star faded. He left Motown in 1976, surfacing on 20th Century Records with a good, tough disco track ("Contact") in 1979.

THE SUPREMES

The story of the Supremes has already passed from history into myth: *Dreamgirls*. Resemblance to any person or persons living or dead is purely coincidental and so on and so on and scooby-dooby-dooby. . . . Call it what you want, history, myth, or speculative fiction, but these are the facts:

The Supremes (Diana Ross, Mary Wilson, and Florence Ballard) came to Motown in 1961. They were still called the Primettes and Barbara Martin was still the fourth member. "I Want a Guy," issued on the *Tamla* label, was their first record as the Supremes. It sounded like they wished they were the Shirelles. Both Barbara Martin and the recording were soon history. Same goes for the Supremes' second 1961 Tamla release, a New Orleans–style dance number ("Buttered Popcorn"), on which Flo Ballard sang lead.

By the end of 1962 the Supremes had another pair of flops to their credit. "Your Heart Belongs to Me" was their first disc to be issued on the Motown Records label, written and produced by Smokey Robinson, and was a poor copy of Mary Wells' "The One Who Really Loves You." Berry Gordy himself wrote and produced the Supremes' second Motown stiff ("Let Me Go the Right Way"), an equally ordinary runaround on Maurice Williams and the Zodiacs' 1960 chartbuster "Stay."

Two more Mary Wells soundalikes ("My Heart Can't Take It Anymore" and "Breathtaking Guy," both 1963) added to the Supremes' rather impressive list of failures, and behind their

46. Which member of the Jackson 5 married Berry Gordy's daughter?
47. Prior to joining Motown, songwriter-producer-label exec Harvey Fuqua sang with what famous doo-wop group?
48. Who were the Rayber Voices?

Baby love. The Supremes—(from left), Mary Wilson, Flo Ballard, and Diana Ross—back when they could only afford costume jewelry.

COURTESY BILLIE JEAN BROWN, ESQ.

backs, whispers of "No-Hit Supremes" filled the halls of Hitsville, U.S.A. Then . . .

Just like in the movies, the group's next record—their *seventh,* mind you—turned everything around. Writers-producers Holland-Dozier-Holland, fresh from their successes with Martha and the Vandellas, took a quick listen to Ellie Greenwich and Jeff Barry's production of the Raindrops' "The Kind of Boy You Can't Forget" and set Diana's cooed vocals against a driving, almost Bo Diddley beat. The result ("When the Lovelight Starts Shining through His Eyes," 1964) rose to number 23 on the pop charts. The follow-up ("Run Run Run") promptly took the gas pipe. Then . . .

The combination of H-D-H and the Supremes upped and exploded with five *consecutive* number one pop hits: "Where Did Our Love Go," "Baby Love," "Come See about Me" (all 1964), "Stop! In the Name of Love," and "Back in My Arms Again" (both 1965). Classics every one.

When the next release ("Nothing But Heartaches") peaked at number 11 pop, H-D-H went for Baroque and came up with the Supremes' third 1965 pop number one: "I Hear a Symphony," an ornate pop record with very little R&B content.

"That song was one of our greatest loves," Mary Wilson recalls, "because it was one of the first songs that H-D-H did for us that was a more mature-type song. It had a very symphonic type of melody to it and we felt very sophisticated, which we were just *dyin'* to feel anyway." She laughs.

After two more 1966 Top 10 hits, the throbbing "My World

Is Empty without You" and the relentless "Love Is Like an Itching in My Heart," the H-D-H/Supremes team roared back with another four *consecutive* pop number ones: "You Can't Hurry Love," "You Keep Me Hangin' On" (both 1966), "Love Is Here and Now You're Gone," and "The Happening" (both 1967).

On their next record ("Reflections," 1967) the group underwent a face-lift with Flo Ballard exiting in favor of Cindy Birdsong, who had been singing with Patti Labelle and the Bluebelles. Along with the change in membership came a change in billing. The trio was now known as Diana Ross and the Supremes.

Flo went solo, cutting discs for the ABC Records label. When those failed, she sued Motown, only to claim that her lawyer wound up with most of the settlement. (He was later disbarred for mishandling funds connected with some other cases.) Over the next nine years Flo would lose her husband, house, and dignity, eventually going on welfare to feed her three daughters. She was also mugged twice and hospitalized twice for "nervous exhaustion." Flo Ballard died of natural causes in 1976. She was all of thirty-two years old.

Although H-D-H left Motown in 1968, Diana Ross and the Supremes' success story continued. "Love Child," written by Pam Sawyer, R. Dean Taylor, Frank Wilson, and Deke Richards and produced by "the Clan" (Taylor, Richards, Wilson, Hank Cosby, and Berry Gordy), topped the 1968 pop charts, and the group starred in their first network TV special, "TCB."

"Someday We'll Be Together" (1969) was Diana Ross and the Supremes' swan song. Produced and cowritten by Johnny Bristol, who as half of Johnny and Jackie (Beavers) recorded the original version of the tune on the Tri-Phi label in 1961, it was also the Supremes' *twelfth*—and last—pop number one.

The group did a second network TV special ("Getting Together on Broadway") later that year, and in 1970 Diana Ross left for a solo career. (See Chapter 10.)

As for the Supremes' music, which admittedly has taken a back seat to the facts here, there's not much to say. The hits are largely interchangeable, all pink tongues and false eyelashes set to an air-hammer beat. It's Diana's persona—coy, demure, ready to give her heart to the Right Guy—that gives them their power. More to the point, she can say "baby" sexier than any woman alive.

However, there is one Supremes disc of more than passing interest: 1965's "The Only Time I'm Happy" (Motown 1079). Collectors are probably screaming that there never was a

Motown 1079. That's true, but this song—bearing that number—did appear on the George Alexander Inc. label (what?) as a promotional item only. What makes the record so fascinating is its flip—the most revealing Supremes interview in the history of Motown. It's one scratch short of a catfight and the trio tells *all*. You wish.

BOBBY TAYLOR AND THE VANCOUVERS

A multiracial outfit, Bobby Taylor and the Vancouvers (guitarist Wes Henderson, bassist Eddie Patterson, organist Robbie King, drummer Ted Lewis, and guitarist Tommy Chong) took their name from the Canadian seaport that was their home. "Does Your Mama Know about Me" (Gordy, 1968), with an interracial love affair theme similar to Janis Ian's 1967 smash "Society's Child," was their only real hit, but the group's contributions to Western Civilization are far greater than their track record alone.

To begin with, it was during a 1968 performance at Chicago's Regal Theater that Bobby Taylor and the Vancouvers discovered the Jackson 5. (Motown lent Diana Ross' name to the legend for the marquee value.)

Not only that, but when the Vancouvers broke up, guitarist Tommy Chong, in what you might call a sino-the-times, became a star of stage, screen, and *High Times* magazine as half of the rock 'n' rolling stoned comedy team Cheech and Chong. Smoke 'em if you got 'em.

Does your mama know about me? Bobby Taylor and the Vancouvers, whose members included (third from left) Thomas Chong of Cheech & . . . Bobby Taylor is at extreme left.

COURTESY TOM DEPIERRO/AIRWAVE INTERNATIONAL

TAMMI TERRELL

If this were a romance novel and not The Motown Story, Tammi Terrell would be one of those characters who are always being described as "tragically beautiful." That she was; she was also half of Motown's most successful male-female duo.

Using her real name, Tammy Montgomery, she began her recording career with James Brown's own Try Me Records while touring with the Godfather of Soul's fold. She also cut discs for the Checker and Wand labels before coming to Motown in 1966.

Her first record as Tammi Terrell was a solo effort ("I Can't Believe You Love Me," 1966), issued on the Motown Records label. It's nothing special—a not-too-subtle knock-off of Little Anthony and the Imperials' 1965 classic "Goin' out of My Head," if you wanna know the truth—and neither were the chart numbers.

"Ain't No Mountain High Enough" (Tamla, 1967) was the first Marvin Gaye and Tammi Terrell duet. It wasn't their

COURTESY TOM DePIERRO/AIRWAVE INTERNATIONAL

Sassoon they forget. The tragically beautiful Tammi Terrell.

biggest hit, but it was definitely their best, building upon a series of shuddering climaxes that left listeners spent and throbbing.

The duo's next four hits, "Your Precious Love," "If I Could Build My Whole World around You" (both 1967), "Ain't Nothing Like the Real Thing," and "You're All I Need to Get By" (both 1968), though less spectacular, all have their moments. Mostly in the singing. Tammi wasn't a bold soul sister, but she had the heartache in her voice.

Also in her personal life. She collapsed onstage in Cleveland in 1967. At first the doctors thought it was simply exhaustion, then they thought it was just Cleveland, and finally they discovered a brain tumor. Eight operations failed to correct the condition and Tammi Terrell, age twenty-four, died in 1970.

THE VELVELETTES

Call them obscure at your own risk, for the Velvelettes (Betty Kelly, Sandra Tilley, and Carolyn Gill) made a pair of

Needle in a haystack. That's what determining the identities of these I.P.G.-period Velvelettes is like, although long-term Velvelette Carolyn Gill is at upper right and future Vandella Betty Kelly is at lower left.

COURTESY MICHAEL OCHS ARCHIVES

truly dangerous records. Check out the way they all—in harmony—take that octave jump on "you better look before you lee-*eap*, yeah!" in "Needle in a Haystack" (V.I.P., 1964).

"He Was Really Sayin' Somethin' " (1965) is no less spine-chilling, with a groove so primal you can practically see the apes dancing around the fire. And what's he saying? "Bop-bop-sookie-do-wah." Of course.

Although the group made another three singles for Motown, including a pretty, tough, Supremes-style stomper, "These Things Will Keep Me Loving You" (Soul, 1966), Motown has never issued a Velvelettes album. Write the company and demand one. (Ask for a Satintones album while you're at it.)

There was, however, a pre-Motown Velvelettes recording, issued on the mysterious I.P.G. Records label in 1962. I.P.G. stood for Independent Producers Group, and the Velvelettes' disc ("There He Goes" b/w "That's the Reason Why") is worth noting not only for its not-so-independent producer (Motown's then A&R chief Mickey Stevenson) but also because the I.P.G.-period Velvelettes were, as pictured, a quintette. The identities of the other two members are . . . well . . . obscure.

JR. WALKER AND THE ALL-STARS

The ultimate dance band, Jr. Walker and the All-Stars (guitarist Willie Woods, organist Vic Thomas, and drummer James Graves) socked out twelve Top 10 R&B hits in five years. A searing tenor saxophonist and splendidly offhand vocalist, Junior had a simple formula for success: set up a rolling, syncopated undertow and let me *blow*, Daddy-O.

"Shotgun" (Soul, 1965) was Junior's first hit, but he had all the elements in place as far back as 1962, when he cut his first record ("Twist Lackawanna") for the Harvey label. There's so little difference between Junior's next two Harvey singles ("Cleo's Mood" and "Brainwasher, Pt. 2") and his Motown work that these same tracks were issued on the Soul label a couple years later.

With its instantly memorable, seven-note theme and a disarmingly soulful vocal, 1969's "What Does It Take (to Win Your Love)" was Junior (born Autry DeWalt, Jr.) and company's second slice of pop perfection, although anyone who finds perfection in Junior's 1966 romp, stomp, and rampage through "(I'm a) Roadrunner" is more than entitled to his opinion.

After 1970 the hits dried up. Only "Walk in the Night" (1972), which sounds like Junior Walker Plays Variations on a

Honk if you love saxophones. Jr. Walker and the All-Stars—(from left), Junior, Vic Thomas, Willie Woods, and James Graves—give us their best shot.

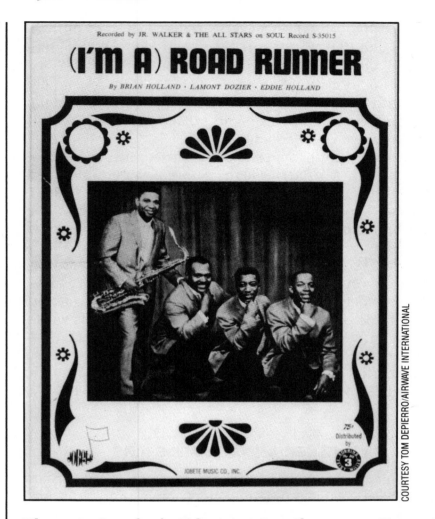

Recorded by JR. WALKER & THE ALL STARS on SOUL Record S-35015

(I'M A) ROAD RUNNER

By BRIAN HOLLAND · LAMONT DOZIER · EDDIE HOLLAND

75¢
Distributed by

JOBETE MUSIC CO., INC.

COURTESY TOM DEPIERRO/AIRWAVE INTERNATIONAL

Theme in Search of a Television Cop Show, went Top 10 R&B, and he left Motown in the late seventies, only to return in 1983.

Junior's stuttering, screeching sax brought him back to the near-top of the pop charts when—in a rare display of good taste from *this* load of hi-gloss metal merchants—he threw down a blistering solo on Foreigner's 1981 smash "Urgent." As Oscar Wilde once wrote, style is forever.

MARY WELLS

Motown's first female star, Mary Wells sang soft soul with a kittenish quality that turned pop confections into purr-fection. "The One Who Really Loves You" (Motown, 1962), "Two Lovers" (also '62), and "My Guy" (1964) are three of the warmest tracks ever waxed.

Also three of the coolest. Pick up on the understated confidence in her delivery of the classic opening line about those other girls who are filling her boyfriend's head with ji-ive in "The One Who Really Loves You." Even when her boyfriend was puttin' on the schiz, as in "Two Lovers"—one of the few pop records besides Lou Christie's "Two Faces Have I" to tackle this issue head-on—Mary never broke a sweat. Mostly she sounded like she wanted to cuddle, or at least rub up against your leg.

While these two discs and the only slightly less incredible "You Beat Me to the Punch" (1962)—talk about a disciplined performance—dipped and swayed to a rhumba rhythm, "My Guy" rode a relaxed, swinging groove that could've passed for a Count Basie chart. A number one pop record, it was Mary's biggest hit. It would also be her last.

Although Motown scored a double-sided hit ("What's the Matter with you Baby" b/w "Once upon a Time") with a Marvin Gaye and Mary Wells duet, issued on the Motown label a couple weeks after "My Guy" took off, Mary beat feet out of Hitsville the day she turned twenty-one.

She went to 20th Century-Fox Records, for a five-figure advance and a two-year contract, during which time her success was marginal. Next stop: Atco Records and another

COURTESY TOM DEPIERRO/AIRWAVE INTERNATIONAL

The one who really loves you. Windblown and in soft focus? This 1964 Mary Wells promo pic was, stylistically, twenty years ahead of its time.

two years of marginal success. Then on to the Jubilee label, where . . .

You really can't blame Mary, though. She came to Motown at seventeen, got a hit ("Bye Bye Baby," 1960) the first time she stepped into a recording studio, and had cut four Top 10 pop records since. How was she supposed to know the dream would ever end?

Besides, say you have a group, the Hungry Arms. Given the choice between fifty grand—in 1964 dollars, remember—and a three-cents-per-record royalty rate, which would you take? Before all of you Hungry Arms shoot up, consider this piece of free advice:

"Take the music as an art," Mary tells young entertainers, "but keep an innocent mind, because when you start noticing too much stuff around you—confusion or a certain amount of politics or whatever—that can freeze your artistic power."

KIM WESTON

Although her own tastes ran to nightclub ballads, all single blue spotlights and skintight gowns, Kim Weston is best remembered for a pair of uptempo performances: the raucous "Take Me in Your Arms (Rock Me a Little While)" and the sparkling "It Takes Two," on which she duetted with Marvin Gaye. She may not have preferred this sort of material but she was certainly quite good at it.

If her rendition of "Take Me in Your Arms" (Gordy, 1965) is eclipsed by the Isleys' 1968 version, it's mainly because producers H-D-H stirred in a few more polyrhythms the second time around and not because of the vocal interpretation. Kim's is definitely tough enough.

She began her recording career in 1963 with "Love Me All the Way," the first of five straight flops to be issued on the Tamla label. During this time she also married Motown A&R head honcho Mickey Stevenson. Switching to the Gordy label in 1965, Kim cut another stiff, then the hit, then another stiff.

Not long after "It Takes Two" (Tamla, 1967) hit, she, too, was down the road and gone, moving to MGM Records for two years of marginal success and by now I'm sure you can guess the rest. . . .

LITTLE STEVIE WONDER

Blind since birth, Stevie Wonder signed his first Motown contract at the ripe old age of eight. Though his real name is Stevland Morris, the "Little Stevie Wonder" tag stems from when Ronnie White of the Miracles brought him in for an

Take me in your arms. More sultry curvaceousness from Kim Weston, then just starting out on the Tamla label. Oh baby, gimme that blue spotlight. . . .

audition and Berry Gordy pronounced Stevie "a little wonder." But of course.

It was four years before Stevie made his first record ("I Call It Pretty Music but the Old People Call It the Blues, Pts. 1 and 2"), a gimmicky, see-the-little-blind-kid-play-blues-harmonica number, issued on the Tamla label in 1962. A year later he would have the number one pop single ("Fingertips, Pt. 2") and the number one best-selling album in America. Recorded live, *Little Stevie Wonder, the 12-Year-Old Genius* was Motown's first number one album. Amazing.

Not really. "Fingertips, Pt. 2" is two minutes and forty-nine seconds of pure hysteria, from the little bit of "Merrily We Roll Along" Stevie tosses into his harmonica solo, to the musician who accidentally finds himself onstage in the middle of this sonic blizzard—you never heard such a racket since the fireworks factory burned down—and blurts, "What key? What key?"

Over the next two years Stevie cut six stiffs and dropped the "Little" Stevie Wonder bit. In 1966 he bounced back with the driving "Uptight." He's had the golden touch ever since. (By the way, the nonalbum flipside of "Uptight" is a ballad

COURTESY TOM DePIERRO/AIRWAVE INTERNATIONAL

Lemme hear you say "yeah." Not Willie Tyler and Lester, but former world heavyweight boxing champion Muhammad Ali (then known as Cassius Clay) and Stevie Wonder (then known as Little Stevie Wonder).

titled "Purple Raindrops." Wanna bet that it's one of Prince's favorites?)

"I Was Made to Love Her" (1967), with its sprung-guitar riff, too-tough rhythm track, and an incredible lead vocal performance—when does he *breathe*?—and "Shoo-Be-Doo-Be-Doo-Dah-Day" (1968), a record which now sounds five years ahead of its time, rounded out Stevie's quartet of sixties classics.

Make that a quintet. His buoyant rendition of the lounge lizard standard "For Once in my Life" (1968) avoids the phony humility and sticky smugness that most of the 200-plus artists who've recorded the song seem to wallow in. Me, I can't take the tune seriously. Too many nights at the Zircon Lounge, listening to Tony Tinpanalli and His Trio giving it the Treatment will do that to you.

Stevie had always been a multi-instrumentalist: drums, keyboards, you name it—the guy could get a hit tune out of a cooked carrot. In 1970 he began to produce his own records. "Signed, Sealed, Delivered I'm Yours" was first. A variation on the company's classic stomp beat, its relentless, tear-away vocals and deft production touches showed that schoolboy Stevie had indeed learned his Motown lessons well.

He spent 1971 renegotiating his contract, which would've expired when he turned twenty-one, and collecting the million-dollar trust fund that Motown had provided for him. When Stevie returned to action the following year with *Talking Book*—the first album by an American artist to enter the *Billboard* LP charts at number one—it was as one of the new breed of black recording artists. Like Marvin Gaye, Stevie Wonder would be his own man: writing, producing, singing, and playing his own music.

Not bad for a child prankster whose idea of a good joke was to call Motown employees on the telephone and—using his elastic vocal skills—pretend to be an angry Berry Gordy! (Again, we'll catch up with Stevie's later career in Chapter 10.)

But right now, ladies and gentlemen, it's time to . . .

Chapter Six

MEET THE TEMPTATIONS

His last falsetto moonshot on the final echoed chorus of *"Girl (Why You Wanna Make Me Blue)" still ringing in the audience's ears, Temptations lead singer Eddie Kendricks throws his hand mike about twenty feet in the air, high enough for bass singer Melvin Franklin to pirouette into a split, catch the mike on the way down, and wind up at the foot of the stage on his knees, singing the opening lines to "Paradise."*

"Hold it. Hold it. Now you see how things get exaggerated over the years," Melvin Franklin says, wagging an accusing finger for emphasis. "That mike-throwing routine was done coming out of 'Paradise' into 'I Want a Love I Can See.' And *I* threw the mike, 'cause I was the only one with the athletic ability to do it right every time, and *David Ruffin* caught it, 'cause he was the only one with the *nerve to catch it [chuckle].* . . ."

Well, now, that makes all the difference in the world, doesn't it? But before we meet the rest of the Temptations, let's make like the Jimmy Castor Bunch and "go back, *way* back, back into time . . . "

The Temptations' story begins in the Distants, which is what Melvin Franklin, Otis Williams, Elbridge "Al" Bryant, Richard Street, and James Crawford called their first group back around 1958–59.

The Distants cut two singles ("All Right" and "Always") for Northern Records, a local Detroit label. "Always," with its flashy harmonies, was something of a regional hit and was license to the New York–based indy Warwick Records.

The first Distants single, entitled "Pecos Kid," had been recorded even before they got to Northern. (Melvin: "No, I can't remember the label. Man, I was fourteen years old.")

Ain't too proud to beg. David Ruffin (kneeling) cops a plea while the rest of the Temptations—(clockwise from top center), Otis Williams, Paul Williams, Melvin Franklin, and Eddie Kendricks—lend suitable support. Custom-tailored, of course.

COURTESY TOM DEPIERRO/AIRWAVE INTERNATIONAL

"In 1960 we left Northern Records," Melvin continues, "and a couple of guys left the group, too. Richard fell in love and naturally he felt more obligation for his love than he did for the group. James sang tenor. He was a Ted Taylor–type singer and, in that day, he was *well received* all the time, so he didn't feel like he needed a place in the group and he went on his own. Like that. [*Hand nosedives.*]

"But it was the best thing that ever happened for us. Richard left and we got Paul Williams. James left and we got Eddie Kendricks. And the wonderful thing about it is that Paul and Eddie brought another dimension to it because they had been in the kind of group that sang ballads and standards and nightclub kind of stuff and we had been a rock 'n' roll, doo-wop–type group, so now we became the best of both worlds."

Paul and Eddie's old group, the Primes, is also noteworthy for its sister group, the Primettes, who would go on to fame and fortune as the Supremes.

"We were doing record hops around town," Melvin backtracks, "and whenever we'd be on a show that the Miracles were on, we always made it plenty hot for them. We didn't have the hit records nationally, but locally we were as hot as anybody. You see, it was where we grew up and I was on the basketball team—Richard and I were All-City—and I was an

COURTESY THE CULTURAL WAREHOUSE

First Temptations. Autographed on the negative by the original lineup, which included Eldrige Bryant (upper left).

honor student, Eagle Scout, minister's son, so like in Detroit we were very popular.

"And we were not happy at Northern Records. We had a record that sold—we thought—and Johnnie Mae Mathews, who was our manager at the time, she got a lot of money and bought cars and all that kind of stuff. I'm not calling her a thief or anything like that but you know how the business starts off. I needed the experience and I was glad to enter through any door. I'd pay twice the price to have the life I've had. [*Laughs.*]

"And it all happened within the same couple, three days. It was kinda like we were not in charge. It was like the hand of fate or the Deity, as one would see it. I do have a deep spiritual background myself, but be that as it may. The thing, the wheel, the force was with us and, as chance would have it, Otis had to go to the men's room.

"It was the same time Mr. Gordy had to go and they were both paying the water bill when Berry said to Otis, 'Man, you guys really are good. If you ever want to come to a real record company, please consider me. Come talk. . . . '

"I wasn't there, so I don't know verbatim what the conversation was, but it all seemed to come together in a week. We got Paul and Eddie and we started singing over at Hitsville, U.S.A. There was no Motown."

Although they originally called themselves the Elgins, by the time their first recording ("Oh, Mother o Mine") was issued on Berry Gordy's short-lived Miracle label in 1961, the quintet (Paul Williams, Eddie Kendricks, Otis Williams, Elbridge Bryant, and Melvin Franklin) was known as the Temptations. The song, yet another rewrite of "Way over There," showed the group's promise, but that was about it.

On "Check Yourself," the Temptations' second 1961 Miracle release, that promise was fulfilled. Written by Elbridge, Otis, Melvin, and Berry Gordy, what begins as a smooch number suddenly jivebombs into a furious, uptempo, minor-key track that features the fabulous harmonies and fast vocal interchanges for which the Temptations are famous. Check out Paul Williams' superfine, grainy lead vocal work and—while you're at it—check yourself.

By 1962 the Miracle label had dissolved into the Gordy Records label, which the Temptations introduced with "Dream Come True," an otherwise undistinguished piece of material. "Paradise" (also 1962), in which we find the Tempts throwing down on the Four Seasons songbook, is a doo-wopper's shangri-la. Cynics will note that the Paradise Lost herein is a dream. Think about it.

"I Want a Love I Can See" was next, in 1963, but neither this nor "Farewell, My Love," released that same year, did much to expand the Temptations' appeal beyond the Motor City limits. (Incidentally, "I Want a Love I Can See" was Smokey Robinson's first Temptations production. "Farewell My Love" and all the rest were Berry Gordy efforts.)

If the Temptations didn't hit the big time until their seventh disc, it wasn't for Motown's lack of ingenuity. Back in 1962 the group went so far as to change its name to the Pirates for one release—a cover of Nolan Strong's "Mind over Matter"—issued on Motown's subsidiary label, Mel-O-Dy Records. Why? Let Melvin Franklin explain:

"You heard me use a phrase earlier, 'Enter through Any Door.' Well, we were trying to get a hit, so we put out two records and whichever one became the hit was who we were gonna be."

Funny, I've always felt the name change was an in-joke stemming from the song having been "pirated" away from Nolan Strong, whose then-current Fortune recording was the more successful of the two.

Whatever the motive, the plan failed. Too bad. 'Cause the Pirates' version is quite good, highlighted by Eddie Kendricks' wailing lead and a too-tuff guitar solo, although that didn't stop whoever used to own the copy I found in a thrift store from writing "CORNY" across the label with a big black felt pen. Everyone's a critic.

That includes Joe Billingslea of the Contours, who notes that for all the attention showered on the Tempts, it was the Contours who beat them to a hit with "Do You Love Me," a song Berry Gordy had originally written with the Temptations in mind.

" 'Twist and Shout' was a big record then," Joe reflects, "and Berry Gordy wanted 'Do You Love Me' sung in the same style as 'Twist and Shout,' and at the time, none of the Temptations could do it. Fortunately for us, we had a guy—Billy Gordon—who could holler and the rest is history."

History is flexible, though. Melvin admits, "Berry Gordy wrote 'Do You Love Me' for us, but we were at church. We went to see the Dixie Hummingbirds and the Harmonizing Four and the Swan Silvertones, because we're really steeped deep in gospel, always had that old gospel-group sound to us. . . . Oh yeah, all on the same bill. Can you dig it? I mean, really. And they're asking for a donation instead of charging you at the door! Those groups couldn't make any money, man. Anyway, nobody would've ever thought to look for the Temptations in *church*, so they couldn't find us.

"And the Contours—not to put 'em down or anything like that—everybody knows that they couldn't outsing us. No more than the Miracles could. They wished—the Miracles had the hit records and we didn't—but they *wished* they had the kind of harmony and that man-thing, that animalness that the Temptations seem to have. We were like a sleeping giant."

When David Ruffin replaced Elbridge Bryant, the giant awoke. Although David didn't sing lead—Eddie Kendricks did—"The Way You Do the Things You Do" was the Temptations' first coast-to-coast hit, rising to number 11 nationally in 1964.

David Ruffin had his own history. He joined the Voice Masters in 1958 shortly after they recorded "Hope and Pray" for the Anna label. Three years later he cut his first solo effort ("I'm in Love"), a midtempo number in the Chuck Jackson mold. This also appeared on Anna. Former Voice Master Lamont Dozier says David's disc, like Ty Hunter's and Lamont's own solo sides, was a group session and that whoever sang lead got the label credit.

David's next stop was Check-Mate Records, where he tore through a pair of '62 uptown R&B workouts: "Mr. Bus Driver, Hurry" and "Action Speaks Louder Than Words." The former is unintentionally comical—like the vehicle, it picks up speed as it goes along—and the latter is unimaginably powerful, an all-stops-out, octave-juggling masterpiece of controlled frenzy. David's vocal alone could levitate a block of condos. Clearly, the man had talent.

49. How old was Michael Jackson when the Jackson 5 first hit with "I Want You Back"?
50. The same bassist and drummer played on almost every Motown record. What were these musicians' names?
51. Which Nobel Peace Prize winner recorded for Motown?

So did the Temptations. What the group needed was a hit song. As Melvin tells it, when Lady Luck smiled on the Temptations, it was because she has a sense of humor.

"The Miracles were playing the Uptown Theater in Philadelphia and they were driving down the Pennsylvania Turnpike, joking. You can tell by the words in 'The Way You Do the Things You Do.' "

"They were just *joking*. When they got back to Detroit, we went right upstairs to where the piano was and Smokey sat down *[sings opening riff: da-DAH da-DAH da da-DAH . . .]* and they played it and said, 'Guys. . . .'

"And we laughed and laughed and laughed, 'cause it was funny. And the 'whoo-hoo'—you know, the 'If good looks was a minute, you know you could've been an hour, whoo-hoo'— well, we could really say 'whoo-hoo.' Made the harmony real nice and everything. And so we recorded it and we went away, up to a place called Muskegon, Michigan—it's up near the Upper Peninsula.

"We went up there in the dead of winter. It was snowed in and no news could get up there. There was a club up there that we worked—the Ebony Ballroom—and they had the hotel in there, so we never had to go outside for like a month.

"When we got back to town, I dropped everybody off. Then I went and picked up my sister, who was on her way home from school. On the way home, 'The Way You Do the Things You Do' came on the radio. We jumped out of the car and

The latter-day Flamingos. That's how bassman Melvin Franklin described the Temptations, and you can certainly see why.

went to dancing together. That was when we knew it was a hit record. Up till then, we had no idea.

"Once again, it happened. [*Snaps fingers twice.*] It wasn't more than two or three weeks, changing from Elbridge Bryant to David Ruffin, that we had a hit record.

"See, Elbridge was a very, very handsome guy. The ladies loved him very much and he was a playboy. He didn't feel he had to do this.

"You know, there are a lot of beautiful ladies in this world, and I thank *each one* of you for the love you've given me. But some people got a chick taking good care of 'em saying, 'Don't go sing: stay here with me.' And what do they do? Some fall weak and stay. *I'm* gonna go sing.

"Hey man, I sang with *people*. I sang with guys that are affected, that are human, that go to the bathroom. And I don't try to make of them what they're not. I accept it. And in their weaknesses, I see some of mine."

With that in mind, here—in Melvin Franklin's words—are the Temptations:

"Otis Williams is the founder of the group. Now, I'm from Mobile, Alabama, and I am the son of an evangelist preacher, one of those old-fashioned kind, and I lived a life sheltered from the ways of the world. So when I came to the big city in '52, I was always afraid of the guys that had processed hair and that other kind of look. You equated it with being in a gang. Well, Otis went to the same high school that Richard [Street] and I went to, so I'd see Otis in school and he'd be around the singers, but he was always quiet.

"Now, my mother had moved from where we lived in kind of a nice neighborhood over closer to town, where it was closer to her work. But it was rougher and I used to always walk from the old neighborhood to where we lived now. In those days Twelfth Street in Detroit was a very rough street and the parallel street to it is Woodrow Wilson, which was relatively quiet, so I would always walk down Woodrow Wilson to avoid all the bad people.

"Well, this particular day, I was walking down Woodrow Wilson and I saw this tall, dark guy with a process coming, and he had on these shiny white shoes and this black leather jacket and stuff. I saw him coming and I crossed the street, because every time guys pass by you they wanna put a stick on your shoulder and knock it off, make you fight with 'em, you know. And I got beat—I didn't have any big brothers. I'm the big brother.

"And so Otis crossed to the other side of the street where I was. That really made me afraid, so I crossed the street *again*. And he crossed the street again. By now, I'm trembling inside

and my eyes are starting to water, 'cause I'm afraid, you know?

"So I took off running and I ran and I stopped at the playground, 'cause there was a junior high school near where I lived. There were some guys out there that I played ball with, so I started playing basketball. I played a couple of games. I figured I'd lost Otis by this time, so I decided to walk on home.

"When I got home, I was on the other side of the street from my house, and I saw Otis up at the door, so I hid behind a tree. I said, 'Oh no. What in the hell is gonna happen to me?' Here *he* is talking to my *mother*.

"And my mother said, 'We see you back there hidin' behind the tree. Come on out.' I'm a kid—this is the God-honest truth—so I came out from behind the tree.

"I didn't know that Otis was looking for me 'cause I had been on records and stuff and his bass singer was one of the pretty boys the girls had pulled away, too. When Otis was up there, he was askin' my mother if I could sing with him in the group.

"That was the first day I met him straightaway, and an hour after that, I was in the studio recording with him. I'd characterize him as stable, serious, a serious man of business. But the greatest compliment I can give to him is that he is my friend. He's been a friend to me and he's never left me. From that day to this one. And I could go on and on. . . .

"Eddie Kendricks was the Lightning. They used to refer to Eddie as the Lightning and me as the Thunder. We were always opposites. I was always husky and big and he was always little and frail.

"Eddie Kendricks is maybe four, five years older than I am and he would never let me be as grown as I wanted to be. He always made me remember that I was a kid, so Eddie and I always had a rough road, a rough, rugged road until—it's surprising like at seventeen how much I thought he didn't know, and by the time I was twenty-one, how much he had learned [chuckles]. So it took a few years for Eddie and I to find out we were really in love with each other.

"But I think probably one of the greatest rifts in my life is the rift between Eddie Kendricks and Otis Williams. To whom am I loyal? See, because Eddie is not a follower. Neither is Otis. Nor will they follow each other. And I'm a great force for uniting and whichever way I'd lean is how it would go and for years that was the problem within the group, because Eddie has great ideas, too.

"But a body can't have two heads, so eventually there came a time for the parting of the ways. I would look at Eddie

Seven easy steps, only six pictures. The group's famous dance routine was obviously unduplicatable. Sophisticates will notice the bottom two photos were mistakenly printed from reversed negatives.

THE 'TEMPTATION WALK'

THE DANCE CRAZE SWEEPING THE COUNTRY
— AS DEMONSTRATED BY —

THE TEMPTATIONS
GORDY RECORDING ARTISTS

The seven basic steps of the "Temptation Walk," a prancing, high-stepping routine created by the sensational Temptations, is shown here.

Kendricks and I'd call him the Prince of Romance and the guy who should've been my brother-in-law.

"Paul Williams. Mr. Professionalism himself. To me the greatest quote-unquote black entertainer that I know—male— is Sammy Davis, Jr. When it comes down to knowing techni- cally what it is to know all twelve positions of the stage and what it's really about, to know your theatrics correctly and to be able to perform and to use all those facilities to your advantage, I mean, the *man* is schooled in it.

"Now, I don't equate Paul Williams to him, but Paul is the closest person that I have known on a one-to-one basis to somebody who is that kind of talented. He knew [one-legged dancer] Pegleg Bates. He knew all the old, old-timers.

"Paul was the oldest of all the original Temptations and his father was a bass singer in a group called the Ensley Jubi- lees—Ensley, Alabama, right outside Birmingham—so Paul had the knowledge. If I were to talk to a young singer now, they'd think my knowledge goes back 'cause I've known the Flamingos and Jackie Wilson and all the people who came back before us. Well, Paul knew people like that back then. So, to me, he was awe-inspiring.

"It's often said that Otis is the head of the Temptations and I'm the heart. Paul was the very soul of the Temptations. Now that he's dead and gone, I personally try to see that all he instilled in me about how to stand onstage, how to be proud of what we do, stays with us. He set the standard on how to keep the Temptations ever professional.

"Even if we don't have anything but a light, a microphone, and just a plain wood floor, we don't need a whole lotta props to do it at its rawest, rarest form. I give it all—I take my hat off—to the late, great Paul Williams. He is my mentor.

"Elbridge Bryant, to me, was an obstacle, 'cause I cannot be part of something and not be integral, be the closest to the leader of anybody. And Al—as we called him—was Otis Williams' best friend. And he was like vice-president and secretary of the group and he was in my way.

"In retrospect—I'm forty years old now—I can look at it and know just what it was. At the time, I did not know. Now I've evaluated the situation, and although I got along with Al very well, I was always competing with him. I'd try to be on time better than him, try to make myself a better group member than he had been, even though he had been the best group member a cat could ever have. And I did it. Al, I like him very much, but he was a quitter. That's my word for him.

"David Ruffin is my mother's first cousin, which makes him my second cousin, and he's also a minister's son. We used to practice how to preach out on the back porch when we were little boys. Now, we did not know that we were cousins when we were growing up. You see, my mother comes from a family of seventeen kids . . .

"But we had been friends. It was David's stepfather, Eddie Bush, that drove me to New York for the Gordys when I went to make my first record. As a matter of fact, it was on David Ruffin's session. For Anna Records. I've forgotten what the song was. That's back in the dinosaur days.

"Okay, like I was sayin', my mother had moved. In order to keep going to the same high school, I couldn't tell anybody that I had moved. And since I couldn't get assistance with my bus fare or anything, I had to walk about a five- or six-mile walk all the time. So one of the places I'd stop off would be over at the hotel where David was living with his stepfather. He would walk me part of the way. I'd be bouncing my basketball.

"You know how guys are buddies? We were *buddies*. David had a white leather coat with sweatered sleeves. The day I first went out for the basketball team, he let me use it and somebody broke in the locker and stole it. I mean, we were that kinda close.

"David Ruffin was probably the most talented individual of anybody I had met up to that particular moment. He could turn flips. He was very acrobatic and he could use that stuff emotionally and bring it into play when he was delivering a song. I thought it was phenomenal.

"But I knew David real well, and I never ever thought of David Ruffin as a group person. David's idols were Jackie Wilson and Sam Cooke. He always wanted to be a solo artist. I told him that when he asked and begged to get in the group. I said, 'David, uh-uh. You're a solo guy. You wanna use the group to launch your own career.' [Imitates David: "No-no-no-no-no-no."] Three years later that's *exactly* what he did.

"But all I can say is he's Mr. Excitement. That's my word for David Ruffin and I love him, okay?

"Dennis Edwards, after fifteen years, he's all the way in. Try living with somebody for fifteen years, and then tell me she's not your wife, yeah. So Dennis and I are brothers of the same blood now, you know? Dennis is also the strongest, most blessed singer I've ever known.

"You see, in the old days, down South—Dennis is the son of an old Baptist minister, too—the old folks used to tell us that babies marked by God would be born very, very large. At birth I weighed twelve pounds—they say I was very blessed and my life was to have been a great life. Evidently, it's true. Dennis is the only person I have ever met who was born bigger than me. He weighed *fifteen pounds at birth!* [Raps on

52. What 1963 Motown hit was recorded in the middle of winter and held for a July release?

53. What Smokey Robinson composition does Richard Gere sing along with in the film *American Gigolo*?

54. When Smokey Robinson left the Miracles, who was his replacement?

First I look at the purse. This later edition of the Contours underscores the one bottom line in rock 'n' soul music that you can always take to the bank: Any decline in a group's earning power is met by an accompanying rise in personnel changes. Pictured (clockwise from top right) are Jerry Green, Council Gay, Hugh Davis, Sylvester Potts, and future Temptation Dennis Edwards.

COURTESY MICHAEL OCHS ARCHIVES

table for emphasis.] That boy was sent here directly from God!

"And right to this very day, I take my hat off to his mother and my mother. I mean, I will respect them, do everything I can for them forever, for they have suffered. I mean, really, really suffered.

"Dennis is a singer's singer. That's my word for Dennis Edwards and I love him. And I thank him for being the man that he has been, because anybody less strong could not have come behind David Ruffin. And he did it. I'm so proud of him. Not only did he do it—and we've sold more records with Dennis than we did with David Ruffin and reached out to far more people—but he never quit. Well, I mean, he had a little hiatus, 'cause the group was in the middle of a little political kind of thing, but he's back in there again and just as solid as ever. [Note: About six months after this interview, Dennis Edwards and the Temptations had a falling out. He's now a Motown solo artist with a couple of R & B hits to his credit.]

"Richard Street is my first cousin and it's almost like he's my brother—we had to share the same bed when we were kids. And we used to sneak up in the living room and play records real late at night and he'd show me how to listen to 'em, 'cause all I had ever heard was church music and that's for real. Sanctified people said, 'No blues. No worldly music.'

"I can remember the first song I ever heard on the radio: 'A

Tisket, A Tasket' by Ella Fitzgerald. I remember because I had never heard anything like that before and I always wanted to hear it again and never got to until I was all the way grown.

"See, Richard put me in tune. Okay, God gave me a great voice and I could sing in the church and I liked it, but singing bass and singing songs are two different concepts, totally. Singing the words and the melody is how we all grow up. *[Sings: Mary had a little lamb. Happy birthday to you.]* Everybody learns the melody. Nobody learns the changes and how to sing those syncopations and do the lip work and all that kinda stuff that a bass singer *[sings: Bom bop-ba ba-oom]* does.

"Richard took away all of my inhibitions. I can still hear my sisters telling my mother, 'Hey, Mama, come make Melvin come out of bathroom. He's in there practicing how to bass.' I would just lock the door and keep on practicing. I mean, *[mimics mother's voice]* 'What's wrong with my child?'

"But late at night Richard would sit by that little bitty record player at his mother's house, playing Frankie Lymon and the Teenagers records and showing me how Sherman Garnes would *[sings: Dip DOOM-wop a-DOOM-wop a-DOOM—intro to "Why Do Fools Fall in Love"]*. And how it really went. And I would *try*.

"I wouldn't be ashamed around him. If I got around somebody and my inhibitions came up, I might. But if Richard was around, I'd *try*. And he would say, 'No, do it like this here.'

"Right to this very day, we could be in a recording studio doing something and there might be a spot where I might want to try something and I might feel inhibited and I won't do it. But Richard'll say, "Doitlikeyeahyeahyeah,' and we will flash all the way back to then. That's Richard. He's my baby and I love him. He's the person that put me in tune. He gave me to the world."

Hold it. Hold it. Now you see how things get confused. That makes seven Temptations—eight counting Melvin—yet the group has always been a quintet. Time to check the seating chart.

From 1964 to 1968 the Temptations consisted of Otis Williams, Melvin Franklin, David Ruffin, Paul Williams, and Eddie Kendricks. When David Ruffin went solo, he was replaced by current member Dennis Edwards, who had been singing with the Contours. (We'll cover David's post-Temptations career in Chapter 10.)

Suffering from exhaustion, Paul Williams left the group on doctor's orders in 1971. His replacement was current member Richard Street, formerly of the Distants and, more recently, the Monitors. Two years later Paul Williams committed sui-

Greetings, this is Uncle Sam. Actually, it's the Monitors—(from left) John "Maurice" Fagin, Warren Harris, Sandra Fagin, and Richard Street—who lost the in-house battle of the bands when ex-Distant Richard Street was drafted into service with the Temptations.

COURTESY TOM DePIERRO/AIRWAVE INTERNATIONAL

cide while sitting in his car, parked two blocks—and about a million miles away—from Hitsville, U.S.A.

Also in 1971 Eddie Kendricks exited for a solo career. (Again, see Chapter 10.) His replacement, Damon Harris, gave way to Glenn Carl Leonard, then current member Ron Tyson. Ollie Woodson is the latest Temptation, having replaced Dennis Edwards in 1984.

By the way, Otis Williams and Paul Williams are unrelated. Otis's real name is Otis Miles. While we're on the subject, Melvin Franklin's real name is David English.

Despite the turnover, the Temptations muscled up fourteen Top 10 pop records, including four number ones: "My Girl" (1965), "I Can't Get Next to You" (1969), "Just My Imagination (Running away with Me)" (1971), and "Papa Was a Rollin' Stone" (1972). And on the R&B charts? *Thirty-two* Top 10 hits, of which *fourteen* went to number one.

"My Girl" was the group's first million-seller and marked

The way you do the things you do. The Temptations—(clockwise from upper right) Melvin Franklin, David Ruffin, Paul Williams, Otis Williams, and Eddie Kendricks—ready to outsing, outdance, and outdress any group in sight.

COURTESY THE CULTURAL WAREHOUSE

the beginning of what has come to be known as the David Ruffin era. Blessed with one of the most distinctive voices on the planet, David was as fine a balladeer ("Since I Lost My Baby," "Don't Look Back," and "I Wish It Would Rain") as he was a screamer ("Ain't Too Proud to Beg," "Beauty Is Only Skin Deep," and "(I Know) I'm Losing You").

It wasn't just the David Ruffin Show, though. Eddie Kendricks had a beautiful, liquid-crystal falsetto that—like David's throaty rasp—was equally effective at either fast ("Get Ready") or slow ("You're My Everything") tempos.

However, since David was getting the lion's share of the leads, it wasn't long before he asked that the name on the marquee be changed to "David Ruffin and the Temptations." The rest of the group decided a nice, simple "David Ruffin" was more appropriate.

"Cloud Nine" was the group's—and Motown's—first Grammy Award winner (Best R&B Record of 1968). It was also the Temptations' first single with Dennis Edwards and the first under their new "five lead voices" format.

"We took a quantum leap," Melvin says proudly. "But you have to take every negative and make it a positive. We didn't ever want to build that kind of a Frankenstein monster again.

"See, we started our group off with five lead singers, okay? Now, if the songwriter can't write songs for everybody in there, that's the songwriter's problem, 'cause everybody in this group can *definitely sing.*

"So with that in mind, we told Norman [Whitfield], 'Lookit, we're not going to do it like that anymore. We want songs that everybody can take parts in.' And we came up with a sound to fit that concept. We kinda stole it from Sly [Stone]."

With all due respect to Sly and the Family Stone, whose "Dance to the Music" predated "Cloud Nine" by ten months, the Temptations' new sound was simply a matter of isolating existing elements and making them the focus. Even their earliest records emphasized flashy harmonies, quick-change rhythms, and a flair for five-part interplay that grew more and more intricate over the years, as on the snowballing vocal arrangement of "It's Growing" (1965).

In the same way five fingers form a fist, the Tempts' new democratic approach enabled the quintet to punch out another eight years of hits. The ensemble performances on "Cloud Nine," "I Can't Get Next to You," and "Ball of Confusion" (1970) are as serious as nuclear waste. I'm also partial to the raucous "Shakey Ground" (1975), but being a native of Los Angeles, it's probably not my fault.

Eddie Kendricks ended his Temptations career on a typi-

55. What year did the first "Motortown Revue" traveling package tours begin?

56. What female Motown recording group sang background vocals on Marvin Gaye's "Can I Get a Witness"?

57. What is the name of the attorney who cowrote Shorty Long's "Here Comes the Judge"?

cally high note. Listening to Eddie's swan song, the ethereal "Just My Imagination (Running away with Me)," is like waking up in someone else's daydream, realizing this is not happening, and then—when you can't get it back—wishing it were.

Now, I'd rather play twenty Temptations tracks than play favorites, but the Grammy-winning "Papa Was a Rollin' Stone," with its deep, throbbing undertow and Norman Whitfield's web-of-sound production (those silences are *loud!*), is one of those rare records that sound *better* the 5,283rd time you play them than they did the 5,282nd (providing, of course, you don't keep playing the same copy).

Commenting on the difference between Smokey Robinson's and Norman Whitfield's productions, Melvin says, "By Smokey being a singer in a group, he was what we call each other lovingly, a 'doo-wopper.' He 'doo-wops,' he understands how a group functions and what it is to be in a group,

I can't get next to you. Dennis Edwards (second from right, top) was the new kid on the street corner when the Temptations' soul became "psychedelicized" under their new "five lead singers" format.

so it was almost like just singin' with your guys. Hangin' around and doin' it the natural way.

"With Norman it was all about technique, because he always came in with huge productions. When I'd hear all that stuff, I'd try to figure out just what we were gonna even *do* on it. You know, where do we fit? With Norman it was just technique and with Smokey it was all in a song.

"As far as Motown itself, I never knew it. We were always working. But we did go through Artist Development, which was just the same as—I went to Wayne Street University— going to school. And they had classes scheduled all day.

"Okay, let's say from ten till twelve the Temptations are in Vocals, with Maurice King and Harvey Fuqua and those people. From twelve-thirty to two-thirty we'd be in Choreography. That's Cholly Atkins, Lon Fontaine, and those people. Johnny Allen wrote arrangements, so he'd be in both departments.

"And then they had departments where they taught you how to walk. They taught you about makeup. They taught you about personal hygiene. They taught us what questions to answer with the press and what not to answer—it's been very hard for me to unlearn some of those things, to go ahead and say what the hell I want to say, but I became very programmed. You represented Motown very well.

"People used to say, 'There's a record industry, then there's Motown.' We were inside of our own capsule, our own world. It was very secure there, and being from the South and Midwest, we didn't feel real hip like New York people, so there was safety in numbers, and the safeness, the security's with your own. It was security from your inabilities, your anxieties—whatever your negative hang-ups are.

"The Motown Revues were also very educational. I learned that I'm really the little boy that ran away with the circus. The sideshow. That's what it really is. It's show business in its rawest state.

"Like when we started off, the transportation we had to use was Brooks Bus Company out of Atlanta, Georgia. They took those old World War II buses—and here it is in the sixties— and put 'em out on the road and those buses would break down.

"I remember one time we were down in Mississippi and the bus broke down across from a little ol' jail, so all of us—the Temptations, Kim Weston, Martha and the Vandellas, Stevie Wonder, and the Supremes—went over to the jail and sang for the people over there. [Ah, to have been thrown in on a drunk charge that night.] But since we were all in it together, I never had a fear.

"Another time we were in [long pause] Roanoke, Virginia. There were these guys and they wore the great big hats and they were really hoodlums. They were walking around with guns and stuff, and they said they were gonna shoot somebody on the stage.

"Yeah, just for the hell of it. You know the chicks were all going for us and all that. And we'd got into town early and gone over to the playground and turned 'em out on the basketball court. It was kinda like comin' in and takin' over their turf, you know?

"Now, the Four Tops' valet, his name was Frazier, was out by the bus. They snuck up on him, took a tire iron, hit him in the forehead, and caved his forehead in—he has a plate up there now, he lived—but all the time we were onstage, everybody else had to watch the wings and everywhere to make sure no one took a shot at us. And it really felt good to have people that were your friends from home, who you could count on almost like you could your family.

"But I think the true Motown Revues happened at the Fox Theater in Detroit. What made them so special was that we always had them during Christmas week. And if there's any part of my life I could live over, it would be at the Fox Theater on the Motown Revue, because we were all there and everybody's family would come backstage and you'd get to meet everybody's mothers and sisters and brothers.

"And then there'd be all your teachers from school, all your old girlfriends, all your best friends—your buddies that you put the blood on the finger with—everybody, you know? That's why I think the true Motown Revues always happened at the Fox Theater in Detroit, and if you talk to anyone else who was there, I'm sure they would agree with me, because that was home for all of us."

Although "Masterpiece" (1973) was the Temptations' last record to go Top 10 pop, the group cut another six Top 10 R&B hits, including three R&B number ones ("Shakey Ground," "Happy People," and "Let Your Hair Down"), before exiting Motown in 1977.

"I didn't want to go to Atlantic Records," Melvin recalls. "But I do want to be a group member, more than I want anything else. And this will be printed and things will be said and all that, but I'll stand by it. 'Cause when it's time to vote, you've gotta go whichever way your head goes. And I felt that we were having our problems here, and the regime that was in here I wasn't getting along with at all.

"But the regime in here has never bothered me because my relationship is not with the regime. I'm the one who used to go to the store for Mrs. Bertha Gordy when I was eleven,

58. Three former and one current Motown recording artists have been awarded stars on Hollywood Boulevard's Walk of Fame. Who are these four acts?

59. How many records did the Supremes release before they scored their first Top 30 hit?

60. What was Motown's first Grammy-winning recording?

twelve years old, so my problem is not with the regime. I could've gone around it. But when we as a group felt more comfortable going somewhere else, I followed suit. But in my heart of hearts I didn't want to go."

After two years of nothing but minor hits and an apparent year in limbo, the Temptations returned to Motown, where the hits didn't come any easier. Then, in 1982, as Melvin puts it, "the time and space came together right" for a Temptation reunion, which saw Eddie Kendricks and David Ruffin return to the fold for an album *(Reunion)* and a tour.

According to Melvin, the album was something of an afterthought, which explains why Eddie and David are heard on only three of the LP's seven songs. However, with a little help from Melvin's nephew Rick James, who wrote, produced, played, and sang along, one of these tunes, the streetsmart, booty-busting "Standing on the Top," gave the Temptations their fourteenth R&B number one.

So, given the Temptations' well-earned-reputation for being able to outsing, outdance, and outdress any group in sight, what's the view like when you're standing on the top?

"Well," Melvin drawls, "we developed our concept of what the Temptations should be by watching a whole lot of groups that came before us—the Flamingos, Harvey and the Moonglows, Frankie Lymon and the Teenagers, the Midnighters, the Five Royales. I mean, I could name 'em, but just sitting here right now maybe I got a little nervous, maybe I can't remember all of 'em bim-bam-boom like that. But we could sit around and I could sing all their songs.

"The Turbans, the Spaniels—you see what I mean? The Dominos, the Drifters, the Platters—classiest group I probably ever saw were the Platters. They were the first black group I ever saw singing really white stuff and they were in those clubs and polished.

"And we came along at a time when the two words in show business stood for that. I remember the first time we met the Flamingos in person. We were the Distants at the time, so it was in the fifties. But all the Flamingos drove up in great big old pretty cars and when they got out of the cars they were all dressed nice and sharp and the whole bit. And when they got onstage, they were a group with five lead singers.

"I think that the Temptations are [*makes quote marks with his fingers*] the latter-day Flamingos. Really, really. I tell it to you. To make a long story short, we're just showing what we learned from some very, very dedicated people to show business. . . ."

Chapter Seven

I SECOND THAT EMOTION

"Al Cleveland and I were in a department store in Detroit, Christmas shopping, and during a conversation with one of the staff, Al meant to say, 'I second the motion,' but instead he said, 'I second that emotion.' We laughed about it, and as we walked out of the store, we both realized—hey, that would make a great song title. And so we went home and wrote that song."
—SMOKEY ROBINSON

"Originally, there was another verse before the last chorus of 'I Second That Emotion.' Mr. Gordy cut it out. Broke Smokey's heart, 'cause he wrote it and that was his baby, but it was just too long."
—BILLIE JEAN BROWN

There you have it. A classic example of what that great rock 'n' roller Mark Twain meant when he described writing as being "1% inspiration and 99% perspiration." After all, "I Second That Emotion" is only two minutes and thirty-nine seconds long. So why did Berry Gordy cut it? In a word—*structure*.

Gordy obviously felt the extra verse caused the song to lose momentum; that is, it didn't get back to the chorus fast enough. Also, shortening the time between repetitions of the chorus automatically gave it more impact. ("Say, what's the name of that song again? Right.")

Second question: What's the first thing you need to make a hit record? You need a hit song. And before there was a Tamla, a Motown, or even a Hitsville, U.S.A., there was a Jobete (Berry Gordy's music publishing company).

Now, fewer than one out of ten people who can carry a tune can write one. Gordy, who knew *he* had what it takes, also had some firm ideas on the subject and graded his staff's songwriting efforts accordingly. Gordy not only wanted all songs written in the present tense ("Write like it's happening now") but insisted they tell a story as well. Someone wanna second that emotion?

> "Gladys Horton, one of the girls in the group, wrote 'Playboy,' but the story has to be strong to be able to do anything, so of course they [Motown writers-producers Brian Holland, Mickey Stevenson, and Robert Bateman] changed it and brought it up to date and all. That's how we got that tune."
> **—KATHERINE ANDERSON, the Marvelettes**

Gordy didn't just sit back and blow slogans either.

> " 'Stubborn Kind of Fellow'—that's interesting because I had written a jazz kind of thing and Berry Gordy was in the control room at the time, listening, and he said, 'Well, now, let's change a few chords.' And we changed a few chords and he said, 'Well, now it sounds pop. Now I think we can get some record sales out of it.' "
> **—MARVIN GAYE**

Above all Motown considered a hit song to be an advertisement for other performers to record the tune.

> "We're signing people with talent to do songs we've already got on hand."
> —BERRY GORDY, 1965

MOTOWN MAGIC MOMENT #20

Once a Motown song was a hit, other artists and producers at the label were encouraged to give it a shot on the theory that it could be an even bigger hit the second time around.

Quite often, Motown was right. Diana Ross' 1970 version of "Ain't No Mountain High Enough," Marvin Gaye's 1968 rendition of "I Heard it Through the Grapevine," and Bonnie Pointer's 1979 remake of "Heaven Must've Sent You" were all more successful than the original hits by Motown stars Mar-

Grinnin' Barrett. Our cover boy, Barrett Strong, not only scored Motown's first hit—the appropriately titled "Money"—but also went on to greater fame and fortune as a staff songwriter.

COURTESY MICHAEL OCHS ARCHIVES

vin Gaye and Tammi Terrell (1967), Gladys Knight and the Pips (1967), and the Elgins (1966), respectively.

There are dozens of other examples. About the only restriction was that if the song had first been a hit for, say, a female group, then Motown wanted it recut with a male group or solo artist in order to give the tune a different interpretation. Motown wasn't always able to top itself, but the company usually got at least an album track out of the process.

Sometimes they did even better. When the Beatles came along in 1964, did Motown know who JohnPaulGeorgeandRingo were? Sure, they were those white boys—English— with the funny haircuts who recorded three of our songs on their second album: "Money" (Barrett Strong, 1960), "Please Mr. Postman" (the Marvelettes, 1961), and "You've Really Got a Hold on Me" (the Miracles, 1962). This meant at least an extra $60,000—in 1964 dollars, yet—to Motown via its music publishing arm, Jobete.

Briefly, music publishing works like this: The publisher collects an automatic two cents per song for every copy sold from the record company. Publishers—the term goes back to the preradio days when successful popular songs were determined by the sales of sheet music—also collect money from one of America's two performing-rights societies: ASCAP or, in Jobete's case, BMI.

These organizations charge radio stations yearly fees for the right to play copyrighted material, namely, phonograph records. Using spot checks, statistics, and other forms of advanced hoodoo, ASCAP and BMI determine how often a song has been played over a three-month period and—at two cents per play—send the publisher the appropriate amount of money.

Without going into detail about jukeboxes, sheet music, foreign rights, or possible film and TV licenses, let's just say these pennies add up to a nice chunk of change. And the checks come in every three months for fifty-six years.

The publisher also collects an equal share of these moneys—called royalties—on behalf of the songwriter. However, if two people wrote the tune, each will wind up with a royalty rate of a penny per copy.

Along with collecting royalties, the publisher tries to persuade other artists to record the song. When that happens, the money-go-round starts all over again.

Jobete has always been Berry Gordy's ace in the hole. Between 1964 and 1981 no fewer than *eighty-six* rerecordings of Jobete-published songs made the *Billboard* Top 100 pop charts, and *seventy-seven* of them by non-Motown artists.

A dozen of these were Top 10 hits. It's an interesting list, ranging from the Vanilla Fudge's "You Keep Me Hangin' On" (1968) and Blood, Sweat and Tears' "You've Made Me So Very Happy" (1969) to the Captain and Tennille's "Shop Around" (1976) and Kim Carnes' "More Love" (1980).

Johnny Rivers scored twice with "Baby, I Need Your Loving" and "The Tracks of My Tears" (both 1967). So did Linda Ronstadt with "Ooh Baby Baby" (1979) and "Heat Wave," one of four such remakes from 1975. The others were James Taylor's "How Sweet It Is," Gloria Gaynor's "Never Can Say Goodbye," and the Carpenter's "Please Mr. Postman," a record which has the dubious distinction of being the only performance of a Jobete-published song by a non-Motown artist to reach number one pop.

"Please Mr. Postman" is also the only tune in the Jobete catalog to top the pop charts twice. (The Marvelettes original 1961 version was the first.) In contrast, Shorty Long's original 1964 recording of "Devil with the Blue Dress," a 1966 pop

Get up, girl, show me what you can do! With no less than "The Corporation" behind you, dough-re-mi was E-Z as 1-2-3 for the Jackson 5.

Top 10 hit for Mitch Ryder and the Detroit Wheels, never made the Top 100.

However, the most recorded Motown song of all, "For Once in My Life," was never published by Jobete. Upon hearing the tune, Berry Gordy reportedly exclaimed, "That sounds like a standard." In order to foster this image, he ordered the creation of a new publishing company, to be given an old, established name—Stein and Van Stock.

Gordy probably didn't have to go to such lengths. Jobete-published songs have been rerecorded by an astonishing range of non-Motown artists, from slumming jazzbos (Mongo Santamaria, Ramsey Lewis, and the Crusaders) to heavy-metal-mongers (Grand Funk Railroad, Motorhead, and Humble Pie), from soul stars (Al Green, Otis Redding, and Aretha Franklin) to pop wimps (Tony Orlando and Dawn, the 5th Dimension, and Donny and Marie Osmond), from hi-class lounge lizards (Tony Bennett, Lou Rawls, and Rod Stewart) to glorified bar bands (Creedence Clearwater Revival, the Beatles, and the Rolling Stones). Long, short, crosswise, consecutive, and with a repeater.

Now, you can argue all night whether it's the singer or the song. You can also argue whether it's hotter in Milwaukee than in July. But we can all agree on one thing—give us what that Jobete catalog earns in one three-month period and we'll tell the whole world to love us or kiss us where it stinks. (And we don't mean New Jersey.)

So what makes these songs so great? Well, it had a lot to do with how they wrote 'em.

"Lamont Dozier was fiddlin' around with it on the piano. He was just doin' the *[sings]* 'lum-de-lum-de-li-i,' because he hadn't really gotten it together, you know? And I asked him to record it on us 'cause I thought just that part there was so strong."
—SMOKEY ROBINSON

MOTOWN MAGIC MOMENT #21

That "lum-de-lum-de-li-i" part Smokey's referring to—the song was "Mickey's Monkey"—is what tunesmiths like to call a "hook" (because it catches the listener's attention). Songwriting is really quite simple: If you don't have a hook, you don't have a hit.

Along with this basic component, songs are made up of two, sometimes three, larger sections, known as verses, choruses, and bridges. Verses lead into choruses—the words

and music that get repeated—and follow a set musical pattern, but the words change. Bridges introduce a third and completely different pattern, usually after the second chorus, and traditionally lead into the third verse.

Warning: We're talking strict theory here. In reality, song structures are much more flexible. Many hits have only two verses (sometimes the first does double duty as the third verse) and get their power from endless repetitions of the chorus/hook, which is often used to open the song as well.

Speaking of intros—and a lot of Motown songs start on the chorus—another favorite Motown trick is to take an instrumental phrase that appears, say, just before the chorus and place it at the beginning of the tune. The horn flourish that kicks off "Beauty Is Only Skin Deep" might be the best example. Hey, first you've gotta get people's attention. . . .

Once you've done that, the real trick is to keep it. Which brings us to the second basic principle of songwriting—flow. It really doesn't matter how a song starts or what form it takes, as long as you get from one section to another smoothly.

For example, let's go back to the million-dollar misunderstanding that began this chapter: "I Second That Emotion." After the opening blast of trombones, the song locks into an unhurried, finger-snapping groove that never lets up. Along the way the rhythmic accents will shift from this basic, punch-every-other beat to a section where all beats are accented equally to a third section, where the emphasis is on the first beat of each measure (the downbeat).

These rhythmic shifts correspond to the melody, which first moves down with, then up against, and finally parallel to the chord changes, which have been rising and falling in steady rolling waves all the way through this particular verse-chorus sequence. The overall effect of this rhythmic/harmonic flow is to create a sense of rising tension until Smokey gets to the hook/title, whereupon he brings everything back to where it started.

That's enough "Motown Songwriting Made E-Z" for now. Once you understand the concepts of hooks and flow, the rest requires talent. Which is what it took to think up the percolating synthesizer riff that powers Stevie Wonder's "Superstition." Once Stevie whipped up that slinky monster, he could've read the previous paragraph over it and still got a hit.

You can't teach that. However, you can improve on it. In the sixties, when Motown got an idea this good, they quickly turned it into another pair of hits. (Nowadays, when artists get an idea this good, they crank out three albums' worth of variations on it. Progress.)

These Motown trilogies were practically written from blueprints. Consider this three-part miniseries from 1966–67: "Reach Out, I'll Be There," "Standing in the Shadows of Love," and "Bernadette," all sung by the Four Tops and all written by Eddie Holland–Lamont Dozier–Brian Holland. All of them sound alike and all of them sound a little different—just like they drew 'em up on the chalkboard.

"Reach Out, I'll Be There" was the first, opening with flutes and exotic percussion over a fast stomp beat. On the first part of the verse the group echoes lead singer Levi Stubbs. On the second half (the "reach out" part) the roles are reversed, with everybody coming in together on the chorus (the "I'll be there" part).

Once H-D-H had these changes, all they had to do was repeat this structure, toss in an extra chorus of background vocals (while playing the introduction over it), and repeat the structure a third time. Next stop: number one.

The follow-up ("Standing in the Shadows of Love") was almost as brilliant. This time, H-D-H begin with the chorus/ title and Levi takes all of the verse, while the group's harmonies build tension in the background. Then H-D-H hit you with the kind of bridge that opens up those golden gates (the "didn't I treat you right, now, baby, didn't I" part), sung by Stubbs and the group in unison, except that the Tops' harmonies are up an octave over Levi's vocal line.

Again, once H-D-H had this chorus-verse-bridge structure in place, they repeated it twice, added another chorus, and faded out. Ho-hum. Another day at the office, another Top 10 record.

The problem of the second follow-up ("Bernadette") was no less creatively solved. This, too, begins on the chorus/title, followed by a verse in which first Levi, then the group, then Levi has the focus before diving back into the chorus. After the third chorus H-D-H give us a break in the form of a bridge, throw down another verse and chorus, and go home. Top 10, again.

Sophisticates will notice that the battle between Levi and the group during the verses parallels and emphasizes the tension created by the alternating chorus-verse structure. Cool.

Hey, as H-D-H themselves slyly noted in an earlier Four Tops' follow-up—"It's the Same Old Song" (and it *was*, too). Very cool.

Which only shows that there's more to Motown's songwriting success than structural one-upmanship. After they cooked up the basic ingredients for a hit, Motown's writers garnished it with endless bits of cleverness designed to tickle the listener's palate.

61. Which Motown recording group had its own Saturday morning cartoon series?

62. What tune does Little Stevie Wonder break into in the middle of his harmonica solo on "Fingertips, Pt. 2"?

63. What former Motown recording artist coscripted the *Lady Sings the Blues* film?

Sometimes these were simple, as in the tiny pause after each "stop" in the phrase "I wanna stop *[stop]* and thank you baby" from Holland-Dozier-Holland's "How Sweet It Is." Sometimes they were complex, like using the bridge—which breaks away from the musical structure of Norman Whitfield and Barrett Strong's "Just My Imagination"—to also break away lyrically and reveal that the singer is only fantasizing. Ice.

Now a few words about lyrics. While it's true they take a back seat to melody, beat, sound, and structure, they also add an extra dimension of meaning to the music. Even nonsense lyrics do this. What does Little Richard's "Tutti Frutti" mean? It means all the squares, go home. So does Bob Dylan's "Like a Rolling Stone," for that matter. The trick is to be as specific as a snapshot and as timeless as, well, "Summertime."

MOTOWN MAGIC MOMENT #22

"The timing [1970] was absolutely perfect, because even the government was saying, 'Wait a minute. Is this ever gonna end?' And thanks to the very creative writing of Barrett Strong, the lyrics never ever said what war was being talked about. It could've been the war in the neighborhood. It could've been the war in Southeast Asia. It simply said, 'War. What is it good for?' "
—EDWIN STARR

And the only thing as timeless as good taste is craftsmanship.

MOTOWN MAGIC MOMENT #23

"Some people say they write from experience. Not me. I write songs no matter what mood I'm in—it's my work, dig?"
—SMOKEY ROBINSON

Or, as the Man himself put it back in '65 when a high-school student asked, "How do you find guys like Smokey Robinson?":

MOTOWN MAGIC MOMENT #24

"We *don't find* guys like Smokey Robinson."
—BERRY GORDY

With all due respect to Eddie Holland, Barrett Strong, and any of the other talented people at Jobete, Smokey Robinson was probably Motown's best lyricist. Certainly, he was the most stylized.

Yes, Bob Dylan once called him "today's greatest American poet," but the man who wrote "You've Really Got a Hold on Me"—one of the few love songs that portray both parties as something less than perfect people (in 1962, yet)—really didn't need the justification.

From his most famous lines ("I've got sunshine on a cloudy day" and "I don't like you, but I love you") to his favorite themes (dreams vs. reality, pleasure vs. pain, and public vs. private feelings), Smokey has built an entire career on an understanding of the contradictions inherent in love.

See, when you're talking pop lyrics, you're really talking about the writer's ability to turn a phrase (tomorrow's clichés today) and make the best lines rhyme. Most songwriters are content to get off one decent crack—usually the hook—and let it go at that. Smokey wouldn't stoop so low.

An inveterate punster ("What's So Good About Good-bye") and a master of the sexual metaphor (who else would've had the Marvelettes sing "I laid such a tender trap/Hoping you would fall into it"?), Smokey knows the value of a vivid image ("You Beat Me to the Punch") and goes for the internal rhyme every time ("Every day I'm more inclined to find my baby"). As a result, Smokey's best tunes had more hooks than a meat-packing plant.

"The Tracks of My Tears" is a typical Smokey construction. During the verses he creates tension by contrasting the singer's public behavior with his private thoughts, which of

COURTESY THE CULTURAL WAREHOUSE

If you can want. The Miracles: going to a go-go, but dressed for the Copa.

course are so painful they cause him to break down uncontrollably by the time the chorus arrives. . . .

The song also sports some of Smokey's finest rhymes: cute/substitute, masquerading/fading. A simple tale, stylishly told (the "secret" of Smokey's success).

Then there's "Pet Names," a nonhit composition for Chuck Jackson, which contains the immortal couplet "I call my baby 'Napalm'/'Cause she's like a fiery bomb." Yeah, Smokey the poet.

Cheap shot. Like his peers Cole Porter and Chuck Berry, Smokey Robinson writes pop songs, not poetry. Without Smokey's flair for stairstep melodies and his fragile falsetto, a tune like "Ooh Baby Baby" looks pretty silly on paper.

More to the point, Smokey was versatile. Many of his biggest hits were written for women singers, and these ranged from sweetly devoted (Mary Wells' "The One Who Really Loves You") to fiercely independent (Brenda Holloway's "When I'm Gone"), even menacing (the Marvelette's "Don't Mess with Bill").

Writing for other male groups, he could be macho (the Temptations' "Get Ready") or intentionally comic (the Contours' "First I Look at the Purse"). Occasionally, he played it straight, as on the Miracles' own "Going to a Go-Go," a record that sticks to strict party lines.

Smokey also wasn't above stealing his own best ideas. The Miracles' "Tears of a Clown" boasts an unusual reference to grand opera's most famous character with the line about Pagliacci keeping his sadness hid. The identical couplet first appeared in a Smokey-composed 1964 nonhit for Carolyn Crawford ("My Smile is Just a Frown Turned Upside Down").

As a songwriter, Smokey's credits include nineteen Top 10 pop records (three of them number ones) and thirty-nine Top 10 R&B hits, of which eleven were number ones. He did it with craftsmanship, cleverness, the ability to write for a wide range of performers, and—most of all—the philosophy expressed in the Miracles' '68 smash, "If You Can Want," wherein Smokey expostulates that if one is able to desire, one is able to require, and if one is able to require, one is able to inspire, and if one is able to inspire, one is able to perspire. Therefore, when desired, he'll perspire.

You guessed it, the man's a card-carrying romantic. After all, it was reportedly Smokey who told Berry Gordy, discouraged at the end of yet another week spent flogging master recordings to record companies all over New York and Chicago, "Why not you be the Man?" Now, that's romantic.

Smokey is also an awfully democratic guy, routinely cowriting tunes with Miracles members Pete Moore, Ronnie

White, and Bobby Rogers as well as the group's guitarist, Marv Tarplin. Few Motown performers were so fortunate.

So who were the other Motown songwriters? Well, unless they had the luxury of working in tandem with a specific producer, as was the case with Barrett Strong and Norman Whitfield, their credits are scattered all over the Motown catalog.

The most successful of these writers were Sylvia Moy ("It Takes Two," "Uptight," "I Was Made to Love Her"), Pam Sawyer ("My Whole World Ended (the Moment You left Me)," "If I Were Your Woman," "Love Child"), and Ron Miller ("For Once in My Life," "Touch Me in the Morning," "Yester-Me, Yester-You, Yesterday"). There were a couple dozen others, but with less spectacular track records.

For the most part the major Motown songwriters were also producers. Berry Gordy, Smokey Robinson, Holland-Dozier-Holland, Norman Whitfield, Nick Ashford and Valerie Simpson, Johnny Bristol and Harvey Fuqua, Frank Wilson, Mickey Stevenson and Ivy Jo Hunter, Clarence Paul, Hal Davis, and Hank Cosby. Some lineup.

However, even with all this talent hammering out tunes day and night, Berry Gordy wasn't taking any chances. He also conducted what would now be called focus group research.

"At the end of the month Berry would bring the neighborhood junior-high school and high school kids in for soft drinks and sandwiches and play all the tapes. And whatever artist got the strongest reaction, that would be the next release."
—**JOE BILLINGSLEA, the Contours**

MOTOWN MAGIC MOMENT #25

And not every Motown hit had its origins within the four walls of Hitsville, U.S.A.

"I used to play in a little club and the kids there were doin' this new dance and they hipped me. They said, 'This is what's happening. This is called the Shotgun and you're gonna have to write a song for this.' "
—**JUNIOR WALKER**

MOTOWN MAGIC MOMENT #26

Now, *that's* pop. That's soul. That's Motown. That's . . .

Chapter Eight

THE SOUND OF YOUNG AMERICA

We were expected to go into the studio and produce four songs in three hours.
—NICK ASHFORD AND VALERIE SIMPSON

hen people talk about the "Motown Sound," they usually mean the sound found on records written and produced by the team of Brian Holland, Lamont Dozier, and Eddie Holland: "Where Did Our Love Go," "I Can't Help Myself," "You Can't Hurry Love," and "Reach Out, I'll Be There," to name but four of their most classic tracks.

Between 1963 and 1967 the trio racked up twenty-five Top 10 pop records, of which twelve were number ones. Eight of these were also R&B number ones, and another twelve H-D-H creations made the R&B Top 10, for a total of thirty-seven hits in five years. Jump back.

Listen. There's no such thing as the "Motown Sound." At its peak the company had a half-dozen different producers, each with his own distinct "sound." Sure, they all recorded in the same studios with the same musicians, but Smokey Robinson's Temptations productions don't sound anything like Norman Whitfield's. Nor does Nick Ashford and Valerie Simpson's production of Diana Ross' "Ain't No Mountain High Enough" resemble Johnny Bristol and Harvey Fuqua's original version with Marvin Gaye and Tammi Terrell.

COURTESY TOM DePIERRO/AIRWAVE INTERNATIONAL

The happening. Seen on the scene at the **Supremes Sing Holland-Dozier-Holland** photo session are (standing, from left) Diana Ross, songwriters-producers Lamont Dozier, Eddie Holland, and Brian Holland; (seated, from left) Mary Wilson and Flo Ballard.

Nevertheless, the size and the sheer number of H-D-H hits have made their "sound" synonymous with Motown's. "A combination of gospel music, pop, country and western, and jazz" is how Lamont Dozier describes it.

"I say that because I've always thought that the 'Motown Sound' started with [1962's] 'Come and Get These Memories,'" Lamont elaborates. "Because that one particular song had a mixture of all these musical elements.

"After we cut 'Come and Get These Memories,' Berry [Gordy] came in and said, 'Well, who did this?' And I got kind of shaken by that statement because I thought he was implying 'What is this mess?' Then he said, 'Wow. That's really different. I like that.'

"And that made me believe we could take this thing and

develop it and get away from that rock 'n' roll, which I thought was . . . it could be done classier. I always thought rock 'n' roll could be done with strings. It's according to how you voice the stuff.

"And 'Come and Get These Memories' did that for me. Because of the voicing of the chords. We were using elevenths and thirteenths and those notes, that before then were just unheard of. I mean, 'Shop Around' was just a regular triad. It was nothin' heavy.

" 'Come and Get These Memories' is the catalyst that opened everybody's ears up to reach out for heavier chords, and to mix those chords with country-type feelings and jazz and gospel.

"The gospel thing was already there naturally, but by expanding it, putting jazz with it and a little country and a little pop, we made it more sophisticated, smoothed it out, fine-tuned the thing.

"And we found that we didn't have to have those bluesy melodies. That we could be as pop as we wanted to be. In other words, going down the whole piano and seeing what our options are [chuckles].

"I also have to say that the people who bought these records had a lot to do with it, because if you don't have the people buying these records—which is a form of approval—you don't have room to expand. You stagnate. You say, 'Well, they don't like it, so let's go back to doin' what we were doin'.' That's what would've happened if people hadn't given us the thumbs up on the stuff."

So what were Brian Holland, Lamont Dozier, and Eddie Holland doing before they cooked up "Come and Get These Memories" (Martha and the Vandellas, 1963)? Not much, although all three Detroiters had been knocking around Motown almost from the very beginning.

Brian had worked his way up from Motown's recording engineer to a producer's spot. The "Brianbert" credited as the producer of the Marvelettes' "Please Mr. Postman" (1961) is a pseudonym for *Brian* Holland and former Satintone *Robert* Bateman. Brian shares writing credits on this, the follow-up ("Twistin' Postman"), and "Playboy," as well.

Lamont, who had recorded with the Romeos (for Fox, leased to Atco), the Voice Masters, and as Lamont Anthony (for Anna and Check-Mate), came to Motown in 1962. After cutting one tune as a solo artist for the Motown subsidiary Mel-O-Dy, he linked up with Brian Holland and writer-performer Freddie Gorman to form the Holland-Dozier-Gorman team that was responsible for a pair of minor Marvelettes hits: "Strange I Know" and "Forever" (both 1963).

COURTESY TOM DEPIERRO/AIRWAVE INTERNATIONAL

Clique to pick. Three slick chicks and three not-so-dumb clucks just crack themselves up in this '66-clicked pic.

Freddie left Motown about this time, only to return a couple years later as a member of the Originals. In between, he's best known as the cowriter of the Reflections' deathless "Just Like Romeo and Juliet" (Golden World, 1964).

When Freddie exited, Brian's brother Eddie, whose experience included singing demo recordings of the songs Berry Gordy wrote for Jackie Wilson at $25 a pop, took his place. Prior to this, Eddie—who had recorded several unsuccessful singles while under contract to Mercury and UA Records—had also been a Motown solo artist.

"Jamie" (1962) was the first of ten Eddie Holland solo Motown efforts. It was also Eddie's only real hit, although 1964's "Leaving Here" has become a rock 'n' roll standard of sorts, having been recorded by legendary Motor City punk

soulsters the Rationals, current Rolling Stone Ronnie Wood's first outfit, the Birds, and, most recently, heavy-metal cases Motorhead.

However, once H-D-H upped and erupted with simultaneous million-dollar hits for the Supremes ("Where Did Our Love Go") and the Four Tops ("Baby, I Need Your Loving"), Eddie gladly put pennies on his eyes for a performing career.

"Eddie has the mentality of an accountant," says Lamont. "That's what he was going to school for and he just wasn't into being a singer. To him that was sort of silly."

Eddie's also very shy, as is his brother Brian. Billie Jean Brown—who, incidentally, passed her bar exam since we last heard from her—remembers that Brian was so bashful he'd turn out all the lights, order everyone out of the studio, and even forbid people to stand in the hallway next to the studio while he laid down vocal tracks on Four Tops demos.

"Brian's very sensitive," Lamont agrees. "More or just as sensitive as I am in a lot of respects. A very give-you-the-shirt-off-his-back type of guy.

"Eddie's an introvert and you'd never really know what his feelings were, 'cause half the time he wouldn't say anything. He'd just sit there and observe. But over a period of years Brian and I knew what his thing was and Eddie is sensitive, too. You have to be to be a songwriter. And we couldn't work together if we weren't all very sensitive toward one another's feelings."

"If I felt that the delivery should be this way and it sounded better than the delivery that Eddie had, or if my lyric was better, he'd say, 'Yeah, that sounds better than what I've got.' Or Brian would say—Brian didn't dabble with the lyrics at all, just made sure that the melody was right—'Well, I don't like either one of your melodies, so do it this way.' Which would be fantastic. And that's the way a team works."

In addition to three heads being better than two, one of the main reasons Holland-Dozier-Holland were Motown's most successful producers was that all three members were specialists.

"Brian was the engineer," Lamont explains. "He was responsible for the sound and the structure of the song. Melody, too. My job was melody, lyrics, and titles—coming up with the basic idea. Eddie's job was lyrics, melody again and teaching the song to the artist, showing them the feeling we wanted to convey to the listener.

"Like, say, 'Where Did Our Love Go.' We were sitting around in our little room, 'cause we were punching the clock then. From nine to six [laughs]. Most of the time we would be in there playing cards 'til somebody came up with something.

64. What was the first Motown TV show to win an Emmy Award?

65. The Supremes' "Love Child" is credited as having been produced by "The Clan." What five people made up this production team?

66. What was the name of the record store Berry Gordy co-owned before he founded Motown?

I didn't gamble, so I was always tinkling at the piano, and I came up with 'Baby, baby, where did our love go? Chink-chink-chink-chink.' Just fooling around. Not even really thinkin' seriously about anything.

"I think then Brian or Eddie—one of the two—made a statement: 'Hey, that sounds like something,' you know? We didn't know quite know *what*, 'cause then again it was different from anything that any of us had ever put out.

"And I was singing, 'Baby, baby, where did our love go? Don't you want me? Don't you want me no more?' That's all I had. And I just kept singing it over and over again. Just chank-chank-chank-chank. Just bangin' away, 'cause I'm not really a piano player as such [chuckles].

"Then Brian and I got together on the structure of the song—where the chorus, verse, and bridge would be—and then we called in Hank Cosby to write the chords out, 'cause neither Brian nor Eddie nor myself write music. So Hank came in and wrote down what we played, and Eddie made sure the key was right for the particular singer.

"We were originally going to give the song to the Marvelettes, because we were going for the fast buck [chuckles]. 'Cause we figured they were powerful enough to handle this, and it was too different for somebody like the Supremes. We thought they needed something a little more [snaps fingers twice] to the point, something that you know is a hit.

"Of course, we had already cut the track and because of Gladys [Horton] singing low like she does, the key was written real low. And it was actually too low for Diana.

"But this song that was in the wrong key is what gave Diana Ross her sound [chuckles]. 'Cause before then they always put Diana in the clouds and, to me, she sounded very thin up there. But because of the way the key was cut, she had to sing it low and it came out very sentimental, very sexy. But anyway, let me get back to . . ."

That's okay, nobody minds a little digression, as long as it's a good story. According to Lamont, the Marvelettes refused "Where Did Our Love Go," claiming—in his words—"they thought it was garbage." Oops.

"After Hank wrote out the chord sheets, the structure, and the repeat signs," Lamont continues, "we went down to Mickey Stevenson's office, and they would tell us who was in the studio and when we could cut. Usually, we got priority, 'cause we were the hottest producers there. So we probably went in the next day. We wouldn't record unless we had four songs ready.

"Once in the studio, Hank would run it down roughly with the musicians, first as an arranger and again after Brian and I listened to it. Hank would have some idea on paper, but then we had to communicate to the guys just what type of feeling we wanted. So Brian and I would split up half the room. Most of the time he'd take the keyboards and guitars and I would take the bass, drums, and vibraphone. But if Brian felt something on the bass or if I felt something on the guitars, we would show it to 'em. Whatever the case may be.

"Now this song was not completed lyrically at all. We just had that little bit I told you I hummed. After we cut the track we'd get a copy, a little tape—a reel-to-reel in those days— and give it to Eddie. I would sit with Eddie for a few minutes and collaborate with him on the lyric and the story. What the situation is here. The beginning, middle, and end. Is it happy? Is it sad? And the whole bit.

"And after jotting some ideas down he would take it, siphon through it, and see if he could use whatever I came up with, you know? Compile it with his own ideas and then go ahead and make demos for the artists.

"Eddie would give them a demo to take home with them. They would usually live with the song a couple of days. Then on the third day they should be in the studio, knowin' this song.

"We would always be there at the dub-in to make sure. While Eddie was laying the vocal down on Diana, I'd be there teaching the girls the harmony parts or whatever the background parts should be."

Eddie was also Motown's designated lyricist, cowriting such modern-jive masterworks as Shorty Long's "Function at the Junction" and the Velvelettes' "He Was Really Sayin' Somethin'." His writing partner on the former was Shorty Long. On the latter it was Norman Whitfield, with whom Eddie shares credit on a number of timeless tunes, including the Temptations' "(I Know) I'm Losing You," "Ain't Too Proud to Beg," "Beauty Is Only Skin Deep," "The Girl's Alright with Me," "Girl (Why You Wanna Make me Blue)," and the Marvelettes' "Too Many Fish in the Sea." What are words worth? Take a look at Eddie's royalty checks.

Along with getting the maximum performance out of the musicians and vocalists, the producer's second most important responsibility lies in the actual sound of the record. Not only the way that the various instruments are recorded—the depth of the drum sound, for example—and the "mix" but the little touches that make your record stand out from the competition.

"We would always be experimenting with different sounds. It wasn't one of our sessions, but I remember Ivy Jo Hunter brought in these big car chains—snow chains—for "Dancing in the Street." He would hit 'em against the floor on a piece of wood. And if you listen to this record, you'll hear these chains: Kr-rrusshhh!"

Lamont laughs. "And I remember Mickey Stevenson underneath the piano. Somebody would press the piano keys down and Mickey would be under the piano with a little light hammer—bang! bang!—and you'd hear the strings ringing. Very weird-sounding. You didn't know what it was, it just sounded different. That was our answer to synthesizers.

"Of course, everything was overdubbed. We never cut everything at one time, 'cause we had limited space. Plus, we didn't have the separation, the equipment wasn't sophisticated enough to do that.

"The rhythm track was first. Everybody was together on that. After the rhythm we'd put the vocals on. After the vocals some extra added percussion—congas, tambourines, guys foot-stomping on a piece of plywood, and what have you. Then the horns and then the strings, which would always come last.

"The first string arrangement we used I'm pretty sure was done by Gil Askey on "Baby I Need Your Loving." Later we started using Paul Riser, who was a trombone player. Paul did most of the strings on our stuff.

"Another thing we did was to fatten the tracks, again on separate sessions. We'd use the Andantes (Jackie Hicks, Marlene Barrow, and Louvain Demps), not so much on the Supremes in those days, but on the Marvelettes. The Marvelettes' harmony was a little rough for my ears [chuckles] and I used to bring the Andantes in. Not when the girls were around. In fact, I don't think they even knew who sang their backgrounds—they thought it was them.

"But I had put the Andantes in there to smooth out the sound, and mixed it in such a way that it would blend and cover up the roughness we were getting from the girls, 'cause they had a harder R&B, church sound, and the Andantes were like really smooth, high-quality, chorus-type singers. We used to use 'em with the Four Tops, too, for the high parts. And that's how it was done in the studio."

During their five-year reign H-D-H's system of specialists was unbeatable. The Supremes and the Four Tops were their one-two-punch, but they also knocked out five Top 10 pop hits for Martha and the Vandellas ("Heatwave," "Nowhere to Run," "Jimmy Mack," "I'm Ready for Love," and "Quicksand") as well as one each for the Miracles ("Mickey's Monkey") and Marvin Gaye ("How Sweet It Is").

Then there were the R&B hits: Junior Walker's "I'm a Roadrunner" and "Come See about Me," Kim Weston's "Take

67. Prior to joining Motown, the songwriting-production team of Nick Ashford and Valerie Simpson were best known for having written one of Ray Charles' biggest hits. What is the title of this song?

68. Why does the Tamla Records label's famous five-digit numbering system begin at 54024?

69. Why are there no pictures of the artists on Motown's earliest albums?

Me in Your Arms (Rock Me a Little While)," the Isley Brothers' "This Old Heart of Mine," and the Elgins' "Darling Baby" and "Heaven Must've Sent You." And then . . .

Holland-Dozier-Holland told Hitsville it was "Splitsville," and exited in the usual cloud of lawsuits, a move which kept the trio out of the studio and off the charts for most of 1968–69. (Motown did release a few things that were lying around in the can.) When the paperwork settled, H-D-H set out to build their own empire and set up the Invictus and Hot Wax labels, to be distributed by Capitol and Buddah records, respectively.

Over the next two years these labels would yield a dozen Top 10 R&B hits, among them such Top 10 pop performances as Freda Payne's shimmering "Band of Gold," female vocal trio the Honey Cone's disarming Jackson 5 rip-off "Want Ads" (a pop number one), the Chairmen of the Board's simmering "Give Me Just a Little More Time," and 100 Proof Aged in Soul's alarming "Somebody's Been Sleeping." By 1974 they were out of business.

What? That's right. It's not enough to collect great talent. Ex-Contour Joe Stubbs fronted 100 Proof Aged in Soul, and former Showmen ("It Will Stand" and "39-21-46") vocalist Norman "General" Johnson led the Chairmen of the Board, while proto-feminist soulstress Laura Lee and funkadelic crazies the Parliaments both parked their slip-in mules under the Invictus/Hot Wax banner.

It's not enough to make great records either. Nor is it enough to get hits. (Seven Invictus/Hot Wax singles were certified million-sellers.) You've got to *get paid*.

"There was very little money being made because of the low [percentage] points we were getting and the loans that we had to pay back to Capitol and Buddah," Lamont sighs. "On the surface it looked great, but I think Capitol and Buddah probably made more money than anybody else did. They were our distributors and they were taking theirs off the top, too. Plus the overhead was just tremendous."

Looking back, perhaps the biggest mistake H-D-H made was to take themselves out of the creative trenches.

"Brian and I came up with 'Band of Gold' and 'Give Me Just a Little More Time,' but we didn't put our names on 'em 'cause we were in a lawsuit and couldn't use our names, so we used Ronnie Dunbar, who was an employee of ours, and Edith Wayne, who was like a friend of the Holland family. But in reality those were Holland-Dozier-Holland songs. Everybody knew it, 'cause . . . [*Lamont laughs*]. So anytime you see that 'E. Wayne,' that's the cue.

"After that, we brought in Greg Perry and General Johnson and they did a lot of the writing. Ronnie Dunbar, too."

Unfortunately, the Perry-Johnson-Dunbar combination wasn't able to sustain the momentum past 1972, and once more the hits turned into writs. As might be expected, certain "philosophical differences" came to a head, and Lamont parted company with the Hollands.

"I felt we should be more instrumental in venturing into other areas, like movies and plays," Lamont reflects. "Getting into the overall picture of music instead of just records, and getting some quick cash, some new blood, some new avenues besides. When I felt they didn't see it that way, I figured that it was time for me to leave."

Before Lamont beat feet, he and the Hollands climbed down out of the executive suites and made several attempts to reverse the company's fortunes: "New Kind of Woman" (performed by Holland-Dozier, 1972) as well as "Don't Leave Me Starvin' for Your Love" and "Slipping Away" (credited to Holland-Dozier featuring Brian Holland, 1973). Only Lamont Dozier's 1972 solo outing, "Why Can't We Be Lovers," made the R&B Top 10, a showing which no doubt prompted Lamont's choice of direction.

"So I went to ABC and got a couple of [Top 10 R&B] hits— "Trying to Hold on to My Woman" [1973] and "Fish Ain't Bitin'" [1974]. Again, I wrote and produced those, but I couldn't use my own name, so I put McKinley Jackson and James Reddick and my brother and one of the engineers— Bobby Perkins—as the writers. I just recently got the rights to my stuff back, although I already controlled the publishing."

By 1975 Lamont had moved to Warner Bros. Records, where all he could do was dent the charts, and the Hollands were back at Motown. Working as independent producers, they managed four Top 10 R&B hits in two years: Michael Jackson's "Just a Little Bit of You" and "We're Almost There," Eddie Kendricks' "Get the Cream off the Top," and the Temptations' "Keep Holding On."

Not bad. But when you're used to living in the upper reaches of the pop charts, this kind of success is no success at all, and all three members of H-D-H more or less went into artistic exile.

There's an upbeat ending to all this, however. Brian, Eddie, and Lamont have recently reunited to write and produce material for pop trumpeter Herb Alpert, kiddie reggae stars Musical Youth, and—get this—the Four Tops, who've returned to Motown after an eleven-year absence. Must be that family atmosphere.

70. Which member of the Supremes sang lead on the group's second single, "Buttered Popcorn"?

71. What former world heavyweight boxing champion recorded for Motown?

72. When Berry Gordy appeared on the TV quiz show "To Tell the Truth" in 1966, how many of the four panelists correctly guessed his identity?

Meanwhile, Lamont's in the process of setting up his own label, Megaphone Records, which he plans to debut with a solo album, *Bigger Than Life*. He's hired execs, signed a pair of self-contained acts, one male (Basic Black) and one female (Caviar), and says he's "firmly committed to the idea of independent distribution." We wish him luck.

By the way, Lamont says, "We've got some two to three hundred unfinished [Holland-Dozier-Holland] tunes in the can at Motown. Most of 'em don't have a lyric on 'em. I wouldn't even know if they're any good. I haven't heard that stuff in years, but one day I will. I'm kind of curious. . . ."

Now, Holland-Dozier-Holland deserve a book of their own, but this isn't it. This is The Motown Story, right? And when H-D-H left, there was still a lot of major-league production talent to be found hanging out around the downtown business section of Hitsville, U.S.A.

Smokey Robinson had already scored his first major hit as the writer and lead singer of the Miracles' "Shop Around" when he began producing records. His behind-the-board debut—Mary Wells' "The One Who Really Loves You" (1962)—was also a huge hit, and the record's gentle sense of swing set the pattern for much of Smokey's later work with Wells ("My Guy"), Brenda Holloway ("When I'm Gone"), and the Marvelettes ("Don't Mess with Bill").

Since we've already covered Smokey the Songwriter in detail in the previous chapter, there's little to add regarding Smokey the Producer. There *is* a distinctive Smokey Robinson "sound," but it's more a result of his highly stylized songwriting than the actual physical sound of his productions, although most of Smokey's uptempo tracks (the Miracles' "Going to a Go-Go," and the Temptations' "Get Ready") have an eerie, airy quality due to the prominent use of blow harmony by the background vocalists.

Smokey's best ballads are similarly atmospheric, almost motionless affairs, mirroring the cool school of doo-wop groups (the Orioles, the Five Keys) that doubtlessly inspired the Miracles in the first place. It's also important to note that for all the lush romanticism of records such as the Temptations' "My Girl" and the Miracles' "The Tracks of My Tears," Smokey always made sure the string arrangements enhanced, rather then overpowered, the background vocals.

Again, this is no doubt due to Smokey himself being a member of a vocal group. Besides, Miracles Pete Moore and Ronnie White were often coproducing the sessions.

Norman Whitfield, on the other hand, never shared a production credit in his life. Not even with his main songwriting partner, lyricist Barrett Strong, who was always sitting in the control booth while Norman stood in the studio putting the vocalists through their paces.

This division of labor was a keynote of the Motown production system and came about for a very simple reason: There's a big difference between the way things sound in the studio and the way they sound in the booth, and you don't want to keep running back and forth to check on it. After all, getting the performance is as important as getting the sound, and when it came to the former, Norman had few peers.

"Norman knew what he wanted, and boy, you'd better give it to him," Billie Jean Brown recalls. "He was *rough*. But he was beautiful to watch. You know those choke collars they use on big dogs? Norman had one, but it was invisible. So when David Ruffin would start to go off on those riffs in places that don't mean anything, Norman would stop him. And that sometimes made the difference between a production that someone else would do on the Temptations and Norman's. He never let an artist destroy the song's melody."

However much he relishes his cheapsteak-tough image, Norman's productions were mostly gourmet-quality filet of soul. He claims to have sold more records than H-D-H even, and he might be right. (Mostly because the market for records has grown geometrically since H-D-H's heyday.) Check out Norman's track record: both Gladys Knight and the Pips' and Marvin Gaye's versions of "I Heard It through the Grapevine," the latter Motown's first platinum (two-million) selling single; Edwin Starr's "War"; the Undisputed Truth's "Smiling Faces Sometimes"; and—duck and cover—*twenty-one* Top 10 R&B hits for the Temptations, including eleven R&B number ones.

The Temptations' macho stylings were obviously Norman's long suit, but occasionally he put on his hot pants and boogalooed down Funky Broadway with the Marvelettes ("Too Many Fish in the Sea"), the Velvelettes ("He Was Really Sayin' Somethin' "), and the Sonnettes ("I've Gotten over You"). This last disc was Norman's first attempt at record production, a pre-Motown effort on the K.O. Records label. Hey, Curtis Mayfield likes it. If he ever heard it, he'd probably swear he wrote it (and he may have a point).

Once he stopped doing Curtis Mayfield impressions, Norman combined the rhythmic body-shots of a boxer working out on the heavy bag with a dramatist's sense of dynamics and came up with his own "sound." When soul became—in the immortal word of the Chambers Brothers—"psychedelicized," Norman freed his mind so that his ass might follow and started cutting nothin' but the intergalactic funk. The next stop was his own Whitfield Records label, which Warner

". . . And the band played on."
Obscure Motown vocalist Gino Parks calls attention to his onetime band of superstar (photo) sessionmen: (from left) songwriter-producer Norman Whitfield, multitalented Marvin Gaye, songwriter-producer Hank Cosby, and songwriter-producer Mickey Stevenson.

COURTESY TOM DEPIERRO/AIRWAVE INTERNATIONAL

Bros. agreed to distribute in 1977. Norman had left Motown in 1975. (Somehow the hits weren't as automatic following Barrett Strong's exit for a solo career with Columbia Records two years earlier.)

After a year in limbo, Norman struck back with a new group (Rose Royce) and a number one pop disc ("Car Wash," 1976) issued on MCA Records, which got the soundtrack rights as a hedge against its parent company's financing of the *Car Wash* film. He chased it with six more hits in two years, five on the Whitfield label, but he's been stone cold since. Barrett hasn't had it any easier, but then it takes *two* sticks to make a fire.

Berry Gordy himself has a list of production credits that any record producer—not to mention any record company president—would be proud to claim: the Contours' "Do You Love Me," the Miracles' "Shop Around," Barrett Strong's "Money," Little Stevie Wonder's "Fingertips, Pt. 2," and Junior Walker's "Shotgun," for openers.

Most of Berry's biggest hits came when Motown was just getting rolling. Once the hits started snowballing, Berry began to spend less time in the studio and more time supervising the entire operation.

However, when a pet project came along, Berry wouldn't hesitate to get his hands dirty. As a member of "the Clan," he coproduced the Supremes' "Love Child," and as a member of "the Corporation" (Freddie Perren, Deke Richards, Fonzie Mizell, and B.G.), he performed the same function for the Jackson 5's incredible opening salvo of hits, including "I Want You Back," "ABC," and "The Love You Save."

If there's one factor that earmarks a Berry Gordy production, it's his love of gimmicks. The fake ending in "Do You Love Me," the shotgun blast at the beginning of "Shotgun," and the opening recitation on "Shop Around" are all fine examples. But since Berry had the final word on anything coming out of Motown, you could also say he left his sonic imprint on every record the company released.

Mickey Stevenson and Ivy Jo Hunter are two of Motown's most underrated producers. True, they weren't as consistently successful as Smokey, Norman, or H-D-H, but individually and collectively they cut records so tough you had to shave 'em with a blowtorch.

Marvin Gaye's "Hitch Hike," "Pride and Joy," and "Stubborn Kind of Fellow," Martha and the Vandellas' "Dancing in the Street," Eddie Holland's "Jamie," and Shorty Long's "Devil with a Blue Dress" were all Mickey's creations. Ivy Jo soloed with the Four Tops' "Loving You Is Sweeter Than Ever," and together they were responsible for the Four Tops' "Ask the Lonely" and the Marvelettes' "I'll Keep Holding On."

Mickey and Ivy Jo were hardly a permanent pairing. Mickey teamed up with Hank Cosby for Marvin Gaye and Kim Weston's "It Takes Two" and Stevie Wonder's "Uptight"; with William Weatherspoon for Jimmy Ruffin's "What Becomes of the Brokenhearted"; and with Clarence Paul for the Contours' "Just a Little Misunderstanding." In turn, Ivy Jo and Clarence posted "Danger Heartbreak Dead Ahead" for the Marvelettes.

In 1967, when MGM offered Mickey a reported million-dollar contract to make its Venture Records subsidiary a presence in the R&B market, he and Kim Weston (his wife) made their Motown association strictly a matter of history. A couple years and no hits later, so were Venture Records, the money, and the Stevensons.

Ivy Jo hung in there a while longer, cutting a couple of flop 1970 singles and an album (*Ivy Jo Is in the Bag*) on the V.I.P. label, before his career went the way of all flesh. Strange? Perhaps not, when you consider that Mickey and Ivy Jo's "sound" was closer to traditional R&B than most of the other Motown producers and, as such, was the first to go out of style with the shift in audiences' tastes that came on the cusp of the seventies.

73. How old was Stevie Wonder when he recorded his first Motown hit?

74. What is Diana Ross' real name?

75. Who were the members of Jr. Walker and the All-Stars and what instruments did they play?

Johnny Bristol and Harvey Fuqua are a second pair of producers whose contributions have been largely overlooked. Harvey didn't do much solo production work—the Junior Walker discs that bear his name are pre-Motown tracks originally issued on the Harvey label—but Johnny did, of which Gladys Knight and the Pips' "I Don't Want to Do Wrong" and Diana Ross and the Supremes' swan song, "Someday We'll Be Together," were his most successful individual efforts. Incidentally, that's Johnny's voice you hear in the background on the latter disc, cuing Diana on how to deliver the tune.

As a team, Johnny and Harvey's productions ranged from Edwin Starr's "25 Miles" and Junior Walker's "What Does It Take (to Win Your Love)," to Marvin Gaye and Tammi Terrell's "Ain't No Mountain High Enough" and "If I Could Build My Whole World Around You" and David Ruffin's "My Whole World Ended (the Moment You Left Me)," making it difficult to build a case for a distinctive Bristol and Fuqua "sound." So we won't.

Johnny left Motown to resume his performing career in 1974, pulling down a Top 10 pop hit with "Hang on in There Baby" for MGM Records that same year. He's been mildly successful since, recording for Atlantic and—most recently—Handshake Records. Meanwhile, Harvey, who exited about the time Motown disbanded its Artist Development Department, moved to Northern California, where he continues to function in an executive capacity for Bay Area independent Fantasy Records.

Nick Ashford and Valerie Simpson are another Motown songwriting-production team who went back to performing when they left the label in 1973. Recording as Valerie and Nick, the duo first kissed success with "I'll Find You" (Glover Records, 1964), but their most famous pre-Motown affair was writing "Let's Go Get Stoned," a number one R&B hit for Ray Charles in 1966.

They parlayed this into a songwriting position with Motown, where they penned Marvin Gaye and Tammi Terrell's "Ain't No Mountain High Enough" and "If I Could Build My Whole World around You." When these became hits, Nick and Valerie became producers, and extended Marvin Gaye and Tammi Terrell's successful catalog of male-female musical dialogues with such sparkling discs as "Ain't Nothing Like the Real Thing" and "You're All I Need to Get By."

Two years later, after Tammi Terrell's sudden illness made it impossible for her to continue recording, Nick and Valerie turned their talents toward Diana Ross, who'd recently split from the Supremes. Reprising their own composition "Ain't No Mountain High Enough," the duo gave Diana the first pop number one of her solo career. They also created a pair of Top 10 R&B hits for La Ross with "Reach Out and Touch (Somebody's Hand)" and "Remember Me."

Valerie recorded a couple of solo discs during her stay at Motown as well. One of these ("Silly Wasn't I") was a minor hit in 1973, the same year that she and Nick decided to become a performing unit again and left Motown for Warner Bros. Records.

It took them five years, but by 1978 Ashford and Simpson—as they are now known—had success licked, and a virtual tongue-bath of Top 10 R&B hits ("Don't Cost You Nothing," "It Seems to Hang On," "Found a Cure," and "Love Don't Make It Right") followed. The duo recently switched to Capitol Records, where they've maintained their hit-making momentum with "Street Corner" (1982).

Through it all, Nick and Valerie's "sound" hasn't changed much. The unorthodox blend of churchy vocals, worldly concerns, and richly textured arrangements that brought them their first Marvin and Tammi hits is still their basic stock-in-trade. It's a formula that's worn well over the years, probably because it was such a revelation in the first place.

Clarence Paul, Hank Cosby, Hal Davis, and **Frank Wilson** were Motown's bench strength. Clarence and, to a lesser degree, Hank are best known for their work with Stevie Wonder. Clarence was responsible for "Blowin' in the Wind" and most of the *Little* Stevie Wonder discs, while Hank was the producer on Stevie's "I Was Made to Love Her," "Shoo-Be-Doo-Be-Doo-Dah-Day," and "For Once in My Life," among others.

As for Hal Davis and Frank Wilson, although they both joined Motown during the sixties, their biggest successes came in the next decade. Hal was the more versatile, producing Diana Ross' burning "Love Hangover" and yearning "My Mistake" (the latter a duet with Marvin Gaye), the Jackson 5's slow cruise "I'll Be There" and footloose "Dancing Machine," and Thelma Houston's churning disco-blues "Don't Leave Me This Way." Hal's also still active at Motown.

In contrast, Frank, whose credits include the Supremes' "Up the Ladder to the Roof," "Stoned Love," and "Nathan Jones" as well as Eddie Kendricks' "Keep on Truckin' " (coproduced by Leonard Wilson) and "Boogie Down" (coproduced by Leonard Caston), left the record business for the ministry a few years back. An odd career shift, to be sure, but perhaps less surprising when you consider that prior to becoming a Motown songwriter-producer, Frank worked as a welfare investigator. *Sic transit gloria mundi.*

The same can be said for the Motown production system.

152

 THE MOTOWN STORY

76. Which two members of the Velvelettes later joined the Vandellas?
77. In what film did Michael Jackson make his acting debut?
78. Who replaced Diana Ross as the lead singer of the Supremes?

Two factors were responsible for its passing. First, the growing number of artists (Marvin Gaye, Stevie Wonder) who insisted on producing their own records. Second, the producers themselves realizing their own hit-making power, which led them to become more like hired guns, negotiating their services on an album-by-album basis.

Some producers took this newfound independence a step further and set up what are known as custom labels, giving one company the sole right to distribute their studio efforts while the producers got their own, colorfully named record label (good for the ego) and a healthier share of the potential profits (good for the wallet). The irony of the situation was that the success of Motown's producers was largely the cause of the system's collapse.

Of course, Motown was not alone in creating the myth of the producer as the man with the Midas touch (Phil Spector, for one, spent as much time engraving his own image as he did cutting hits for the Crystals, Ronettes, and Righteous Brothers), but the influence of Motown's producers went far beyond mere money matters.

As Lamont Dozier, who walked into Motown at age twenty-one with "Heat Wave," "Come and Get These Memories," and "Locking up My Heart" already written out on brown paper grocery sacks, proudly notes, "[Seventies superstar writers-producers] Kenny Gamble and Leon Huff and Thom Bell give us [H-D-H] the credit for being innovative enough to change the sound of R&B to 'crossover music' or pop/R&B, which Berry and the Publicity Department started calling 'The Motown Sound,' subtitled 'The Sound of Young America.'

"And that's what it became. It was no longer 'race music,' because everybody was buying it—all colors—and when it got to be world-renowned, it was still 'The Motown Sound,' but it was also 'The Sound of Young America.'

"For example, bass figures. 'I Can't Help Myself' is probably one of the most well known bass figures there is. That started the whole country—the whole world—using that [sings] 'Dun-dun-da-dun Duh-da-da da-duh da-dun.' That's the most famous riff I came up with. That Spanish group Los Bravos used it on 'Black Is Black.' I mean, everybody's done it. And they *still* use it.

"I still hear that line on commercials and sports things today. At least four bars of it. And I always think back to when I first came up with that thing. I was just rolling my fingers [sings] 'Dun-dun da-dun.' And we started a lot of things like that. We were very innovative, very instrumental in creating sounds."

Innovation. Creativity. How do you define those words,

especially when you're dealing with an industry that calls everyone from Johnny Ace to Pia Zadora a recording *artist*? A psychologist might tell you that you could measure Brian Holland, Lamont Dozier, or Eddie Holland's creativity quotient by their scores on a Thematic Apperception Test (TAT). Billie Jean Brown prefers the following story:

"There was an out-of-town show and the lineup was such that the Marvelettes went on before Eddie Holland, 'cause he had a hot record—'Jamie'—at the time, so he had to follow them.

"Now, the Marvelettes used to do 'Locking up My Heart' with Wanda Young singing as their closing number then. That was in the days of the miniskirts and they left the stage *smokin'*. So here's Eddie, who was never very comfortable about performing and definitely not a jumper-arounder like a James Brown or a Jackie Wilson, and he's worried about how he's gonna fill this stage.

"But Eddie had the mind. Oh, he had the mind. I remember all the stage lights going . . . dead. And then the introduction to "Jamie' and then the spotlight and Eddie Holland stepping in, and the spotlight would move. And by the time he hit center stage, the place was going wild. Absolutely fabulous. He'd thought of it right there backstage, 'cause he couldn't figure out how the hell he was going to get on. . . ."

"We were a little more extreme than the rest of the guys," is Lamont's own explanation. "Because we would reach out and bring in some Russian stuff *[chuckles]*. You know, different kinds of beats. Boleros or whatever. 'Cause we were trying everything.

"Once the musicians knew what we were going after, they would fall into the part *fast*, mind you. Really fast. I mean, I wouldn't have to hum it but once and they'd be right on top of it, creating, adding, and building. Helping to arrange this thing."

Hmnn, sounds like there was one more key to "The Sound of Young America.". . .

Chapter Nine

THE FUNK BROTHERS

"Man, he [drummer Benny Benjamin] was one of the major forces in the Motown sound. He could've very well been the baddest; you wouldn't even need a bass, that's how bad he was."

—STEVIE WONDER, 1972

Of course, Motown had a bass. And a bass player—the incomparable James Jamerson. He and Benny Benjamin, together with guitarist Robert White and keyboardist Earl Van Dyke, made up the inner circle of Motown studio musicians, or Funk Brothers, as they liked to call themselves.

"James Jamerson came up with the name the Funk Brothers," Earl Van Dyke recalls, " 'cause producers were always telling us to play it funky. Shorty Long used to come in and say, 'Today we ain't playin' nuthin' but funk. If you don't feel funky, take a drink of this.' And then he'd reach in his coat and pull out a bottle."

Earl, whose credits stretched from Aretha Franklin and Jackie Wilson to a stint with Chris Columbo's Gentlemen of Jazz, joined Motown in 1962. By the time he left Motown in 1974 Earl estimates he'd played on more than two hundred charted records.

During the seventies, Earl led road bands for such diverse performers as Aretha Franklin, Freda Payne, Kelly Garrett, and Soupy Sales. Through his association with Motown, he's performed with the Grosse Pointe Symphony (1976), the West

COURTESY TOM DEPIERRO/AIRWAVE INTERNATIONAL

Chunk o' funk. Earl Van Dyke. Between cutting million-sellers, Motown's studio bandleader gave Stevie Wonder free keyboard lessons.

Bloomfield Hills Symphony (1977), and the Atlanta Ballet Company (1980). He still lives in Detroit—only recently moved from the house he bought with the bonus Berry Gordy gave him for acting as the Supremes' road manager/ bandleader on a nineteen-day tour back in the sixties—and, at age fifty-four, still plays professionally.

If you're ever in the Motor City, you can catch the Earl Van Dyke Trio working out at the Fairlane Athletic Club on a regular basis, or look for them backing local sing-sation Michie Braden, whom Earl describes as a female jazz vocalist "like Ella Fitzgerald and Betty Carter." He also does volunteer work in conjunction with the music department at Osbourne High School ("giving back what I've received," he calls it). On Sundays he plays golf or goes fishing on his new boat.

Reminiscing about those endless days in the "Snakepit"— otherwise known as Studio A, located in the basement of the Hitsville, U.S.A., offices—Earl quickly points out that Motown's sessionmen were "all older guys, married, with families, and all *solid* jazz musicians."

Most of them were also from Detroit, and because of their family obligations, preferred local studio work to the constant wear and tear of touring. Besides, Motown paid them between $25,000 and $50,000 a year for their services. Talk about your Most Valuable Players.

Naturally, Berry Gordy didn't start out paying these kinds of wages, and the Funk Brothers didn't all arrive at once, either, although according to Earl, drummer William "Benny" Benjamin was with Motown from the very beginning, and guitarist Robert White, then a neighbor of Marv Johnson's, claims to have played on the "Come to Me" session. However, Robert didn't join Motown full-time until Berry Gordy absorbed his previous employers, the Anna and the Harvey/Tri-Phi labels.

Smokey Robinson brought in bassist James Jamerson, whom Temptation Melvin Franklin recalls as being something of a local legend for putting around the Motor City with his upright bass strapped to the top of his Volkswagen bug. (Before Robert and James came in, Motown's guitarist and bassist were Larry Vita and Clarence Isabell respectively.) As for Earl, he replaced Ivy Jo Hunter when the latter traded in his piano bench for a Motown producer's chair.

Now, Mr. and Mrs. Funk came to Detroit from way out in the country where they didn't have TV, so there were fourteen Funk Brothers in all.

Benny, James, Robert, and Earl were the hard-core four. They're the ones who used to get off work at Motown around

Band of gold. Another day at the studio, another night at the Chit-Chat club. The Funk Brothers— (from left) Robert White, Dan Turner, Earl Van Dyke, Uriel Jones, and James Jamerson—always remembered that the first three letters of funk spell f-u-n.

COURTESY E. VAN DYKE

6 or 7 P.M., meet back over at the nearby Chit-Chat club at 9:30 that evening, and, as Earl puts it, "let off steam," playing jazz till 2 A.M. About which time Clarence Paul or Norman Whitfield or Johnny Bristol or Ivy Jo Hunter or Shorty Long would walk in the door and call everybody back to Motown for a late session, starting at 3 A.M.

When they got there, they'd find food, booze, and the rest of the Funk Brothers (guitarists Eddie Willis and Joe Messina, keyboardist James Gittens, and—when needed—percussionist Jack Ashford) waiting. Three hours later they'd all stumble out of the studio. "And by that time," says Earl, "we'd be so drunk we'd just sleep there until it was 10 A.M. and time to go to work again."

Admittedly, this sounds more like they were the Drunk Brothers than the Funk Brothers, but these seven, eight, nine characters (Johnny Griffith replaced James Gittens, who died in a 1965 car crash) were not only cutting four songs every three hours, they were cutting maybe four hits a *day* as well. Hey, it helps to have a good buzz on.

So pick yourself up a six-pack, put on a stack of Motown wax, sit back, relax, forget about the vocalists, and just dig the track. One-two, one-two-three . . .

"I started to play. Benny started the beat. We'd look at each other and know whether we needed a triplet, quarter triplet, double time, or whatever. We didn't need sheet music. We could feel the groove together."
—JAMES JAMERSON

MOTOWN MAGIC MOMENT #27

James might not have needed sheet music, but he was such a monster when it came to "sight reading" (to play a written piece of music perfectly without even having seen it before), the rest of the Funk Brothers nicknamed him "Igor." James was also blessed with perfect pitch, which means he could do all sorts of nifty parlor tricks like tell you the exact note your teakettle whistled when it boiled.

When his son, James Jamerson, Jr., was eight years old, James Senior stuck a bass in the boy's hands and began teaching him how to play. By the time the kid was in high school, his father was bringing him in to play alongside him on sessions. If Junior missed a note, his dad would slap him upside the head. As a result, the younger Jamerson developed what is known as "relative pitch." (Ouch! Bad joke. Hey, the guys in the band are laughing. . . .)

"Igor was *brainy*," exclaims Earl, and aside from an obvious

Bass ace. Said to have perfect pitch, the late James Jamerson nevertheless claimed to have developed one of his heaviest bass lines from watching a fat woman's walk.

COURTESY E. VAN DYKE

fascination with B. F. Skinner's principles of behavior modification, the elder Jamerson was one of the first people to electrically amplify an upright bass, using a makeshift pickup he'd developed himself. To Billie Jean Brown, he was "eccentric." To Marvin Gaye, he was "a genius."

To P-Funk mastermind and onetime Motown staff songwriter George Clinton, "James Jamerson was the epitome. He started Fender bassing. All that funk bassing, Jamerson was it. He started all that bottom thing, and even though Motown had a pop sound, they still had some serious bass in that shit. Like Stevie's record [sings] 'I was born in Little Rock . . .' Man, the track to that would *kick ass.*"

For those readers who do not speak jive, Mr. Van Dyke will now provide a translation: "The basis for the whole Motown sound was the way Benny's foot (the one playing the bass drum) and James' bass functioned as a unit."

What Earl's talking about here is the tiny space between the beat and the accents James and Benny actually played. When you hear a classic Motown record, your mind reacts logically, to where it thinks the beat is going to be. But your body reacts physically, to where the beat actually *is.*

This creates tension and releases it almost immediately, which is what makes you want to move along with the music and thereby unify your mind and body. Getting into the beat, it's called.

Among musicians the trick is to see how long or how cleverly this tension between beat and accent can be sustained without losing the song's momentum. In order to do this, all the players, but especially the drummer and bassist, have to be completely synchronized—not to the mind's rhythms, but to the body's. When you're doing this *without thinking about it,* you're "playing the groove," so called because the rhythm is both well defined and traveling in a straight line.

The tragically hip will also note that when Benny and James are really burning down the house, they're actually

COURTESY E. VAN DYKE

Brush with greatness. At the seat of the beat, the man it took two drummers to replace, the late Benny Benjamin.

"interplaying the groove." In other words, they don't always play the same beat at the same time. Instead, they punch in and out of each other, yet the effect is, as Earl mentioned four paragraphs earlier, that of a unified whole. And you can't beat that with a lickin' stick.

Speaking of shticks, there's more to being a great drummer than a right foot that kicks. Benny was famous not for his ability to keep four different rhythms going at the same time—any quality drummer can handle that—but for the incredible speed and accuracy of his stickwork.

"Benny was our leader," says Earl. "He'd been at Motown the longest, so our nickname for Benny was Papa Zita, 'cause he was from Bimini [part of the Bahamas, located off the east coast of Florida] originally. He used to do quarter-note triplet pickups and eighth-note pickups on the tom-toms. When he got sick, Motown had to bring in *two drummers* to replace him! And that's God's truth.

"In 1964 Uriel Jones came in. He was the meter man. Kept strict time, 'cause Benny had trained both him and Richard 'Pistol' Allen, who started around 1965. Pistol did the pickups when Benny wasn't there."

Which was often. "Benny was always late and always had some lie for an excuse," Earl continues. "Probably his *best* lie was the time he showed up for a session an hour late, and when the producer asked him why, Benny told him, 'Well, I was on the freeway and the circus was in town. And the elephant got loose from the circus and blocked traffic on the freeway, so that's why I'm late. Now, if you want a session, count it off. . . .' "

Benny was also generous to a fault. Mickey Stevenson used to have to cash Benny's checks and turn them over to his wife; otherwise Benny might not have any money by the time he got home. Of course, Benny expected everyone else to be as accommodating.

"One time Berry Gordy was bringing some of our European distributors through the studio on a tour of Motown," Earl recalls. "Benny got up from behind his drums, went over to them, and said, 'Hey, Berry, let me have a fin.'

"But Berry loved Benny and he knew it had to be that way. We'd hear Berry yelling to his secretary, Rebecca Jiles, 'Rebecca! Rebecca! Give him [Benny] anything he wants, but don't let him catch me.' "

By 1968 Benny's physical condition had deteriorated to the point where if you could just set him upright, everything was cool. A lot of times, you couldn't even find him.

"You see, Benny was a drug addict," says Earl, a note of sadness creeping into his voice. "And when he couldn't get drugs, he'd disappear, stay drunk for two, three days. But he was a beautiful person and we all loved him.

"When Benny died [*of a stroke, in 1969*], Motown paid all the funeral expenses, a limousine for his wife, everything. And all the producers chipped in—I don't know—$500 apiece for his wife so she would have something. I think that day was the saddest I've ever seen Stevie Wonder. When he sang at the funeral, he broke down and cried.

"See, Stevie hung out with us all the time, because of Clarence Paul. Benny taught him things on the drums—when you hear Stevie Wonder, you're hearing Benny Benjamin. I gave Stevie organ lessons. And we talked to him like he was our son, and because he respected us, he believed us.

"You know, Ted Hull, his tutor, and Clarence, they raised Stevie. They took care of him when he was on the road. Clarence would even get him a woman if that was what Stevie wanted. Of course, that was when he was just a young man.

"When Stevie was around, all he wanted to do was jam. But we had no mercy on Stevie. We used to play tricks on him. We'd slap him on the head, run and stop. He'd listen. And he'd find us every time, run right to where we were and hit us back. He knew every foot of that studio."

The point being, Stevie could seriously hear. Studio A wasn't that large, although Motown managed to pack forty people into the former photography studio when they recorded the strings on "Baby, I Need Your Loving."

"We took sawhorses and laid plywood across 'em and miked the strings up in the air," Earl remembers. "After that, Pops Gordy went up to Berry and said, 'Son, you need more room.'"

Berry Gordy followed up on that suggestion right away, and Pops reconstructed the studio, which remained the focus of Motown's recording activity until its four, then eight, then sixteen-track recording capabilities were outdated.

As recording techniques grew more sophisticated, the number of Funk Brothers increased. Jack Brokenshaw, a veteran of the Australian Jazz Quintet, joined as a percussionist. The other brothers nicknamed him White Jack to distinguish him from Black Jack (Jack Ashford), who was also a percussionist.

According to Earl, "Jack Ashford's contributions get overlooked, but he was the best. Marvin Gaye brought him in from Philly and he played vibes, tambourine, slapped sticks, did foot stomps. He was very creative."

A little later, Eddie "Bongo" Brown, who played congas and—obviously—bongos, came in as a third percussionist, while first Dennis Coffey, then Wah-Wah Watson (real name: Melvin Raglin) took on what Earl calls the "free" guitar

One bad mother plucker. Guitarist Robert White and thumbnail.

COURTESY E. VAN DYKE

parts—all those semipsychedelic effects Norman Whitfield was so fond of sticking in the Temptations' records. (Earl: "Norman used to always tell Dennis, 'Bring your gimmicks.' ")

Which, in turn, brings us to the second most important element of "The Motown Sound": the interplay between guitarists Robert White, Eddie Willis, and Joe Messina. Or, as the Funk Brothers called 'em, Heckle and Jeckyl and Son.

"Joe Messina was an Italian," Earl explains, "and he was self-taught. He was playing professionally with Soupy Sales at WXYZ when he was seventeen. He'd played with Charlie Parker, and I guess we all owe quite a bit to Joe. He coached the rest of the guitar players.

"Joe had a fantastic sense of time. He'd sit there with his legs crossed, smiling, and never miss a backbeat. That was his function, he was the backbeat guitar player, and Eddie Willis was funky rhythms, definitely funky rhythms.

"Robert White was the main reason we called 'em Heckle and Jeckyl and Son. He'd talk from time in to time out, but the other two were almost as bad. The minute the producers passed out the lead sheets, they'd all start talking. Joe'd be switching around, making it different, and suddenly Robert 'd yell, 'I'm ready! I'm ready!' "

As a charter member of the Funk Brothers, Robert White also had another, more common, nickname. But Earl shot me a measured look and refused to cough up this tidbit of information. ("Let's just say we called him 'Lover.' ")

While Joe and Eddie played off each other's rhythm guitar parts, Robert—who picked with his thumbnail—handled all the guitar lines, working off the lines Earl laid down on piano or organ. Study that last sentence carefully, because, in Earl's words, "The secret to the whole Motown sound was that nobody played the same chord in the same damn position."

Instead, the Funk Brothers all played the same chord, but each one played it in a different spot on the neck of the guitar or the keyboard of the piano. In musical terms this is called playing "inversions." Now, when everyone plays a different inversion of the same chord at the same time, the result sounds like ONE HUGE CHORD.

For example, check out the Temptations' "My Girl." The relationship between Robert's guitar line and James' bass line is fairly obvious, but listen closely to what Earl and second pianist Johnny Griffith are doing on the chords during the bridge. You say you can't hear *two* pianos? That's exactly the point.

Earl notes that Johnny also played lead piano on some of the sessions. "My hands would get tired playing acoustic piano, so I'd switch over to organ 'cause you don't have to put so much weight behind it. Johnny knew the system. We all knew each other's styles from working together so long. It was a family thing.

"Like when we'd go into the studio with a producer, we knew his style. And if there was a problem, we knew how to straighten it out. We'd take the most intricate thing they had and jump on it first 'cause everything else was just a cakewalk.

"First, we'd play it as it was written. Then we'd start messing around with it. And within ten minutes we'd have what he wanted. We'd do three or four takes and that'd be it. We *never* did any more than that. The whole thing would take about twenty minutes. Then we'd take a ten-minute break and go on to the next tune.

"As far as any particular favorites, all the tunes we liked, the Contours' 'Just a Little Misunderstanding,' the Four Tops' 'Loving You Is Sweeter Than Ever'—we liked that one 'cause it was difficult and we really worked hard on that to get it right—they weren't any kind of hits. Whereas 'I Can't Help Myself,' that was a fluke.

"When we did 'Where Did Our Love Go,' we thought that was a piece of shit. We couldn't believe it when that was a hit. Now, the other Supremes hits were better. After that, we knew the sound and the style that they wanted."

All this proves is that musicians are no better judges of what makes a hit than anyone else. Probably less so, because most of them listen to music from a completely different perspective than the average yard-ape. Besides, whoever said you have to know how to play guitar to buy a record?

"Among the hits," Earl continues, "we enjoyed Marvin Gaye's 'How Sweet It Is'—that whole album's good—the Temptations' 'Psychedelic Shack,' '(I Know) I'm Losing You,' and 'Get Ready.' We enjoyed Stevie's stuff, Tammi Terrell's 'Ain't No Mountain High Enough' and 'Ain't Nothing Like the Real Thing'—Ashford and Simpson always came in with these intricate arrangements, so that would be interesting.

"See, at Motown, the producer was like a dictator—we used to call Berry Gordy 'Der Führer' and Mickey Stevenson 'Il Duce'—but naturally, we had our favorites.

"Number one was Clarence Paul. He couldn't read music, couldn't play anything. But he had ears. He knew what he wanted. He'd hum the parts and we'd find the chords. He'd listen and when he heard the right note, he had this habit of turning his head like a dog, you know?

"He was closest to us. He'd always come in at 2 A.M. and say, 'I wanna cut.' We'd go in from 3 to 6 A.M. and he'd order us steak 'n' eggs. We always got four tunes with Clarence.

"Our number two favorite was Norman Whitfield. He

79. Who sang with both the Contours and the Temptations?
80. Which member of the Gordy family was married to Marvin Gaye?
81. Who were the original members of the Temptations?

couldn't play anything either. Oh, he plays piano now, and he started out playing tambourine in Popcorn Wylie's band, but when he first came to Motown, he just sat on the steps in the studio, listening and watching, for about a year. So he was always real good to us and we always got four tunes with Norman.

"And our number three favorite was George Gordy because he used to say, 'You know, I don't know what I'm doing. I need some help.' We'd tell him, 'Fine. Go up in the booth and count it off.'"

Other favorites, according to Earl, were Harvey Fuqua, Shorty Long, Holland-Dozier-Holland, Ivy Jo Hunter, and Johnny Bristol. You might say this is one of those lists where certain names are conspicuous by their absence. . . .

Earl also says that when they were cutting rhythm tracks, the producers didn't allow the artists in the studio, so the Funk Brothers' contact with the stars of Motown was somewhat limited. "I suppose the Four Tops were our favorites—they were closer to our age range—them and Pete [Moore] and Bobby [Rogers] of the Miracles.

"Sometimes, particularly with the younger artists, they'd get an attitude, you know? And whenever they did, Benny would always tell 'em: 'We've seen 'em come and we've seen 'em go, and we're still here.'

"See, Berry Gordy didn't let anyone fool with his musicians. He did everything he could for us. He'd loan us money, buy us instruments. One time somebody wanted a bass trombone. Berry Gordy came down and asked us if we needed it. We told him, 'Well, you'll get a better sound.' He said, 'Buy it.'

"He bought me my first organ. I had never played organ before, and I wasn't sure I wanted to. He told me, 'If you'll play it, you can have it.' And he bought me a brand-new Hammond B-3, the same one I play today."

However, there was a flip side to working at Motown. The Funk Brothers never got any credit for their contributions, mostly because Berry Gordy feared the publicity might cause his winning team to break up.

"Berry Gordy was so tight on us, he never let us out of the country," Earl chuckles. "Oh, Robert and I went over to England once on the Motortown Revue, but he kept Benny and James back in Detroit.

"He *never* let the four of us go out on the road at the same time. We did go out once, for a pair of weekend dates with Kim Weston. Berry heard about it and first thing Monday morning he called Mickey Stevenson into his office and chewed him out good. He told Mickey that was 'never ever to take place again. If they're not making enough here, pay 'em more.' "

Nevertheless, the foursome soon found another way to supplement their Motown salaries. They started doing outside sessionwork, fitting their time around Motown. At first these moonlight drives were strictly local runs.

"We did some sessions for Mike Hanks' D-Town label and did a lot of work out of United Sound Studios," Earl recalls, "or we'd go over to Artie Fields and do jingles for McCann-Erickson [the giant advertising agency].

"Pretty soon, people would come into town, ask around, and find out about us. It got so producers were calling us and we'd have to tell 'em to wait. Our weekends were all booked up.

"They'd fly us down to Muscle Shoals, Memphis—we did a lot of Willie Mitchell's early stuff—Toronto, Chicago—we did Jimmy McCracklin sessions and a whole lot of stuff on Brunswick Records for producers Sonny Sanders and Tom-Tom Washington, working with the Chicago guys like Raynard Minor, Phil Upchurch, Maurice Jennings, and Billy Butler.

"It got so we'd hear a record on the radio and say, 'Damn, that sounds like us.' And we'd have to check back with the producer to see if it was."

Perhaps the Funk Brothers' most famous non-Motown sessions were done in Detroit for Eddie Wingate's Ric-Tic and Golden World labels. Berry Gordy fined the Bros. Funk $1,000 apiece for playing on Edwin Starr's 1965 Top 10 R&B hit, "Agent Double-O-Soul" (Ric-Tic 103).

"When Wingate found out about it, he Bogarted his way into the Motown Christmas party and paid our fines," Earl laughs. "He said he didn't care, he'd pay our fines and use us again. He gave us a bonus on the session, too."

So if you've ever wondered about who was responsible for that cruise-control bass line or those pristine piano fills on the Top 30 pop instrumental "Hungry for Love," issued under the name the San Remo Golden Strings (Ric-Tic 104), don't.

The Funk Brothers weren't doing all this serious moonlighting because Motown wasn't treating them well. Far from it. Berry Gordy, Motown controller Ed Pollack, and company troubleshooter Ralph Seltzer gathered the band together for a series of lectures on deferred income plans and the wisdom of investments.

"Some of 'em kinda listened," says Earl. "Joe Messina was one. He always said when he reached forty-two, he was gonna retire. We all used to laugh, but he did quit. He's rich. He bought a string of washracks and he owns the land they built this new shopping center on.

"But all the musicians bought beautiful homes here in Detroit. I've got three houses and three cars for working at Motown. I've got no regrets."

82. What Motown recording artist cowrote the 1966 hit "Oh How Happy" by the Shades of Blue?

83. What was the first Motown album to reach number one on the *Billboard* charts?

84. What film was directed by Motown founder Berry Gordy?

Well, maybe a few. Earl cut two albums and five singles for Motown under his own name. He says he's "not happy with any of 'em. See, none of 'em are really me. On the *Earl Van Dyke Plays That Motown Sound* LP (1965), I just played organ on top of the tracks, and on *The Earl of Funk* album (1970), that was recorded live and suffers from poor engineering."

"About 1970 I began to see the handwriting on the wall, and I went out on the road with Freda Payne. I was going to get a band together with [legendary session saxophonist] King Curtis—we met in Texas—but before we could do it, he got killed. [Born Curtis Ousley, he was stabbed outside of the apartment building he owned in New York City in 1971.] Motown moved out of Detroit in 1972, and by 1975 they weren't doing any more cutting here.

"I could've lived out there, but they left the musicians behind when they took it out of Detroit. Some of the guys did move. Eddie 'Bongo' Brown, Robert White, Jack Ashford, and James Jamerson, they're all out there. [On August 2, 1983, less than two months after this interview, James Jamerson, forty-five, died from complications following a heart attack.] But they broke up the combination when Motown moved to L.A.

"Detroit musicians seem to stick together more than other musicians. And Detroit is basically a jazz city—we've got festivals here all summer—and a lot of real good jazz talent has come out of Detroit: Kenny Burrell, Sir Roland Hanna, Tommy Flanagan, Yusef Lateef, Hank Jones, Barry Harris. . . .

"You know, Motown has a whole lot of good stuff that they cut on the Workshop Jazz label. Most of it never got released, but they cut sessions with Charles 'Lefty' Edwards, George Bohannon, Pepper Adams, Blue Mitchell, Tate Houston, Johnny Griffith, and Dave Hamilton, among others.

"That was all Mickey Stevenson's idea. See, what they'd do is get the Horace Silver Quintet, but without Horace, 'cause he was under contract. They'd use everybody else, with Wade Legge on piano instead of Horace, and put it down as [drummer] Roy Brooks' session. They did that with the MJQ, too.

"It was good stuff, but Berry Gordy was not a jazz fanatic. He wanted the money, bam! He wanted the quick hit.

"Now, there's some other Motown musicians that you should mention: Our horn section, which was Paul Riser, George Bohannon, and Patrick Lanier on trombones and Floyd Jones and Herbie Williams on trumpets. Mike Terry played baritone sax, Teddy Bucker played alto sax, and Ka-suku Mafie [born Norris Patterson] played tenor sax after Hank Cosby became assistant A&R director—Hank does the solo on my 1964 record 'Soul Stomp' and Norris does the solo on the Temptations' 'Get Ready' (1966)—you can hear the difference in their styles."

You also might notice that Earl hasn't said much about his own style of playing. "Well," he drawls, "they used to say that my timing was impeccable, that I never played my chords too clean, and that I wasn't afraid to use the bottom of the piano. They used to call me Chunk o' Funk 'cause I was heavy back then and 'cause of my funky chords.

"We also had musicians who were arrangers: Abdul Saleem, Dave Van de Pitte, and Willie Shorter. Hank Cosby and Paul Riser, too. Johnny Allen—he's the guy who *actually* wrote 'Shaft'—and Maurice King were musicians and arrangers who worked out of the Artist Development Department.

"Choker Campbell, who played tenor sax, was the road bandleader. A lot of people think because he led the road band, he was the session leader, too. That's not true. He led the big band that we used for recording people like Tony Martin, Bobby Breen, Billy Eckstine, Barbara McNair, and Diahann Carroll. It was either Choker or, when he was out of town, Jimmy Wilkins or John Trudeau.

"We did those sessions over at the Greystone Ballroom 'cause it had such great natural acoustics. We used to bring in the Detroit Symphony and do strings there, too. Matter of fact, we played with the Detroit Symphony for a fashion show at Hudson's department store in 1966. But nine out of ten times—whatever the session—it was the Funk Brothers who played on it."

For the final word on the relative importance of the Funk Brothers to Motown, let's go directly to their leader, Benny Benjamin.

"We were supposed to do a session over at the Golden World studios with Berry Gordy producing," Earl recalls. "So I went out to Benny's house and picked him up. We're driving back through the North End of Detroit, when Benny says, 'I'm hungry. I've gotta get something to eat. Drop me off here.'

"I told him 'Okay, but the session starts in half an hour.' 'Cause Benny always caught cabs. So what happens?

"He comes in *an hour and a half late*. To Berry's session! He'd walked back. He was high and eating ice cream, so he walked. All the way across town. Berry turned around to us and said, 'Why does this guy do this to me?'

"Benny said, 'Do what, man?'

"'But I'm the president,' says Berry.

"Benny looked at him and said, 'The president of *what*?'

"Berry just shook his head and walked away. . . ."

Chapter Ten

DON'T LEAVE ME THIS WAY

Don't . . .
Leave me
This way

Credit where credit is due—or, more accurately, contractually obligated: The above-quoted song, which topped the pop and R&B charts for Tamla recording artist Thelma Houston in 1977, was produced by Hal Davis, arranged by Art Wright, and written by Kenny Gamble, Leon Huff, and Cary Gilbert. Gamble and Huff also produced the original version of "Don't Leave Me This Way," recorded by Harold Melvin and the Bluenotes on the duo's own Philadelphia International Records label two years earlier.

Granted, this is one of the rare instances where Motown went outside its own doors to get a hit, but as a symbol for how much not only the company's system but also the pop music scene itself had changed since the label left Detroit in 1972, it makes a lovely clash. (Especially considering Philadelphia International was Motown's biggest rival when it came to mass-producing pop/R&B music in the early seventies.)

These multiplatinum overtones even end on a suitably ironic note; we haven't heard so much as a rumor of a hit from Gamble and Huff for the last couple of years, while B. G. and Company are writing new chapters in The Motown Story as you read this sentence.

In September 1983 Motown won its first Emmy Award, when the "Motown 25: Yesterday, Today, Forever" television special was named the year's "Outstanding Music/Variety

COURTESY TOM DEPIERRO/AIRWAVE INTERNATIONAL

Looking for Mr. Goodbar? Thelma Houston's masterpiece of disco (deca)dance music lent its peculiar aural simulation of oral stimulation to the soundtrack of the 1977 Diane Keaton film.

Program." Featuring an all-star lineup of Motown performers past and present, the two-hour spectacle was the top-rated television broadcast of the week May 16–22, with an estimated *47 million viewers*. Wanna bet we'll be seeing more of Motown on TV in the near future?

After all, conquering the worlds of television and film was Berry's main reason for moving Motown from Detroit to Los Angeles in the first place. Berry began relocating in 1969—Motown had maintained a Los Angeles office since the midsixties—and by 1972 the company's headquarters had shifted to Hollywood. Motown kept its downtown Detroit office and recording studios operating until 1975, when it cut everything but whatever spiritual ties still bind Berry's "conglamourate" to the Motor City.

There were other changes besides the address. You don't have to be as sharp as Berry Gordy to know that the success that comes from hit records is only temporary: *films* are what cement a singer's image and give a pop artist real staying power. Accordingly, Berry took his biggest name, Diana Ross, and set to finding an appropriate vehicle for her.

Lady Sings the Blues, starring Diana Ross as the late great jazz vocalist Billie Holiday, was released in 1972. Based upon Billie's autobiography, which she wrote with William Duffy, the film took in $15 million at the box office. Paramount, the studio that originally backed the project, had predicted between a $6 - $8 million gross. Motown, unimpressed by this lack of confidence, bought out the studio, brought the film in for under $4 million, and watched the Paramount execs pass the bucks.

Besides being a box-office hit, the film earned Diana Ross an Academy Award nomination for Best Actress—the first black woman so honored. Additional Oscar nominations went to the film's score, conductor Gil Askey, and to Terence McCloy, Motown VP Suzanne DePasse, and former Motown recording-artist-turned-label-exec Chris Clark, who collaborated on the script.

No winners, but by any other standards the Sidney Furie–directed film was a certified smash. Not only did Diana Ross prove she could act, but her vocal interpretation of the tunes associated with Billie Holiday was perhaps Diana's finest singing to date. As they say down at Loucye's Orbit Room, she did it her way.

The film also launched male lead Billy Dee Williams' film career (he'd first come to attention for his portrayal of pro football star Gale Sayers in the TV movie *Brian's Song*) and gave funnyman Richard Pryor his first chance to showcase his considerable dramatic skills.

The only real drag was the liberties Motown took with Billie's book; notably, it was most likely a black musician who introduced her to heroin and not—as shown in the film—a white bandleader. As dramatic license goes, that's a dog.

Flushed by this first-time success, Motown followed *Lady Sings the Blues* with another Diana Ross vehicle, *Mahogany.* In this 1975 production Diana played a ghetto-born model/fashion designer who finds "success means nothing unless you have someone you love to share it with." Billy Dee Williams was on hand again as Diana's love interest, and Anthony Perkins took on the familiar white villain's role as a fashion photographer who attempts to rape Diana, finds himself impotent, and therefore decides to buy the farm. Most film critics indicated they would've liked to join him.

Nevertheless, *Mahogany* made money, grossing $12 million at the box office. (It cost less than $4 million to produce.) Along with marking Berry Gordy's directorial debut, *Mahogany* merits attention for one of La Ross' most outrageous lines—namely, the clothes she designed for her character.

COURTESY TOM DEPIERRO/AIRWAVE INTERNATIONAL

M-1440

Paying the cost to be La Ross. If it's lonely at the top, it's only because it's crowded at the bottom. Right, Diana?

In contrast, Motown's third film, *Bingo Long and the Traveling All-Stars and Motor Kings*, was a better than average movie, but went belly-up at the box office, losing $4 million of Motown's and coproducer Universal's money. Adapted from William Brashler's book about playing baseball in the old Negro leagues, the 1976 production starred James Earl Jones, Richard Pryor, and—once again—Billy Dee Williams. Catch it on TV sometime.

The legendary ragtime pianist Scott Joplin won a posthumous Pulitzer Prize for his music in 1974, so it was only natural that two years later Motown would make a movie of his life. *Scott Joplin* starred Art Carney as a "good white" (music publisher John Stark) and—doncha just know it— Billy Dee Williams as Scott Joplin. The movie took the Big Sleep; Motown and Universal took the tax write-off.

This might not look like much on paper, but on-screen an even ratio of hits to flops will get you a German car, your own parking space, and a good table at Spago any night of the week. However, soaring production costs have made Hollywood filmmaking an expensive gamble that not even the Berry Gordys of this world can afford, and Motown's last two film ventures have been relatively modest affairs.

Thank God It's Friday, a 1978 coproduction with Casablanca Records and FilmWorks and Columbia Studios, was an equally modest box-office hit. Released near the tail end of the disco boom, the film's bottom line was designed to shake teen jeans loose from some of *Saturday Night Fever's* booty. The Commodores and Donna Summer were featured.

Motown produced a second teen-oriented film that year. *Almost Summer*, starring Didi Conn and Tim Matheson, was simply one of many attempts to ape the King Kong monkey business of *Animal House*, a film that has become the *Beach Blanket Bingo* of the seventies. Motown's version was no better, no worse, and no more successful than the rest.

If these films seem calculated, the same cannot be said for Motown's decision to make a black musical version of *The Wizard of Oz*. Which is what *The Wiz* was. Broadway hit or no, a less commercial idea couldn't have been dreamed up in a month of lunches.

Motown and Universal coproduced, at a cost of $23 million. (Director Sidney Lumet and star Diana Ross each got a million for their efforts.) The producers spent another $6 million promoting the 1978 epic, which rewarded their faith by returning less than $8 million at the theaters. And to think that Michael Jackson made his acting debut as the Scarecrow, too.

The Wiz, Mahogany, and *Thank God It's Friday* all spawned successful soundtrack albums, however; and during the after-*Shaft* heyday of blaxploitation films, several Motown acts laid down soundtracks for such reel-life experiences as *Hell up in Harlem* (Edwin Starr), *Big Time* (Smokey Robinson), *The Mack* (Willie Hutch), and *Trouble Man* (Marvin Gaye). Marvin even got a hit record for his trouble, man.

A few Motown acts also appeared in another youth-market staple of seventies cinema: the Concert Movie. Marvin Gaye, the Temptations, Gladys Knight and the Pips, and the Jackson 5 were all captured live for future generations in the 1974 film *Save the Children*.

The forerunner of all these concert movies and still the best pop musical showcase of the sixties was *The T. A. M. I. Show*. This early (1965) video production, although more famous for its James Brown (follow *this*, suckers) vs. the Rolling Stones finale, featured live performances from Marvin Gaye, the Supremes, and the Miracles, the last of whom contributed a chest-beating, scratching-each-other's-fleas dance routine on "Mickey's Monkey" that must be seen to be believed.

Same goes for Robert DeNiro's modified cool-jerk as the same tune blasts out of Harvey Keitel's car radio in Martin

Scorcese's classic *Mean Streets*. Not to mention the poolroom brawl set to the Marvelettes' "Please Mr. Postman" in the same 1973 flick, or the incredible, pre-MTV promotional film of Martha and the Vandellas singing "Dancing in the Street" while rolling down an auto assembly line in a '64 Mustang convertible. Such marriages of sound and image are rare, unfortunately, but that hasn't stopped less talented filmmakers from copping a handful of hoary oldies for that cheap period feel.

While listing every film that ever featured a Motown song somewhere in its soundtrack is a task better left to less imaginative authors, Motown itself has relatively few soundtrack LPs, notably 1975's *Cooley High*, a not-unsuccessful attempt to do a black *American Graffiti*; 1978's *Fastbreak*, a "high concept" Gabe Kaplan as a basketball coach tune-out whose "With You I'm Born Again" theme answered Billy Preston and Syreeta Wright's prayers for a hit; and 1983's *The Big Chill*, which milked the Pepsi Generation's lost innocence, sixties nostalgia, and Motown's music for all their considerable worth. By this time Motown was shrewd enough to demand rights to the soundtrack LP in return for the use of the songs in the film, and was rewarded with a platinum album—which cost them next to nothing to produce—for their foresight.

Motown's television productions made less of a media splash than its movies, but on the whole the company's small-screen efforts were more profitable. From 1969 on, Motown first coproduced, then self-produced a half dozen TV specials starring the Supremes, the Temptations, Diana Ross, and the Jackson 5.

One for the time capsule: The Jackson 5 are the only other live pop music act besides the Beatles to be granted a certain measure of immortality as the animated stars of their own Saturday morning cartoon show (1971–73).

The third stage in Motown's development from a record label into a multimedia entertainment complex was Broadway. Motown invested $140,000 in *Pippin* in 1972. The play ran six years and earned Motown several million dollars in the process.

Once again, after an initial explosive success, Motown's further theatrical ventures, notably a 1976 coproduction of *The Baker's Wife* with big-time Broadway financier David Merrick and the production of an original-cast LP for a black version of the musical *Guys and Dolls*, were duds.

There were dozens of other projects—theater and film— planned, but as Willie the Shake spake, "There's many a slip

betwixt the cup and the lip," and most of these entrées never got any further than some executive's in-tray. (Everybody sing: "*Hol*-ly-wood, da-dada-da-da-dada. . . .")

Okay, now time to face the music. Here, too, Motown tried to diversify, either by signing distribution agreements with English rock (Manticore and Gull) and U.S. jazz (Chisa and C.T.I./Kudu) labels or by setting up a half dozen subsidiaries of its own.

Some of this activity predated Motown's move to Los Angeles. Inferno Records, formed in 1968, was folded into Motown's major rock subsidiary, Rare Earth Records, that same year. Two of the Inferno releases, veteran local vocal group the Volumes' "Ain't That Loving You" and the Mitch Ryder-less Detroit Wheels' acronymically titled "Linda Sue Dixon," were also issued under the Rare Earth logo. There was a second Detroit Wheels single ("Think") on Inferno and Rare Earth as well.

Buoyed by hits from R. Dean Taylor and the group that called itself Rare Earth, the label continued until 1973. The problem was that Motown was geared toward getting pop hits and—back in those daze of hallucinogenic enlightenment—this was definitely NOT HIP.

Motown never really came to grips with the new, "freeform" FM radio stations, so when a single on the Rare Earth label nosedived, as far as Motown was concerned the act might as well have fallen off the edge of the world. By the early seventies, when the gray suits with the clipboards managed to screw FM radio playlists down tighter than any old-line Top 40 station's and it was no longer possible to break a rock act until maybe their third album, all the while spending four times the gross national product of El Salvador on tour support, Motown had lost its chance to get in on the underground floor.

Too bad. Along with Love Sculpture and the Easybeats, whom you'll no doubt remember from Chapter 3, the Rare Earth roster included such cult heroes as Limey punk blooze-crushers-turned-"rock opera"-composers the Pretty Things as well as such future hitmakers as British female pop/rock singer Kiki Dee ("I've Got the Music in Me" and "Don't Go Breaking My Heart," the latter a duet with Elton John) and the male-female duo Stoney and Meatloaf. (Yes, the same Mr. Loaf whose oafish *Bat Out of Hell* album made him a ton of bread five years back.)

Less successful—although marginally more interesting—were Toe Fat, a heavy-metal combo led by veteran British R&B/rock vocalist Cliff Bennett; Blue Scepter, a later edition of semilegendary Motor City garage-rockers the SRC (Scott

Richards Case); and the Sunday Funnies, a Detroit rock group whose two albums were produced by former Rolling Stones manager-producer Andrew Loog Oldham.

Then there were solo singles by Motown songwriter Leonard Caston and ex–Bobby Taylor and the Vancouvers guitarist Wes Henderson as well as several albums from the appropriately named XIT, a rock band who tried to make heap big wampum out of its members being American Indians. Talk about your claim to fame. . . .

In 1969 Motown penned a distribution pact with South African pop/jazz trumpeter Hugh Masekela's jazz label, Chisa Records. Despite several releases from the Jazz Crusaders, bassist Monk Montgomery, and Masekela himself, Chisa failed to put much cash in the parent company's coffers and two years later Motown's first distribution deal was down and out.

Motown's next subsidiary, Black Forum Records, met a similar fate. Beginning in 1970 there were eight albums issued on this spoken-word label: the Reverend Dr. Martin Luther King's *Why I Oppose the War in Vietnam*, literary heavyweight Langston Hughes' *Writers of the Revolution*, noted politico Stokley Carmichael's *Free Huey*, poetess Elaine Brown's *Elaine Brown*, actors Bill Cosby and Ossie Davis' *The Congressional Black Caucus*, a collection of black Vietnam War veterans' thoughts entitled *Guess Who's Coming Home?* by the Black Fighting Men, and *Black Spirits* and *It's Nation Time* by the multitalented author Imamu Amiri Baraka (born Leroi Jones).

As you might've guessed, this mixture of politics and poetry didn't cause too many revolutions at 33⅓, and Motown declared Black Forum adjourned in 1973.

Formed in 1971 and folded in 1973, the Mowest Records subsidiary managed only one Top 10 pop record: Tom Clay's 1971 sound collage "What the World Needs Now/Abraham, Martin and John," a period piece that blended gunfire, on-site news reports, and little kids' inability to define segregation while session vocalists the Blackberries cooed the Dionne Warwick/Dion hits in the background. (Evidently Tom's sociopolitical awareness didn't extend to matters of nutrition as the follow-up "Whatever Happened To" found him fondly reminiscing about all the sugar sandwiches he used to eat as a kid.)

Nowadays, Mowest is best remembered for being the label where the Commodores and Thelma Houston made their Motown recording debuts, and a number of lesser Motown stars—G. C. Cameron, Syreeta Wright, and Bobby Taylor—passed through. So did the Jazz Crusaders, Frankie Valli and

85. What was the first Motown single to reach number one on the *Billboard* pop charts?

86. When Holland-Dozier-Holland left Motown to start their own company, what were the names of their two record labels?

87. What was Motown's first platinum (2 million-selling) single?

the Four Seasons and every teenage girl's sob sister of 1964, the lovely and talented Lesley Gore. Current Motown executive Susan Wendy Ikeda cut a couple of singles for Mowest as well.

The V.I.P. Records subsidiary, established in 1964, survived until '72, when Motown introduced yet another short-lived pop subsidiary, Natural Resources Records. A couple years and a half dozen stiffs later (sound familiar?) Motown's Natural Resources vanished—almost.

The label came back as a budget-line in 1978–79, offering vintage Motown LPs at a reduced price. In 1981 Motown decided to treat its catalog right and reissued more than sixty of its most classic albums on the original labels. But we're getting ahead of ourselves. . . .

Having blown out five of its subsidiary labels in the past two years, Motown tried another assault on the rock market, signing a 1974 distribution agreement with British "progressive rock"—now *there's* a contradiction for you—group Emerson, Lake and Palmer's ego trip, er, custom label, Manticore Records.

Unfortunately for Motown, ELP was under contract to Atlantic Records' Cotillion subsidiary in the United States and therefore wasn't part of the Manticore roster, which included such world-beaters as Italian progressive rockers P.F.M. and Banco, British folkie Keith Christmas, and U.S. schlockbusters Thee Image, who used to be known as Blues Image when they cut their 1970 hit "Ride Captain Ride."

Oh yeah, there was another progressive-rock group in there, too. England's Stray Dog. Wow, doncha wish *artists* could run the world?

Truthfully, the only real keyboard genius Manticore ever had was the undisputed Queen of Rock 'n' Roll himself, Little Richard, who cut one single ("Call My Name," 1975) before the Motown-Manticore agreement ended in 1976.

Also in 1974 Motown inked an agreement with jazz producer Creed Taylor, giving the company distribution rights to the C.T.I. and Kudu labels. On paper the deal looked good. With A&M Records distributing, Kudu had been successful for a couple of years now, and both rosters were loaded with talent.

George Benson (guitar), Grover Washington (alto sax), Hubert Laws (flute), and the late Esther Phillips (vocals) were the most commercially successful. Esther, who began her career singing R&B with the Johnny Otis Orchestra while still a teenager, even scored a Top 10 R&B hit with a remake of Dinah Washington's "What a Difference a Day Makes" in 1975. But the roster also included guitarists Kenny Burrell,

Joe Beck, and Gabor Szabo, pianists Bill Evans and Bob James, bassist Ron Carter, drummer Idris Muhammed, trumpeters Freddie Hubbard and Chet Baker, vibraphonist Milt Jackson, and saxophonists Stanley Turrentine, Paul Desmond, Joe Farrell, and Hank Crawford.

The music, however, was something less spectacular: heavily orchestrated, funky pop/jazz mung that mostly sounded like themes in search of a car chase. Nevertheless, by jazz standards the stuff sold well and the Motown-C.T.I./Kudu association lasted until 1978, when the relationship sank under a ton of lawsuits.

Apparently, Creed's creativity extended to his accounting practices and Motown won the legal battle—it usually does—retaining all rights to the C.T.I./Kudu catalog for its troubles. Motown hasn't agreed to distribute anyone's records since.

The last distribution deal Motown did sign was with a British label, Gull Records, in 1975. Two years and a half dozen releases later—stop me if you've heard this before—this was also history. Which is more than can be said for most of the talent involved. Exceptions: heavy-metal mediocrities Judas Priest, who hung in long enough to hang platinum Stateside nowadays, and grand bizarro Arthur Brown, whose Crazy World of Arthur Brown burned up sales charts with the nightmarish "Fire" back in 1968.

Motown took a final fling at the pop market with its Prodigal Records subsidiary (1975–79). No hits, but when the biggest names on the label were former Raspberries member Wally Bryson, leader of the rock group Tattoo; Delaney Bramlett, minus Bonnie and Friends; Michael Quatro, better known as Leather Tuscadero, uh, Suzie Quatro's brother; and Joe Frazier, better known as the former heavyweight boxing champion of the world, that was no surprise, either.

The surprise came in 1982, when a tune that was originally issued on Prodigal five years earlier, the dewy ballad "I've Never Been to Me," sold a million copies for Motown Records and femme vocalist Charlene (Duncan), mostly because a certain Tampa, Florida, radio program director—Scott Shannon, now a wildly successful PD/morning air personality at WHTZ, New York—looking to increase his eighteen-to-thirty five female audience, remembered the tune from way back, started playing it and watched the station's request lines glow with radio-activity. You've no doubt heard of prodigal sons. Well, this time it was a Prodigal daughter, who upon her return, bore prodigal sums.

Strange? So's the story of Motown's country music subsidiary, Melodyland Records. In 1975 Motown rounded up some good ol' country record honchos to ride herd on some tal-

ented buckaroos (current country star T. G. Sheppard and ex-pop star Ronnie Dove, former rockabillys Jerry Naylor and Dorsey Burnette, and—the man with the white-buck cowboy boots—Pat Boone) and lassoed a passel of country hits.

One of these, Jud Strunk's novelty number "The Biggest Parakeets in Town," attracted the attention of the Melodyland–Christian Center Church, whose members worshiped in a defunct theater-in-the-round located across the street from Disneyland. The church had been releasing gospel records on its own (unregistered) Melodyland Records label for several years and objected to having its name muddied by what church members felt were dirty "leer-ics."

Motown could've probably won the rights to the Melodyland name in court, but it would've been a publicist's nightmare, so they simply said the hell with it and, in 1976, rechristened their country subsidiary Hitsville Records. Motown knew they had the rights to *that* one, having released a couple of stray pop discs, notably an album by sixties schizoid screecher Lou ("Two Faces Have I") Christie, under the Hitsville Records name two years earlier.

The second version of Hitsville Records lasted until 1977, when Motown decided the difference between a Top 10 country record's chart success and its sales figures wasn't worth the investment. (A pure country hit—one that doesn't become a pop hit as well—generally sells fewer copies than a pure R&B hit.)

This track record might sound like it's broken (hit-flop-flop, hit-flop-flop . . .), but every successful record company has similar skeletons in the mailroom. We're dealing with a business where 86 percent of the records released don't make their costs back, and that's a .140 batting average, sports fans.

As for all those artists who found success after they left Motown, that story's as old as wax cylinders. Same goes for the practice of signing up artists who had one hit way back when. . . .

The Soul Records subsidiary, established in 1964, was axed in '78. Keep in mind that while all these subsidiaries are drowning in red ink, Motown's three remaining labels—Tamla, Motown, and Gordy Records—are still pumping platinum from such veteran hitmakers as Stevie Wonder, Marvin Gaye, and Diana Ross as well as newcomers the Jackson 5, the Commodores, and Rick James.

We'll focus on Motown's brightest stars of the seventies in a hot flash, but a solitary subsidiary of semisignificance remains: Lasting for only one release, Valentino's confessional "I Was Born This Way" (1975), the Gaiee Records label was perhaps the shortest-lived—certainly the queerest—Motown spin-off of all.

Enough tasteless jokes. On to the artists, although sometimes it's hard to tell the difference. In another time and place I might make a case for the best artists being the most tasteless clowns of all. But then somebody might consider that argument a vindication of Rod Stewart's career, when what I'm really talking about is the nervy genius of the minds responsible for Sam the Sham and the Pharoahs' "Wooly Bully" or the Swingin' Medallions' "Double Shot (Of My Baby's Love)" or—lest anyone think this sort of thing went out in the sixties—Kool and the Gang's "Hollywood Swinging" or the Sex Pistols' "God Save the Queen."

But that's the rock 'n' roll party line, and Motown doesn't always mean rock 'n' roll. Motown is pop music, remember, and therefore covers a wider spectrum of sounds, such as . . .

THE COMMODORES

The biggest-selling group in Motown history, this sextet (guitarist Thomas McClary, bassist Ronald LaPread, trumpeter William King, drummer-vocalist Walter Orange, keyboardist Milan Williams, and saxophonist-vocalist Lionel

The Commodores meet the Jackson 5. The eyes of taxes were upon this meeting of the future superstars: (back row, from left) Commodores Thomas McClary, Lionel Richie, and Milan Williams, and Jackson 5 member Jackie Jackson; (front row, from left) Michael, Marlon, and Tito Jackson and Commodore William King.

COURTESY MICHAEL OCHS ARCHIVES

Too hot ta trot. At ease with their stage-warmer status, the Commodores: (from left) Lionel Richie, William King, Ronald LaPread, Thomas McClary, Milan Williams, and (front) Walter Orange.

COURTESY MICHAEL OCHS ARCHIVES

Richie) got together while college students at Tuskegee Institute in Alabama during the late sixties. A couple years later they got their first break as the opening act on Jackson 5 tours.

The Commodores' first success, however, came when the Mowest subsidiary, where they had recorded for two years, was absorbed by the Motown Records label in 1974. Their initial Motown release, the percolating instrumental "Machine Gun," was the first of the group's fourteen Top 10 R&B hits, of which six were R&B number ones.

Early hits such as "I Feel Sanctified" (1974) and "Slippery When Wet" (1975) are best described as clean-cut, "collegiate funk," although on 1977's "Brick House," the Commodores proved they could get jivey in the halls of ivy and tear the roof off the structure, too. The whole record stands as a monument to man's edifice complex, albeit one that's more likely to be found within the pages of *Penthouse* than *Architectural Digest.* Yowl.

Funk might've launched their career, but the Commodores' ship came in when Lionel Richie sat down at the piano and apparently extracted a magic formula for writing million-selling ballads. "Sweet Love" (1975) was the group's first of nine Top 10 pop hits, followed by "Just to Be Close to You" (1976), "Easy" (1977), and "Three Times a Lady" (1978), the last of which gave the Commodores their first pop number one. A year later another Lionel Richie ballad, "Still," would be their second. *Yowl.*

"When we first got to Motown, we went through every writer, every producer, everybody that had talent in the business. And a guy kept telling us, 'It looks like if you really want to find out what the Commodores are all about, you're going to have to find it inside.' We didn't believe that—we wanted to come in and be made stars—but out of frustration we just started looking into ourselves and slowly we discovered that the whole sound was right here in the Commodores."
—LIONEL RICHIE

The Commodores are due for another voyage of self-discovery soon as Lionel recently embarked on a solo career, a move foreshadowed by his chart-topping duet with Diana Ross on the title track to a Brooke Shields film ("Endless Love," 1981). Not to mention little things like Lionel's first solo album selling platinum-plus and giving him yet another number one, this time a midtempo tune ("You Are," 1982).

For all the Commodores' success—over 25 million records sold, half of those being albums—the group has never been accused of innovation. Instead, the group's records are cited for their cleanliness, craftsmanship, straightforwardness, even their subtle production touches. (Credit: James Carmichael). But never for their personality or point of view. Which goes a long way toward explaining the Commodores' $UCCE$$. They don't offend anyone. Is this a strength or a weakness? Well, now, depends on *your* point of view, doesn't it?

As for their ultimate impact, it's too soon to know. The Commodores' early hits enabled Motown to come to grips with the new self-contained funk bands that all but replaced vocal groups by the mid-seventies. The group's ability to attract a huge pop audience without losing black record-buyers is even more significant. (Isn't that what Motown has always been about?)

Nevertheless, questions as to staying power and whether or

Easy. From the Commodores' tenor saxophonist to a multiplatinum solo artist, Lionel Richie has done it with simple songs that seemingly anyone could write, but apparently only Lionel can.

not Lionel Richie's ballads belong in the same class with Motown's sixties classics will have to be decided by future generations. Although slipping in just under deadline, Lionel's solo smash, the uncharacteristically uptempo transworld rhythm salad, "All Night Long (All Night)," is arguably the finest thing he's ever done and probably answers our first question—at least as far as Lionel's career is concerned.

Lionel's second multiplatinum solo album cemented his current superstar status (some weeks Lionel's LP sales account for 90 percent of Motown's total album sales), and he was recently seen lip-synching a special version of "All Night Long (All Night)" before a global viewing audience of millions at the closing ceremonies of the 1984 Summer Olympic Games.

MARVIN GAYE

"Terrible" and "That sucks" were two of the milder opinions aired at the 1971 Motown staff meeting where Marvin Gaye premiered his new *What's Going On* LP. The album, released only after Marvin threatened never to make another record for Motown, went on to sell a million copies and spawned three R&B number ones: the title track, "Mercy Mercy Me (the Ecology)," and "Inner City Blues (Make Me Wanna Holler)." All three were Top 10 pop hits, too.

Through the miracle of twenty-twenty hindsight, it's not hard to see why Motown didn't understand Marvin's disc. Simultaneously spacey, spiritual, and soulful, the album was such a quantum leap beyond the old "Motown Sound" that

COURTESY TOM DePIERRO/AIRWAVE INTERNATIONAL

Pride and joy. Marvin Gaye, 1939–1984.

Marvin never bothered to change it much again. And why should he? Marvin became an *artiste* —wrote, produced, sang, and played most of the instruments on his records himself—so he did what he wanted.

However, Marvin's mama didn't raise no fools, and whenever he really needed a hit, he went back to the Main Thing. "Let's Get It On," (1973) distinguished by Marvin's marvelous multitracked vocals, remains one of the most seductive, sensual records in all of popular music. You can practically hear cherries popping by the thousands in the background.

Both this record and 1977's "Got to Give It Up, Pt. 1," which finds Marvin's most fragile falsetto awash in oceans of exotic percussion and an appropriately loose, party-down atmosphere, went to number one on the pop as well as the R&B charts. Even more incredible, both sold more than 2 million copies *as singles*.

Those were Marvin's twin monsters, although 1976's "I Want You," written by T-Boy Ross and Leon Ware, is a great record if you're looking for something pretty to play while you chew your fingernails to bleeding stumps. No lie. It's one of the most twisted expressions of desire this side of the Velvet Underground.

Marvin never lost his sense of humor, though. When the judge told him to hand over $60,000 worth of royalties on his next LP to his ex-wife, Anna Gordy, Marvin responded with *Here, My Dear*, an album basically devoted to describing their failed marriage in all its gory details. Marvin became a tax exile, living in Europe, after that one.

When Motown issued 1981's *In Our Lifetime*, an album Marvin claimed he hadn't completed, he vowed never to record again. He was stone serious about this, and a year later Motown let him out of his contract, whereupon he signed with Columbia Records and promptly whipped out a king-size comeback hit with "Sexual Healing." He put the finishing touches on the legend with his first American tour in several years and—Marvin being the kind of *artiste* that he was—climaxed each show by appearing stripped to a pair of gold lamé bikini briefs.

On April 1, 1984—the day before his forty-fifth birthday—Marvin Gaye was shot to death by his father, Marvin Gay, Sr. The incident, which took place at the Los Angeles residence that Marvin sometimes shared with his parents, was reportedly the result of a family quarrel.

For the last word on the subject, let's go to Marvin himself. The man who once claimed he tried to commit suicide after the breakup of his second marriage (to Janie Hunter) by

88. What was the first album by an American artist to debut at number one on the *Billboard* charts?

89. What was the Jackson 5's first record?

90. What was Motown's first gold (million-selling) single?

ingesting an ounce of pure cocaine also said he "used it all, the bad stuff and the good, in the music."

THE JACKSON 5

Before he even had his big teeth, Michael Jackson was onstage with his four brothers (Jermaine, Marlon, Jackie, and Tito) wowing Gary, Indiana, audiences with his castrati vocals and his "I may be only five years old, but I know I can be *super* bad" routines.

Six years later the Jackson 5 was having the same effect on the nation, thanks to "I Want You Back" (1969), the brotherhood's first Motown Records release and the first of what would be four *consecutive* double number ones—number one R&B and number one pop—for the group. Can you say 'superbad'?

Although it's not widely known, the group had cut at least three singles for the Steeltown Records label previously: 1967's "Let Me Carry Your Schoolbooks," credited to the Ripples and Waves featuring Michael; 1968's "Big Boy," their first as the Jackson 5; and "You Don't Have to Be Twenty-one to Fall in Love," also from that same year and also under the Jackson 5 name. All three discs are crudely produced affairs, but you don't have to be Diana Ross to fall in love with the talent that was there. (This last single was later issued on the Dynamo Records label in an attempt to cash in on the group's newfound fortunes. Motown put a stop to that real quick.)

Tossing objectivity aside for a paragraph, I'd like to say that "I Want You Back" is probably the best pop record ever made. And when I say "pop," I mean the way the record just explodes off your turntable. The arrangement is faultless—the bass playing alone is enough to turn your hair into snakes—and a ten-year-old Michael sings as if his lungs are about to burst into flames any second.

After a fiendishly clever follow-up ("ABC," 1970), the next disc ("The Love You Save," also 1970) seemed like a case of stepping on the formula one too many times, and the fourth Jackson 5 release was a pristine ballad ("I'll Be There," again 1970) that completed the group's incredible opening salvo of chart-toppers.

They cooled off a little bit after that, but only a few degrees. Over the next five years all ten singles they cut for Motown went Top 10 R&B, and two of these (1971's "Never Can Say Goodbye" and 1974's "Dancing Machine") were R&B number ones. The former later became a bona fide, disco-fied Top 10 pop hit for Gloria Gaynor and MGM Records in 1975, while

the latter goes down smooth and bubbly like champagne and orange juice and does your body about as much damage, too.

So what do you do with a phenomenon like the Jackson 5? You do what the TV networks do and create a couple of spin-offs. Michael started making solo records in 1971. Ranging from watery ballads ("Got to be There" and "I Wanna Be Where You Are") to remakes of old rock 'n' roll numbers (Bobby Day's "Rockin' Robin"), these were also hits. If there was ever any question about the depth of Michael's talent, consider this: Who else could've turned a love song to a rat ("Ben") into a number one pop record?

In 1972 Jermaine went solo. He, too, upheld the Jackson standard of success with a remake of Shep and the Limelites 1961 doo-wop classic "Daddy's Home" (1973). When the group left Motown for Epic Records in 1975, Jermaine—who had married Berry Gordy's daughter, Hazel Joy, two years earlier—decided to remain a solo artist, and he was replaced by brother Randy Jackson.

See, folks, love is thicker than blood. Unfortunately for Jermaine, hits were thinner than both, although with a little help from Stevie Wonder—who produced, cowrote, and shared lead vocals—he battled his way back to the top of the R&B charts with the punchy "Let's Get Serious" (1980). Nowadays, Jermaine spells love M-O-N-E-Y and records for Arista Records.

Rechristened the Jacksons, Jermaine's brothers maintained their usual two-hits-per-year average, including such gems as "Enjoy Yourself" (1976), "Blame It on the Boogie" (1978), and the superb, Miracles-influenced "Shake Your Body down to the Ground" (1979). Sisters LaToya and Janet Jackson also took the solo route, for Polydor and A&M Records respectively. So far they've been only slightly more successful than brother Jackie's brief—one album on Motown in 1973—solo flight. Or brother Randy's—one album on Epic in 1978—for that matter.

Michael's solo career, however, has pushed the Jackson standard of success somewhere out into the stratosphere. 1979's *Off the Wall* album, Michael's first solo effort in five years, sold more than 3 million copies and yielded three million-selling singles to boot: the title track, "Rock with You," and—best of all—the aquatic ray-gun boogie-woogie "Don't Stop 'Til You Get Enough." Tough act to follow, but when he did . . .

At last count, sales of Michael's 1982 *Thriller* LP stood at 35 million units and rising: With titanic tracks such as "Wanna Be Startin' Somethin'," all debts to Manu Dibango's "Soul Makossa" paid in full; "Beat It," featuring a brilliant

Can you say, "superbad"? Having outgrown their matching suits, the Jackson 5—(from left) Tito, Marlon, Michael, Jackie, and Jermaine—entered their fringe period.

guitar solo from Eddie Van Halen; and the loose-jointed neon heartbeat of "Billie Jean," it seems obvious that from here on in, Michael Jackson competes only with himself.

It should also be noted that during the Jacksons' stay at Motown all their hits came from writers outside the group. Shortly after the brothers joined Epic they began writing and producing their own material. Same goes for Michael, who not only coproduced *Thriller* with his usual collaborator, veteran jazzman Quincy Jones, but also produced "Muscles," a 1982 hit for Diana Ross. In return, Diana comes over to Michael's house and helps him peel the skin off his pet six-foot boa constrictor, for which the song was named.

RICK JAMES

With his tongue-in-groove "punk funk" and his gladiator smirk, Rick James (born James Johnson) is anything but your typical R&B multitalent. Rick not only writes, produces, sings, and plays most of the instruments on his records himself but also controls his music publishing, chooses his own cover art, and even dictates his band's hairstyles.

Bustin' out of L-7. No square roots here. Funkmeister Rick James cometh all over his bad self with streetwise songs of teenage tongue baths and taking tea with Mary Jane.

COURTESY THE CULTURAL WAREHOUSE

Rick first came to Motown as a member of a rock group, the Mynah Birds, back in the mid-sixties. When nothing happened, he cut out for Canada, then Europe, before shuffling off to Buffalo—his hometown—in 1977 or thereabouts.

The following year he showed up in L.A. with a finished album under his arm. Motown expressed interest, but the once-bitten, twice-shy Rick saddled the company with such strict contractual demands that the Chairman himself was asked to authorize the deal.

 "I played him the tapes of 'You and I' and 'Mary Jane' and all that stuff, and Berry Gordy didn't halfway understand it *[laughs],* but he said, 'Okay.' "
—**RICK JAMES**

Hey, Berry might've been getting a little old for this sort of thing, but he certainly wasn't deaf. "You and I" (Gordy Records, 1978) cut a groove the size of the Grand Canyon all the way up to the top of the R&B charts, while "Mary Jane"— Rick's hymn to herb—was a Top 10 R&B number. *Smoke.*

Another hunk of burnin' funk, 1979's "Bustin' Out," earned Rick a third Top 10 R&B hit, but his real commercial breakthrough came two years later when sales of his *Street Songs* LP topped 3 million units.

Talk about monster hits, *Street Songs* featured two: "Give It to Me Baby"—Rick's second R&B number one—and the million-selling single "Super Freak," both of which sounded something like Godzilla doing the Pop-Lock with King Kong. As for cross-cultural impact, watching a dozen blue-mohawked punk rockers skanking furiously atop the tables down at Danny's Oki Dog while the radio blasts the latter track is a sight neither easily forgotten nor dismissed.

Matter of fact, the song was *so* successful, Rick—and every other funk act worth its weight in smoke bombs—promptly went out and recorded sixty-nine variations of the little sucker. At one album a year it's getting so you can't even steal your own ideas anymore 'cause some practical joker has already beaten you to it.

Rick learned this the hard way. His last several smokers have been respectable—but not spectacular—R&B hits, of which 1983's "Cold Blooded" and his gorgeous duet with Smokey Robinson, "Ebony Eyes," have burned the brightest and the best. Yo, Rick. Time to twist up another one of those inspirational numbers.

EDDIE KENDRICKS

When his showcase ballad "Just My Imagination" topped the pop and R&B charts, Eddie Kendricks found that the temptation to become a solo artist was greater than actually being a Temptation, and he left the group in 1971. "Keep on Trucking, Pt. 1" (Tamla Records, 1973), featuring Eddie's feathery falsetto floating over stuttering synthesizers and a deep, climbing bass line, was his first solo hit. It was also his best, with a sound as light as it was percussive—just like the jazzy vibraphone solo in the middle of this double number one disc.

Eddie scored another six hits over the next three years, including the prime proto-disco cut, 1974's "Boogie Down," a number one R&B record that stiffed out at number 2 on the pop charts. "Shoeshine Boy" (1975) which despite the title is an exceptionally dull record, was also an R&B number one.

That's the good news. The bad news was that Eddie didn't write his mega-hits. Frank Wilson, Leonard Caston, and Anita Poree did, and when the team ran short of ideas, Eddie ran out of hits, out the door—to Arista Records in 1978, to Atlantic Records in 1981—and, apparently, out of time.

TEENA MARIE

A funky little white girl from the seaside slum of Venice, California, Teena Marie had been under contract to the company for three and a half years without ever having a record released when Rick James overheard this *voice* coming through the wall of Motown's music room. Impressed by what he heard and surprised by what he saw, Rick offered to do the honors as her next record producer. Teena honored his offer. And for the next six months it was offer-and-honor, honor-and-offer. . . .

Old joke. But after all, anyone who makes a record titled "I'm a Sucker for Your Love" (Gordy Records, 1979) is obviously a very sensitive artist and should be given all the respect due her. Which is a lot, 'cause it's a too-tough funk track—Rick wrote it—and you gotta respect Teena's vocals. Besides, it was a Top 10 R&B hit.

So were "I Need Your Lovin'" (1980), a sleek slice of *moderne* soul, and "Square Biz" (1981), a gum-flappin' rap 'n' funk number. Both were written and produced by Teena, which makes her not only one of the few successful female record producers but also one of the rare white artists who sell a lot of records to an audience that's almost exclusively black.

After four albums in two years Motown found out what all

this R-E-S-P-E-C-T meant to Lady T and she left the label in a huff. (Which she found conveniently parked outside the offices.) It took Teena across town to Epic Records, where she scored her fourth major R&B hit with "Fix It" (1983).

THE MIRACLES

Following Smokey Robinson's departure in 1972, Miracles Ronnie White, Bobby Rogers, and Warren "Pete" Moore recruited a new lead singer, Smokey soundalike Billy Griffin, and soldiered on. The pneumatic "Love Machine, Pt. 1" (1976) was the new outfit's biggest hit, huffing and puffing its way to the top of the pop charts and deservedly selling a million copies in the process. Written by Pete Moore and Billy Griffin, it's a classic examination of contemporary dehumanization and the track kicks ass.

"Don't Cha Love It," recorded a year earlier, is almost as good, with a smooth, relentless groove and vocals that keep climbing higher (and higher). The post-Smokey group's second Top 10 R&B hit (1974's musically strong, lyrically weak "Do It Baby" was the first), it's hard to believe the record stalled at number 78 on the pop charts.

Evidently, the Miracles found this sort of success equally mysterious, and they attempted to solve the problem by switching to Columbia Records in 1977. Here they found even getting an R&B hit could be a mystery, and the group disbanded two years later.

SMOKEY ROBINSON

Although Berry Gordy had made him a Motown vice-president back in the early sixties, Smokey Robinson was not one to sit back and rest on his royalty checks. The main reason he left the Miracles was so he could watch his kids grow up. He certainly didn't stop making records.

He had a few R&B hits, but nothing myth-making. "Quiet Storm" (1976) was appropriately tense and "Baby Come Close" (1974) suitably warm; however, most of Smokey's seventies material was strictly electric wallpaper.

Smokey had been two years without a hit when an enterprising Chicago DJ began playing a cut off Smokey's new album instead of his current single. Audience reaction was such that Motown quickly turned the album cut ("Cruisin' ") into a single that wound up not only selling a million copies but also becoming Smokey's first Top 10 pop hit since 1970. Another one of Smokey's patentedly ethereal, slow-drag specialties, the song is destined to be a low-rider favorite for as long as there are *barrios*.

91. Marvin Gaye has recorded duets with four Motown female vocalists. What are their names, and in what order did these pairings take place?

92. Which Motown recording artist is also a vice-president of the label?

93. Which Motown recording artist has been nominated for an Academy Award?

Same goes for "Being with You" (1980), a second puff of vintage Smokey, his second solo Top 10 pop hit, and his second million-selling single in as many years. Even if these two records were his only claims to fame, Smokey Robinson would remain indisputably the coolest vice-president in town.

DIANA ROSS

To Berry Gordy she was "my star." To her fans she's D*I*A*N*A R*O*S*S, a perception doubtlessly reinforced by her having titled no fewer than six different albums either *Diana Ross* (1970 and 1976), *Diana* (1971 and 1980), or *Ross* (1978 and 1983). Lord, it's hard to be humble.

Say what you want about imagination as well, but remember that Diane became D*I*A*N*A for the same reason Robert Zimmerman became Bob Dylan: All performers are applause junkies and it takes someone with a habit the size of King Kong to scale the Empire State Building.

It also takes talent. And the right persona. Unlike their competition, the Supremes came on neither as teenage rock 'n' rollers nor blues-shouting mamas, but as hip black airline stewardesses.

When Diana flew solo, all it took was a couple number one records and—most crucial—a successful film role and *presto!* the skinny girl from the Brewster Projects was now one of the great ladies of the entertainment world. Dream, girl.

The films, the TV specials, the ads for Blackglama minks certainly helped, because Diana the solo artist wasn't exactly an automatic hit machine. During her ten-year tenure at Motown she managed only six Top 10 pop tunes, but five of these were number ones. Ashford and Simpson's melodramatic, symphonic soul remake of "Ain't No Mountain High Enough" (1970) was the first, followed by the adult pop of "Touch Me in the Morning" (1973) and the soapy, music-box melody of "Theme from Mahogany (Do You Know Where You're Going To)," Diana's contribution to America's bicentennial effort.

With its air of sophisticated despair, "Love Hangover" (also 1976) not only proved Diana could be every inch the equal of Roxy Music's Bryan Ferry in the tongue-in-chic department but also established a new Diana the Disco Diva persona that was tailor-made for the feline funk eleganza of Bernard Edwards and Nile Rodger's "Upside Down" (1980), her fifth pop number one.

"I'm Coming Out," another 1980 Edwards and Rodgers creation, was even better, sporting the most electrifying intro since the Chiffons' "One Fine Day" (1963)—dig how the drums enter and STOP!—and the sort of disguise-in-love-with-you lyrics that made it almost impossible to drive through Boys Town that summer without hearing the sucker blasting out of every other bar. A true pop experience, just like when Blondie walked onstage at the Greek Theater around the time "Heart of Glass" was a hit and the whole place—outdoors, yet—suddenly smelled like dirty feet from all the amyl nitrite capsules bursting under youngmen's noses.

However, most of Diana's material seemed to be tailored to the young black woman who reads *Cosmopolitan*. Ashford and Simpson's "The Boss" and "It's My House" (both 1979) are perhaps the best examples, but off-beat singles such as 1973's "Good Morning Heartache" from the *Lady Sings the Blues* album and 1974's "Sleepin'," with its chilling Billie Holliday Meets the Shangri-Las story line, are infinitely more interesting discs.

Similarly, Diana's 1973 duet with Marvin Gaye, "You're a Special Part of Me," pulled the bigger chart numbers, while the 1974 follow-up, "My Mistake," which found Marvin's fourth and final female partner singing with an intensity she's seldom displayed since, walks away the aesthetic winner.

In 1981 Diana Ross walked away from Motown to RCA Records, where she supports herself and her three daughters from her 1971–77 marriage to Robert Ellis Silverstein in the style to which she's grown accustomed, with everything from remakes of old Frankie Lymon and the Teenagers tunes ("Why Do Fools Fall in Love") to sleek Michael Jackson productions ("Muscles"). And if it's lonely at the top, it's only because it's so crowded at the bottom, right?

DAVID RUFFIN

As a vocalist, David's talent was incomparable. As an ex-Temptation, it was almost invisible. Two hits in ten years isn't much of a track record and 1969's "My Whole World Ended (the Moment You Left Me)"—Top 10 pop and R&B chart numbers notwithstanding—isn't much of a record, period. It's the same sort of dreary, overblown codswallop that worked similar wonders for his brother Jimmy's career.

Seven years later veteran independent producer Van McCoy found David a song that showcased his wracked, lemon-and-honey tone, giant range, and pinpoint control, and David responded with the performance of a lifetime. "Walk away from Love" is one part class, two parts pain, and *all* David Ruffin.

Tunes like that don't come knockin' every day, unfortunately, and without a sharp producer custom-fitting him with songs to suit his voice, David was completely at the mercy of his material. He left the Motown label for Warner Bros. Records in 1979. Two years later he was not only looking for mercy but looking for a recording contract as well.

THE SUPREMES

In the seven years after Diana Ross went solo, the Supremes went through a dizzying series of personnel changes. Jean Terrell, who had been singing with her brother heavyweight boxer Ernie Terrell's group the Knockouts, replaced Diana in 1970. She, in turn, gave way to Freda's sister and former Glass House member Scherrie Payne in 1975. Cindy Birdsong, a Supreme since 1967, left in 1972, only to return in 1975. Her first replacement, Lynda Lawrence, lasted about a year. Her second, Susaye Greene, hung in until the group finally disbanded in 1977.

Les Supremes après la Ross. This particular edition of the Supremes—(from left) Mary Wilson, Jean Terrell, and Lynda Lawrence—lasted less than a year, but no matter how many times the faces changed, the style remained the same: According to the caption attached to the original press release, "each gown has over 10,000 hand-sewn imported French jeweled beads in the design."

COURTESY TOM DEPIERRO/AIRWAVE INTERNATIONAL

Confusing? You bet. The only thing constant was the presence of original Supreme Mary Wilson. Hits were another matter entirely.

The Jean Terrell–Cindy Birdsong–Mary Wilson edition was the most successful, responsible for a pair of 1970 Top 10 pop numbers: the neoclassic, semipsychedelic "Stoned Love"— oh baby, break out those body paints—and the underrated "Up the Ladder to the Roof." You might notice that the vocal line mirrors the story line on the choruses of the latter record. Then again, you might not.

With a murky phasing effect running through the track and gloomy, almost chanted vocals, "Nathan Jones" (1971), the Jean-Cindy-Mary combination's last Top 10 R&B hit, rivals only the Jaynetts' 1963 classic "Sally, Go 'round the Roses" in the pop-records-with-a-Venusian atmosphere-of-weirdness sweepstakes. A year later the Jean-*Lynda*-Mary lineup scored the Supremes' final Top 10 R&B hit: Smokey Robinson's "Floy Joy."

After that there was a nonhit album produced by Jimmy Webb and another, produced by Stevie Wonder, that was shelved when various frictions kept the group out of action for almost two years. By then neither the Holland brothers' production efforts nor several attempts to pick up on the disco market could revive much interest in the Supremes, no matter whether it was Scherrie-Cindy-Mary or Scherrie-Susaye-Mary doing the singing, and the group went straight to Jukebox Heaven in 1977.

Both Mary Wilson and the Scherrie Payne–Susaye Greene duo issued albums in 1979. These were consigned to limbo almost immediately. Nowadays, Mary sings a bit, travels a lot, and remains something of the Supremes' official spokesperson; Scherrie, who recorded on Motown's V.I.P. label back in 1969, plays in Vegas musicals; and, for all we know, Susaye is still out there limboing.

THE UNDISPUTED TRUTH

Joe Harris was the lead singer of this relatively minor act, whose personnel shifted so frequently Motown issued at least four albums by the group without ever bothering to identify its members. Beginning as a two-man, two-woman vocal quartet, the group first dropped one of the women, then added musicians and became a self-contained unit before finally settling back into a three-man, one-woman lineup.

Along with the changes in size, there was an awful lot of turnover within the group as well, and all we really know for sure is that Chaka Khan's sister—Taka Boom—was a member at one point. Wowie zowie.

Smiling faces sometimes. One of the following statements is the Undisputed Truth: (a) pictured (from left) are Michele, Joe Harris, and Billie Calvin; (b) the woman on the left lost her last name in the war; (c) the other original male member is hiding somewhere in the girl's wigs; (d) you make your own heaven and hell right here on earth.

COURTESY MICHAEL OCHS ARCHIVES

"Smiling Faces Sometimes" (Gordy, 1971), as cold-blooded a record as has ever existed, was the group's first and only hit, but it was monster-cool, thanks to a great, swirling production from Norman Whitfield and the profound lyrics of Barrett Strong. The follow-up is one of those rare discs where reading the label is almost as much fun as playing the record ("You Make Your Own Heaven and Hell Right Here on Earth"—The Undisputed Truth) and was one of Jean-Paul Sartre's personal favorites. Albert Camus would've liked it, too.

The rest of the Undisputed Truth's recordings were somewhat less existential, most of the time sounding like a more polished version of the P-Funk's psychedelic groove thang. Which is okay by this geepie, but when you consider that the Undisputed Truth's rendition of "Papa Was a Rolling Stone" hit the lower reaches of the pop charts *four months* before the Temptations took the tune to the top of the same, then perhaps you'll understand not only the former group's revolving-door membership but also the reason they followed Norman to his Whitfield Records label in 1976 and why they were ultimately no more successful there than they had been at Motown. And that's the Undisputed Truth.

STEVIE WONDER

With an attitude that ranges from the sublime—lobbying Congress to declare the Reverend Dr. Martin Luther King's birthday a national holiday—to the ridiculous—making fun of himself doing comedy skits opposite Eddie Murphy on network TV—Stevie Wonder deserves to be what he is: the most respected figure in contemporary music. As a singer, songwriter, or producer, he has few peers; as a musician whose albums consistently sell multiplatinum, he has no equals.

Once the 1971 recording contract that guaranteed him not only more money but also more freedom than any previous Motown act was signed and sealed, Stevie delivered his first double number one in almost a decade. "Superstition" (1972), with its crunching riff, rolling keyboards, and punchy horn lines, was such a strong piece of material that even a

Master blasters jammin'. Stevie Wonder (left) and late great reggae singer-songwriter Bob Marley duet to it uptown style. Any better illustration of Motown's—and Stevie's—cross-cultural impact?

KIA

94. What was Smokey Robin's first non-Miracles recording?

95. Who recorded the original version of the Supremes' 1969 hit "Someday We'll Be Together"?

96. Three of the five original Marvelettes continued on as a trio. What are their names?

"supergroup" such as Beck, Bogert and Appice couldn't ruin it.

In fact, the sound has proved so durable that all Stevie has needed to do is modify it slightly since. The too-tough "I Wish" (1976), the goofy "Boogie on Reggae Woman" (1974), and the relentless "Higher Ground" (1973) are all fine examples of this. That's not a put-down either. The same could be said about any pop artist. What has the self-proclaimed "greatest rock 'n' roll band in the world" done except run off endless variations on "Brown Sugar" for the past ten years?

While that might've been all Stevie needed to do, it wasn't the only thing he did. "You Are the Sunshine of My Life" (1974) was a pretty ballad, sentimental as a greeting card; 1977's "Sir Duke" was a jazzy riot, with a fantabulous Ellingtonian horn arrangement; and 1980's "Master Blaster (Jammin')" was a tougher, more celebrative reggae record than anything that came out of Jamaica that year.

Although too often Stevie wastes brilliant musical structures in support of syrupy love songs and Pollyanna-like visions of universal brotherhood, he occasionally digs deeper, as evidenced by the double-edged social commentary of "Living for the City" (1974)—check out the album version for the hero's fate. What's more, all eight of these songs were Top 10 pop hits and half of those were pop number ones. (Only 1974's "You Haven't Done Nothin'," which also topped the pop charts, and "You Are the Sunshine of My Life" failed to make number one R&B as well.)

Had not Stevie's career been interrupted for almost two years as the result of a 1973 auto accident which cost him his sense of smell, his track record might be even more astonishing. Not that it seems to matter much to Stevie, who apparently does whatever he wants, whether that be the cosmic instrumental meanderings of his *Journey through the Secret Life of Plants* soundtrack LP (1979) or writing and producing outside hits such as "Tell Me Something Good" for Rufus featuring Chaka Khan (ABC Records, 1974).

Besides, as long as he puts at least one song as classy and commercial as the slinky "That Girl" (1982) on his albums, Stevie's records will sell as easily as ice cubes in hell. He's already won fourteen Grammy Awards (five each in 1974 and 1975) and toured with the Rolling Stones twice—they opened for him in 1964 and returned him the favor in 1972—what more does he have to prove?

Answer: nothing. Oh, artists will come along who surpass Stevie's achievements, but records were meant to be played, not broken. And as long as he continues to keep an open mind, then whenever a new Stevie Wonder album hits the street, you can be sure that every working musician will be paying *close* attention. More than a "superstar," the man is music incarnate.

These were Motown's stars of the seventies. There were others who landed individual hits, but with the exception of Thelma Houston, whose "Don't Leave Me This Way" hovers over this chapter like Indian summer, these were all performed by artists who are still part of Motown's current talent roster.

Since I don't have a crystal ball, I'm not going to speculate on the ultimate fates of the Dazz Band, DeBarge, High Inergy, Bonnie Pointer, Switch, Syreeta Wright, and all the rest. We're dealing with history, not conjecture, here. And it would be both unwise and unjust to close the book on anyone just yet.

In the interest of history, however, those notables who passed through the company's major labels—Tamla, Motown, Gordy, Soul, and V.I.P. Records—deserve mention, despite their lack of success. Tamla had Keith and Darrell, better known as Smokey Robinson's cousins. Soul was, appropriately enough, home to minor soulstars Major Lance, Joe

Someday we'll be together. Motown's founding family backstage in Las Vegas circa 1970. Pictured (from left) are songwriter-producer-executive and Gwen Gordy's former husband, Harvey Fuqua; songwriter-producer-recording artist and Iris Gordy's former husband, Johnny Bristol; La Ross; Berry Gordy; Smokey Robinson; and Berry's brother, former Motown recording artist and head of Jobete music publishing Robert Gordy.

COURTESY TOM DEPIERRO/AIRWAVE INTERNATIONAL

Hinton, Yvonne Fair, and the Fantastic Four as well as songwriters Frank Wilson and Jack Hammer, white rock group the Messengers, and Abdullah, whose "I Comma Zimba Zio" (1968) is stark, dark, and on the mark.

On the V.I.P. list were soulstirrers Chuck Jackson and King Floyd, white rock group the Hornets, whose 1964 disc "Give Me a Kiss" just might be the worst Beatles imitation ever made, and the Abbey Tavern Singers. Say *what?*

The Gordy family of talent included Eivets Rednow, his former wife, Syreeta Wright—whose first record ("I Can't Give Back the Love I Feel for You") was issued under the *nom de chanson* Rita Wright in 1968—songwriter Leon Ware, pop/soul dorks Jay and the Techniques, and the brilliant Chicago blues guitarist Luther Allison, whose three Gordy albums (1972, '74, '76) are hard to find, but worth the search.

The Motown label itself had the largest collection of soul survivors. Chuck Jackson's first and Yvonne Fair's last records for the company appeared under the Motown logo; so did efforts by Jerry Butler, Betty Lavette, Bloodstone, former Tower of Power vocalist Larry Williams, ex–Main Ingredient mainman Cuba Gooding, and cult heroine Gloria Jones, who went on to become the late T. Rex leader Marc Bolan's jeepster of love.

Then there were discs from jazzmasters Ahmad Jamal and Jonah Jones, Motown's road-band leader Choker Campbell, and jump blues kingpin Amos Milburn. Staff songwriter Leonard Caston and veteran keyboardist-vocalist Billy Preston, too.

In the talent-is-relative category Motown Records had mellow fellow Severin Browne—Jackson's brother—and T-Boy ("Don't call me Arthur") Ross—Diana's brother. Moving from young whippersnappers to old fingersnappers, the company issued adult-oriented pop from the likes of Sammy Davis, Jr., the late Bobby Darin, male-female vocal group the 5th Dimension, and noted English actor Albert Finney.

Perhaps the all-time weirdest Motown act was Black Russian, a male-female pop vocal group who were, in fact, white and from the USSR. Contrary to what Bobby Marchan and the Clowns prophesized on their great Ace recording of 1958, the Rooskis aren't exactly "Rockin' Behind the Iron Curtain" just yet.

However, when NASA receives the first message from outer space, it'll probably read: "We would like intergalactic distribution rights to the Motown 50 Hits mail-order package." And you know that's right.

What's *true*—and more germane—is that Motown was responsible for some of the best records of the seventies. Check the chart: sixty-two Top 10 pop hits, including twenty-four pop number ones, and eight more discs that went to number one R&B, for a grand total of seventy king-size hits in ten years.

Granted, this nowhere rivals the company's peak mid-sixties period, but remember that Motown's seventy hits of the seventies not only sold more copies per disc but also sold at least four times as many albums—at more than four times the profit margin—during the past decade than in the sixties. Its worst year, the company probably made around $43 million.

Inside Motown things had changed greatly. The Artist Development Department was dismantled in 1970. (You could think of the Jackson 5 as the last graduating class.) And the System itself, that familiar four-way combination of songwriters, producers, vocalists, and musicians, was no more. For one thing, many of these people had decided to take their talent across the street. For another, the new breed of do-it-all-yourself artists had made the Motown system of specialists obsolete.

More important, Berry Gordy—the man who appeared on the TV quiz show *To Tell the Truth* in 1966 and not one of the four panelists guessed his correct identity—was greatly changed. The same person who in 1963 could see directly into the reception area of the Hitsville U.S.A. building was someone who in 1971 left work faithfully every day at 6 p.m. to have dinner with his family.

The famous Motown "family atmosphere," however, surfaced only occasionally, such as at the 1973 wedding of Hazel Joy Gordy and Jermaine Jackson, which featured 175 doves in white cages, seven thousand camelias, and Smokey Robinson singing a song he'd composed especially for the couple. A closed-circuit TV broadcast carried the ceremony to the "B" list, while luminaries such as Jim Brown, Dionne Warwick, Chuck Connors, Leslie Uggams, Beau Bridges, Rona Barret, and the *Los Angeles Times* society editor who covered the event made up a partial "A" list. The soiree put proud papa out a couple hundred grand, but the tab included Christmas dinner for twelve hundred needy black families, so it was charity, baby. The same way the old USC grads down at the Newport Yacht Club practice it.

The flip side of the family atmosphere showed up in the wake of Berry ("Pops") Gordy, Sr.'s passing at age ninety in 1978, an event commemorated by the rush release of an A-side "Pops, We Love You" (Motown, 1978), on which Marvin Gaye, Diana Ross, Smokey Robinson, and Stevie Wonder pooled their vocal talents in tribute to the dearly departed.

97. What 1982 Motown million-selling single had been a flop when it was first released in 1977?

98. Who sang lead on the Temptations' first pop hit?

99. What two films starred Frankie Avalon and Annette Funicello and featured musical performances from Little Stevie Wonder?

100. What are the names of the members of the Four Tops?

Weddings and funerals. Otherwise, the family atmosphere was greatly mist.

MOTOWN MAGIC MOMENT #30

"I don't think economics would ever let it be like it was with us again. Now that everyone not only has a mind of their own but also an attorney's mind and an agent's mind as well, it's not the same atmosphere, because it's more money-motivated."
—BERRY GORDY

The record business had grown up. By 1976 New York City's legendary Apollo Theater had discontinued its Wednesday night showcase of live amateur talent, mostly because no one was discovered at the Apollo anymore. Instead, they all came through the record companies' doors via a demo tape in an attorney's or a producer's or an ex-promotion man's briefcase.

The situation was similar to the transformation that professional baseball went through at almost the same time. Taking this sports analogy the full nine innings, Motown was not unlike those teams who had previously relied on the strength of their organizations to attract and develop hot hitters. Now that the common draft and free agency had thrown them a curve and a knuckler, the clubs weren't getting around on the high, hard one as well as they used to.

While it's true that Motown didn't develop much in the way of new talent, even if current R&B star Stephanie Mills was really the only one that got away, the obvious defense is that the company was too busy taking the old, established talent to new sales heights. The Chrysler Corporation, the Mob, and the Trilateral Commission all do business the same way.

The payback comes when the talent takes a hike, turns cold, or turns the tables and starts holding you up for more money than your end of the deal is worth. When that happens, you've gotta have a new face to take their place. Trouble is, superstars aren't made as easily as K-cars, cocaine, or prime interest rates.

Which is why you find Motown working its one thing of constant value—that incredible catalog of hits—overtime nowadays.

Think about it. And when you do, consider this:

Thirty years ago the Houston Juvenile Delinquency and

Crime Commission displayed a keen sense of the Orwellian when it declared the lyrics of some thirty R&B songs, including Lowell Fulson's classic "Everyday I Have the Blues" (Swing Time, 1950), objectionable and told local radio stations not to play these records. In the mid-sixties U.S. Senator Gordon Allot (R-Colorado) stumbled into "It's What's Happening, Baby!" a TV program on soul music promoted by the Office of Economic Opportunity, and reported, "For one and a half hours the intelligence of the public was insulted. . . . If I were a Communist, I would ask for nothing more than to show this film in underdeveloped countries."

He probably didn't watch the "Motown: 25" special either.

Of course, Motown didn't win the cultural battle all by its lonesome. But it is the only record company that began as a noun and wound up as an adjective: The Motown Sound. A Motown bass line. A Motown chorus. "Gimme that Motown feel."

More than the music, even, Motown has the Myth. Call it a phenomenon, call it _____ or call it a cab. Whatever version of The Motown Story you prefer, you'd have to agree it's something we're not likely to see again.

Or at least not until some crazy whiteboy like Keith Morris, leader of L.A. hard-core punk outfit the Circle Jerks, gets his dream band—"Me 'n' six dusted-out bloods off the Crenshaw [bus] line"—together.

> Doot-doot-doot-WOW!
> Say yeah yeah yeah
> Say yeah yeah yeah
> *One more time . . .*

Discography

Take a good look. This is the most complete Motown discography money can buy. Beginning with the Tamla label in 1959, it covers every 45 rpm single and 33⅓ rpm album issued by the Motown Record Corporation in the United States as of December 1984. It's not perfect, and we'll get to that, but first let's all start on the One:

One purpose of a discography is to provide an easy reference source, of use to working professionals and barroom bettors alike. That's why we've chosen the simplest format possible: labels appear in alphabetical order, and records are listed according to catalog number, followed by title, artist, and date of release.

Due to the scope of the project—twenty-five years, an even greater number of subsidiary labels, and more than 600 releases on the Motown label alone—we've omitted foreign pressings, 12-inch "disco" singles, and jukebox EPs. Pre-Motown recordings, non-Motown recordings of Jobete-published songs, and recordings on labels for which Motown only served as a distributor—such as Gull, Manticore, CTI, and Kudu—are likewise not found here. Same goes for cassettes, compact discs, and the company's incredible line of mid-priced reissue LPs. Not to mention a whole batch of midline "greatest hits" albums and the entire "Yesteryear's" series of reissue 45s.

We have, however, managed to identify the correct titles and artists for dozens of missing catalog numbers. All such information has been verified by a close inspection of test pressings, promotion-only records, and yellowing, twice-photocopied paperwork. For one reason or another—bad timing, an adjudged lack of commercial potential, company politics, etc.—most of these discs were never made available to the record-buying public and are therefore listed as "not released" (NR). In cases where, say, the title and artist are known but not the date of release, we've left the space for such unconfirmed information blank. Ditto for a known non-release, for which the title and artist cannot be confirmed.

You'll also notice that a significant number of these records were not issued in strict chronological order. Again, there are countless reasons for this, ranging from the artist's failure to complete the recording on time, to the company holding the disc off the market in order to give it a stronger promotional effort. This should explain why when we were certain of the year, but not the month of release, we've left the latter information blank.

Sophisticats and sophistikittens alike will doubtlessly question our use of the plural pronoun "we," customarily reserved for editors and other royalty. Quite simply, this discography was a collective operation, and before we proceed to define the various codes used herein, I should like to take this opportunity to thank three people without whom this document would be filled with even more blank spaces than it already is. For all this and more, I am eternally indebted to record collectors, Motown fanatics, wonderful entertainers, and great humanitarians Ken Barnes, Tom DePierro, and Doug Moody. You're all beautiful cats. Now get out of here. I hate you.

But seriously, folks, we love all people. Even the ones who are going to write me c/o Radio & Records, 1930 Century Park West, Los Angeles, CA 90067 and complain about whatever chunks of missing information they are now only too glad to supply. Great. Just enclose a photocopy of the record or other official source and I'll be sure and credit you when we update future editions. No joke.

Wish the same could be said for our attempt at a uniform dating system. Basically, when we had the month/day/year at our fingertips, we went with it. And when we didn't—well, you can guess the rest.

Although we've tried to keep footnotes to a minimum, there are a few cases where more detailed explanations were necessary, such as the alternate LP titles listed in parenthesis. At other times, the abbreviations are almost self-explanatory: "Soundtrack" means that the music was used in a film or TV show, and "various artists" is shorthand for a disc that contains recordings by more than one performer.

As for 45 rpm singles, it's obvious that we are several B-sides short of a load, mostly because it's not easy to locate commercial (two-sided) copies of non-hits. (Record companies like to minimize their losses and don't press up too many copies of flops. Not if they want to stay in business for twenty-five years, anyway.) Furthermore, since not all these records were hits—and we didn't always have copies of the discs so we could check and see which side had the lower matrix number—we've probably listed a few singles backwards, or a B-side first. Oops.

Speaking of matrix numbers—also known as those funny little scratchings found in the wax between the grooves and the record label—a couple of discs are listed with more than one of these multiple digits in parenthesis. That's because, in these cases, the change in numbering indicates a radically different version of the same song.

Songs that share the same *catalog* number were either issued with two different B-sides or were mistakes on the company's part. Oops again.

Completing our discussion of B-sides, those records labeled "instrumental" feature the same song (minus vocals) on the flip, while those marked "Pts. 1 and 2" sport the same song, but split in half to accommodate fast-moving radio formats. (Better to play two three-and-a-half-minute songs and maybe lose your listeners for one of 'em than to play one seven-minute song and lose your listeners for all of it, or so the theory goes.)

With that in mind, here is our final disclaimer: As a rule of thumb, this discography is most accurate from 1959 to 1970 or thereabouts, which is the period in which the majority of Motown collectors are most interested anyway. Those who are not record collectors can take pleasure in yet another view of Motown that only this particular brand of historical evidence can provide—which records were the innovations and which were the imitations is but one application. The ratio of hits to misses is another.

Better yet, the names and number of the record labels as well as the song titles and groups' names themselves combine to create an overwhelming wave of proper nouns that could only be titled "The Motown Story" . . .

SINGLES

BLACK FORUM

This spoken-word label spawned some of the rarest discs in the parent company's history. Lotta famous names here. (45s/LPs)

20000	No Time/Until We're Free	Elaine Brown	4/9/73

BLAZE

Apparently the only disc on this singles-only subsidiary. Jack Ashford was a Motown session percussionist of long-standing. (45s)

1107	Do the Choo Choo (Parts 1 and 2)	Jack Ashford and the Sound of New Detroit	9/24/69

CHISA

Established by expatriate black South African trumpeter Hugh Masekela as an outlet for jazz and Afro-pop artists. When Motown stopped distributing the label after scant success, they retained rights to the following string of curiosities. (45s/LPs)

8001	Home on the Range (Everybody Needs a Home)/Mend This Generation	Stu Gardener	9/24/69
8001	Home on the Range (Everybody Needs a Home)/It's a Family Thang	Stu Gardener	9/24/69
8002	A Place in the Sun/Your Love	Monk Montgomery	9/29/69
8003	It's Private Tonight/Let's Make Some Love	Arthur Adams	10/8/69
8004	Can We Talk to You (For a Little While)/Love and Peace	Anonymous Children of Today	11/25/69
8005	Gonna Put It on Your Mind/Henry Blake	Dorothy, Oma and Zelpha	5/11/69
8006	I Will Never Love Another/Love unto Me	Five Smooth Stones	12/29/69
8007	Expressin' My Love/I Don't Dream No More	Stu Gardener	2/17/70
8008	My Baby's Love/Loving You	Arthur Adams	4/15/70
8009	You Keep Me Hangin' On/Make Me a Potion	Hugh Masekela and the Union of South Africa	10/1/70
8010	Way Back Home/Jackson!	Jazz Crusaders	9/24/70
8011	Can't Wait to See You Again/It's Private Tonight	Arthur Adams	2/11/71
8012	I Won't Weep No More/You Touched Me	Letta	3/30/71
8013	Pass the Plate/Greasy Spoon	Jazz Crusaders	6/15/71
8014	Dyambo (Dee-Yambo) Weary Day Is Over/Shebeen	Hugh Masekela and the Union of South Africa	6/17/71
8015	Uncle Tom/Mornin' Train	Arthur Adams	NR

DIVINITY

Early—and Motown's only—attempt at a gospel label. (45s)

99004	That's What He Is to Me/Pilgrim of Sorrow	Wright Specials	7/31/62
99005	Ninety-Nine and a Half Won't Do/I Won't Go Back	Wright Specials	6/7/63
99006	Give God a Chance/Have You Any Time for Jesus	Gospel Stars	7/12/63
99007	First You've Got to Recognize God/I'm Going Home	Burnadettes	5/20/63
99008	We Shall Overcome/Trouble in This Land	Liz Lands	—

ECOLOGY

When Sammy and B.G. had a falling-out, plans for this exceptionally short-lived label returned to that from whence they came. (45s)

1000	In My Own Lifetime/I'll Begin Again	Sammy Davis, Jr.	3/11/71

GAIEE

As the name implies, disguise in love with the commercial potential behind this one-off single. (45s)

90001	I Was Born This Way/Liberation	Valentino	4/9/75

GORDY

The third of the major Motown subsidiary labels. Still active. (45s/LPs)
Note: Gordy 7001 to 7056 are purple with the Gordy logo in yellow at the top and bear the "It's what's in the grooves that counts" slogan. 70055 to date are purple with the Gordy logo in a yellow arrowhead at the side. Some later numbers may still bear the older design, as pressing plants sought to use up all the old labels they had sitting around gathering dust. At any rate, discs bearing the older label are always more valuable, regardless of whether they were officially issued that way or not.

7001	Dream Come True/Isn't She Pretty	Temptations	3/16/62
7002	Come into My Palace/Trying to Make It	Lee and the Leopards	4/14/62
7003	While I'm Away/Because I Love Her	Valadiers	5/21/62
7004	—	—	—
7005	Do You Love Me/Move Mr. Man	Mike and the Modifiers	7/11/62
7006	I've Found Myself a Brand New Baby/It's Too Bad	Mike and the Modifiers	7/11/62
7007	Your Love is Wonderful/Here You Come	Hattie Littles	1/8/63
7008	Hold on Pearl/Toodle Loo	Bob Kauli	—

7009	Camel Walk/The Chaperone	LaBrenda Ben and the Beljeans	—
7010	Paradise/Slow Down Heart	Temptations	10/1/62
7011	I'll Have to Let Him Go/My Baby Won't Come Back	Martha and the Vandellas	9/27/62
7012	Shake Sherry/You Better Get in Line	Contours	11/15/62
7013	I Found a Girl/You'll Be Sorry Someday	Valadiers	1/8/63
7014	Come and Get These Memories/Jealous Lover	Martha and the Vandellas	2/22/63
7015	I Want a Love I Can See/The Further You Look, The Less You See	Temptations	3/18/63
7016	Don't Let Her Be Your Baby/It Must Be Love	Contours	3/8/63
7017	We're Only Young Once/I'm Hooked	Bunny Paul	5/28/63
7018	Going Steady Anniversary/Pushing Up Daisys	Stylers	6/11/63
7019	Pa, I Need a Car/You Get Ugly	Contours	6/11/63
7020	Farewell My Love/May I Have This Dance	Temptations	6/25/63
7021	Just Be Yourself/I Can't Help It, I Gotta Dance	LaBrenda Ben	8/30/63
7022	Heat Wave/A Love Like Yours (Don't Come Knocking Every Day)	Martha and the Vandellas	7/10/63
7023	I Have a Dream/We Shall Overcome	Rev. Martin Luther King and Liz Lands	—
7024	Too Hurt to Cry/Come on Home	Darnells	11/4/63
7025	Quicksand/Darling, I Hum Our Song	Martha and the Vandellas	11/4/63
7026	May What He Lived for Live/—	Liz Lands	12/6/63
7027	Live Wire/Old Love (Let's Try It Again)	Martha and the Vandellas	1/17/64
7028	The Way You Do the Things You Do/Just Let Me Know	Temptations	1/23/64
7029	Can You Do It/I'll Stand by You	Contours	2/28/64
7030	Keep Me/Midnight Journey	Liz Lands	3/11/64
7031	In My Lonely Room/A Tear for the Girl	Martha and the Vandellas	3/23/64
7032	The Girl's Alright with Me/I'll Be in Trouble	Temptations	4/29/64
7033	Dancing in the Street/There He Is (At My Door)	Martha and the Vandellas	7/31/64
7034	Baby I Miss You/Leaving Here	Tommy Good	7/31/64
7035	Girl (Why You Wanna Make Me Blue)/Baby Baby I Need You	Temptations	8/20/64
7036	Wild One/Dancing Slow	Martha and the Vandellas	11/3/64
7037	Can You Jerk Like Me/That Day When She Needed Me	Contours	11/16/64
7038	My Girl/Nobody but My Baby	Temptations	12/21/64
7039	Nowhere to Run/Motoring	Martha and the Vandellas	2/5/65
7040	It's Growing/What Love Has Joined Together	Temptations	3/18/65
7041	A Thrill a Moment/I'll Never See My Love Again	Kim Weston	4/21/65
7042	Why Do You Want to Let Me Go/I'm Not a Plaything	Marv Johnson	5/28/65
7043	Since I Lost My Baby/You Got to Earn It	Temptations	6/1/65
7044	First I Look at the Purse/Searching for a Girl	Contours	6/23/65
7045	Love Makes Me Do Foolish Things/You've Been in Love Too Long	Martha and the Vandellas	7/26/65
7046	Take Me in Your Arms (Rock Me a Little While)/Don't Compare Me with Her	Kim Weston	9/2/65
7047	Don't Look Back/My Baby	Temptations	9/30/65
7048	My Baby Loves Me/Never Leave Your Baby's Side	Martha and the Vandellas	1/4/66
7049	Get Ready/Fading Away	Temptations	2/7/66
7050	Helpless/A Love Like Yours (Don't Come Knocking Every Day)	Kim Weston	2/14/66
7051	I Miss You Baby (How I Miss You)/Just the Way You Are	Mary Johnson	3/4/66
7052	Just a Little Misunderstanding/Determination	Contours	4/18/66
7053	What Am I Going to Do Without Your Love/Go Ahead and Laugh	Martha and the Vandellas	5/19/66
7054	Ain't Too Proud to Beg/You'll Lose a Precious Love	Temptations	5/3/66
7055	Beauty Is Only Skin Deep/You're Not an Ordinary Girl	Temptations	8/4/66
7056	I'm Ready for Love/He Doesn't Love Her Anymore	Martha and the Vandellas	10/6/66
7057	(I Know) I'm Losing You/I Couldn't Cry If I Wanted To	Temptations	11/2/66
7058	Jimmy Mack/Third Finger, Left Hand	Martha and the Vandellas	2/3/67
7059	It's So Hard Being a Loser/Your Love Grows More Precious Everyday	Contours	3/9/67
7060	Festival Time/Joy Road	San Remo Golden Strings	4/6/67
7061	All I Need/Sorry Is a Sorry Word	Temptations	4/13/67
7062	Love Bug Leave My Heart Alone/One Way Out	Martha and the Vandellas	8/3/67
7063	You're My Everything/I've Been Good to You	Temptations	6/13/67
7064	I Can't Give Back the Love I Feel For You/Something on My Mind	Rita Wright	1/11/68
7065	(Loneliness Made Me Realize) It's You That I Need/Don't Send Me Away	Temptations	9/26/67
7066	I Want My Baby Back/Gonna Keep on Trying 'Till I Win Your Love	Edwin Starr	10/5/67
7067	Honey Chile/Show Me the Way	Martha Reeves and the Vandellas	10/31/67
7068	I Wish It Would Rain/I Truly Truly Believe	Temptations	12/21/67
7069	Does Your Mama Know About Me/Fading Away	Bobby Taylor and the Vancouvers	2/7/68
7070	I Promise to Wait My Love/Forget Me Not	Martha Reeves and the Vandellas	4/4/68
7071	I Am the Man for You Baby/My Weakness Is You	Edwin Starr	3/21/68
7072	I Could Never Love Another (After Loving You)/Gonna Give Her All the Love I've Got	Temptations	4/18/68
7073	I Am Your Man/If You Love Her	Bobby Taylor and the Vancouvers	6/27/68
7074	Please Return Your Love to Me/How Can I Forget	Temptations	7/16/68
7075	I Can't Dance to That Music You're Playing/I Tried	Martha Reeves and the Vandellas	7/25/68
7076	Alfie/More than a Dream	Eivets Rednow	8/27/68
7077	I'll Pick a Rose for My Rose/You Got the Love I Love	Marv Johnson	10/3/68
7078	Way Over There/If My Heart Could Tell the Story	Edwin Starr	10/26/68
7079	Melinda/It's Growing	Bobby Taylor and the Vancouvers	10/8/68

7080	Sweet Darlin'/Without You	Martha Reeves and the Vandellas	10/10/68
7081	Cloud Nine/Why Did She Have to Leave Me	Temptations	10/25/68
7082	Rudolph the Red-Nosed Reindeer/Silent Night	Temptations	11/27/68
7083	Twenty-Five Miles/Love Is My Destination	Edwin Starr	1/2/69
7084	Runaway Child, Running Wild/I Need Your Love	Temptations	1/30/69
7085	We've Got Honey Love/I'm in Love	Martha Reeves and the Vandellas	3/20/69
7086	Don't Let the Joneses Get You Down/Since I've Lost You	Temptations	5/1/69
7087	I'm Still a Struggling Man/Pretty Little Angel	Edwin Starr	5/21/69
7088	Oh I've Been Blessed/It Should Have Been Me Loving Her	Bobby Taylor	NR
7089	Cheating Is Telling on You/Need Your Love	Lollipops	NR
7090	Oh How Happy/Ooo Baby Baby	Edwin Starr & Blinky	7/20/69
7091	My Springtime/Suzie	Terry Johnson	NR
7092	My Girl Has Gone/It Should Have Been Me Loving Her	Bobby Taylor	7/29/69
7093	I Can't Get Next to You/Running Away (Ain't Gonna Help You)	Temptations	7/30/69
7094	Taking My Love (And Leaving Me)/Heartless	Martha Reeves and the Vandellas	8/14/69
7095	What'cha Gonna Do/Suzie	Terry Johnson	1/9/70
7096	Psychedelic Shack/That's the Way Love Is	Temptations	12/29/69
7097	Time/Running Back and Forth	Edwin Starr	1/20/70
7098	I Should Be Proud/Love, Guess Who	Martha Reeves and the Vandellas	2/12/70
7099	Ball of Confusion (That's What the World Is Today)/It's Summer	Temptations	5/7/70
7100	Stone Soul Booster/Sandy	Buzzie	8/28/70
7101	War/He Who Picks a Rose	Edwin Starr	6/8/70
7102	Ungena Za Ulimwengu (Unite the World)/Hum Along and Dance	Temptations	9/15/70
7103	I Gotta Let You Go/You're the Loser Now	Martha Reeves and the Vandellas	10/1/70
7104	Stop the War Now/Gonna Keep on Trying 'Till I Win Your Love	Edwin Starr	11/19/70
7105	Just My Imagination (Running Away with Me)/You Make Your Own Heaven and Hell Right Here on Earth	Temptations	1/14/71
7106	Save My Love for a Rainy Day/Since I've Lost You	Undisputed Truth	2/2/71
7107	Funky Music Sho Nuff Turns Me On/Cloud Nine	Edwin Starr	3/30/71
7108	Smiling Faces Sometimes/You Got the Love I Need	Undisputed Truth	5/13/71
7109	It's Summer/I'm the Exception to the Rule	Temptations	6/24/71
7110	Bless You/Hope I Don't Get My Heart Broke	Martha Reeves and the Vandellas	9/14/71
7111	Superstar (Remember How You Got Where You Are)/Gonna Keep on Trying 'Till I Win Your Love	Temptations	10/19/71
7112	You Make Your Own Heaven and Hell Right Here on Earth/Ball of Confusion (That's What the World Is Today)	Undisputed Truth	11/16/71
7113	In and Out of My Life/Your Love Makes It All Worthwhile	Martha Reeves and the Vandellas	12/16/71
7114	What It Is/California Soul	Undisputed Truth	1/25/72
7115	Take a Look Around/Smooth Sailing from Now On	Temptations	2/3/72
7116	It's Too Much for a Man to Take Too Long/Time Don't Wait	Eric and the Vikings	4/25/72
7117	Papa Was a Rolling Stone/Friendship Train	Undisputed Truth	5/9/72
7118	Tear It on Down/I Want You Back	Martha and the Vandellas	5/23/72
7119	Mother Nature/Funky Music Sho Nuff Turns Me On	Temptations	6/1/72
7120	Green Grow the Lilacs/So in Love	Festivals	7/11/72
7121	Papa Was a Rolling Stone/Instrumental	Temptations	9/28/72
7122	Girl You're Alright/With a Little Help from My Friends	Undisputed Truth	10/10/72
7123	Robot Man/I'll Be Here	Jay and the Techniques	11/27/72
7124	Mama I Got a Brand New Thing (Don't Say No)/Gonna Keep on Trying 'Till I Win Your Love	Undisputed Truth	2/15/73
7125	Feel Like Givin' Up/Once You Had a Heart	Paul Williams	NR
7126	Masterpiece/Instrumental	Temptations	2/1/73
7127	I Won't Be the Fool I've Been Again/Baby (Don't You Leave Me)	Martha Reeves	NR
7128	The Little Red Rooster/Raggedy and Dirty	Luther Allison	NR
7129	Plastic Man/Hurry Tomorrow	Temptations	5/10/73
7130	Law of the Land/Just My Imagination (Running Away with Me)	Undisputed Truth	6/5/73
7131	Hey Girl (I Like Your Style)/Ma	Temptations	7/24/73
7132	I'm Truly Yours/Where Do You Go (Baby)	Eric and the Vikings	10/11/73
7133	Let Your Hair Down/Ain't No Justice	Temptations	11/27/73
7134	Help Yourself/What's Going On	Undisputed Truth	2/14/74
7135	Heavenly/Zoom	Temptations	2/12/74
7136	You've Got My Soul on Fire/I Need You	Temptations	5/16/74
7137	Now You Got It/Part Time Love	Luther Allison	5/28/74
7138	Happy People/Instrumental	Temptations/Temptations Band	11/21/74
7139	I'm a Fool for You/The Girl's Alright with Me	Undisputed Truth	6/25/74
7140	Lil' Red Riding Hood/Big John Is My Name	Undisputed Truth	10/17/74
7141	Earthquake Shake/Spaced Out	Undisputed Truth	NR
7142	Shakey Ground/I'm a Bachelor	Temptations	2/17/75
7143	UFO's/Gotta Get My Hands on Some Lovin'	Undisputed Truth	8/4/75
7144	Glasshouse/The Prophet	Temptations	6/18/75
7145	Higher Than High/Spaced Out	Undisputed Truth	8/4/75
7146	Keep Holding On/What You Need Most (I Do Best of All)	Temptations	1/5/76
7147	Boogie Bump Boogie/I Saw You When You Met Her	Undisputed Truth	10/21/75
7148	Comfort/Share Your Love	Leon Ware	NR
7149	I Want to Make It Easy for You/Two Shoes	Leslie Uggams	4/22/76

7150	Up the Creek (Without a Paddle)/Darling Stand by Me (Song for My Woman)	Temptations	4/29/76
7151	Who Are You (And What Are You Doing the Rest of Your Life)/Darling Stand by Me (Song for My Woman)	Temptations	NR
7152	Who Are You (And What Are You Doing the Rest of Your Life)/Let Me Count the Ways (I Love You)	Temptations	9/23/76
7153	I'm in Love/Don't Fan the Flame	Frankie Kah'rl	11/30/76
7154	Tailgate/Mr. Disco Radio	21st Creation	4/7/77
7155	You Can't Turn Me Off (In the Middle of Turning Me On)/Save It for a Rainy Day [original B-side]	High Inergy	8/2/77
7155	You Can't Turn Me Off (In the Middle of Turning Me On)/Let Me Get Close to You	High Inergy	3/16/78
7156	You and I/Hollywood	Rick James	3/16/78
7157	Love Is All You Need/Some Kinda Magic	High Inergy	—
7158	Girls Let's Keep Dancing Close/Funk Machine	21st Creation	3/21/78
7159	There'll Never Be/You Pulled a Switch	Switch	6/15/78
7160	We Are the Future/High School	High Inergy	4/27/78
7161	Lovin' Fever/Beware	High Inergy	8/3/78
7162	Mary Jane/Dream Maker	Rick James	9/25/78
7163	I Wanna Be Closer/Somebody's Watchin' You	Switch	1/79
7164	High on Your Love Suite/Stone City Bank High	Rick James	2/79
7165	Astro Disco (Pts. 1 and 2)	Apollo	—
7166	Shoulda Gone Dancing/Peaceland	High Inergy	—
7167	Bustin' Out/Sexy Lady	Rick James	4/79
7168	Best Beat in Town/It's So Real	Switch	5/79
7169	I'm a Sucker for Your Love/Deja Vu (I've Been There Before)	Teena Marie	5/79
7170	You Have Inspired Me/—	Mira Waters	8/79
7171	Fool on the Street/Jefferson Ball	Rick James	—
7172	Come and Get It/Midnight Music Man	High Inergy	—
7173	Don't Look Back/I'm Gonna Have My Cake	Teena Marie	—
7174	Skate to the Rhythm/Midnight Music Man	High Inergy	—
7175	I Call Your Name/Best Beat in Town	Switch	9/79
7176	Love Gun/Stormy Love	Rick James	10/79
7177	Come into My Life (Pts. 1 and 2)	Rick James	1/80
7178	I Love Makin' Love (To the Music)/Somebody Somewhere	High Inergy	—
7179	F.I.M.A. (Funk in Mama Afrika)/Strut Your Stuff	Stone City Band	2/80
7180	Can It Be Love/Too Many Colors	Teena Maria	2/80
7181	Don't Take My Love Away (Pts. 1 and 2)	Switch	5/80
7182	Little Runaway/South American Sneeze	Stone City Band	5/80
7183	Power (Pts. 1 and 2)	Temptations	4/80
7184	Behind the Groove/You're All the Boogie I Need	Teena Marie	4/80
7185	Big Time/Island Lady	Rick James	7/80
7186	Rock and Roll Me/You're Moving Out Today	Mira Waters	—
7187	I Love Makin' Love/Make Me Yours	High Inergy	8/80
7188	Struck by Lightning Twice/I'm Coming Home	Temptations	7/80
7189	I Need Your Lovin'/Irons in the Fire	Teena Marie	8/80
7190	My Friend in the Sky/Next to You	Switch	—
7191	Summer Love/Gettin' It On (In the Sunshine)	Rick James	—
7192	Hold on to My Love/If I Love You Tonight	High Inergy	—
7193	Love Over and Over Again/Keep Movin' On	Switch	10/80
7194	Young Love/First Class Love	Teena Marie	1/81
7195	All Day and All of the Night/Instrumental	Stone City Band	1/81
7196	Messin' Up a Good Thing/Face on the Photograph	Nolen and Crossley	'81
7197	Give It to Me Baby/Don't Give Up on Love	Rick James	3/81
7198	—		—
7199	You and I/Get Back with You	Switch	4/81
7200	Freaky/Party Girls	Stone City Band	'81
7201	I Just Wanna Dance with You/Take My Life	High Inergy	5/81
7202	Square Biz/Opus III (Does Anybody Care)	Teena Marie	6/81
7203	What's Your Name/You're So Gentle, So Kind	DeBarge	'81
7204	This Is It/Again	Tony Travalini	'81
7205	Super Freak (Pts. 1 and 2)	Rick James	7/81
7206	—		—
7207	Goin' through the Motions/I Just Can't Help Myself	High Inergy	8/81
7208	Aiming at Your Heart/The Life of a Cowboy	Temptations	8/81
7209	—		—
7210	—		—
7211	Don't Park Your Loving/Now That There's You	High Inergy	'81
7212	It Must Be Love/Yes Indeed	Teena Maria	10/81
7213	Oh What a Night/Isn't the Night Fantastic	Temptations	10/81
7214	I Do Love You/Without You in My Life	Switch	11/81
7215	Ghetto Life/Below the Funk (Pass the J)	Rick James	11/81
7216	Portuguese Love/The Ballad of Cradle, Rob and Me	Teena Marie	11/81

HITSVILLE

The country label that picked up where Motown let the legally troubled Melodyland label off. (45s/LPs)

6032	Solitary Man/Shame	T. G. Sheppard	5/18/76
6033	—	—	—
6034	—	—	—
6035	I Heard a Song/Plans That We Made	Rick Tucker	6/10/76
6036	—	—	—
6037	Texas Woman/It's Gone	Pat Boone	6/10/76
6038	Tragedy/Songs That We Sang as Children	Ronnie Dove	7/15/76
6039	I've Been There Too/She Made Me Love You More	Kenny Seratt	7/15/76
6040	Show Me a Man Just Live Here (We Don't Love Here Anymore)	T. G. Sheppard	8/26/76
6041	The Bad Part of Me/I Hate to Drink Alone	Jerry Naylor	8/26/76
6042	Oklahoma Sunshine/Won't Be Home Tonight	Pat Boone	9/16/76
6043	I Knew You When/One	Jerry Foster	10/7/76
6044	My Eyes Adored You/Devil Woman	Marty Mitchell	10/7/76
6045	Why Daddy/The Morning After the Night Before	Ronnie Dove	11/2/76
6046	The Last Time You Love Me/Born to Fool Around	Jerry Naylor	11/2/76
6047	Lovelight Comes a Shining/Country Days and Country Nights	Pat Boone	11/11/76
6048	May I Spend Every New Year's with You/I'll Always Remember That Song	T. G. Sheppard	11/30/76
6049	Daddy, They're Playing a Song About You/I Threw Away a Rose	Kenny Seratt	1/4/77
6050	I Will/Show Me the Way	Wendel Adkins	1/4/77
6051	She Gives Me Love/Little Sister	Lloyd Schoonmaker	1/25/77
6052	Family Man/Just Another Song Away	Jerry Foster	1/25/77
6053	Lovin' On/I'll Always Remember That Song	T. G. Sheppard	2/3/77
6054	Colorado Country Morning/Don't Want to Fall Away from You	Pat Boone	2/3/77
6055	Texas Moon/Laid Back Country Picker	Wendel Adkins	3/31/77

INFERNO

A Detroit-based indie label that issued discs before and after its brief association with Motown. (45's)

5001	Ain't That Loving You/I Love You Baby	Volumes	5/12/68
5002	Linda Sue Dixon/Tally Ho	Detroit Wheels	4/23/68
5003	Think (About the Good Things)/For the Love of a Stranger	Detroit Wheels	9/10/68

JU-PAR

Another Detroit-based indie label that released records before and after its Motown distribution deal went the way of all flesh. (45s)

8001	Don't Freeze Up/Instrumental	Flavor	2/3/77
8002	Funky Music/Time	Ju-Par Universal Orchestra	4/12/77

M.C.

M.C. was Mike Curb, record business *wunderkind* and former Lt. Governor of California. The country label that bore his initials wasn't nearly so successful. (45s/LPs)

5001	Whatever Happened to the Good Old Honky Tonk/Ain't Goin' Down in the Ground Before My Time	Pat Boone	9/22/77
5002	Julieanne (Where Are You Tonight?)/She Gives Me Love	Wendel Adkins	10/6/77
5003	Like a Gypsy/$10 Room	Marty Cooper	10/11/77
5004	If You Don't Want to Love Her/Love Away Her Memory Tonight	Jerry Naylor	1/5/78
5005	You Are the Sunshine of My Life/Yester-Me, Yester-You, Yesterday	Marty Mitchell	1/19/78
5006	What We Do Two by Two/Broken Bones	Porter Jordan	2/16/78
5007	She's the Trip I've Been On (Since You've Been Gone)/She Only Made Me Love You More	Kenny Serratt	2/16/78
5008	You've Lost That Loving Feeling/Show Me the Way	Wendel Adkins	3/14/78
5009	Neon Riders and Sawdust Gliders/The Very Last Love Letter	Ernie Payne	4/11/78
5010	Rave On/Lady Would You Like to Dance	Jerry Naylor	4/11/78
5011	All Alone in Austin/Virginia	Marty Mitchell	5/11/78
5012	Baby I Need Your Lovin'/Why Not Try Lovin' Me	E. D. Wooford	5/11/78
5013	Angel in Your Eyes (Brings Out the Devil in Me)/Song We Sang As Children	Ronnie Dove	8/3/78
5014	Try Me/Big Red Roses (And Little White Lies)	Kay Austin	7/13/78
5015	The Little Man's Got the Biggest Smile in Town/Another Pretty Country Song	Arthur Blanch	7/13/78

MELODY

After four discs as an R&B subsidiary, this here-and-gone label became Motown's first venture into the country music field. (45s)

101	This Is Our Night/My Inspiration	Creations	7/22/62
102	Dearest One/Fortune Teller Tell Me	Lamont Dozier	6/15/62

103	You'll Never Cherish a Love So True ('Till You Lose It)/There He Is (At My Door)	Vells	10/1/62
104	—	—	—
105	Mind Over Matter/I'll Love You 'Till I Die	Pirates	9/29/62
106	Sugar Cane Curtain/Dingbat Diller	Chuck a Luck	2/7/63
107	Peaceful/Summit Chanted Meeting	Jack Haney and "Nikiter" Armstrong	NR
108	—	—	—
109	The Big Wheel/That Silver Haired Daddy of Mine	Howard Crockett	12/30/63
110	Shambles/Beautiful Women	Gene Henslee	1/21/64
111	Bringing in the Gold/I've Been a Long Time Leaving	Howard Crockett	3/30/64
112	Satisfied Mind/That's What's Happenin'	Bruce Channel	3/30/64
113	Little Acorn/Cold As Usual	Dorsey Burnette	5/4/64
114	You Make Me Happy/You Never Looked Better	Bruce Channel	7/29/64
115	My Lil's Run Off/Spanish Lace and Memories	Howard Crockett	'64
116	Jimmy Brown/Everybody's Angel	Dorsey Burnette	6/24/64
117	Love Makes the World Go Round, But Money Greases the Wheel/Come on Back (And Be My Love Again)	Dee Mullins	1/15/65
118	Ever Since the World Began/Long Long Time Ago	Dorsey Burnette	11/30/64
119	Put Me in Your Pocket/The Miles	Howard Crockett	12/22/64
120	You Only Pass This Way One Time/Rain Is a Lonesome Thing	Hillsiders	3/26/65
121	All the Good Times Are Gone/The Great Titanic	Howard Crockett	4/27/65

MELODYLAND

Motown's second effort at becoming a country powerhouse. Folded into the Hitsville label when an Orange County ministry claimed rights to a name they hadn't bothered to patent. (45s/LPs)

6001	Candy Lips/Young Girl	Pat Boone	10/22/74
6002	Devil in the Bottle/Rollin' with the Flow	T. G. Sheppard	11/7/74
6003	Is This All There Is to a Honky Tonk/You're the One	Jerry Naylor	11/12/74
6004	Please Come to Nashville/Pictures on Paper	Ronnie Dove	2/13/75
6005	Indiana Girl/Young Girl	Pat Boone	2/13/75
6006	Tryin' to Beat the Morning Home/I'll Be Satisfied	T. G. Sheppard	3/14/75
6007	Molly (I Ain't Gettin' Any Younger)/She's Feelin' Low	Dorsey Burnette	4/10/75
6008	The Dessert/Annie	Karen Kelly	4/10/75
6009	Darling Think It Over/I Can't Find It	Terry Stafford	4/10/75
6010	Baby, I Love You Too Much/You've Been Doing Wrong for So Long	Barbara Wyrick	5/15/75
6011	Things/Here We Go Again	Ronnie Dove	5/15/75
6012	He'll Have to Go/Once Again	Jerry Naylor	5/15/75
6013	She Satisfies/How Important Can It Be	Sheila Taylor	5/23/75
6014	If I Could Have It Any Other Way/Not Too Old to Cry	Kenny Seratt	5/23/75
6015	The Biggest Parakeets in Town/I Wasn't Wrong About You	Jud Strunk	5/23/75
6016	Another Woman/I Can't Help Myself (Sugar Pie, Honey Bunch)	T. G. Sheppard	7/18/75
6017	Say Love (Or Don't Say Anything At All)/He Makes the Wrong Seem Right	Darla Foster	9/3/75
6018	I'd Do It with You/Yester Me, Yester You, Yesterday	Pat Boone w/ Shirley Boone	8/20/75
6019	Lyin' in Her Arms Again/Doggone the Dogs	Dorsey Burnette	8/20/75
6020	Prayin' for My Mind/What's a Nice Girl Like You Doing in a Honky Tonk	Jerry Naylor	9/3/75
6021	Drina (Take Your Lady Off For Me)/Your Sweet Love	Ronnie Dove	9/26/75
6022	Reba/(She's A) Fire Out of Control	Terry Stafford	NR
6023	Pity Little Billy Jo/Crazy Love	Barbara Wyrick	9/26/75
6024	Let's Hold on to What We've Got/Truly Great American Blues	Kenny Serratt	9/26/75
6025	Anything to Keep from Going Home/Rubie Is a Groopie	Joey Martin	10/6/75
6026	Take Me (The Way That I Am)/Talk to Jeanette	Ernie Payne	12/29/75
6027	Pamela Brown/They're Tearing Down a Town	Jud Strunk	12/29/75
6028	Motels and Memories/Pigskin Charade	T. G. Sheppard	12/1/75
6029	Glory Train/U.F.O.	Pat Boone	2/6/76
6030	Right or Wrong/Guns	Ronnie Dove	3/9/76
6031	Ain't No Heartbreak/I Dreamed I Saw	Dorsey Burnette	3/9/76

MIRACLE

Some exceptionally good but rare R&B releases to be found here among the lackluster country numbers that made up the bulk of the discs issued. (45s)

1	Don't Feel Sorry for Me/Heart	Jimmy Ruffin	1/31/61
2	When I Need You/Continental Street	Little Eva and Band[1]	NR
3	Blibber Blabber/Don't Say Bye Bye	Gino Parks	NR
4	Rosa Lee/Shoo Ooo	Andre Williams	NR
5	Oh, Mother O Mine/Romance without Finance	Temptations	7/24/61
6	Greetings (This Is Uncle Sam)/Take a Chance	Valadiers	10/23/61
7	Someone to Call My Own/You're My Desire	Equadors	9/15/61

[1] The Little Eva in Question is Raynoma Gordy.

8	Love Me/Darling Tonight	Pete Hartfield	9/15/61
9	Angel in Blue/Blue Cinderella	Joel Sebastian	10/2/61
10	Whose Heart Are You Going to Break Now/I'll Call You	Don McKenzie	1/23/61
11	The Day Will Come/Just for You	Freddie Gorman	10/20/61
12	Check Yourself/Your Wonderful Love	Temptations	11/7/61

MOTOWN

Not the first—unless you wanna get technical and count the Miracles' test pressings—but the biggest of the company's major labels. Still active, naturally. (45s/LPs)

Note: Motown 1000–1011 pink labels with stripes; Motown 1011 to date feature the now-famous map design.

TLX2207[2]	Bad Girl/I Love Your Baby	Miracles	—
1000	My Beloved [MT 12345/MT 1000 G3][3]/Sugar Daddy	Satintones	9/7/61
1001	You Never Miss a Good Thing/Hold Me Tight	Eugene Remus	—
1001	You Never Miss a Good Thing [H55510, L8027990]/Gotta Have Your Lovin'	Eugene Remus	—
1002	Custer's Last Man/Shimmy Gully	Popcorn and the Mohawks	—
1003	Bye Bye Baby/Please Forgive Me	Mary Wells	2/28/61
1004	That's Why I Love You So/Oh Lover	Singin' Sammy Ward and Sherri Taylor	9/23/61
1005	I've Got a Notion/We Really Love Each Other	Henry Lumpkin	1/11/61
1006	Tomorrow and Always [H55596, H625]/A Love That Can Never Be	Satintones	4/24/61
1006	Angel/A Love That Can Never Be	Satintones	—
1007	Don't Let Him Shop Around/A New Girl	Debbie Dean	9/25/61
1008	Whole Lotta Woman/Come on and Be Mine	Contours	2/20/61
1009	Money/I'll Be Around	Richard Wylie	4/6/61
1010	I Know How It Feels/My Kind of Love	Satintones	6/24/61
1011[4]	I Don't Want to Take a Chance/I'm So Sorry	Mary Wells	6/3/61
1012	Funny/The Stretch	Contours	8/22/61
1013	What Is a Man/Don't Leave Me	Henry Lumpkin	1/22/62
1014	But I'm Afraid/Itty Bitty Pity Love	Debbie Dean	8/25/61
1015	I'm Bound/Precious Memories	Gospel Harmonettes	3/7/62
1016	Strange Love/Come to Me	Mary Wells	10/6/61
1017	—	—	—
1018	—	—	—
1019	Real Good Loving/Have I the Right	Richard Wylie	10/20/61
1020	Zing Went the Strings of My Heart/Faded Letter	Satintones	10/20/61
1021	Jamie/Take a Chance on Me	Eddie Holland	1/20/61
1022	White House Twist/Christmas Twist	Twistin' Kings	11/27/61
1023	Congo Twist (Pts. 1 and 2)	Twistin' Kings	12/18/61
1024	The One Who Really Loves You/I'm Gonna Stay	Mary Wells	2/8/62
1025	Everybody's Talking About My Baby/I Cried All Night	Debbie Dean	3/12/62
1026	You Deserve What You Get/Last Night I Had a Vision	Eddie Holland	4/6/62
1027	Your Heart Belongs to Me/(He's) Seventeen	Supremes	5/8/62
1028	Sleep (Little One)/Uptight	Herman Griffin	6/7/62
1029	Mo Jo Hanna/Break Down and Sing	Henry Lumpkin	7/11/62
1030	If Cleopatra Took a Chance/What About Me	Eddie Holland	5/7/62
1031	If It's Love (It's All Right)/It's Not Too Late	Eddie Holland	8/3/62
1032	You Beat Me to the Punch/Old Love (Let's Try It Again)	Mary Wells	7/17/62
1033	Camel Walk/Chaperone [G7009]	Beljeans	NR
1034	Let Me Go the Right Way/Time Changes Things	Supremes	11/5/62
1035	Two Lovers/Operator	Mary Wells	10/29/62
1036	Just a Few More Days/Darling I Hum Our Song	Eddie Holland	1/8/63
1037	Goodbye Cruel Love/Envious	Linda Griner	1/25/63
1038	I'll Make It Up to You Somehow/My Baby Gave Me Another Chance	Amos Milburn	3/4/63
1039	Laughing Boy/Two Wrongs Don't Make a Right	Mary Wells	2/1/63
1040	My Heart Can't Take It Anymore/You Bring Back Memories	Supremes	2/2/63
1041	Oh Freddie/It Hurt Me Too	Connie Van Dyke	3/11/63
1042	Your Old Standby/What Love Has Joined Together	Mary Wells	4/24/63
1043	Baby Shake/Brenda	Eddie Holland	4/24/63
1044	A Breath Taking Guy/Rock and Roll Banjo Man	Supremes	6/12/63
1045	What Goes Up Must Come Down/Come On Home	Holland-Dozier	6/12/63
1046[5]	If Your Heart Says Yes/I'll Cry Tomorrow	Serenaders	NR
1047	Back to School Again/Pig Knuckles	Morocco Muzik Makers	8/23/63
1048	You Lost the Sweetest Boy/What's Easy for Two Is Hard for One	Mary Wells	8/30/63
1049	I'm on the Outside Looking In/I Couldn't Cry If I Wanted To	Eddie Holland	10/16/63
1050	Forget About Me/Devil in His Eyes	Carolyn Crawford	11/6/63
1051	When the Lovelight Starts Shining through His Eyes/Standing at the Crossroads of Love	Supremes	10/31/63

[2] Also appears with the record numbers G1 and G2.
[3] Matrix numbers are listed to indicate where Motown issued two different takes of a song under the same record number.
[4] A few copies of Motown 1011 had the new Motown label with a map showing Detroit.
[5] Issued as VIP 25002.

1052	Leaving Here/Brenda	Eddie Holland	12/19/63
1053	How Can We Tell Him/Better Late than Never	Bobby Breen	1/31/64
1054	Run Run Run/I'm Giving You Your Freedom	Supremes	2/7/64
1055	Right Now/Only You	Sammy Turner	2/14/64
1056	My Guy/Oh Little Boy (What Did You Do to Me)	Mary Wells	3/13/64
1057	Once Upon a Time/What's the Matter with You Baby	Marvin Gaye and Mary Wells	4/14/64
1058	Just Ain't Enough Love/Last Night I Had a Vision	Eddie Holland	4/24/64
1059	You're Just Like You/Here Comes That Heartache	Bobby Breen	1/31/64
1060	Where Did Our Love Go/He Means the World to Me	Supremes	6/17/64
1061	T.G.'s Voodoo Lounge/Snoots 'n' Thangs	Joy Buzzers	9/1/64
1062	Baby I Need Your Loving/Call on Me	Four Tops	7/10/64
1063	Candy to Me/If You Don't Want My Love	Eddie Holland	7/29/64
1064	My Smile Is Just a Frown Turned Upside Down/I'll Come Running	Carolyn Crawford	8/4/64
1065	Whisper You Love Me/I'll Be Available	Mary Wells	NR
1066	Baby Love/Ask Any Girl	Supremes	9/17/64
1067	Sweet Thing/How Can I	Spinners	10/9/64
1068	Come See About Me/Always in My Heart	Supremes	10/27/64
1069	Without the One You Love/Love Has Gone	Four Tops	—
1070	When Someone's Good to You/My Heart	Carolyn Crawford	11/12/64
1071	Our Rhapsody/Talkin' to Your Picture	Tony Martin	11/27/64
1072	Come See About Me/Pride and Joy	Choker Campbell	12/21/64
1073	Ask the Lonely/Where Did You Go	Four Tops	1/5/65
1074	Stop! In the Name of Love/I'm in Love Again	Supremes	2/8/65
1075	Back in My Arms Again/Whisper You Love Me Boy	Supremes	4/15/65
1076	I Can't Help Myself/Sad Souvenirs	Four Tops	4/23/65
1077	Down to Earth/Had You Been Around	Billy Eckstine	5/17/65
1078	I'll Always Love You/Tomorrow May Never Come	Spinners	6/4/65
1079[6]	The Only Time I'm Happy/Supremes Interview	Supremes	NR
1080	Nothing but Heartaches/He Holds His Own	Supremes	7/16/65
1081	It's the Same Old Song/Your Love Is Amazing	Four Tops	7/9/65
1082	The Bigger Your Heart Is/The Two of Us	Tony Martin	8/16/65
1083	I Hear a Symphony/Who Could Ever Doubt My Love	Supremes	10/6/65
1084	Something About You/Darling I Hum Our Song	Four Tops	10/21/65
1085	Children's Christmas Song/Twinkle Twinkle Little Me	Supremes	11/18/65
1086	I Can't Believe You Love Me/Hold Me Oh My Darling	Tammi Terrell	11/15/65
1087	The Touch of Time/You're Gonna Love My Baby	Barbara McNair	11/15/65
1088	Ask Any Man/Spanish Rose	Tony Martin	12/23/65
1089	My World Is Empty without You/Everything Is Good About You	Supremes	12/29/65
1090	Shake Me, Wake Me (When It's Over)/Just As Long as You Need Me	Four Tops	2/2/66
1091	Slender Thread/I Wish You Were Here	Billy Eckstine	3/7/66
1092	What's Easy for Two Is Hard for One/Walk in Silence	Connie Haines	3/11/66
1093	Truly Yours/Where Is That Girl	Spinners	4/8/66
1094	Love Is Like an Itching in My Heart/He's All I Got	Supremes	4/8/66
1095	Come on and See Me/Baby Don'tcha Worry	Tammi Terrell	4/7/66
1096	Loving You Is Sweeter than Ever/I Like Everything About You	Four Tops	5/9/66
1097	You Can't Hurry Love/Put Yourself in My Place	Supremes	7/25/66
1098	Reach Out, I'll Be There/Until You Love Someone	Four Tops	8/18/66
1099	Everything Is Good About You/What a Day	Barbara McNair	9/12/66
1100	And There You Were/A Warmer World	Billy Eckstine	9/12/66
1101	You Keep Me Hanging On/Remove This Doubt	Supremes	10/12/66
1102	Standing in the Shadows of Love/Since You've Been Gone	Four Tops	11/28/66
1103	Love Is Here and Now You're Gone/There's No Stopping Us Now	Diana Ross and the Supremes	1/11/67
1104	Bernadette/I Got a Feeling	Four Tops	2/16/67
1105	I Wonder Why/I've Been Blessed	Billy Eckstine	4/6/67
1106	Here I Am Baby/My World Is Empty without You	Barbara McNair	3/16/67
1107	The Happening/All I Know About You	Diana Ross and the Supremes	3/20/67
1108	Chained/Don't Let It Happen to Us	Paul Petersen	5/11/67
1109	For All We Know/I Cross My Heart	Spinners	5/11/67
1110	7 Rooms of Gloom/I'll Turn to Stone	Four Tops	5/4/67
1111	Reflections/Going Down for the Third Time	Diana Ross and the Supremes	7/24/67
1112	Steal Away Tonight/For Once in My Life	Barbara McNair	NR
1113	You Keep Running Away/If You Don't Want My Love	Four Tops	8/29/67
1114	From Head to Toe/The Beginning of the End	Chris Clark	9/7/67
1115	Oh What a Good Man He Is/There Are Things	Tammi Terrell	NR
1116	In and Out of Love/I Guess I'll Always Love You	Diana Ross and the Supremes	10/25/67
1117	You Haven't Seen My Love/Happy Days	Ones	11/13/67
1118	(You Can't Let the Boy Overpower) The Man in You/Girls, Girls, Girls	Chuck Jackson	2/1/68
1119	Walk Away Renee/Your Love Is Wonderful	Four Tops	1/18/68
1120	Thank You Love/Is Anyone Here Going My Way	Billy Eckstine	2/6/68
1121	Whisper You Love Me Boy/The Beginning of the End	Chris Clark	2/13/68
1122	Forever Came Today/Time Changes Things	Diana Ross and the Supremes	2/29/68

[6]Issued as a promotional record on the George Alexander Inc. label

1123	Where Would I Be Without You/For Once in My Life	Barbara McNair	3/26/68
1124	If I Were a Carpenter/Wonderful Baby	Four Tops	4/11/68
1125	What the World Needs Now/Your Kiss of Fire	Diana Ross and the Supremes	NR
1126	Some Things You Never Get Used To/You're Been So Wonderful to Me	Diana Ross and the Supremes	5/21/68
1127	Yesterday's Dreams/For Once in My Life	Four Tops	6/27/68
1128	His Eyes Is on the Sparrow/Just a Closer Walk with Thee	Marvin Gaye/Gladys Knight and the Pips	9/10/68
1129	A Little Bit for Sandy/Your Love's Got Me Burnin' Alive	Paul Peterson	8/8/68
1130	Don't Let Me Lose This Dream/I've Been Good to You	Ones	8/22/68
1131	For Love of Ivy/A Woman	Billy Eckstine	8/9/68
1132	I'm in a Different World/Remember When	Four Tops	9/19/68
1133	You Could Never Love Him/Fancy Passes	Barbara McNair	10/1/68
1134	I Wouldn't Change the Man He Is/I'll Always Love You	Blinky	11/7/68
1135	Love Child/Will This Be the Day	Diana Ross and the Supremes	9/30/68
1136	Bad Bad Weather (Till You Come Home)/Together We Can Make Such Sweet Music	Spinners	10/24/68
1137	I'm Gonna Make You Love Me/A Place in the Sun	Diana Ross and the Supremes and the Temptations	11/21/68
1138	Just Too Much to Hope For/This Old Heart of Mine	Tammi Terrell	12/6/68
1139	I'm Living in Shame/I'm So Glad I Got Somebody	Diana Ross and the Supremes	1/6/69
1140	My Whole World Ended (The Moment You Left Me)/I've Got to Find Myself a Brand New Baby	David Ruffin	1/20/69
1141	Muck-Arty-Park/Green Grow the Lilacs	Soupy Sales	1/21/69
1142	I'll Try Something New/The Way You Do the Things You Do	Diana Ross and the Supremes and the Temptations	2/20/69
1143	My Cup Runneth Over/Ask the Lonely	Billy Eckstine	NR
1144	Are You Lonely for Me/Your Wonderful Love	Chuck Jackson	3/12/69
1145	For Better or Worse/Don't Mess with Bill	Jonah Jones	NR
1146	The Composer/The Beginning of the End	Diana Ross and the Supremes	3/27/69
1147	What Is a Man/Don't Bring Back Memories	Four Tops	4/10/69
1148	No Matter What Sign You Are/The Young Folks	Diana Ross and the Supremes	5/9/69
1149	I've Lost Everything I Ever Loved/We'll Have a Good Thing Going On	David Ruffin	9/20/69
1150	Stubborn Kind of Fellow/Try It Baby	Diana Ross and the Supremes and the Temptations	NR
1151	The Luney Landing/The Luney Take-Off	Captain Zap and the Motortown Cut Ups	7/16/69
1152	Honey Come Back/What Am I Going to Do without You	Chuck Jackson	8/8/69
1153	The Weight/For Better or Worse	Diana Ross and the Supremes and the Temptations	8/21/69
1154	Midnight Cowboy/Green Grow the Lilacs	Joe Harnell	9/25/69
1155[7]	In My Diary/At Sundown	Spinners	NR
1156	Someday We'll Be Together/He's My Sunny Boy	Diana Ross and the Supremes	10/14/69
1157	I Want You Back/Who's Lovin' You	Jackson 5	10/7/69
1158	I'm So Glad I Fell for You/I Pray Everyday You Won't Regret Loving Me	David Ruffin	11/18/69
1159	Don't Let Him Take Your Love From Me/The Key	Four Tops	11/6/69
1160[8]	Baby I'll Get It/The Day My World Stood Still	Chuck Jackson	NR
1161	My Cherie Amour/Green Grow the Lilacs	Joe Harnell	1/13/70
1162	Up the Ladder to the Roof/Bill, When Are You Coming Home	Supremes	2/16/70
1163	ABC/The Young Folks	Jackson 5	5/13/70
1164	It's All in the Game/Love (Is the Answer)	Four Tops	3/21/70
1165	Reach Out and Touch (Somebody's Hand)/Dark Side of the World	Diana Ross	4/6/70
1166	The Love You Save/I Found That Girl	Jackson 5	5/13/70
1167	Everybody's Got the Right to Love/But I Love You More	Supremes	6/25/70
1168	How You Gonna Keep It/This Time Last Summer	Blinky	NR
1169	Ain't No Mountain High Enough/Can't It Wait Until Tomorrow	Diana Ross	7/16/70
1170	Still Water (Love)/Still Water (Peace)	Four Tops	8/6/70
1171	I'll Be There/One More Chance	Jackson 5	8/28/70
1172	Stoned Love/Shine on Me	Supremes	10/15/70
1173	River Deep, Mountain High/Together We Can Make Such Sweet Music	Supremes and the Four Tops	11/5/70
1174	Santa Claus Is Comin' to Town/Christmas Won't Be the Same This Year	Jackson 5	11/25/70
1175	Just Seven Numbers (Can Straighten Out My Life)/I Wish I Were Your Mirror	Four Tops	12/28/70
1176	Remember Me/How About You	Diana Ross	12/8/70
1177	Mama's Pearl/Darling Dear	Jackson 5	1/7/71
1178	Each Day Is a Lifetime/Don't Stop Loving Me	David Ruffin	2/4/71
1179	Never Can Say Goodbye/She's Good	Jackson 5	3/16/71
1180	Strung Out/Sounds of the Zodiac	Gordon Staples and the String Things	3/23/71
1181	You Gotta Have Love in Your Heart/I'm Glad About It	Supremes and the Four Tops	5/11/71
1182	Nathan Jones/Happy Is a Bumpy Road	Supremes	4/15/71
1183	Melodie/Someday We'll Be Together	Bobby Darin	'71

[7] Issued on VIP 25050
[8] Issued on VIP 25052

1184	Reach Out (I'll Be There)/Close to You	Diana Ross	4/8/71
1185	In These Changing Times/Right Before My Eyes	Four Tops	5/27/71
1186	Maybe Tomorrow/I Will Find a Way	Jackson 5	6/22/71
1187	You Can Come Right Back to Me/Dinah	David Ruffin	7/20/71
1188	Surrender/I'm a Winner	Diana Ross	7/29/71
1189	MacArthur Park (Pts. 1 and 2)	Four Tops	8/10/71
1190	Touch/It's So Hard for Me to Say Goodbye	Supremes	9/7/71
1191	Got to Be There/Maria (You Were the Only One)	Michael Jackson	10/7/71
1192	I'm Still Waiting/A Simple Thing Like Cry	Diana Ross	10/13/71
1193	I'll Be Your Baby Tonight/Simple Song of Freedom	Bobby Darin	11/24/71
1194	Sugar Daddy/I'm So Happy	Jackson 5	11/23/71
1195	Floy Joy/This Is the Story	Supremes	'71
1196	A Simple Game/L.A. My Town	Four Tops	1/4/72
1197	Rockin' Robin/Love Is Here and Now You're Gone	Michael Jackson	2/17/72
1198	I Can't Quit Your Love/Happy (Is a Bumpy Road)	Four Tops	4/20/72
1199	Little Bitty Pretty One/If I Have to Move a Mountain	Jackson 5	4/4/72
1200	Automatically Sunshine/Precious Little Things	Supremes	4/11/72
1201	That's How Love Goes/I Lost My Love in the Big City	Jermaine Jackson	7/14/72
1202	I Wanna Be Where You Are/We've Got a Good Thing Going	Michael Jackson	5/2/72
1203	Sail Away/Hard Hearted Woman	Bobby Darin	6/2/72
1204	A Little More Trust/A Day in the Life of a Working Man	David Ruffin	6/8/72
1205	Lookin' through the Windows/Love Song	Jackson 5	6/23/72
1206	Your Wonderful Sweet Sweet Love/The Wisdom of Time	Supremes	7/11/72
1207	Ben/You Can Cry on My Shoulder	Michael Jackson	7/12/72
1208	The Good Things/Me and My Brother	Naturals	9/20/72
1209	Duck You Sucker/It Happened on a Sunday	Jerry Ross Symposium	7/28/72
1210	It's the Way Nature Planned It/I'll Never Change	Four Tops	8/1/72
1211	Good Morning Heartache/God Bless the Child	Diana Ross	12/18/72
1212	Average People/Something in Her Love	Bobby Darin	11/3/72
1213	I Guess I'll Miss the Man/Over and Over	Supremes	9/15/72
1214	Corner of the Sky/To Know	Jackson 5	10/2/72
1215	Take It Out on Me/It's the Same Old Song	Jerry Ross Symposium	NR
1216	Daddy's Home/Take Me in Your Arms	Jermaine Jackson	11/15/72
1217	Happy/Something in Your Arms	Bobby Darin	11/20/72
1218	With a Child's Heart/Morning Glow	Michael Jackson	4/12/73
1219	Love Theme from "Lady Sings the Blues"/Any Happy Home	Diana Ross	1/30/73
1220	Don't Explain/C.C. Ryder	Gil Askey	2/15/73
1221	No Time at All/Time (To Believe in Each Other)	Irene Ryan	2/19/73
1222	Brother's Gonna Work It Out/I Choose You	Willie Hutch	2/14/73
1223	Blood Donors Needed/Go on with Your Bad Self	David Ruffin	2/27/73
1224	Hallelujah Day/You Made Me What I Am	Jackson 5	2/26/73
1225	Bad Weather/Oh Be My Love	Supremes	3/22/73
1226	Shame and Scandal in the Family/Never Been to Spain	Vin Cardinal	NR
1227	—	—	—
1228	I'll See You Through/Help the People	Ruben Howell	4/26/73
1229	Thinkin' Bout My Baby/Best Friends	Martin and Finley	'73
1230	Boogie Man/Don't Let Your Baby Catch You	Jackson 5	NR
1231	I See Your Name Up in Lights/When Yesterday Was Tomorrow	Irene Ryan	NR
1232	—	—	—
1233	Tangle in Your Life Line/This Man of Mine	Blinky	5/10/73
1234	No Matter Where You Are/Have I Lost You	G. C. Cameron	5/1/73
1235	Together We Can Make Sweet Music/Bad Bad Weather	Supremes	4/3/73
1236	Woman in My Eyes/Every Little Bit Hurts	Stacie Johnson	7/10/73
1237	Time for Me to Go/Zip-A-Dee-Doo-Dah	Suzee Ikeda	4/3/73
1238	Since I Met You There's No Magic/The Circle Again	Celebration	NR
1239	Touch Me in the Morning/I Won't Last a Day without You	Diana Ross	5/3/73
1240	Darlin' Christina/All American Boy and His Dog	Severin Browne	NR
1241	When the Hurt Is Put Back on You/Sending Good Vibrations	Different Shades of Brown	7/24/73
1242	It's Another Sunday/Best Friends	Martin and Finley	5/29/73
1243	Plainsville U.S.A./High Road	Jimmy Randolph	'73
1244	You're in Good Hands/Does Your Mama Know About Me	Jermaine Jackson	9/11/73
1245	Piano Man/I'm Just a Part of Yesterday	Thelma Houston	3/29/73
1246	Let's Make Love Now/I've Given You the Best Years of My Life	Art & Honey	7/5/73
1247	Follow Me—Mother Nature/And I Thought You Loved Me	Marbaya	7/31/73
1248	Let Me Down Easy/It's Always Me	Stoney	4/26/73
1249	Sunshine Man/Soul Long	Earthquire	7/31/73
1250	Rollin' Down a Mountain Side/It's Just a Phase	3rd Creation	7/26/73
1251	You've Got Your Troubles/Listening to Yesterday	Franki Valli	5/29/73
1252	Slick/Mother's Theme	Willie Hutch	6/21/73
1253	There'll Be No City on the Hill/Never Been to Spain	Vin Cardinal	6/26/73
1254	Hey Man—We Gotta Get You a Woman/How Can I Forget You	Four Tops	NR
1255	How Come/Life and Breath	Four Seasons	5/29/73
1256	Why Can't You Be Mine/Baby Don't You Know	Gloria Jones	2/5/74

1257[9]	Truly Yours/Where Do You Go Baby	Eric and the Vikings	NR
1258	Darlin' Christina/Snowflakes	Severin Browne	8/24/73
1259	Common Man/I'm Just a Mortal Man	David Ruffin	7/31/73
1260	Do You Know Where You're Going/Together	Thelma Houston	9/25/73
1261	Let Me Down Easy/Time	G. C. Cameron	9/25/73
1262	Relove/Give It One More Try	Charlene Duncan	—
1263	That's How It Was from the Start/It's So Sad	Devastating Affair	11/15/73
1264	Lady/You Make Me Happy	Puzzle	7/5/73
1265	God Bless Conchita/Song of Long Ago	Riot	9/4/73
1266	—	—	—
1267	—		
1268	Are You Happy/There's a Song in My Heart	Commodores	8/24/73
1269	My Mistake/Include Me in Your Life	Diana Ross and Marvin Gaye	1/17/74
1270	Doggin' Around/Up Again	Michael Jackson	NR
1271	To a Gentler Time/Can't Give Back the Love	Diahann Carroll	NR
1272	Still Holding On/Say It Like the Children	C. P. Spencer	NR
1273	—	—	—
1274	When You Take Another Chance/Can't Stop the Man	Reuben Howell	10/30/73
1275	My Love Is Yours Until the End of Time/You've Got My Mind	Sisters Love	9/13/73
1276	You've Got My Soul on Fire/Love the Lonely People Prayer	Edwin Starr	8/21/73
1277	Get It Together/Touch	Jackson 5	8/3/73
1278	Last Time I Saw Him/Save the Children	Diana Ross	12/6/73
1279	And I Will Love You (The Scalliwag Song)/Listening to Yesterday	Frankie Valli	'73
1280	You're a Special Part of Me/I Think I'm Falling in Love	Diana Ross and Marvin Gaye	9/13/73
1281	I'd Hate Myself in the Morning/Take My Word	Zell Black	NR
1282	Sunshine Lady/I Just Wanted to Make Her Happy	Willie Hutch	10/18/73
1283	Mary Mary/On with the Show	Puzzle	11/8/73
1284	Ain't It Hell Up in Harlem/Don't It Feel Good to Be Free	Edwin Starr	12/20/73
1285	All That Love Went to Waste/Give It One More Try	Charlene Duncan	1/17/74
1286	Dancing Machine/It's Too Late to Change the Time	Jackson 5	2/19/74
1287	If You Ain't Got No Money (Pts. 1 and 2)	Willie Hutch	1/24/74
1288	Hickory/Charisma	Four Seasons	2/21/74
1289	Roxanne/Roll It Over	Mike Campbell	2/21/74
1290	I've Been Had by the Devil/Confessions (Gotta Get Back to Myself)	Zell Black	2/26/74
1291	You're My Life/Gonna Find a True Love	Bottom and Co.	2/28/74
1292	Foxy Brown/Love Theme	Willie Hutch	3/19/74
1293	Dan the Banjo Man/Londonderry	Dan the Banjo Man	2/19/74
1294	White Bird/He Still Plays On	Martin and Finley	4/23/74
1295	Sleepin'/You	Diana Ross	4/4/74
1296	Don't Knock My Love/Just Say Just Say	Diana Ross and Marvin Gaye	6/18/74
1297	Come Get My Stuff/Black Maybe	Syreeta	6/11/74
1298	Where Were You When the Ship Went Down/Tidal Wave	Dickie and the Poseidons	3/28/74
1299	—	—	—
1300	Big Papa/Like We Used to Be	Edwin Starr	4/23/74
1301	Streakin' Down the Avenue/Commercial Break	Matrix	'74
1302	Everybody Wants to Be Somebody/State of Mind	Puzzle	5/2/74
1303	Love Song/Snow Flakes	Severin Browne	7/25/74
1304	I Need Your Love/Movin' from the City	Xit	5/13/74
1305	Rings/I'll Bell Your Brother	Reuben Howell	5/15/74
1306	Funky Music Sho Nuff Turns Me On/Let Your Hair Down	Yvonne Fair	5/28/74
1307	Machine Gun/There's a Song in My Heart	Commodores	4/23/74
1308	Whatever You Got I Want/I Can't Quit Your Love	Jackson 5	10/1/74
1309	Spread the News/Love Pain	Bottom and Co.	9/19/74
1310	I Am Love (Pts. 1 and 2)	Jackson 5	12/23/74
1311	If You Don't Love Me/Topics	G. C. Cameron	10/1/74
1312	Just Beyond/It's Been Oh So Long	Riot	NR
1313	I've Been There Before/Can't Give Back the Love	Diahann Carroll	NR
1314	Please Mr. Postman/Friend	Boone Family	'74
1315	Where Do I Belong/Penny Annie Fortune Lady	3rd Creation	NR
1316	You've Been Doing Wrong for So Long/Pick of the Week	Thelma Houston	8/1/74
1317	I'm Going Left/Heavy Day	Syreeta	6/11/74
1318	Put Your Gun Down Brother/It's Been Oh So Long	Riot	8/1/74
1319	I Feel Sanctified/It's As Good As You Make It	Commodores	10/1/74
1320	Renegade/Cement Prairie	Xit	NR
1321	You Don't Know How Hard It Is to Make It/Instrumental	Devastating Affair	8/15/74
1322	High Tide/Don't Make Me Wait Too Long	Allens	NR
1323	Walk Out the Door If You Wanna/It Should Have Been Me	Yvonne Fair	9/12/74
1324	Shoe Shoe Shine/Release Me	Dynamic Superiors	8/22/74
1325	Constant Disappointment/I Believe (When I Fall In Love It Will Be Forever)	Reuben Howell	9/19/74
1326	Who's Right or Wrong/Lonely Rainy Days in San Diego	Edwin Starr	10/1/74

[9]Issued on Gordy 7132

1327	Me and Rock and Roll Are Here to Stay/Smiling Faces (Sometimes)	David Ruffin	10/10/74
1328	Your Kiss Is Sweeter [or] Just a Little Piece of You/Spinnin' and Spinnin'[10]	Syreeta	NR
1329	What Becomes of a Broken Heart/Baby I've Got It	Jimmy Ruffin	1/8/75
1330	Power Is/Take It Now	Stephen Cohn	1/2/75
1331	I'm Gonna Stay/Woman You Touched Me	Willie Hutch	NR
1332	Take Me Clear from Here/I Just Want to Celebrate	David Ruffin	NR
1333	Romance/Sweet Sound of Your Song	Severin Browne	1/31/75
1334	When the Lovelight Starts Shining through His Eyes/Viva Espana	Boones	2/26/75
1335	Sorry Doesn't Always Make It Right/Together	Diana Ross	2/11/75
1336	Superstar/No Matter Where You Are	David Ruffin	1/31/75
1337	Do You Wanna Do a Thing/Ticket to the Moon	Bottom and Co.	4/2/75
1338	Slippery When Wet/The Bump	Commodores	4/2/75
1339	Get Ready for the Get Down/Don't Let Nobody Tell You How to Do Your Thing	Willie Hutch	1/31)75
1340	A Bird in the Hand/California Music	Allens	3/27/75
1341	We're Almost There/Take Me Back	Michael Jackson	2/6/75
1342	Leave It Alone/One Nighter	Dynamic Superiors	3/3/75
1343	All I Wanna Do/For You	Sue Shifrin	3/12/75
1344	It's Bad for Me to See You/You Can't Judge a Book	Yvonne Fair	4/17/75
1345	You've Got to Try a Little Love/Static Free	Bob Horn	5/6/75
1346	Love City/—	Kathe Green	4/17/75
1347	If You're Ever Gonna Love Me/Tippin'	G. C. Cameron	4/17/75
1348	—	—	—
1349	Just a Little Bit of You/Dear Michael	Michael Jackson	4/29/75
1350	It's All Been Said Before/—	Supremes	NR
1351	High Tide/California Music	Allens	'75
1352	Country Boy/What Does It Take	Jr. Walker and the All Stars	5/8/75
1353	Harbour Love/Cause We've Ended As Lovers	Syreeta	5/23/75
1354	Love Ain't No Toy/You Can't Judge a Book	Yvonne Fair	5/16/75
1355	Good Lovin' Is Just a Dime . . ./Nothin' Can Take the Place . . .	Originals	5/23/75
1356	Forever Came Today/All I Do Is Think of You	Jackson 5	6/10/75
1357	Romeo/I Got Away	Dynamic Superiors	NR
1358	He's My Man/Give Out, But Don't Give Up	Supremes	6/12/75
1359	Nobody's Gonna Change Me/I Got Away	Dynamic Superiors	7/18/75
1360	Love Power/Talk to Me	Willie Hutch	7/9/75
1361	This Is Your Life/Look What You've Done to Me	Commodores	8/18/75
1362	Control Tower/Scratchin'	Magic Disco Machine	7/29/75
1363	Here for the Party/Ticket to the Moon	Bottom and Co.	8/18/75
1364	It's So Hard to Say Goodbye to Yesterday/Haulin'-Cold Blooded	G. C. Cameron	8/12/75
1365	Deception/One Nighter	Dynamic Superiors	9/5/75
1366	Wide Open/—	Commodores	NR
1367	Wait Until September/Dreamtime Lover	Chip Hand	8/14/75
1368	Come Live with Me/Share My Love	Leon Ware	NR
1369	Since I Met You/Motion	Lenny Williams	9/11/75
1370	50 Years/Financial Affair	Originals	NR
1371	Party Down/Just Another Day	Willie Hutch	'75
1372	Beautiful Changes/What Kind of Man Are You	Kathe Green	10/14/75
1373	Spirit of '76 (I Am America)/Southern Comfort	William Goldstein	12/29/75
1374	Where Do I Go from Here/Give Out but Don't Give Up	Supremes	9/5/75
1375	Body Language/Call of the Wild	Jackson 5	NR
1376	Walk Away from Love/Love Can be Hazardous . . .	David Ruffin	10/21/75
1377	Theme from "Mahogany" (Do You Know Where You're Going To)/No One's Gonna Be a Fool Forever	Diana Ross	9/24/75
1378	First Round Knock Out/Looky Looky (Look at Me Girl)	Joe Frazier	9/17/75
1379	Everybody's Got to Do Something/Instrumental	Originals	11/25/75
1380	I'm So Glad/Hot Shot	Jr. Walker	NR
1381	Sweet Love/Better Never than Forever	Commodores	11/25/75
1382	This Empty Place/I See You for the First Time	Stephanie Mills	12/1/75
1383	Whole New Thing/What Am I Gonna Do (With My Life)	Rose Banks	4/1/76
1384	It Should Have Been Me/Tell Me Something Good	Yvonne Fair	1/30/76
1385	The Bingo Long Song (Steel on Home)/Razzle Dazzle (Instrumental)	Thelma Houston/William Goldstein	6/10/76
1386	She's the Ideal Girl/I'm So Glad You Chose Me	Jermaine Jackson	NR
1387	I Thought It Took a Little Time (But Today I Fell in Love)/After You	Diana Ross	2/20/76
1388	Heavy Love/Love Can Be Hazardous to Your Health	David Ruffin	2/6/76
1389	My Guy/When the Lovelight Starts Shining through His Eyes	Boones	2/27/76
1390	Love City/What Kind of Man Are You	Kathe Green	2/13/76
1391	I'm Gonna Let My Heart Do the Walking/Early Morning Love	Supremes	3/16/76
1392	Love Hangover/Kiss Me Now	Diana Ross	3/16/76
1393	Everything's Coming Up Love/No Matter Where	David Ruffin	5/18/76
1394	Come Inside/Time	Commodores	NR

[10] Neither A-side was released.

1395	—	—	—
1396	Selling My Heart to the Junkman/Love Proposition	Ronnie McNair	8/5/76
1397	Dream Lady/Tippin'	G. C. Cameron	7/29/76
1398	One Love in My Lifetime/Smile	Diana Ross	7/8/76
1399	High on Sunshine/Thumpin' Music	Commodores	NR
1400	Midnight Rhapsody (Pts. 1 and 2)	William Goldstein and the Magic Disco Machine	7/15/76
1401	Let's Be Young Tonight/Bass Odyssey	Jermaine Jackson	8/5/76
1402	Just to Be Close to You/Thumpin' Music	Commodores	8/9/76
1403	The Devil in Mrs. Jones/Don't Wanna Be Reminded	Jerry Butler	8/19/76
1404	Right's Alright/Darling Baby	Rose Banks	9/16/76
1405	On and Off/Status of a Fool	David Ruffin	9/16/76
1406	Let Me Be the One Baby/She's Just Doing Her Thing	Willie Hutch	9/16/76
1407	You're My Driving Wheel/You're What's Missing in My Life	Supremes	9/30/76
1408	Fancy Dancer/Cebu	Commodores	11/18/76
1409	You Need to Be Loved/My Touch of Madness	Jermaine Jackson	9/22/77
1410	Have You Ever Seen Them Shake (Shake It Baby)/It Won't Be Long (When We're All Gone)	Ronny McNair	11/11/76
1411	Shake It, Shake It/I Feel Like We Can Make It	Willie Hutch	11/9/76
1412	You're What's Missing in My Life/Kiss Me When You Want To	G. C. Cameron	2/8/77
1413	I Can't Stay Away (From Someone I Love)/Supersensuousensation (Try Some Love)	Dynamic Superiors	1/11/77
1414	I Wanna Do It to You/Don't Wanna Be Reminded	Jerry Butler	1/25/77
1415	Let Yourself Go/You Are the Heart of Me	Supremes	1/25/77
1416	We Gonna Have a House Party/I Never Had It So Good	Willie Hutch	3/8/77
1417	Do It For Me/Boogie Boogie Love	Jennifer	4/14/77
1418	Easy/Can't Let You Tease Me	Commodores	5/5/77
1419	Nowhere to Run (Pts. 1 and 2)	Dynamic Superiors	6/21/77
1420	Just Let Me Hold You for a Night/Rode by the Place (Where We Used to Stay)	David Ruffin	6/30/77
1421	Chalk It Up/I Don't Want Nobody to Know	Jerry Butler	6/21/77
1422	It's a Lifetime Thing/Kiss Me Now	Thelma Houston and Jerry Butler	7/21/77
1423	Those Other Men/What Have They Done (To My Home Town)	Albert Finney	6/23/77
1424	We Gonna Party Tonight/Precious Pearl	Willie Hutch	7/21/77
1425	Brick House/Captain Quick Draw	Commodores	8/11/77
1426	Let's Make a Deal/Love to the Rescue	G. C. Cameron and Syreeta	8/11/77
1426	Let's Make a Deal (Pts. 1 and 2)	G. C. Cameron & Syreeta	—
1427	Gettin' Ready for Love/Confide in Me	Diana Ross	10/11/77
1428	You're What I Need/Here Comes That Feeling Again	Dynamic Superiors	9/8/77
1429	Solar Flight (Opus I)/Money (That's What I Want)	Mandre	9/22/77
1430	When It's Gone/A State of Grace	Albert Finney	10/11/77
1431	When I Looked at Your Face/Fly	Scherrie Payne	10/24/77
1432	Too Hot Ta Trot/Funky Situation	Commodores	11/17/77
1433	What You Gonna Do After the Party/I Feel Like We Can Make It	Willie Hutch	11/17/77
1434	Keep Tryin'/Third World Calling (Opus II)	Mandre	12/8/77
1435	You're My Peace of Mind/Rode by the Place (Where We Used to Stay)	David Ruffin	12/15/77
1436	Your Love Is So Good for Me/Baby It's Me	Diana Ross	1/24/78
1437	You Are the Reason (I Feel Like Dancing)/Slipping into Something New	5th Dimension	1/24/78
1438	I Was Born This Way/Instrumental	Carl Bean	3/9/78
1439	Star Love/I Found the Feeling	3 Ounces of Love	3/14/78
1440	Mind Pleaser/Where Would I Be without You	Cuba Gooding	4/11/78
1441	Castles of Sand/I Love Every Little Thing About You	Jermaine Jackson	4/27/78
1442	You Got It/Too Shy to Say	Diana Ross	4/11/78
1443	Three Times a Lady/Look What You've Done to Me	Commodores	6/8/78
1444	"Good Times" Theme/"Carter Country" Theme	Prime Time	7/13/78
1445	Sticks and Stones (But the Funk Won't Never Hurt You)/Strokin'	Finished Touch	8/10/78
1446	Give Me Some Feeling/Does Your Chewing Gum Lose It's Flavor on the Bedpost Overnight	Three Ounces of Love	7/18/78
1447	Hooked for Life/Gotta Find a Woman	Platinum Hook	7/20/78
1448	Fair Game/Light Years (Opus IV)	Mandre	7/13/78
1449	Top of the World/The Same Love That Made Me Laugh	Diana Ross	NR
1449	Everybody's Gotta Give It Up/You Are the Most Important Person in Your Life	5th Dimension	NR
1449	I Love to See You Dance/You Danced into My Life	Finished Touch	'78
1450	Lovin' Livin' and Givin'/Baby It's Me	Diana Ross	NR
1451	Free Me from My Freedom—Tie Me to a Tree (Handcuff Me)/Instrumental	Bonnie Pointer	9/25/78
1452	Flying High/X-Rated Movie	Commodores	8/31/78
1453	I Love to See You Dance/Trying to Kick the Habit	Finished Touch	—
1454	Do Dat Santa Cruzin/Reed Seed	Grover Washington, Jr.	—
1455	Pops We Love You/Instrumental	Marvin Gaye, Diana Ross, Smokey Robinson, and Stevie Wonder	—

1456	What You Gave Me/Together	Diana Ross	1/79
1457	—	—	—
1458	Just Want to Get the Feel of It/It's Been a Long Long Time	Bloodstone	—
1459	Heaven Must Have Sent You [Disco Mix]/LP Version	Bonnie Pointer	2/79
1460	With You I'm Born Again/Go for It	Billy Preston and Syreeta	—
1461	M 3000 (Opus IV)/Spirit Groove	Mandre	—
1462	The Boss/I'm in the World	Diana Ross	5/79
1463	Down Sound (Pts. 1 and 2)	Finished Touch	—
1464	Give Me Time to Say/Lover What You've Done (To Me)	Platinum Hook	—
1465	Cop An Attitude/My Song in G	Patrick Gammon	—
1466	Sail On/Thumpin' Music	Commodores	7/79
1467	Red Hot/Midnight Dancer	Mary Wilson	—
1468	Roll-Her Skater (Pts. 1 and 2)	Finished Touch	—
1469	Let's Get Serious/Je Vous Aime Beaucoups	Jermaine Jackson	2/80
1470	All I Wanted Was You/It Will Come in Time	Billy Preston	—
1471	It's My House/Sparkle	Diana Ross	11/79
1472	Freakin's Fine/Spirit Groove	Mandre	—
1473	Leavin' Me Was the Best Thing You've Ever Done/When the Day Comes	Scherrie and Susaye	—
1474	Still/Such a Woman	Commodores	9/79
1475	—	—	—
1476	Pinball Playboy/Reach Out for Love	Cook Country	—
1477	With You I'm Born Again/All I Wanted Was You	Billy Preston and Syreeta	—
1478	I Can't Help Myself (Sugar Pie Honey Bunch)/I Wanna Make It (In Your World)	Bonnie Pointer	11/79
1479	Wonderland/Lovin' You	Commodores	12/79
1480	—	—	—
1481	Little Girls and Ladies/Olympiad '84	Cook County	—
1482	Body in Motion (Want Your Body in Motion With Mine)/You Gotta Keep Dancin'	Clifton Dyson	—
1483	Blue Lodge/Struttin'	Dr. Strutt	—
1484	Deep Inside My Soul/I Love To Sing To You	Bonnie Pointer	—
1485	Break It to Me Gently/Secret	Planets	—
1486	Love/Snake Eyes	Grover Washington, Jr.	—
1487	This Is Funkin' Insane/Walk On	Ozone	—
1488	Medley of Hits/Where Did We Go Wrong	Diana Ross and the Supremes/Diana Ross	—
1489	Old Fashioned Love/Sexy Lady	Commodores	6/80
1490	You're Supposed to Keep Your Love for Me/Let It Ride	Jermaine Jackson	7/80
1491	I'm Coming Out/Friend to Friend	Diana Ross	9/80
1492	I Won't Remember Ever Loving You/Hungry	Charlene	—
1493	Leave Me Now/Love's Enough	Black Russian	—
1494	Upside Down/Friend to Friend	Diana Ross	6/80
1495	Heroes/Funky Situation	Commodores	8/80
1496	It's My Turn/Together	Diana Ross	10/80
1497	Move Together/Mystified	Black Russian	9/80
1498	Ecstasie Paradise/Words of Love	Platinum Hook	—
1499	Little Girl Don't You Worry/We Can Put It Back Together	Jermaine Jackson	11/80
1500	Only Love/Shake It Up	Dazz Band	—
1501	Take Me Away/There's More Where That Came From	Temptations	11/80
1502	Jesus Is Love/Mighty Spirit	Commodores	12/80
1503	You Like Me Don't You/Instrumental	Jermaine Jackson	2/81
1504	Theme from "Raging Bull"/Joey's Theme	Joel Diamond	'81
1505	Hope/Sock-It, Rocket	Billy Preston	'81
1506	I Who Have Nothing/Instrumental	Midnight Blue	'81
1507	Invitation to Love/Magnetized	Dazz Band	'81
1508	One More Chance/After You	Diana Ross	3/81
1509	—	—	—
1510	Ozonic Bee Bop/The Preacher's Gone Home	Ozone	'81
1511	A Change Is Gonna Come/You	Billy Preston	'81
1512	One Day in Your Life/Take Me Back	Michael Jackson	3/81
1513	Cryin' My Heart Out for You/To Love Again	Diana Ross	5/81
1514	Lady (You Bring Me Up)/Gettin' It	Commodores	6/81
1515	Knock! Knock!/Sooner or Later	Dazz Band	'81
1516	Flame/Superstar of Love (Instrumental)	Tommy Hill	'81
1517	Everybody Loves Me/The Drought Is Over	Jose Feliciano	'81
1518	Mighty-Mighty/Rock and Roll, Pop and Soul	Ozone	'81
1519	Endless Love/Instrumental	Diana Ross and Lionel Richie	7/81
1520	Searchin'/Hey You	Billy Preston and Syreeta	'81
1521	Gigolette/Instrumental	Ozone	12/81
1522	Just for You (Put the Boogie in Your Body)/Hey You	Billy Preston and Syreeta	'81
1523	Medley of Hits/Where Did We Go Wrong	Supremes	'81
1524	—	—	—
1525	I'm Just Too Shy/All Because of You	Jermaine Jackson	10/81

1526	Shame on You/Look Out Below	Lovesmith	'81
1527	Oh No/Lovin' You	Commodores	9/81
1528	Let the Music Play/Hello Girl	Dazz Band	'81
1529	—	—	—
1530	I Wanna Be Where You Are/Let's Make Love over the Telephone	Jose Feliciano	'81
1531	My Old Piano/Now That You're Gone	Diana Ross	'81
1532	Right in the Middle/Ya Seen One Ya Seen 'Em All	Betty Lavette	'81
1532	Right in the Middle/—	Betty Lavette	—

MOTOWN CONSOLIDATED SERIES

G = Gordy, T = Tamla, M = Motown, ML = Motown Latino, MR = Morocco. Motown Latino is Motown's recent fling at the Spanish-speaking market (45s and LPs), and Morocco is Motown's latest attempt at gaining a foothold in the rock and pop marketplace 45s and LPs. The name stems from MOtown ROCk COmpany, you dig?

1600M	Paradise in Your Eyes/I'm My Brother's Keeper	Jermaine Jackson	2/82
1601T	Tell Me Tomorrow (Pts. 1 and 2)	Smokey Robinson	12/81
1602T	That Girl/All I Do	Stevie Wonder	1/82
1603G	Call on Me/Fallin'	Switch	2/82
1604M	Why You Wanna Try Me/Fallin'	Commodores	1/82
1605M	Do What Cha Wanna/Come on In	Ozone	'82
1606	—	—	—
1607M	I Fooled Ya/You're a Fox (On the Box)	Lovesmith	'82
1608G	Ready or Not/A Place in My Heart	Nolen and Crossley	'82
1609M	Let It Whip/Everyday Love	Dazz Band	4/82
1610T	I Must Be in Love/Wish upon a Star	Syreeta	'82
1611M	I've Never Been to Me/—	Charlene	'82
1612T	Do I Do/Rocket Love	Stevie Wonder	5/82
1613G	First Impressions/Could This Be Love	High Inergy	5/82
1614M	I Can't Stop/Either Way We Lose	Bettye Lavette	—
1615T	Old Fashioned Love/Destiny	Smokey Robinson	3/82
1616G	Standing on the Top (Pts. 1 and 2)	Temptations	4/82
1617	—	—	—
1618M	I Second That Emotion/—	Jose Feliciano	'82
1619G	Dance Wit' Me (Pts. 1 and 2)	Rick James	5/82
1620M	If You Don't Know Me By Now/Completeness	Jean Carn	'82
1621M	It Ain't Easy Coming Down/If I Could See Myself	Charlene	'82
1622M	Keep It Live/This Time It's Forever	Dazz Band	7/82
1623M	Love Changes/Got to Know	O. C. Smith	'82
1624ML	Nunca He Ido A Mi/—	Charlene	'82
1625M	I'm Never Gonna Say Goodbye/I Love You So	Billy Preston	'82
1626M	We Can Never Light That Flame Again/Old Funky Rolls	Diana Ross	'82
1627M	Lil' Suzy/I'm Not Easy	Ozone	7/82
1628M	Let Me Tickle Your Fancy/Maybe Next Time	Jermaine Jackson	7/82
1629M	Strung Out on Motown/Strung Out on Commodores	Regal Funkharmonic Orchestra	—
1630T	Yes It's You Lady/Are You Still Here	Smokey Robinson	6/82
1631G	More on the Inside/Money's Hard to Get	Temptations	7/82
1632G	Wrong Man, Right Touch/Beware	High Inergy	'82
1633ML	Angelito/Esta Vez	Isela Sotelo	'82
1634G	Hard to Get/My Love	Rick James	7/82
1635G	Stop! Don't Tease Me/Hesitated	DeBarge	'83
1636M	I Betcha/—	O. C. Smith	'82
1637M	In and Out/—	Willie Hutch	'82
1638	—	—	—
1639T	Ribbon in the Sky/Black Orchid	Stevie Wonder	8/82
1640	—	—	—
1641G	Journey to Love/—	High Inergy	'82
1642T	You've Got Me Where I Want You/One	Gene Van Buren	'82
1643M	She's Just a Groupie/—	Bobby Nunn	9/82
1644M	Truly/Just Put Some Love in Your Heart	Lionel Richie	10/82
1645G	I Like It/Hesitated	DeBarge	11/82
1646G	She Blew My Mind (69 Times)/Instrumental	Rick James	10/82
1647ML	Samba Pa Ti/Malas Costumbres	Jose Feliciano	'82
1648	—	—	—
1649M	Very Special Part/You're Givin' Me the Runaround	Jermaine Jackson	10/82
1650M	Used to Be/—	Charlene and Stevie Wonder	'82
1651M	Painted Picture/Reach High (Instrumental)	Commodores	11/82
1652G	Let's Stay Together/Charlie's Backbeat	Bobby Militello w/Jean Carn	'82
1653M	Got to Get Up on It/You Need Non-Stop Lovin'	Bobby Nunn	12/82
1654G	Silent Night/Everything for Christmas	Temptations	12/82
1655T	I've Made Love to You 1000 Times/Into Each Rain Some Life Must Fall	Smokey Robinson	1/83

1656	—	—	—
1657M	You Are/You Mean More to Me	Lionel Richie	1/83
1658G	Teardrops/Throwdown	Rick James	'83
1659M	On the One for Fun/Just Believe in Love	Dazz Band	1/83
1660G	All This Love/I'm in Love With Ya	DeBarge	4/83
1661M	Reach High/Sexy Lady	Commodores	2/83
1662G	He's a Pretender/Don't Let Up on the Groove	High Inergy	1/83
1663M	I Want to Go Back There Again/Richie's Song	Charlene	'83
1664M	Bread and Butter/If You Don't Want My Love	Robert John	1/83
1665M	Dancing Machine/I'll Be There	Monalisa Young	'83
1666G	Love on My Mind Tonight/Bring Your Body Home	Temptations	3/83
1667	—	—	—
1668M	Strutt My Thang/Don't Leave Me Now	Ozone	4/83
1669M	Skip to My Lou/I'd Rather Be Gone	Finis Henderson	6/83
1670G	Candy Man/Instrumental	Mary Jane Girls	3/83
1671M	Sexy Sassy/Instrumental	Bobby Nunn	'83
1672M	At 15/Dirty Rats	Kagny and the Dirty Rats	'83
1673	—	—	—
1674M	Let's Find Each Other Tonight/¡Cuidado!	Jose Feliciano	'83
1675T	Forever Is Not Enough/She's Leaving Home	Syreeta	'83
1676M	Cheek to Cheek/Can We Dance	Dazz Band	4/83
1677M	My Love/Round and Round	Lionel Richie	4/83
1678T	Touch the Sky/All My Life's a Lie	Smokey Robinson	4/83
1679M	Lonely Teardrops/¡Cuidado!	Jose Feliciano	5/83
1680M	Party Right Here/Gamble with My Love	Dazz Band	6/83
1681G	Bad Lady/Instrumental	Stone City Band	6/83
1682	—	—	—
1683G	Surface Thrills/Made in America	Temptations	'83
1684T	Blame It on Love/Even Tho'	Smokey Robinson w/Barbara Mitchell	6/83
1685M	Baby I Will/What's the Bottom Line	Michael Lovesmith	7/83
1686	—	—	—
1687G	Cold Blooded/Instrumental	Rick James	7/83
1688G	Back in My Arms Again/So Right	High Inergy	7/83
1689M	Blow the House Down/Ball Baby	Junior Walker	10/83
1690G	All Night Long/Musical Love	Mary Jane Girls	7/83
1691M	Our Hearts (Will Always Shine)/Here I Go Again	Ozone	'83
1692MR	Get Crazy/Hot Shot	Sparks/Malcolm McDowell	8/83
1693G	Ladies Choice/Instrumental	Stone City Band	9/83
1694M	Only You/Cebu	Commodores	8/83
1695M	Private Party/Get It While You Can	Bobby Nunn	9/83
1696M	Lovers/School Girl	Finis Henderson	9/83
1697M	Let's Break/Instrumental	Motor City Crew	'83
1698M	All Night Long/Wandering Stranger	Lionel Richie	9/83
1699	—	—	—
1700T	Don't Play Another Love Song/Wouldn't You Like to Know	Smokey Robinson	10/83
1701M	Joystick/Don't Get Caught in the Middle	Dazz Band	11/83
1702M	Somebody's Watching Me/Instrumental	Rockwell	1/84
1703G	U Bring the Freak Out/Money Talks	Rick James	10/83
1704G	Boys/Instrumental	Mary Jane Girls	10/83
1705G	Time Will Reveal/I'll Never Fall in Love Again	DeBarge	10/83
1706G	I Just Can't Walk Away/Hang	Four Tops	10/83
1707G	Miss Busy Body/Instrumental	Temptations	10/83
1708	—	—	—
1709M	Sweet Remedy/Don't Mess with Bill	Monalisa Young	'83
1710M	Running with the Night/Serves You Right	Lionel Richie	11/83
1711M	Hangin' Out at the Mall/The Lady Killer	Bobby Nunn	12/83
1712T	Work That Body/The Things You're Made Of	Keith and Darrell	3/84
1713G	Silent Night/Everything for Christmas	Temptations	12/83
1714G	Ebony Eyes/You, Her and Me	Rick James and Smokey Robinson/Rick James	11/83
1715G	Don't Look Any Farther/I Thought I Could Handle It	Dennis Edwards w/Siedah Garrett	1/84
1716MR	Flashes/Roses for Lydia	Tiggi Clay	2/84
1717MR	Good Clean Fun/Street Angel	Kidd Glove	3/84
1718M	Make Yourself Right at Home/Sing a Song of Yesterday	Four Tops	'84
1719M	Turn Off the Lights/Been Lovin' You	Commodores	11/83
1720G	Sail Away/Isn't the Night Fantastic	Temptations	2/84
1721G	Jealous/You Are My Heaven	Mary Jane Girls	1/84
1722M	Hello/—	Lionel Richie	2/84
1723G	Love Me in a Special Way/Dance the Night Away	DeBarge	2/84
1724M	Do You Look That Good in the Morning/Sex Maniac	Bobby Nunn	3/84
1725M	Sweep/Bad Girl	Dazz Band	4/84
1726M	Lovequake/Fall in Love	Bobby King	4/84
1727T	You Excite Me/I Love You More (Than I Hate What You Do)	Gene Van Buren	'84

1728MR	The Winner Gets the Heart/Who Shot Zorro	Tiggi Clay	4/84
1729MR	Don't Take the Candy/War of Nerves	Wolf and Wolf	'84
1730G	17/Instrumental	Rick James	6/84
1731M	Obscene Phone Caller/Instrumental	Rockwell	4/84
1732M	Gotta Get Out Tonight/Sorry Won't Cut It	Michael Lovesmith	'84
1733M	Baby Sister/Instrumental	KoKo-Pop	6/84
1734M	We're Both in Love with You/I Want the World to Know He's Mine	Charlene	7/84
1735T	And I Don't Love You/Dynamite	Smokey Robinson	5/84
1736MR	Little Lady/(I've Got A) Little Black Book	Duke Jupiter	4/84
1737G	(You're My) Aphrodisiac/Shake Hands (Come Out Dancin')	Dennis Edwards	5/84
1738M	Hello Detroit/Instrumental	Sammy Davis, Jr.	'84
1739M	Farewell My Summer Love/Call on Me	Michael Jackson	5/84
1740	—	—	—
1741	—	—	—
1742MR	Straight from the Heart (Into Your Life)/Echo	Coyote Sisters	6/84
1743M	Sugar Don't Bite/You Keep Me Hangin' On	Sam Harris	9/84
1744M	Sundown on Sunset/Nothin' but Pocket	Kagny	'84
1745M	I Just Called to Say I Love You/Instrumental	Stevie Wonder	8/84
1746M	Stuck on You/Round and Round	Lionel Richie	6/84
1747M	Close to Me/Love in the Fire	Bobby King w/Alfie Silas	7/84
1748MR	Rescue Me/Me and Michelle	Duke Jupiter	7/84
1749M	I Can't Give Her Up/He Only Looks the Part	Michael Lovesmith	'84
1750MR	Hell Is on the Run/Don't Ever Let Go	Jakata	7/84
1751	—	—	—
1752M	Pretty Mess/Instrumental	Vanity	8/84
1753	—	—	—
1754MR	Talk of the Town/War of Nerves	Wolf and Wolf	'84
1755G	Another Place in Time/Let's Go Up	Dennis Edwards	8/84
1756T	I Can't Find/Gimme What You Want	Smokey Robinson	8/84
1757M	Girl You're So Together/Touch the One You Love	Michael Jackson	8/84
1758M	Candlelight Afternoon/Back in the Race	Phyllis St. James	'84
1759M	I'm in Love with You/On the Beach	Koko-Pop	'84
1760M	Let It All Blow/Now That I Have You	Dazz Band	9/84
1761M	Hit and Run Lover/The Last Song	Charlene	—
1762M	Penny Lover/Tell Me	Lionel Richie	10/84
1763G	You Turn Me On/Fire and Desire	Rick James	10/84
1764	—	—	—
1765G	Treat Her Like a Lady/Isn't the Night Fantastic	Temptations	10/84
1766MR	I've Got a Radio/I'll Do It	Coyote Sisters	10/84
1767M	Mechanical Emotion/Crazy Maybe	Vanity	11/84
1768M	Thin Walls/—	Thomas McClary	11/84
1769M	Love Light in Flight/It's More Than You	Stevie Wonder	11/84
1770	—	—	—
1771M	Hearts on Fire/—	Sam Harris	12/84

MOWEST

The first subsidiary label established after Motown's move to the West Coast, hence the name. (45s/LPs)

5001	I want to Be Humble/My Place	Devastating Affair	1/27/72
5002	What the World Needs Now Is Love—Abraham, Martin and John/The Victors	Tom Clay	6/71
5003	Happiness/I Hope I See It in My Lifetime	Lodi	8/18/71
5004	Zip-A-Dee-Doo-Dah/Bah-Bah-Bah	Suzee Ikeda	10/14/71
5005	Act Like a Shotgun/Girl, I Really Love You	G. C. Cameron	8/30/71
5006	Hey Lordy/Just a Little Bit Closer	Bobby Taylor	11/2/71
5007	Whatever Happened to Love/Baby I Need Your Loving	Tom Clay	10/14/71
5008	I Want to Go Back There Again/Pick of the Week	Thelma Houston	11/2/71
5009	The Zoo (The Human Zoo)/I'm Looking for Love	Commodores	3/16/72
5010	—	—	—
5011	Love Isn't Here (Like It Used to Be)/Poor Fool	Frankie Valli	2/29/72
5012	I'm Gonna Get You (Pts. 1 and 2)	G. C. Cameron	NR
5013	Me and Bobby McGee/No One's Gonna Be a Fool Forever	Thelma Houston	3/28/72
5014	Mr. Fix-It Man/You've Got to Make the Choice	Sisters Love	3/9/72
5015	What It Is, What It Is/You Are That Special One	G. C. Cameron	3/28/72
5016	I Love Every Little Thing About You/Black Maybe	Syreeta	9/20/72
5017	I Can't Give Back the Love I Feel for You/Mind Body and Soul	Suzee Ikeda	6/8/72
5018	Just Not Gonna Make It/Spend Some Time Together	Michelle Aller	8/18/72
5018	The Morning After/Spend Some Time Together	Michelle Aller	—
5019	Money (That's What I Want)/For Your Precious Love	Blinky	6/22/72
5020	Somebody Up There/But I Love Him	Blackberries	NR
5021	To Know You Is to Love You/Happiness	Syreeta	7/5/72
5022	Our Lives Are Shaped by What We Love/Broken Road	Odyssey	8/3/72

5023	Where Do You Go Baby/—	Devastating Affair	NR
5024	—	—	
5025	The Night/Sun Country	Four Seasons	NR
5026	Walk On, Don't Look Back/Sun Country	Frankie Valli and the Four Seasons	8/23/72
5027	What If/There Is a God	Thelma Houston	NR
5028	Spanish Harlem/Papa Hooper's Barrelhouse Groove	Crusaders	10/12/72
5029	She Said That/The Road I Walk	Leslie Gore	10/12/72
5030	You've Got My Mind/Try It, You'll Like It	Sisters Love	NR
5031	Songwriter/Fiddler	Repairs	NR
5032	Glad That You're Not Me/Child He Die	Kubie	NR
5033	T'ain't Nobody's Bizness If Do/What More Can I Do	Blinky	1/3/73
5034	Since I Met You There's No Magic/The Circle Again	Celebration	NR
5034	A House Is Not a Home/—	Celebration	NR
5035	Come Get This Thang/My Woman	G. C. Cameron and Willie Hutch	NR
5036	Don't Wanna Play Pajama Games/Jesus Help Me Find Another Way	G. C. Cameron	1/9/73
5037	When the Brothers Come Marching Home/A Heart Is a House	Nu Page	2/8/73
5038	Don't You Be Worried/Determination	Commodores	1/6/73
5039	Long Life and Success to the Farmer/Half Crazed	Martin and Finley	11/28/72
5040	Angel Got a Book Today/The People in the Family	Mike Campbell	1/23/72
5041	(I Could Never Make) A Better Man Than You/Give Me Your Love	Sisters Love	1/25/73
5042	Give It to Me Sweet Thing/Don't Want to Be One	Leslie Gore	NR
5043	Thinkin' 'Bout My Baby/Best Friends	Martin and Finley	NR
5044[11]	Follow Me—Mother Nature/And I Thought You Loved Me	Music Makers	NR
5045[12]	Let Me Down Easy/It's Always Me	Stoney	NR
5046	If It's the Last Thing I Do/And I Never Did	Thelma Houston	NR
5047[13]	Woman in My Eyes/A Carbon Copy	Stacie Johnson	NR
5048[14]	Let's Make Love Now/(I've Given You) The Best Years of My Life	Art and Honey	NR
5049	—	—	—
5050[15]	Piano Man/I'm Just a Part of Yesterday	Thelma Houston	3/29/73

NATURAL RESOURCES

The three-digit number series were pop and rock issues. The four-digit number series were repackages and reissues of classic Motown tracks. The *From the Vaults* LP is notable in that none of the performances included had been previously issued. (45s/LPs)

6001	Angelina (The Waitress at the Pizzeria)/Ramona	Gaylord and Holiday	12/10/76

PRODIGAL

Another attempt at a pop and rock label with a few stray R&B sides in there, too. (45s/LPs)

611	I Hear Those Church Bells Ringing—Chapel of Love/I Do Love You	Shirley	12/2/74
612	Grandma's Washboard Band/Believing You	Gary U.S. Bonds	1/16/75
613	—	—	
614	Wendy Is Gone/Give Me a Sign	Ronnie McNair	3/15/75
615	Bump in Your Jeans/Such a Long Time	Fox Fire	3/24/75
616	I'd Rather Not Be Loving You/Can't Stop Singin' ('Bout the Boy I Love)	Shirley Alston	5/9/75
617	Body Chains/Instrumental	Eddie Parker	'75
618	After You Give Your All (What Else Is There To Give)/Say That You Love Me Boy	Softouch	7/30/75
619	For Your Love/You Better Come on Down	Ronnie McNair	8/5/75
620	Sagittarian Affair/You Better Come on Down	Ronnie McNair	11/14/75
621	Who's Cheating on Who/I'm in Love	Orange Sunshine	'75
622	Eh! Cumpari/The Little Shoemaker	Gaylord and Holiday	'76
623	Little Dog Heaven/What Ya Gonna Do When the Rain Starts Fallin'	Joe Frazier	4/8/76
624	Funky Cocktail (Pts. 1 and 2)	Disco Stan	4/8/76
625	Wait Until September/Dreamtime Lover	Chip Hand	NR
626	Rich Man, Poor Man/I'll Hold Out My Hand	Rita Graham	6/10/76
627	Minne Ha Ha/Stay with Me	Fantacy Hill	6/29/76
628	The Stripper/Children of Tomorrow	Michael Quatro	NR
629	Imaginary Girl/Two	Dunn & Rubini	1/20/77
630	Diggin' It/Just Keep Laughin'	Dunn & Rubini	6/29/76
631	Pure Chopin/One by One	Michael Quatro	10/21/76
632	It Ain't Easy Comin' Down/On My Way to You	Charlene	11/9/76
633	Freddie/Instrumental	Charlene	3/31/77
634	—	—	—

[11] Same as Motown 1247
[12] Same as Motown 1248
[13] Issued on Motown
[14] Same as Motown 1246
[15] Same as Motown 1245

635	"Star Wars" Theme/Long Version	Graffiti Orchestra	7/7/77
636	I've Never Been to Me/It's Really Nice to Be in Love Again	Charlene	7/28/77
637	Is Your Teacher Cool/Crazy Love	Rare Earth	9/29/77
638	—	—	—
639	Just How Does It Feel/Feelin' Fresh	Fresh	3/29/78
640	Warm Ride/Would You Like to Come Along	Rare Earth	3/29/78
641	Sanity Baby/Your Mama	Fantacy Hill	6/8/78
642	Summertime/Feelin' Fresh	Fresh	6/22/78
643	S.O.S. (Stop Her on Sight)/I Can Feel My Love Risin' (From Future Shock and Beyond)	Rare Earth	'78

RARE EARTH

The company's first real stab at the growing "underground" rock market. In retrospect, the talent roster should've been enough to keep the label afloat today. (45s/LPs)

5005	Private Sorrow/Balloon Burning	Pretty Things	7/14/69
5006	Temptation 'Bout to Get Me/Look Away	Virgil Brothers	8/15/69
5007	In Bed/Reality	Wes Henderson	8/15/69
5008	Love at First Sight/Love You Too	Sounds Nice	9/23/69
5009	St. Louis/Can't Find Love	Easybeats	9/11/69
5010	Generation (Light Up the Sky)/Magic Key	Rare Earth	11/10/69
5011	Can't You Hear the Music Play/I Guess This Is Goodbye	Rustix	11/28/69
5012	Get Ready/Magic Key	Rare Earth	2/18/70
5013	Indiana Wants Me/Love's Your Name	R. Dean Taylor	4/10/70
5014	Come on People/Free Again (Non . . . C'est Rien)	Rustix	4/10/70
5015	Just Another Morning/Arma'Geden	Michael Denton	5/21/70
5016	Marian/Somewhere Up There	Cats	6/4/70
5017	(I Know) I'm Losing You/When Joanie Smiles	Rare Earth	7/9/70
5018	As Long As I've Got You/One Little Teardrop	Danny Hernandez and the Ones	9/16/70
5019	Just Like Me/Bad Side of the Moon	Toe Fat	10/23/70
5020	Coming Apart/Let the Music Play	Allan Nichols	11/12/70
5021	Born to Wander/Here Comes the Night	Rare Earth	11/23/70
5022	Sweet Water/You Keep Me Hangin' On	Brass Monkey	1/7/71
5023	Ain't It a Sad Thing/Back Street	R. Dean Taylor	1/19/71
5024	Don't Pay Me No Mind/Listen to Your Soul	Ken Christie and the Sunday People	2/2/71
5025	Love Makes the World Go Round/Jimmy	Kiki Dee	2/12/71
5026	Gotta See Jane/Back Street	R. Dean Taylor	3/18/71
5027	What You See Is What You Get/She's a Lady	Stoney and Meatloaf	4/14/71
5028	Never Can Say Goodbye/So Far, So Good	Impact of Brass	4/23/71
5029	The Rev. John B. Daniels/Jesus Is the Key	Ken Christie and the Sunday People	6/10/71
5030	Candy Apple Red/Woman Alive	R. Dean Taylor	6/17/71
5031	I Just Want to Celebrate/The Seed	Rare Earth	6/21/71
5032	That's the Way a Woman Is/In the Jungle	Messengers	7/15/71
5033	It Takes All Kinds of People/The Way You Do the Things You Do	Stoney and Meatloaf	7/21/71
5034	My Piece of Heaven/Down Down	Rustix	NR
5035	Walk Down the Path of Freedom/It's Just a Dream	Sunday Funnies	9/9/71
5036	I'm an Easy Rider/Concrete and Clay	My Friends	8/19/71
5037	We All End Up in Boxes/Down Down	Rustix	11/5/71
5038	He Big Brother/Under God's Light	Rare Earth	11/4/71
5039	The Greatest Man Who Ever Lived/A Child Is Waiting	Dave Prince	11/30/71
5040	Out in the Night/Gypsy Eyes	Blue Scepter	1/20/72
5041	Taos New Mexico/Shadow	R. Dean Taylor	3/9/72
5042	I Can Make It Alone/Come Clean	Vincent Dimirco	4/25/72
5043	What'd I Say/Nice to Be with You	Rare Earth	3/23/72
5044	Nihaa Shil Hozho (I Am Happy About You)/End	Xit	4/20/72
5045	Long Way from Home/Why Do You Cry	Howl The Good	4/25/72
5046	Get Me Some Help/If Time Could Stand Still	Chris Holland and T Bone	5/72
5047	Somebody Oughta Turn Your Head Around/Earth People	Crystal Mansion	7/8/72
5048	Good Time Sally/Love Shines Down	Rare Earth	10/5/72
5049	Ballad of the Unloved/Tale of Two Cities	Wolfe	NR
5050	It's Not the Last Time/On with the Show	Puzzle	NR
5051	The Battle Is Over/Take Time to Love Me	John Wagner Coalition	1/25/73
5052	We're Gonna Have a Good Time/Would You Like to Come Along	Rare Earth	12/8/72
5053	Ma/Instrumental	Rare Earth	3/14/73
5054	Hum Along and Dance/Come with Me	Rare Earth	8/21/73
5055	Reservation of Education/Color Nature Gone	Xit	9/11/73
5056	Big John Is My Name/Me	Rare Earth	10/25/73
5057	Chained/Fresh from the Can	Rare Earth	5/16/74
5058	It Makes You Happy/Boogie with Me Children	Rare Earth	10/3/75
5059	Keepin' Me Out of the Storm/Let Me Be Your Sunshine	Rare Earth	8/7/75
5060	Midnight Lady/Walking Schtick	Rare Earth	5/18/76

SOUL

Long-lasting, now defunct, Motown subsidiary label. (45s/LPs)
Note: Soul 35001 to 35019 labels are white with logo in pink on side; Soul 35020 to end-of-run labels are purple/pink swirl design.

35001	Devil with the Blue Dress/Wind It Up	Shorty Long	3/23/64
35002	Since I've Lost You/I Want Her Love	Jimmy Ruffin	7/16/64
35003	Satan's Blues/Monkey Jump	Jr. Walker and the All Stars	8/24/64
35004	You've Got to Change/Bread Winner	Sammy Ward	8/24/64
35005	It's a Crying Shame/Out to Get You	Shorty Long	8/24/64
35006	Soul Stomp/Hot 'n' Tot	Early Van Dyke and the Soul Bros.	9/30/64
35007	Thumpin'/Do the Pig	Merced Blue Notes	NR
35008	Shotgun/Hot Cha	Jr. Walker and the All Stars	1/14/65
35009	All for You/Too Many Fish in the Sea	Earl Van Dyke and the Soul Bros.	NR
35010	Never Say No to Your Baby/Let's Dance	Hit Pack	3/24/65
35011	My Baby/Brown Eyes	Freeman Brothers	3/31/65
35012	Do the Boomerang/Tune Up	Jr. Walker and the All Stars	5/13/65
35013	Shake and Fingerpop/Tune Up	Jr. Walker and the All Stars	7/8/65
35014	I Can't Help Myself/How Sweet It Is	Earl Van Dyke and the Soul Bros.	9/30/65
35015	(I'm a) Road Runner/Shoot Your Shot	Jr. Walker and the All Stars	3/21/66
35016	As Long As There Is L-O-V-E Love/How Can I Say I'm Sorry	Jimmy Ruffin	10/11/65
35017	Cleo's Mood/Baby You Ain't Right	Jr. Walker and the All Stars	12/23/65
35018	The Flick (Pts. 1 and 2)	Earl Van Dyke and the Soul Bros.	11/29/65
35019	Do I Love You/Sweeter As the Days Go By	Frank Wilson	12/31/65
35020	Keep on Lovin' Me/Fight Fire with Fire	Frances Nero	3/11/66
35021	Function at the Junction/Call on Me	Shorty Long	3/17/66
35022	What Becomes of the Brokenhearted/Baby I've Got It	Jimmy Ruffin	6/3/66
35023	Just Walk in My Shoes/Stepping Closer to Your Heart	Gladys Knight and the Pips	6/7/66
35024	How Sweet It Is (To Be Loved By You)/Nothing but Soul	Jr. Walker and the All Stars	7/8/66
35025	These Things Will Keep Me Loving You/Since You've Been Loving Me	Velvelettes	8/25/66
35026	Money (That's What I Want) (Pts. 1 and 2)	Jr. Walker and the All Stars	10/27/66
35027	I've Passed This Way Before/Tomorrow's Tears	Jimmy Ruffin	11/15/66
35028	6 × 6/There Is No Greater Love	Earl Van Dyke and the Soul Bros.	12/21/66
35029	Goodnight Irene/Need Your Lovin' (Want You Back)	Originals	12/27/66
35030	Pucker Up Buttercup/(Dance) Anyway You Wanna	Jr. Walker and the All Stars	1/17/67
35031	Chantilly Lace/Your Love Is Amazing	Shorty Long	1/26/67
35032	Gonna Give Her All the Love I've Got/World So Wide, Nowhere to Hide (From Your Heart)	Jimmy Ruffin	2/23/67
35033	Take Me in Your Arms and Love Me/Do You Love Me Just a Little Honey	Gladys Knight and the Pips	3/16/67
35034	Everybody Needs Love/Stepping Closer to Your Heart	Gladys Knight and the Pips	6/12/67
35035	Don't You Miss Me a Little Bit Baby/I Want Her Love	Jimmy Ruffin	6/29/67
35036	Shoot Your Shot/Ain't It the Truth	Jr. Walker and the All Stars	6/22/67
35037	Window Shopping/California Soul	Messengers	9/7/67
35038	I Got a Feeling/Hurtin' All Over	Barbara Randolph	9/14/67
35039	I Heard It through the Grapevine/It's Time to Go Now	Gladys Knight and the Pips	9/28/67
35040	Night 'Fo Last/Instrumental	Shorty Long	1/11/68
35041	Come See About Me/Sweet Soul	Jr. Walker and the All Stars	11/7/67
35042	The End of Our Road/Don't Let Her Take Your Love from Me	Gladys Knight and the Pips	1/25/68
35043	I'll Say Forever My Love/Everybody Needs Love	Jimmy Ruffin	2/13/68
35044	Here Comes the Judge/Sing What You Wanna	Shorty Long	5/7/68
35045	It Should Have Been Me/You Don't Love Me No More	Gladys Knight and the Pips	5/16/68
35046	Don't Let Him Take Your Love From Me/Lonely Lonely Man Am I	Jimmy Ruffin	6/20/68
35047	I Wish It Would Rain/It's Summer	Gladys Knight and the Pips	8/8/68
35048	Hip City (Pts. 1 and 2)	Jr. Walker and the All Stars	7/23/68
35049	Step by Step (Hand in Hand)/Time Is Passin' By	Monitors	8/22/68
35050	Can I Get a Witness/You Got Me Hurtin' All Over	Barbara Randolph	8/10/68
35051	I Comma Zimba Zio (Here I Stand the Mighty One)/Why Them, Why Me	Abdullah	10/22/68
35052	I Love You Madly/Instrumental	Fantastic Four	9/24/68
35053	Gonna Keep on Trying 'Till I Win Your Love/Sad and Lonesome Feeling	Jimmy Ruffin	11/7/68
35054	I Had a Dream/Ain't No Justice	Shorty Long	2/11/69
35055	Home Cookin'/Mutiny	Jr. Walker and the All Stars	12/23/68
35056	We've Got a Way Out Love/You're the One	Originals	1/16/69
35057	Didn't You Know (You'd Have to Cry Sometime)/Keep an Eye	Gladys Knight and the Pips	2/13/69
35058	I Feel Like I'm Falling in Love Again/Pinpoint It Down	Fantastic Four	3/13/69
35059	Runaway Child Running Wild/Gonna Give Her All the Love I Got	Earl Van Dyke	3/25/69
35060	If You Will Let Me, I Know I Can/Farewell Is a Lonely Sound	Jimmy Ruffin	10/7/69
35061	Green Grow the Lilacs/You're the One	Originals	5/6/69
35062	What Does It Take (To Win Your Love)/Brainwasher (Pt. 1)	Jr. Walker and the All Stars	4/25/69
35063	The Nitty Gritty/Got Myself a Good Man	Gladys Knight and the Pips	6/26/69
35064	A Whiter Shade of Pale/When You are Available	Shorty Long	8/28/69
35065	Just Another Lonely Night/Don't Care Why You Want Me (Long As You Want Me)	Fantastic Four	9/23/69

35066	Baby I'm for Real/The Moment of Truth	Originals	8/12/69
35067	These Eyes/Got to Find a Way to Win Maria Back	Jr. Walker and the All Stars	10/2/69
35068	Friendship Train/Cloud Nine	Gladys Knight and the Pips	10/6/69
35069	The Bells/I'll Wait for You	Originals	1/9/70
35070	Gotta Hold on to This Feeling/Clinging to the Thought She's Coming Back	Jr. Walker and the All Stars	1/29/70
35071	You Need Love Like I Do (Don't You)/You're My Everything	Gladys Knight and the Pips	3/3/70
35072	On the Brighter Side of a Blue World/I'm Gonna Carry On	Fantastic Four	4/23/70
35073	Do You See My Love (For You Growing)/Groove and Move	Jr. Walker and the All Stars	6/17/70
35074	We Can Make It Baby/I Like Your Style	Originals	7/7/70
35075	Stay a Little Longer/We Should Never Be Lonely My Love	Yvonne Fair	7/9/70
35076	Stand by Me/Your Love Was Worth Waiting For	David and Jimmy Ruffin	9/22/70
35077	Maria (You Were the Only One)/Living in a World I Created for Myself	Jimmy Ruffin	12/28/70
35078	If I Were Your Woman/The Tracks of My Tears	Gladys Knight and the Pips	10/29/70
35079	God Bless Whoever Sent You/Desperate Young Men	Originals	11/18/70
35080	Let's Save All the Children/You Are Blue	Joe Hinton	1/5/71
35081	Holly Holy/Carry Your Own Load	Jr. Walker and the All Stars	11/24/70
35082	When My Love Hand Comes Down/Steppin' on a Dream	David & Jimmy Ruffin	3/30/71
35083	I Don't Want to Do Wrong/Is There a Place in His Heart for Me	Gladys Knight and the Pips	5/6/71
35084	Take Me Girl I'm Ready/Right on Brothers and Sisters	Jr. Walker and the All Stars	7/8/71
35085	Keep Me/A Man without Love	Originals	7/15/71
35086	Lo and Behold/The Things We Have to Do	David and Jimmy Ruffin	NR
35087	Funky Rubber Band/Instrumental	Popcorn Wylie	8/12/71
35088	Color Combination/Swim	Jack Hammer	9/16/71
35089	How You Gonna Keep It (After You Get It)/This Time Last Summer	Blinky	NR
35090	Way Back Home/Instrumental	Jr. Walker and the All Stars	11/4/71
35091	Make Me the Woman That You Go Home To/It's All Over but the Shoutin'	Gladys Knight and the Pips	11/18/71
35092	Our Favorite Melody/You Gave Me Love	Jimmy Ruffin	1/6/72
35093	I'm Someone Who Cares/Once I Have You (I Will Never Let You Go)	Originals	1/18/72
35094	Help Me Make It Through the Night/If You Gonna Leave (Just Leave)	Gladys Knight and the Pips	3/6/72
35095	Walk in the Night/I Don't Want to Do Wrong	Jr. Walker and the All Stars	2/29/72
35096	Take Me Clear from Here/Ball of Confusion (That's What the World Is Today)	Edwin Starr	3/2/72
35097	Groove Thang/Me and My Family	Jr. Walker and the All Stars	2/29/72
35098	Neither One of Us (Wants to Be the First to Say Goodbye)/Can't Give It Up No More	Gladys Knight and the Pips	12/26/72
35099	What Is Black/I Can Take It All	Billy Proctor	7/13/72
35100	Who Is the Leader of the People/Don't Tell Me I'm Crazy	Edwin Starr	8/23/72
35101	Gospel Truth/Running Like a Rabbit	Bob Babbit	NR
35102	Be My Love/Endlessly Love	Originals	4/17/73
35103	There You Go/Instrumental	Edwin Starr	3/29/73
35104	Gimme That Beat (Pts. 1 and 2)	Jr. Walker and the All Stars	1/11/73
35105	Daddy Could Swear (I Declare)/For Once in My Life	Gladys Knight and the Pips	4/9/73
35106	I Don't Need No Reason/Country Boy	Jr. Walker and the All Stars	5/1/73
35107	All I Need Is Time/The Only Time You Love Me Is When You're Losing Me	Gladys Knight and the Pips	7/10/73
35108	Peace and Understanding Is Hard to Find/Soul Clappin'	Jr. Walker and the All Stars	7/3/73
35109	There's a Chance When You Love You'll Lose/First Lady (Sweet Mother's Love)	Originals	9/20/73
35110	Dancin' Like They Do on Soul Train/I Ain't That Easy to Lose	Jr. Walker and the All Stars	5/9/74
35111	Between Her Goodbye and My Hello/This Child Needs Its Father	Gladys Knight and the Pips	5/22/74
35112	Supernatural Voodoo Woman (Pts. 1 and 2)	Originals	1/10/74
35113	Game Called Love/Ooh You (Put a Crush on Me)	Originals	5/2/74
35114	You Are the Sunshine of My Life/Until You Come Back to Me	Jr. Walker	NR
35115	You're My Only World/So Near (And Yet So Far)	Originals	11/7/74
35116	I'm So Glad/Soul Clappin'	Jr. Walker	1/5/76
35117	Touch/Ooh You (Put a Crush on Me)	Originals	4/27/76
35118	You Ain't No Ordinary Woman/Hot Shot	Jr. Walker	5/27/76
35119	Down to Love Town/Just to Be Closer to You	Originals	7/15/76
35120	If Love Is Not the Answer (Baby Right Ain't Right)/Nothing Is Too Good (For You Baby)	Jamal Trice	11/2/76
35121	(Call on Your) Six Million Dollar Man/Mother Nature's Best	Originals	NR
35122	Hard Love/Whopper Bopper Show Stopper	Jr. Walker	8/22/77
35123	I Never Thought I'd Be Losing You/Chicago Disco	Major Lance	3/29/78

TAMLA

The genesis of the Motown empire. Still active, but you knew that. (45s/LPs)
   Note: Tamla 101 and 102 labels are solid green; Tamla 54024 to 54044 labels are yellow with stripes; Tamla 54045 to 54140 labels are yellow with globe at top; Tamla 54141 to date are yellow with brown bar at top.

101	Come to Me/Whisper	Marv Johnson	1/59
102	Merry Go Round/It Moves Me	Eddie Holland	12/59
5501	Cool and Crazy/Ich-I-Bon #1	Nick and the Jaguars	'59

54024	Snake Walk (Pts. 1 and 2)	Swingin' Tigers	—
54025	Solid Sender/I'll Never Love Again	Chico Leverett	—
54025	It/Don't Say Goodbye	Ron and Bill	5/59
54026	Motor City/Going to the Top	Satintones	—
54027	Money/Oh, I Apologize	Barrett Strong	8/59
54028	You Can Depend on Me/The Feeling Is So Fine	Miracles	—
54028	You Can Depend on Me/Way Over There [H55501, H5501 T-3]	Miracles	4/4/60
54029	Yes, No, Maybe So/You Knows What to Do	Barrett Strong	7/6/60
54030	That Child Is Really Wild/What Makes You Love Him	Singin' Sammy Ward	9/19/60
54030	That Child Is Realy Wild/Who's the Fool	Singin' Sammy Ward	—
54031	Who Wouldn't Love a Man Like That/You Made a Fool of Me	Mabel John	8/26/60
54032	True Love/It's You	Herman Griffin	10/10/60
54033	I'm Gonna Cry/Whirlwind	Barrett Strong	8/31/60
54034	Shop Around [H55518-A2, L13]/Who's Lovin' You	Miracles	10/15/60
54035	Money and Me/You Got What It Takes	Barrett Strong	2/8/61
54036	Ain't It Baby/The Only One I Love	Miracles	3/15/61
54037	He Lifted Me/Behold the Saints of God	Gospel Stars	3/7/62
54038	I Want a Guy/Never Again	Supremes	3/9/61
54039	Poor Sam Jones/They Rode through the Valley	Mickey Wood	3/29/61
54040	No Love [H632, H667]/Looking for a Man	Mabel John	6/12/61
54041	Let Your Conscience Be Your Guide/Never Let You Go	Marvin Gaye	5/25/61
54042	Same Thing/That's No Lie	Gino Parks	6/17/61
54043	Misery/Two Wrongs Don't Make a Right	Barrett Strong	6/3/61
54044	Mighty Good Lovin'/Broken Hearted	Miracles	6/3/61
54045[16]	Buttered Popcorn/Who's Loving You	Supremes	7/21/61
54046	Please Mr. Postman/So Long Baby	Marvelettes	8/21/61
54047	Jesus Loves/They Shall Be Mine	Rev. Columbus Mann	3/7/62
54048	Everybody's Gotta Pay Some Dues/I Can't Believe	Miracles	9/19/61
54049	Don't Take It Away/What Makes You Love Him	Sammy Ward	11/2/61
54050	Action Speaks Louder than Words/Take Me	Mabel John	'61
54051	Small Sad Sam/Tie Me Tight	Bob Kayli	11/22/61
54052	Please Mr. Kennedy/They Call Me Cupid	Mickey Woods	2/12/62
54053	What's So Good About Goodbye/I've Been Good to You	Miracles	12/14/61
54054	Twistin' Postman/I Want a Guy	Marvelettes	12/6/61
54055	I'm Yours, You're Mine/Sandman	Marvin Gaye	1/19/62
54056	Your Baby's Back/Request of a Fool	Downbeats	2/8/62
54057	Big Joe Moe/Everybody Knew It	Singin' Sammy Ward	3/1/62
54058	I Out Duked the Duke/Baby I Need You	Little Otis	3/13/62
54059	I'll Try Something New/You Never Miss a Good Thing	Miracles	4/9/62
54060	Playboy/All the Love I've Got	Marvelettes	4/9/62
54061	I Call It Pretty Music but the Old People Call It the Blues (Pts. 1 and 2)	Little Stevie Wonder	8/16/63
54062	—		—
54063	Soldier's Plea/Taking My Time	Marvin Gaye	5/8/62
54064	Same Old Story/I'll Cry a Million Tears	Mickey McCullers	6/18/62
54065	Beachwood 45789/Someday, Someway	Marvelettes	7/11/62
54066	For This I Thank You/Fire	Gino Park and the Love Tones	8/3/62
54067	It's Gonna Be Hard Times/Camel Walk	Sandra Mallett and the Vandellas	'62
54068	Stubborn Kind of Fellow/It Hurt Me Too	Marvin Gaye	7/23/62
54069	Way Over There/If Your Mother Only Knew	Miracles	8/17/62
54070	La La La La La/Little Water Boy	Little Stevie Wonder	10/3/62
54071	Part Time Love/Someday Pretty Baby	Singin' Sammy Ward	8/27/62
54072	Strange I Know/Too Strung Out to Be Strung Along	Marvelettes	10/29/62
54073	You've Really Got a Hold On Me/Happy Landing	Miracles	11/9/62
54074	Contract on Love/Sunset	Little Stevie Wonder	12/26/62
54075	Hitch-Hike/Hello There Angel	Marvin Gaye	12/19/62
54076	Love Me All the Way/It Should Have Been Me	Kim Weston	2/7/63
54077	Lockin' Up My Heart/Forever	Marvelettes	2/15/63
54078	A Love She Can Count On/I Can Take a Hint	Miracles	3/11/63
54079	Pride and Joy/One of These Days	Marvin Gaye	4/18/63
54080	Fingertips (Pt. 1 and 2)	Little Stevie Wonder	5/21/63
54081	Who Wouldn't Love a Man Like That/Say You'll Never Let Me Go	Mabel John	6/12/63
54082	My Daddy Knows Best/Tie a String Around Your Finger	Marvelettes	7/1/63
54083	Mickey's Monkey/Whatever Makes You Happy	Miracles	7/26/63
54084	—		—
54085	Just Loving You/Another Train Coming	Kim Weston	10/24/63
54086	Workout, Stevie, Workout/Monkey Talk	Little Stevie Wonder	9/13/63
54087	Can I Get a Witness/I'm Crazy 'Bout My Baby	Marvin Gaye	9/20/63
54088	As Long As I Know He's Mine/Little Girl Blue	Marvelettes	10/14/63
54089	I Gotta Dance to Keep from Cryin'/Such Is Love, Such Is Life	Miracles	10/31/63
54090	Castles in the Sand/Thank You	Little Stevie Wonder	1/16/64
54091	He's a Good Guy (Yes He Is)/Goddess of Love	Marvelettes	1/29/64

[16] Tamla 54045 was the first Tamla release with globes rather than stripes on the label.

54092	(You Can't Let the Boy Overpower) The Man in You/Heartbreak Road	Miracles	1/13/64
54093	You're a Wonderful One/When I'm Alone I Cry	Marvin Gaye	2/20/64
54094	Every Little Bit Hurts/Land of a Thousand Boys	Brenda Holloway	3/26/64
54095	Try It Baby/If My Heart Could Sing	Marvin Gaye	5/21/64
54096	Hey Harmonica Man/This Little Girl	Little Stevie Wonder	5/21/64
54097	You're My Remedy/A Little Bit of Sympathy, A Little Bit of Love	Marvelettes	6/8/64
54098	I Like It Like That/You're So Fine and Sweet	Miracles	6/3/64
54099	Sad Song/I'll Always Love You	Brenda Holloway	7/3/64
54100	Looking for the Right Guy/Feel Alright Tonight	Kim Weston	8/7/64
54101	Baby Don't You Do It/Walk on the Wild Side	Marvin Gaye	9/2/64
54102	That's What Love Is Made Of/Would I Love You	Miracles	8/28/64
54103	Happy Street/Sad Boy	Stevie Wonder	9/14/64
54104	What Good Am I Without You/I Want You 'Round	Marvin Gaye and Kim Weston	9/30/64
54105	Too Many Fish in the Sea/A Need for Love	Marvelettes	10/14/64
54106	A Little More Love/Go Ahead and Laugh	Kim Weston	11/6/64
54107	How Sweet It Is (To Be Loved By You)/Forever	Marvin Gaye	11/4/64
54108	Pretty Little Angel/Tears in Vain	Stevie Wonder	NR
54109	Come on Do the Jerk/Baby Don't You Go	Miracles	11/20/64
54110	I'm Still Lovin' You/Go Ahead and Laugh	Kim Weston	1/29/65
54111	When I'm Gone/I've Been Good to You	Brenda Holloway	2/9/65
54112	I'll Be Doggone/You've Been a Long Time Coming	Marvin Gaye	2/26/65
54113	Ooo Baby Baby/All That's Good	Miracles	3/5/65
54114	Kiss Me Baby/Tears in Vain	Stevie Wonder	3/26/65
54115	Operator/I'll Be Available	Brenda Holloway	5/14/65
54116	I'll Keep Holding On/No Time for Tears	Marvelettes	5/11/65
54117	Pretty Little Baby/Now That You've Won Me	Marvin Gaye	6/18/65
54118	The Tracks of My Tears/A Fork in the Road	Miracles	6/23/65
54119	High Heel Sneakers/Music Talk	Stevie Wonder	8/2/65
54119	High Heel Sneakers/Funny (How Time Slips Away)	Stevie Wonder	8/65
54120	Danger Heartbreak Dead Ahead/Your Cheating Ways	Marvelettes	7/23/65
54121	You Can Cry on My Shoulder/How Many Times Did You Mean It	Brenda Holloway	8/24/65
54122	Ain't That Peculiar/She's Got to Be Real	Marvin Gaye	9/14/65
54123	My Girl Has Gone/Since You Won My Heart	Miracles	9/22/65
54124	Uptight (Everything's Alright)/Purple Raindrops	Stevie Wonder	11/22/65
54125	Together 'Till the End of Time/Sad Song	Brenda Holloway	1/11/66
54126	Don't Mess with Bill/Anything You Wanna Do	Marvelettes	11/26/65
54127	Going to A-Go-Go/Chossey Begger	Miracles	12/6/65
54128	This Old Heart of Mine/There's No Love Left	Isley Brothers	1/28/66
54129	One More Heartache/When I Had Your Love	Marvin Gaye	1/31/66
54130	Nothing's Too Good for My Baby/With a Child's Heart	Stevie Wonder	3/24/66
54131	You're the One/Paper Boy	Marvelettes	4/4/66
54132	Take This Heart of Mine/Need Your Lovin', Want You Back	Marvin Gaye	5/2/66
54133	Take Some Time Out for Love/Who Could Ever Doubt My Love	Isley Brothers	4/29/66
54134	Whole Lot of Shakin' in My Heart (Since I Met You)/Oh Be My Love	Miracles	5/27/66
54135	I Guess I'll Always Love You/I Hear a Symphony	Isley Brothers	6/17/66
54136	Blowin' in the Wind/Ain't That Asking for Trouble	Stevie Wonder	6/28/66
54137	Hurt a Little Everday/Where Were You	Brenda Holloway	8/25/66
54138	Little Darling (I Need You)/Hey Diddle Diddle	Marvin Gaye	7/26/66
54139	A Place in the Sun/Sylvia	Stevie Wonder	10/24/66
54140	Come 'Round Here, I'm the One You Need/Save Me	Miracles	10/19/66
54141	It Takes Two/It's Got to Be a Miracle (This They Called Love)	Marvin Gaye and Kim Weston	12/2/66
54142	Someday at Christmas/The Miracles of Christmas	Stevie Wonder	11/22/66
54143	The Hunter Gets Captured by the Game/I Think I Can Change You	Marvelettes	12/27/66
54144	'Till Johnny Comes/Where Were You	Brenda Holloway	NR
54149[17]	Ain't No Mountain High Enough/Give a Little Love	Marvin Gaye and Tammi Terrell	4/20/67
54145	The Love I Saw in You Was Just a Mirage/Come Spy with Me	Smokey Robinson and the Miracles	1/27/67
54146	Got to Have You Back/Just Ain't Enough Love	Isley Brothers	3/30/67
54147	Travelin' Man/Hey Love	Stevie Wonder	2/9/67
54148	Just Look What You've Done/Starting the Hurt All Over Again	Brenda Holloway	3/9/67
54150	When You're Young and in Love/The Day You Take One You Have to Take the Other	Marvelettes	4/6/67
54151	I Was Made to Love Her/Hold Me	Stevie Wonder	5/18/67
54152	More Love/Swept for You Baby	Smokey Robinson and the Miracles	5/26/67
54153	Your Unchanging Love/I'll Take Care of You	Marvin Gaye	6/12/67
54154	That's the Way Love Is/One Too Many Heartaches	Isley Brothers	6/29/67
54155	You've Made Me So Very Happy/I've Got to Find It	Brenda Holloway	8/17/67
54156	Your Precious Love/Hold Me Oh May Darling	Marvin Gaye and Tammi Terrell	8/22/67
54157	I'm Wondering/Everytime I See You I Go Wild	Stevie Wonder	9/14/67
54158	My Baby Must Be a Magician/I Need Someone	Marvelettes	'67
54159	I Second That Emotion/You Must Be Love	Smokey Robinson and the Miracles	10/12/67
54160	You/Change What You Can	Marvin Gaye	12/21/67

[17] First pressing with brown bar at the top of the label

54161	If I Could Build My Whole World Around You/If This World Were Mine	Marvin Gaye and Tammi Terrell	11/14/67
54162	If You Can Want/When the Words from Your Heart Get Caught Up in Your Throat	Smokey Robinson and the Miracles	2/8/68
54163	Ain't Nothing Like the Real Thing/Little Ole Boy, Little Ole Girl	Marvin Gaye and Tammi Terrell	3/28/68
54164	Take Me in Your Arms/Why When Love Is Gone	Isley Brothers	3/14/68
54165	Shoo-Be-Doo-Be-Doo-Be-Doo-Da-Day/Why Don't You Lead Me to Love	Stevie Wonder	3/19/68
54166	Here I Am Baby/Keep Off, No Tresspassing	Marvelettes	5/2/68
54167	Yester Love/Much Better Off	Smokey Robinson and the Miracles	5/13/68
54168	You Met Your Match/My Girl	Stevie Wonder	6/25/68
54169	You're All I Need to Get By/Two Can Have a Party	Marvin Gaye and Tammi Terrell	7/9/68
54170	Chained/At Last (I Found a Love)	Marvin Gaye	8/20/68
54171	Destination: Anywhere/What's Easy for Two Is Hard for One	Marvelettes	8/27/68
54172	Special Occasion/Give Her Up	Smokey Robinson and the Miracles	7/30/68
54173	Keep on Lovin' Me Honey/You Ain't Livin' Till You're Lovin'	Marvin Gaye and Tammi Terrell	9/24/68
54174	For Once in My Life/Angie Girl	Stevie Wonder	10/15/68
54175	All Because I Love You/Behind a Painted Smile	Isley Brothers	11/5/68
54176	I Heard It through the Grapevine/You're What's Happening	Marvin Gaye	11/30/68
54177	I'm Gonna Hold on As Long As I Can/Don't Make Hurting Me a Habit	Marvelettes	12/23/68
54178	Baby Baby Don't Cry/Your Mother's Only Daughter	Smokey Robinson and the Miracles	12/12/68
54179	Good Lovin' Ain't Easy to Come By/Satisfied Feeling	Marvin Gaye and Tammi Terrell	1/14/69
54180	My Cherie Amour/Don't Know Why I Love You	Stevie Wonder	1/28/69
54181	Too Busy Thinking About My Baby/Wherever I Lay My Hat	Marvin Gaye	4/2/69
54182	Just Ain't Enough Love/Take Some Time Out for Love	Isley Brothers	5/1/69
54183	Doggone Right/Here I Go Again	Smokey Robinson and the Miracles	5/28/69
54184	Abraham, Martin and John/Much Better Off	Smokey Robinson and the Miracles	6/11/69
54185	That's the Way Love Is/Gonna Keep on Tryin'	Marvin Gaye	8/4/69
54186	That's How Heartaches Are Made/Rainy Mourning	Marvelettes	9/23/69
54187	What You Gave Me/How You Gonna Keep It	Marvin Gaye and Tammi Terrell	11/6/69
54188	Yester-Me, Yester-You, Yesterday/I'd Be a Fool Right Now	Stevie Wonder	9/30/69
54189	Point It Out/Darling Dear	Smokey Robinson and the Miracles	11/18/69
54190	How Can I Forget/Gonna Give Her All the Love I've Got	Marvin Gaye	12/16/69
54191	Never Had a Dream Come True/Somebody Knows, Somebody Cares	Stevie Wonder	1/13/70
54192	Onion Song/California Soul	Marvin Gaye and Tammi Terrell	3/20/70
54193	The Day Will Come Between Sunday and Monday/My Whole World Ended	Kiki Dee	6/17/70
54194	Who's Gonna Take the Blame/I Gotta Thing for You	Smokey Robinson and the Miracles	4/28/70
54195	The End of Our Road/Me and My Lonely Room	Marvin Gaye	5/19/70
54196	Signed Sealed Delivered (I'm Yours)/I'm More than Happy (I'm Satisfied)	Stevie Wonder	6/3/70
54197	To Be Young, Gifted and Black/Peace of Mind	Bob & Marcia	7/23/70
54198	Marionette/After All	Marvelettes	11/3/70
54199	The Tears of a Clown/Promise Me	Smokey Robinson and the Miracles	9/24/70
54200	Heaven Help Us All/I Gotta Have a Song	Stevie Wonder	9/29/70
54201	What's Going On/God Is Love	Marvin Gaye	1/21/71
54202	We Can Work It Out/Never Dreamed You'd Leave in Summer	Stevie Wonder	2/18/71
54203	So Hard for Me to Say Goodbye/This Used to Be the Home of Johnnie Mae	Eddie Kendricks	5/71
54204	Back to Nowhere/Can't It Wait Until Tomorrow	Valerie Simpson	'71
54205	I Don't Blame You at All/That Girl	Smokey Robinson and the Miracles	3/71
54206	Crazy About the La La La/Oh Baby Baby I Love You	Smokey Robinson and the Miracles	7/71
54207	Mercy Mercy Me (The Ecology)/Sad Tomorrows	Marvin Gaye	7/71
54208	If You Really Love Me/Think of Me As Your Soldier	Stevie Wonder	8/71
54209	Inner City Blues (Make Me Wanna Holler)/Wholly City	Marvin Gaye	10/71
54210	Can I/I Did It All for You	Eddie Kendricks	12/71
54211	Satisfaction/Flower Girl	Smokey Robinson and the Miracles	11/71
54212	I Can't Believe You're Really Leaving/You Ain't Saying Nothing New	Virgil Henry	'71
54213	A Breath Taking Guy/You're the One for Me Baby	Marvelettes	'71
54214	What Christmas Means to Me/Bedtime for Toys	Stevie Wonder	12/71
54215	It Takes a Man to Teach a Woman to Love/TLC	P.J.	'72
54216	Superwoman (Where Were You When I Needed You)/I Love Every Little Thing About You	Stevie Wonder	5/72
54217	It's the Same Old Love/Last Row First Balcony	Courtship	6/72
54218	Eddie's Love/Let Me Run into Your Lonely Heart	Eddie Kendricks	6/72
54219	Label Me Love/Life's a Ball	Different Shades of Brown	'72
54220	We've Come Too Far to End It Now/When Sundown Comes	Smokey Robinson and the Miracles	6/72
54221	You're the Man (Pts. 1 and 2)	Marvin Gaye	5/72
54222	If You Let Me/Just Memories	Eddie Kendricks	9/72
54223	Keep on Running/Evil	Stevie Wonder	9/72
54224	Silly Wasn't I/This Ride I Believe I'm Gonna Take	Valerie Simpson	12/72
54225	I Can't Stand to See You Cry/With Your Love Came	Smokey Robinson and the Miracles	12/72
54226	Superstition/You've Got It Bad Girl	Stevie Wonder	11/72
54227	Oops, It Just Slipped Out/Love Ain't Love	Courtship	'72
54228	Trouble Man/Don't Mess with Mr. T	Marvin Gaye	12/72

54229	Xmas in the City/I Want to Go Home	Marvin Gaye	12/72
54230	Girl You Need a Change of Mind (Pts. 1 and 2)	Eddie Kendricks	2/73
54231	Genius/One More Baby Child Born	Valerie Simpson	'73
54232	You Are the Sunshine of My Life/Tuesday Heartbreak	Stevie Wonder	3/73
54233	Sweet Harmony/Wanna Know My Mind	Smokey Robinson	7/73
54234	Let's Get It On/I Wish It Would Rain	Marvin Gaye	7/73
54235	Higher Ground/Too High	Stevie Wonder	8/73
54236	Darlin' Come Back Home/Lovin' You the Second Time Around	Eddie Kendricks	6/73
54237	Don't Let It End ('Til You Let It Begin)/Wigs and Lashes	Miracles	7/73
54238	Keep on Truckin' (Pts. 1 and 2)/Trouble Man	Eddie Kendricks	8/73
54239	Baby Come Close/A Silent Partner in a Three Way Love Affair	Smokey Robinson	11/73
54240	Give Me Just Another Day/I Wanna Be with You	Miracles	12/73
54241	Come Get to This/Distant Lover	Marvin Gaye	11/73
54242	Living for the City/Visions	Stevie Wonder	11/73
54243	Boogie Down/Can't Help What I Am	Eddie Kendricks	12/73
54244	You Sure Love to Ball/Just to Keep You Satisfied	Marvin Gaye	1/2/74
54245	Don't You Worry 'Bout a Thing/Blame It on the Sun	Stevie Wonder	3/14/74
54246	It's Her Turn to Live/Just My Soul Responding	Smokey Robinson	4/18/74
54247	Son of Sagittarius/Trust Your Heart	Eddie Kendricks	4/16/74
54248	Do It Baby/I Wanna Be with You	Miracles	6/20/74
54249	Tell Her Love Has Felt the Need/Lovin' You the Second Time Around	Eddie Kendricks	7/2/74
54250	Virgin Man/Fulfill Your Need	Smokey Robinson	7/16/74
54251	I Am I Am/The Family Song	Smokey Robinson	11/7/74
54252	You Haven't Done Nothin'/Big Brother	Stevie Wonder	7/23/74
54253	Distant Lover (Live)/Trouble Man (Live)	Marvin Gaye	9/5/74
54254	Boogie on Reggae Woman/Seems So Long	Stevie Wonder	10/23/74
54255	One Tear/The Thin Man	Eddie Kendricks	11/5/74
54256	Don't Cha Love It/Up Again	Miracles	11/15/74
54257	Shoeshine Boy/Hooked on Your Love	Eddie Kendricks	1/13/75
54258	Baby That's Backatcha/Just Passing Through	Smokey Robinson	2/17/75
54259	Gemini/You Are Love	Miracles	3/17/75
54260	Get the Cream Off the Top/Honey Brown	Eddie Kendricks	6/18/75
54261	Agony and the Ecstasy/Wedding Song	Smokey Robinson	7/29/75
54262	Love Machine (Pts. 1 and 2)	Miracles	9/19/75
54263	Happy/Deep and Quite Love	Eddie Kendricks	9/11/75
54264	I Want You/Instrumental	Marvin Gaye	'75
54265	Quiet Storm/Asleep on My Love	Smokey Robinson	11/21/75
54266	He's a Friend/All of My Love	Eddie Kendricks	1/16/76
54267	Open/Coincidentally	Smokey Robinson	5/76
54268	Night Life/Smog	Miracles	5/76
54269[18]	When You Came/Coincidentally	Smokey Robinson	5/76
54270	Get It While It's Hot/Never Gonna Leave You	Eddie Kendricks	6/76
54271	Full Speed Ahead/Just As Long As There Is You	Tata Vega	7/29/76
54272	Take My Love/—	Miracles	NR
54273	After the Dance/Feel All My Love Inside	Marvin Gaye	7/15/76
54274	I Wish/You and I	Stevie Wonder	11/18/76
54275	One Out of Every Six (Censored)/Pick of the Week	Thelma Houston	9/23/76
54276	An Old-Fashioned Man/Just Passing Through	Smokey Robinson	9/23/76
54277	Goin' Up in Smoke/Thanks for the Memories	Eddie Kendricks	10/26/76
54278	Don't Leave Me This Way/Today Will Soon Be Yesterday	Thelma Houston	11/16/76
54279	There Will Come a Day (I'm Gonna Happen to You)/The Humming Song (Lost for Words)	Smokey Robinson	1/13/77
54280	Got to Give It Up (Pts. 1 and 2)	Marvin Gaye	3/15/77
54281	Sir Duke/He's Misstra Know It All	Stevie Wonder	3/22/77
54282	You'll Never Rock Alone/Just When Things Are Getting Good	Tata Vega	4/14/77
54283	If It's the Last Thing I Do/If You Won't Let Me Walk on the Water	Thelma Houston	4/7/77
54284	Vitamin U/Holly	Smokey Robinson	5/17/77
54285	Born Again/Date with the Rain	Eddie Kendricks	4/21/77
54286	Another Star/Creepin'	Stevie Wonder	8/9/77
54287	I'm Here Again/Sharing Something Perfect Between Ourselves	Thelma Houston	9/13/77
54288	Theme from "Big Time" (Pts. 1 and 2)	Smokey Robinson	8/11/77
54289	Baby/I Want to Live (My Life with You)	Eddie Kendricks	NR
54290	Intimate Friends/Baby	Eddie Kendricks	12/22/77
54291	As/Contusion	Stevie Wonder	10/14/77
54292	I Can't Go on Living without Your Love/Any Way You Like It	Thelma Houston	1/19/78
54293	Daylight and Darkness/Why You Wanna See My Bad Side	Smokey Robinson	2/7/78
54294	Passion Flower/Kiss Me Now	Kenny Lupper	3/14/78
54295	I'm Not Strong Enough to Love You Again/Triflin'	Thelma Houston	8/10/78
54296	Shoe Soul/I'm Loving You Softly	Smokey Robinson	9/28/78
54297	Saturday Night Sunday Morning/Come to Me	Thelma Houston	2/79
54298	A Funky Space Reincarnation (Pts. 1 and 2)	Marvin Gaye	5/79
54299	I Just Keep Thinking About You Baby/Music in My Heart	Tata Vega	—

[18] Issued only in Canada

54300	—	—	—
54301	Get Ready/Ever Had a Dream	Smokey Robinson	6/79
54302	I Just Need More Money (Pts. 1 and 2)	Shades	—
54303	Send One Your Love/Instrumental	Stevie Wonder	10/79
54304	I Need You Now/In the Morning	Tata Vega	—
54305	Ego Tripping Out/Instrumental	Marvin Gaye	10/79
54306	Cruisin'/Ever Had a Dream	Smokey Robinson	8/79
54307	Feel the Fever/Things You're Made Of	Keith and Darrell	—
54308	Outside My Window/Same Old Story	Stevie Wonder	2/80
54309	Kickin' It Around/I Met This Girl	Keith and Darrell	—
54310	Only You (Pts. 1 and 2)	Quiet Storm	—
54311	Let Me Be the Clock/Travelin' Through	Smokey Robinson	2/80
54312	One More Time for Love/Dance for Me Children	Syreeta and Billy Preston/Syreeta	—
54313	Heavy on Pride (Light on Love)/I Love the Nearness of You	Smokey Robinson	6/80
54314	Heartbreak Graffiti/—	Quiet Storm	—
54315	Lay Your Body Down/Shake It Lady	Legend	—
54316	You Better Watch Out—You Keep Me Hangin' On	Tata Vega	—
54317	Master Blaster/Dub	Stevie Wonder	9/80
54318	Wine Woman and Song/I Want to Be Your Love	Smokey Robinson	9/80
54319	Please Stay/Signed Sealed Delivered (I'm Yours)	Syreeta and Billy Preston	—
54320	I Ain't Gonna Stand for It/Knocks Me Off My Feet	Stevie Wonder	11/80
54321	Being with You/What's In Your Life for Me	Smokey Robinson	1/81
54322	Praise/Funk Me	Marvin Gaye	2/81
54323	Lately/If It's Magic	Stevie Wonder	2/81
54324	—	—	—
54325	Aqui Con Tigo/Being with You—Aqui Con Tigo	Smokey Robinson	4/81
54326	Heavy Love Affair/Far Cry	Marvin Gaye	5/81
54327	You Are Forever/I Hear the Children Singing	Smokey Robinson	5/81
54328	Did I Hear You Say You Love Me/As If You Read My Mind	Stevie Wonder	7/81
54329	You're My Gardener/Don't Be Afraid	Keith and Darrell	'81
54330	When You Came/I Let You Go	Quiet Storm	'81
54331[19]	Happy Birthday/Instrumental	Stevie Wonder	—
54332	Who's Sad/Food for Thought	Smokey Robinson	8/81
54333	Quick Slick/I Don't Know	Syreeta	11/81

VIP

Semi-successful, moderately long-lived subsidiary that appeared to get all the records that Motown didn't know quite what to do with. Too bad. (45s/LPs)
    Note: V.I.P. 25000 to 25023 labels are yellow with plain block lettering; V.I.P. 25024 to end of run are multi-colored with logo at side.

25000	—	—	—
25001	—	—	—
25002	If Your Heart Says Yes/I'll Cry Tomorrow	Serenaders	1/23/64
25003	After the Showers Come Flowers/Don't Be a Cry Baby	Joanne and the Triangles	2/7/64
25004	Give Me a Kiss/She's My Baby	Hornets	2/19/64
25005	—	—	—
25006	(Like A) Nightmare/If You Were Mine	Andantes	NR
25007	Needle in a Haystack/Should I Tell Them	Velvelettes	9/3/64
25008	Lifetime Man/Mr. Lonely Heart	Oma Heard	NR
25009	Who You Gonna Run to/Same Old Story	Mickey MuCullers	10/7/64
25010	—	—	—
25011	Tonight's the Night/You're Bad News	Headliners	10/9/64
25012	Randy the Newspaper Boy/Happy Ghoultide	Ray Oddis	11/25/64
25013	He Was Really Sayin' Somethin'/Throw a Farewell Kiss	Velvelettes	12/28/64
25014	—	—	—
25015	—	—	—
25016	Buttered Popcorn/Tell Me	Vows	5/17/65
25017	Lonely Lonely Girl Am I/I'm the Exception to the Rule	Velvelettes	5/7/65
25018	By Some Chance/He's an Oddball	Lewis Sisters	5/24/65
25019	Please Don't Turn the Lights Out/This Time Last Summer	Danny Day	—
25020	—	—	—
25021	A Bird in the Hand (Is Worth Two in the Bush)/Since You've Been Loving Me	Velvelettes	NR
25022	I Don't Know What to Do/What Now My Love	Richard Anthony	8/20/65
25023	Hang on Bill/Puppet on a String	Little Lisa	8/20/65
25024[20]	Moonlight on the Beach/You Need Me	Lewis Sisters	8/31/65
25025	I've Been Cheated/Something's Bothering You	Dalton Boys	10/25/65
25026	Voodoo Plan/We Call It Fun	Headliners	10/15/65
25027	Let's Go Somewhere/Poor Girl	R. Dean Taylor	10/25/65
25028	All For Someone/Say You	Monitors	11/12/65

[19] Released only in Australia

[20] V.I.P. label begins new logo.

25029	Put Yourself in My Place/Darling Baby	Elgins	12/31/65
25030	A Bird in the Hand (Is Worth Two in the Bush)/Since You've Been Loving Me	Velvelettes	11/22/65
25031	Do Right Baby, Do Right/Don't Be Too Long	Chris Clark	12/2/65
25032	Greetings (This Is Uncle Sam)/No. 1 in Your Heart	Monitors	2/24/66
25033	—	—	—
20534	—	—	—
25035	Three Choruses of Despair/Cause You Know Me	Rick, Robin and Him	6/3/66
25036	La La La La La/This Is True	La Salles	6/22/66
25037	Heaven Must Have Sent You/Stay in My Arms	Elgins	8/25/66
25038	Love's Gone Bad/Put Yourself in My Place	Chris Clark	7/14/66
25039	Since I Lost You Girl/Don't Put Off 'Till Tomorrow What You Can Do Today	Monitors	11/21/66
25040	Love's Gone Bad/Mo Jo Hanna	Underdogs	1/4/67
25041	I Want to Go Back There Again/I Love You	Chris Clark	2/23/67
25042	There's a Ghost in My House/Don't Fool Around	R. Dean Taylor	3/30/67
25043	I Understand My Man/It's Been a Long Long Time	Elgins	6/8/67
25044	Why Am I Lovin' You/Stay My Love	Debbie Dean	2/1/68
25045	Gotta See Jane/Don't Fool Around	R. Dean Taylor	4/9/68
25046	Bring Back the Love/The Further You Look, The Less You See	Monitors	4/2/68
25047	Baby/Cherie	Honest Man	4/23/69
25048	—	—	—
25049	—	—	—
25050	In My Diary/(She's Gonna Love Me) At Sundown	Spinners	10/21/69
25051	Cheating Is Telling on You/Need Your Love	Lollipops	10/23/69
25052	Baby, I'll Get It/The Day the World Stood Still	Chuck Jackson	11/24/69
25053	Blackmail/Oh, I've Been Blessed	Bobby Taylor	1/8/70
25054	Message from a Black Man/(She's Gonna Love Me) At Sundown	Spinners	2/12/70
25055	I Remember When (Dedicated to Beverly)/Sorry Is a Sorry Word	Ivy Jo	3/11/70
25056	Let Somebody Love Me/Two Feet from Happiness	Chuck Jackson	5/7/70
25057	It's a Shame/Together We Can Make Such Sweet Music	Spinners	6/11/70
25058	It's a Lonesome Road/Yesterday's Love Is Over	Hearts of Stone	9/30/70
25059	Pet Names/Is There Anything Love Can't Do	Chuck Jackson	1/12/71
25060	We'll Have It Made/My Whole World Ended (The Moment You Left Me)	Spinners	12/21/70
25061	Heartaches/Together We Can Do Anything	King Floyd	4/29/71
25062	(I've Given You) The Best Years of My Life/It Takes a Man to Teach a Woman How to Love	P.J.	4/8/71
25063	I Still Love You/I Can Feel the Pain	Ivy Jo	5/26/71
25064	If I Could Give You the World/You Gotta Sacrifice (We Gotta Sacrifice)	Hearts of Stone	6/10/71
25065	Heaven Must Have Sent You/Stay in My Lonely Arms	Elgins	9/9/71
25066	What Is Love/Where Did the Children Go	Stylists	6/6/71
25067	Who You Gonna Run To/Forgive My Jealousy	Chuck Jackson	NR
25068	We've Only Just Begun—I'll Be There/I Can Get Away From You	Tony and Carolyn	11/1/71
25069	Feel Like Givin' Up/Take Somebody Like You	Posse	2/1/72

WORKSHOP JAZZ

Early jazz—not fusion—label that ended about the time B.G. got a look at the sales figures. This stuff is so rare that Motown's books are still bleeding red ink. (45s/LPs)

2001	Exodus/I Remember You	Hank and Carol Diamond	5/12/62
2002	Opus No. II/March Lightly	Earl Washington	5/16/62
2003	I Want to Talk About You/So in Love	Paula Greer	—
2004	Lat Freight/Mellow in Coli	Dave Hamilton	5/24/62
2005	I'll See You Later/I Did	Johnny Griffith	5/24/62
2006	Bobbie/El Rig	George Bohanon	5/24/62
2007	I Did/Falling in Love with Love	Paula Greer	5/24/62

ALBUMS

BLACK FORUM

451	Why I Oppose the War in Vietnam	Dr. Martin Luther King	10/70
452	Free Huey	Stokley Carmichael	10/70
453	Writers of the Revolution	Langston Hughes and Margaret Danner	10/70
454	Guess Who's Coming Home	Black Fighting Men (Recorded Live in Vietnam)	2/72
455	The Congressional Black Caucus	Ossie Davis and Bill Cosby	4/72
456	Black Spirits	Imanu Amiri Baraka	4/72
457	It's Nation Time	Imanu Amiri Baraka	4/72
458	Elaine Brown	Elaine Brown	4/73

END OF LABEL

CHISA

801	It's Never Too Late	Monk Montgomery	1/70
802	—	—	—
803	Reconstruction	Hugh Masekela	7/70
804	Old Socks New Shoes, New Socks Old Shoes	Jazz Crusaders	7/70
805	Letta	Letta	9/70
806	Bass Odyssey	Monk Montgomery	5/71
807	Pass the Plate	Crusaders	5/71
808	Hugh Masekela and the Union of South Africa	Hugh Masekela and the Union of South Africa	5/71
809	Mosadi	Letta	NR

END OF LABEL

GORDY[21]

901	Do You Love Me	Contours	10/62
902	Come and Get These Memories	Martha and the Vandellas	6/63
903	Modern Innovations on C&W Themes	Ralph Sharon	6/63
904	—	—	—
905	—	—	—
906	The Great March to Freedom	Rev. Martin Luther King	8/63
907	Heatwave	Martha and the Vandellas	9/63
908	The Great March on Washington	Rev. Martin Luther King	10/63
909	—	—	—
910	—	—	—
911	Meet the Temptations	Temptations	3/64
912	Sing Smokey	Temptations	2/65
913	—	—	—
914	The Temptin' Temptations	Temptations	11/65
915	Dance Party	Martha and the Vandellas	4/65
916	—	—	—
917	Greatest Hits	Martha and the Vandellas	5/66
918	Gettin' Ready	Temptations	6/66
919	Greatest Hits	Temptations	11/66
920	Watchout!	Martha and the Vandellas	12/66
921	Live!	Temptations	3/67
922	With a Lot o' Soul	Temptations	7/67
923	Hungry for Love	San Remo Golden Strings	8/67
924	In a Mellow Mood	Temptations	8/67
925	Live!	Martha Reeves and the Vandellas	8/67
926	Ridin' High	Martha Reeves and the Vandellas	4/68
927	I Wish It Would Rain	Temptations	4/68
928	Swing	San Remo Golden Strings	6/68
929	Free at Last	Rev. Martin Luther King	6/68
930	Bobby Taylor and the Vancouvers	Bobby Taylor and the Vancouvers	8/68
931	Soul Master	Edwin Starr	8/68
932	Alfie	Eivets Rednow	11/68
933	The Temptations Show	Temptations	7/69
934	—	—	—
935	Motown Winners Circle Vol. 1	Various Artists	1/69
936	Motown Winners Circle Vol. 2	Various Artists	1/69
937	—	—	—
938	Live! At the Copa	Temptations	12/68
939	Cloud Nine	Temptations	2/69
940	25 Miles	Edwin Starr	4/69
941	—	—	—
942	Taylor Made Soul	Bobby Taylor	7/69
943	Motown Winners Circle Vol. 3	Various Artists	7/69
944	Sugar 'n' Spice	Martha Reeves and the Vandellas	9/69
945	Just We Two	Edwin Starr and Blinky	9/69
946	Motown Winners Circle Vol. 4	Various Artists	10/69
947	Psychedelic Shack	Temptations	3/70
948	War and Peace	Edwin Starr	8/70
949	Puzzle People	Temptations	9/69
950	Motown Winners Circle Vol. 5	Various Artists	3/70
951	Christmas Card	Temptations	10/70
952	Natural Resources	Martha Reeves and the Vandellas	9/70

[21] Gordy, Tamla, and Motown labels were consolidated in December 1981.

953	Live! At London's Talk of the Town	Temptations	7/70
954	Greatest Hits Vol. 2	Temptations	9/70
955	Undisputed Truth	Undisputed Truth	6/71
956	Involved	Edwin Starr	6/71
957	Sky's the Limit	Temptations	4/71
958	Black Magic	Martha Reeves and the Vandellas	3/72
959	Face to Face with the Truth	Undisputed Truth	1/72
960	—	—	—
961	Solid Rock	Temptations	1/72
962	All Directions	Temptations	7/72
963	Law of the Land	Undisputed Truth	6/73
964	Bad News Is Coming	Luther Allison	12/72
965	Masterpiece	Temptations	2/73
966	1990	Temptations	12/73
967	Luther's Blues	Luther Allison	2/74
968	Down to Earth	Undisputed Truth	7/74
969	A Song for You	Temptations	1/75
970	Cosmic Truth	Undisputed Truth	2/75
971	Wings of Love	Temptations	3/76
972	Higher than High	Undisputed Truth	9/75
973	House Party	Temptations	11/75
974	Night Life	Luther Allison	2/76
975	The Temptations Do the Temptations	Temptations	8/76
976	Musical Massage	Leon Ware	9/76
977	Rock Bottom	Bottom and Co.	11/76
978	Turnin' On	Hi Inergy	9/77
979	Break Thru	21st Creation	1/78
980	Switch	Switch	7/78
981	Come Get It	Rick James	4/78
982	Steppin' Out	High Inergy	6/78
983	21st Creation	21st Creation	NR
984	Bustin' Out	Rick James	1/79
985	Apollo	Apollo	3/79
986	Wild and Peaceful	Teena Marie	3/79
987	Shoulda Gone Dancin'	High Inergy	4/79
988	Switch II	Switch	4/79
989	Frenzy	High Inergy	10/79
990	Fire It Up	Rick James	10/79
991	In 'n' Out	Stone City Band	2/80
992	Lady T	Teena Marie	2/80
993	Reaching for Tomorrow	Switch	3/80
994	Power	Temptations	4/80
995	Garden of Love	Rick James	7/80
996	Hold On	High Inergy	8/80
997	Irons in the Fire	Teena Marie	8/80
998	Give Love at Christmas	Temptations	8/80
999	This Is My Dream	Switch	10/80
1000	Nolen and Crossley	Nolen & Crossley	1/81
1001	The Boys Are Back	Stone City Band	1/81
1002	Street Songs	Rick James	4/81
1003	The DeBarges	DeBarges	4/81
1004	It Must Be Magic	Teena Marie	5/81
1005	High Inergy	High Inergy	5/81
1006	The Temptations	Temptations	8/81
1007	Switch V	Switch	10/81

HITSVILLE

404	Solitary Man	T. G. Sheppard	9/76
405	Texas Woman	Pat Boone	9/76
406	Sundowners	Wendel Adkins	1/77

END OF LABEL

JU-PAR

1001	Moods and Grooves	Ju-Par Universal Orchestra	1/77
1002	In Good Taste	Flavor	5/77
1003	Sly, Slick and Wicked	Sly, Slick and Wicked	8/77

END OF LABEL

MELODYLAND

401	T. G. Sheppard	T. G. Sheppard	5/75
402	—		
403	Motels and Memories	T. G. Sheppard	3/76

END OF LABEL

M.C.

501	The Country Side of Pat Boone	Pat Boone	8/77
502	Love Away Her Memory Tonight	Jerry Naylor	NR
503	Once Again	Jerry Naylor	NR
504	Porter Jordan Sings	Porter Jordan	NR
505	Country Days and Country Nights	Pat Boone	NR
506	—		—
507	Presenting	Bob and Penny	NR
508	Kenny Seratt	Kenny Seratt	NR
509	—		—
510	—	Susie Allanson	NR
511	You Are the Sunshine of My Life	Marty Mitchell	11/77
512	Wendell Adkins	Wendell Adkins	NR
513	Tucker and Schoonmaker	Tucker and Schoonmaker	NR
514	—		—
515	Please Take Me Back	Larry Groce	12/77

END OF LABEL

MOTOWN[22]

600	Bye Bye Baby	Mary Wells	—
601	Twistin' the World Around	Twistin' Kings	12/63
602	—		—
603	Motown Special Vol. 1	Various Artists	5/62
604	Eddie Holland	Eddie Holland	5/62
605	The One Who Really Loves You	Mary Wells	6/62
606	Meet the Supremes	Supremes	12/63
607	Two Lovers	Mary Wells	1/63
608	The Return of Amos Milburn	Amos Milburn	4/63
609	Motortown Revue Vol. 1 Recorded Live! At the Apollo	Various Artists	4/63
610	Supremes Sing Ballads and Blues	Supremes	NR
611	Live! On Stage	Mary Wells	9/63
612	Second Time Around	Mary Wells	NR
613	Together	Mary Wells and Marvin Gaye	4/64
614	A Package of 16 Hits	Various Artists	10/63
615	Motortown Revue Recorded Live! Vol. 2	Various Artists	4/64
616	Greatest Hits	Mary Wells	4/64
617	My Guy	Mary Wells	6/64
618	—		—
619	My Son the Sit-in	Stepin Fetchit	'66
620	Hits of the Sixties	Choker Campbell	8/64
621	Where Did Our Love Go	Supremes	1/65
622	Four Tops	Four Tops	10/64
623	A Bit of Liverpool	Supremes	10/64
624	16 Big Hits Vol. 3	Various Artists	12/64
625	Sing C&W and Pop	Supremes	2/65
626	Live Live Live	Supremes	NR
627	More Hits	Supremes	7/65
628	There's a Place for Us	Supremes	NR
629	We Remember Sam Cooke	Supremes	5/65
630	Nothing but a Man (film soundtrack)	Various Artists	3/65
631	That Motown Sound	Earl Van Dyke and the Soul Brothers	5/65
632	The Prime of My Life	Billy Eckstine	11/65
633	A Collection of 16 Big Hits Vol. 4	Various Artists	11/65
634	Second Album	Four Tops	11/65
635	—		—
636	At the Copa	Supremes	11/65
637	Tribute to the Girls	Supremes	NR
638	Merry Christmas	Supremes	11/65

[22] Gordy, Tamla, and Motown labels were consolidated in December 1981.

639	The Original Spinners	Spinners	8/67
640	Live at Lake Tahoe	Billy Eckstine	NR
641	—		
642	In Loving Memory	Various Artists	8/68
643	I Hear a Symphony	Supremes	2/66
644	Here I Am	Barbara McNair	11/66
645	At the American	Tony Martin	NR
646	My Way	Billy Eckstine	11/66
647	On Top	Four Tops	7/66
648	Pure Gold	Supremes	NR
649	A Go-Go	Supremes	8/66
650	Sing Holland-Dozier-Holland	Supremes	1/67
651	A Collection of 16 Big Hits Vol. 5	Various Artists	8/66
652	Irresistable	Tammi Terrell	1/68
653	Vintage Stock	Mary Wells	11/66
654	Live!	Four Tops	11/66
655	A Collection of 16 Big Hits Vol. 6	Various Artists	1/67
656	—		—
657	On Broadway	Four Tops	3/67
658	—		
659	Sing Rogers and Hart	Supremes	5/67
660	Reach Out	Four Tops	7/67
661	A Collection of 16 Big Hits Vol. 7	Various Artists	8/67
662	Greatest Hits	Four Tops	8/67
663	Greatest Hits (2-LP set)	Diana Ross and the Supremes	8/67
664	Soul Sounds	Chris Clark	8/67
665	Reflections	Diana Ross and the Supremes	3/68
666	A Collection of 16 Big Hits Vol. 8	Various Artists	11/67
667	Arrives	Chuck Jackson	2/68
668	A Collection of 16 Big Hits Vol. 9	Various Artists	8/68
669	Yesterday's Dreams	Four Tops	8/68
670	Love Child	Diana Ross and the Supremes	11/68
671	—		—
672	Sing and Perform Funny Girl	Diana Ross and the Supremes	8/68
673	—		—
674	—		—
675	Now (Mac Arthur Park)	Four Tops	5/69
676	Live! At London's Talk of the Town	Diana Ross and the Supremes	8/68
677	For the Love of Ivy	Billy Eckstine	10/68
678	—		—
679	Diana Ross and the Supremes Join the Temptations	Diana Ross and the Supremes and the Temptations	11/68
680	The Real Barbara McNair	Barbara McNair	4/69
681	Merry Christmas From Motown	Various Artists	12/68
682	T.C.B.	Diana Ross and the Supremes and the Temptations	12/68
683	Along Came Jonah	Jonah Jones	1/69
684	A Collection of 16 Big Hits Vol. 10	Various Artists	4/69
685	My Whole World Ended	David Ruffin	5/69
686	A Bag of Soup	Soupy Sales	4/69
687	Going Back to Chuck Jackson	Chuck Jackson	5/69
688	Motortown Revue Recorded Live!	Various Artists	7/69
689	Let the Sun Shine In	Diana Ross and the Supremes	5/69
690	A Little Dis, A Little Dat	Jonah Jones	9/69
691	Red Jones Strikes Back	Red Jones	8/69
692	Together	Diana Ross and the Supremes and the Temptations	9/69
693	A Collection of 16 Big Hits Vol. 11	Various Artists	9/69
694	Cream of the Crop	Diana Ross and the Supremes	11/69
695	Soul Spin	Four Tops	11/69
696	Doin' His Thing	David Ruffin	11/69
697	—		—
698	Moving On	Joe Harnell	11/69
699	On Broadway	Diana Ross and the Supremes and the Temptations	11/69
700	Diana Ross Presents the Jackson 5	Jackson 5	12/69
701	Shades of Gospel Soul	Various Artists	3/70
702	Greatest Hits Vol. 3	Diana Ross and the Supremes	12/69
703	Motown at the Hollywood Palace	Various Artists	3/70
704	Still Waters Run Deep	Four Tops	3/70
705	Right On	Supremes	5/70
706	—		—
707	Motown Chartbusters Vol. 1	Various Artists	9/70

708	Farewell (2-LP Set)	Diana Ross and the Supremes	4/70
709	ABC	Jackson 5	5/70
710	Something for Everyone	Sammy Davis Jr.	4/70
711	Diana Ross	Diana Ross	5/70
712	Sunny and Warm	Blinky	NR
713	Christmas Album	Jackson 5	10/70
714[23]	—	Jonah Jones	NR
715	Motown Chartbusters Vol. 2	Various Artists	9/70
716	Gimme Dat Ding	Ding Dongs	7/70
717	The Magnificent Seven	Supremes and the Four Tops	9/70
718	Third Album	Jackson 5	9/70
719	Diana! (TV special)[24]	Diana Ross	3/71
720	New Ways but Love Stays	Supremes	9/70
721	Changing Times	Four Tops	9/70
722	Strung Out	Gordon Staples and the Motown Strings	9/70
723	Surrender	Diana Ross	7/71
724	Everything Is Everything	Diana Ross	10/70
725[25]	Christmas Gift Rap	Various Artists	10/70
726	The Motown Story (5-LP Set)	Various Artists	2/71
727	The Motown Story Vol. 1	—	—
728	The Motown Story Vol. 2	—	—
729	The Motown Story Vol. 3	—	—
730	The Motown Story Vol. 4	—	—
731	The Motown Story Vol. 5	—	—
732	Motown Chartbusters Vol. 3	Various Artists	5/71
733	—	David Ruffin	NR
734	Motown Chartbusters Vol. 4	Various Artists	5/71
735	Maybe Tomorrow	Jackson 5	4/71
736	Return of the Magnificent Seven	Supremes and the Four Tops	5/71
737	Touch	Supremes	5/71
738	Live! At the Desert Inn	Bobby Darin	NR
739[26]	Souvenir Album (1971 Sterling Ball Benefit)	Various Artists	'71
740	Greatest Hits Vol. 2	Four Tops	8/71
741	Greatest Hits	Jackson 5	12/71
742	Goin' Back to Indiana	Jackson 5	9/71
743	The Key to the Kingdom	Various Artists	9/71
744	Motown Chartbusters Vol. 5	Various Artists	12/71
745	Dynamite	Supremes and the Four Tops	12/71
746	Promises Kept	Supremes	NR
747	Got to Be There	Michael Jackson	1/72
748	Nature Planned It	Four Tops	4/72
749	—	—	—
750	Lookin' through the Windows	Jackson 5	5/72
751	Floy Joy	Supremes	5/72
752	Jermaine	Jermaine Jackson	7/72
753	Bobby Darin	Bobby Darin	7/72
754	Jerry Ross Symposium Vol. 2	Jerry Ross Symposium	7/72
755	Ben	Michael Jackson	8/72
756[27]	Produced and Arranged by Jimmy Webb	Supremes	10/72
757	Jackie Jackson	Jackie Jackson	NR
758	Lady Sings the Blues (2-LP Set)	Diana Ross	12/72
759[28]	—	—	—
760	Pippin (original cast album)	—	12/72
761	Skywriter	Jackson 5	3/73
762	David Ruffin	David Ruffin	2/73
763[29]	Lady Sings the Blues (7-inch EP)	Various Artists	—
764[30]	The Best of the Four Tops (2-LP Set)	Four Tops	4/73
765	—	—	—
766	The Mack	Willie Hutch	4/73
767	Music and Me	Michael Jackson	4/73
768	Puzzle	Puzzle	4/73
769	The Best of the Spinners	Spinners	4/73
770	Softly	Blinky	NR

[23] The title of this unreleased album was never established.

[24] The "TV special" note is to differentiate this Diana! album from the later LP known simply as Diana.

[25] This is the same album as Motown 681. Only the cover and the title were changed.

[26] This was an inter-company only promotional item, never released to the general public.

[27] The Jackie Jackson album was originally scheduled to be released as Motown 757. It was eventually issued as Motown 785.

[28] The Motown 759 number was assigned to the 8-track and cassette versions of Motown 758, most likely to reflect the need for two tapes to handle the extra length.

[29] This was a 7-inch EP that was issued for promotional purposes only.

[30] See Footnote 28.

771	Reuben Howell	Reuben Howell	4/73
772	Touch Me in the Morning	Diana Ross	6/73
773	—		—
774	Severin Browne	Severin Browne	5/73
775	Come into My Life	Jermaine Jackson	5/73
776	Stacie	Stacie Johnson	NR
777	Big Ben Sings	Scatman Crothers	6/73
778	Anthology (2-LP set)	Martha Reeves and the Vandellas	8/74
779	The New Improved Severin Browne	Severin Browne	11/74
780	Dancing Machine	Jackson 5	9/74
781	Devastating Affair	Devastating Affair	NR
782	Anthology/10th Anniversary Special (3-LP set)	Temptations	8/73
783	Get It Together	Jackson 5	9/73
784	Fully Exposed	Willie Hutch	9/73
785	Jackie Jackson	Jackie Jackson	9/73
786	Anthology (2-LP set)	Jr. Walker and the All Stars	7/74
787	Relocation	Xit	NR
788	Inside Out	Frankie Valli and the Four Seasons	NR
789	Stephen Cohn	Stephen Cohn	9/73
790	Share My Love	Gloria Jones	9/73
791	Anthology (3-LP set)	Marvin Gaye	4/74
792	Anthology (2-LP set)	Gladys Knight and the Pips	1/74
793	Anthology (3-LP set)	Smokey Robinson and the Miracles	1/74
794	Anthology (3-LP set)	Diana Ross and the Supremes	5/74
795	A Motown Christmas (2-LP set)	Various Artists	9/73
796	At Their Best	Crusaders	9/73
797	Dazzle 'Em with Footwork	Martin and Finley	6/74
798	Machine Gun	Commodores	7/74
799	Rings	Reuben Howell	6/74
800	Save the Children (film soundtrack) (2-LP set)	Various Artists	4/74
801	Live! At Caesar's Palace	Diana Ross	5/74
802	Hell Up in Harlem (film soundtrack)	Edwin Starr	5/74
803	Diana and Marvin	Diana Ross and Marvin Gaye	10/73
804	Looking Back (3-LP set)	Stevie Wonder	12/77
805	Diahann Carroll	Diahann Carroll	5/74
806	Welcome to the World of Riot	Riot	5/74
807	Second Album	Puzzle	2/74
808	Stevie Wonder Presents . . . Syreeta	Syreeta	6/74
809	Anthology (3-LP set)	Four Tops	7/74
810	Michael Edward Campbell	Michael Edward Campbell	4/74
811	Foxy Brown	Willie Hutch	4/74
812	Last Time I Saw Him	Diana Ross	12/73
813	Darin 1936–1973	Bobby Darin	2/74
814	Caston and Majors	Caston and Majors	11/74
815	Mark of the Beast	Willie Hutch	11/74
816	How Do We Get Out of the Business Alive	Puzzle	NR
817	Rickenstein	Rickenstein	NR
818	Me and Rock n' Roll Are Here to Stay	David Ruffin	11/74
819	Love Songs and Other Tragedies	G. C. Cameron	11/74
820	Caught in the Act	Commodores	2/75
821	Discotech	Magic Disco Machine	5/75
822	Dynamic Superiors	Dynamic Superiors	1/75
823	—	H.U.B.[31]	—
824	Discotech 1	Various Artists	5/75
825	Forever, Michael	Michael Jackson	1/75
826	California Sunset	Originals	3/75
827	Anthology (2-LP set)	Marvelettes	5/75
828	The Supremes	Supremes	5/75
829	Moving Violation	Jackson 5	5/75
830	—	Thelma Houston	NR
831	Discotech 2	Various Artists	5/75
832	The Bitch Is Black	Yvonne Fair	5/75
833	Discotech 3	Various Artists	NR
834	Free Delivery	Sonny Burke	NR
835	Motortown Revue (groups)	Various Artists	NR
836	Love Ballads	Various Artists	NR
837	Mellow Moods	Various Artists	NR
838	Ode to My Lady	Willie Hutch	6/75
839	Murph the Surf (film soundtrack)	—	6/75
840	Cooley High (film soundtrack) (2-LP set)	Various Artists	6/75

[31]H.U.B. was a name created from the initials of the group's members, all of whom were formerly of the group Rare Earth. This album was eventually released by Capitol Records.

841	Pure Pleasure	Dynamic Superiors	7/75
842	My Name Is Jermaine	Jermaine Jackson	8/76
843	Rise Sleeping Beauty	Lenny Williams	7/75
844	—	Syreeta	NR
845	Rose	Rose Banks	5/76
846	Leslie Uggams	Leslie Uggams	8/75
847	Libra	Libra	8/75
848	Movin' On	Commodores	10/75
849	Who I Am	David Ruffin	10/75
850	Love's on the Menu	Jerry Butler	6/76
851	The Best of Michael Jackson	Michael Jackson	8/75
852	Inside You	Frankie Valli	9/75
853	Motown Discotech 3	Various Artists	1/76
854	Concert in Blues	Willie Hutch	2/76
855	G. C. Cameron	G. C. Cameron	10/76
856	Kathe Green	Kathe Green	NR
857	Motown Magic Disco Machine Vol. 2	Magic Disco Machine	5/76
858	Mahogany (film soundtrack)	Diana Ross	10/75
859	For the First Time	Stephanie Mills	11/75
860	Motown Original Versions	Various Artists	2/76
861	Diana Ross	Diana Ross	2/76
862	Sky's the Limit	Dynamic Superiors	NR
863	High Energy	Supremes	4/76
864	Winter's Day Nightmare	Libra	5/76
865	Joyful Jukebox Music	Jackson 5	10/76
866	Everything's Coming Up Love	David Ruffin	5/76
867	Hot on the Tracks	Commmodores	6/76
868	Anthology (3-LP set)	Jackson 5	6/76
869	Greatest Hits	Diana Ross	7/76
870	Love's Coming Down	Ronnie McNeir	8/76
871	Color Her Sunshine	Willie Hutch	9/76
872	Motown Discotech 4	Various Artists	8/76
873	Mary, Scherrie, Susaye	Supremes	10/76
874	Havin' a House Party	Willie Hutch	5/77
875	You Name It	Dynamic Superiors	10/76
876	Guys and Dolls (original cast album)	—	12/76
877	An Evening with Diana Ross (2-LP set)	Diana Ross	1/77
878	Suite for the Single Girl	Jerry Butler	1/77
879	Give and Take	Dynamic Superiors	5/77
880	You're What's Missing in My Life	G. C. Cameron	1/77
881	Motown's Preferred Stock, Stock Option No. 1	Various Artists	2/77
882	Motown's Preferred Stock, Stock Option No. 2	Various Artists	2/77
883	Motown's Preferred Stock, Stock Option No. 3	Various Artists	2/77
884	Commmdores	Commodores	3/77
885	In My Stride	David Ruffin	5/77
886	Mandre	Mandre	4/77
887	Thelma and Jerry	Thelma Houston and Jerry Butler	5/77
888	Feel the Fire	Jermaine Jackson	6/77
889	Albert Finney's Album	Albert Finney	6/77
890	Baby It's Me	Diana Ross	9/77
891	Rich Love, Poor Love	Syreeta and G. C. Cameron	8/77
892	It All Comes Out in My Song	Jerry Butler	10/77
893	—	—	
894	Live! (2-LP set)	Commodores	10/77
895	At His Best	David Ruffin	1/78
896	Star Dancing	5th Dimension	1/78
897	The First Cuba Gooding Album	Cuba Gooding	2/78
898	Frontiers	Jermaine Jackson	2/78
899	Platinum Hook	Platinum Hook	3/78
900	Mandre II	Mandre	3/78
901	Three Ounces of Love	Three Ounces of Love	4/78
902	Natural High	Commodores	5/78
903	Two to One	Thelma Houston and Jerry Butler	6/78
904	At Their Best	Supremes	6/78
905	Motown Presents Prime Time	Various Artists	7/78
906	Need to Know You Better	Finished Touch	7/78
907	Ross	Diana Ross	9/78
908	Space Dance	Motown Sounds	1/79
909	Don't Stop	Bloodstone	1/79
910	Reed Seed	Grover Washington	9/78
911	Bonnie Pointer	Bonnie Pointer	10/78
912	Greatest Hits	Commodores	10/78
913	Changes	T-Boy Ross	2/79
914	High on Sunshine	5th Dimension	1/79

915	Music from the Motion Picture "Fastbreak"	Billy Preston and Syreeta	3/79
916	—		—
917	M 3000	Mandre	2/79
918	It's Time	Platinum Hook	3/79
919	Love Dancer	Cuba Gooding	4/79
920	Partners	Scherrie and Susaye	10/79
921	Pops, We Love You, The Album	Various Artists	4/79
922	Don't Touch Me	Patrick Gammon	5/79
923	The Boss	Diana Ross	5/79
924	Dr. Strut	Dr. Strut	5/79
925	Late at Night	Billy Preston	7/79
926	Midnight Magic	Commodores	7/79
927	Mary Wilson	Mary Wilson	8/79
928	Let's Get Serious	Jermaine Jackson	3/80
929	Bonnie Pointer	Bonnie Pointer	11/79
930	Pinball Playboy	Cook County	11/79
931	Struttin'	Dr. Strut	2/80
932	Excursion Beyond	Flight	2/80
933	Skylarkin'	Grover Washington Jr.	2/80
934	The Planets	Planets	2/80
935	—		—
936	Diana	Diana Ross	5/80
937	20/20—Twenty No. 1 Hits from Twenty Years at Motown (2-LP set)	Various Artists	3/80
938	Walk On	Ozone	4/80
939	Heroes	Commodores	6/80
940	Baddest (2-LP set)	Grover Washington Jr.	8/80
941	The Way I Am	Billy Preston	2/81
942	Black Russian	Black Russian	5/80
943	—		—
944	Serenade for the City	Michael Urbaniak	8/80
945	Night Song	Ahmad Jamal	10/80
946	Invitation to Love	Dazz Band	10/80
947	It's My Turn (soundtrack)	Diana Ross and Others	10/80
948	Loving Couples (soundtrack)	Various Artists	11/80
949	Jermaine	Jermaine	11/80
950	Jump on It	Ozone	1/81
951	To Love Again	Diana Ross	2/81
952	I Like Your Style	Jermaine Jackson	8/81
953	Jose Feliciano	Jose Feliciano	10/81
954	—		—
955	In the Pocket	Commodores	6/81
956	One Day in Your Life	Michael Jackson	3/81
957	Let the Music Play	Dazz Band	5/81
958	Billy Preston and Syreeta	Billy Preston and Syreeta	7/81
959	Lovesmith	Lovesmith	8/81
960	All the Great Hits (2-LP set)	Diana Ross	10/81
961	Grover Washington Jr. Anthology (2-LP set)	Grover Washington Jr.	9/81
962	Send It	Ozone	9/81

MOWEST

101	Happiness	Lodi	10/72
102	Thelma Houston	Thelma Houston	7/72
103	What the World Needs Now Is Love	Tom Clay	7/71
104	—		—
105	—	Devastating Affair	NR
106	—	Blackberries	NR
107	7th Son	G. C. Cameron	NR
108	Chameleon	Frankie Vallie and the Four Seasons	5/72
109	—	Sisters Love	NR
110	—	Commodores	NR
111	—	Blinky Williams	NR
112	—		—
113	Syreeta	Syreeta	6/72
114	—	Frankie Valli	NR
115	Odyssey	Odyssey	5/72
116	—		—
117	Someplace Else Now	Lesley Gore	7/72
118	Hollywood	Crusaders	7/72
119	Celebration	Celebration	7/72
120	Dazzle 'Em with Footwork	Martin and Finley	NR
121	Repairs	Repairs	11/72
122	Kubie	Kubie	NR

| 123 | — | Stacie Johnson | NR |
| 124 | — | G. C. Cameron and Willie Hutch | NR |

END OF LABEL

MOTOWN CONSOLIDATED SERIES

6000M	Tell Me a Lie	Bettye Lavette	1/82
6001T	Yes It's You Lady	Smokey Robinson	1/82
6002T	Stevie Wonder's Original Musiquarium (2-LP set)	Stevie Wonder	5/82
6003G	Ambience	Nolen and Crossley	2/82
6004M	Keep It Live	Dazz Band	2/82
6005G	Throwin' Down	Rick James	5/82
6006G	So Right	High Inergy	4/82
6007M	Lionel Richie	Lionel Richie	'82
6008G	Reunion	Temptations	4/82
6009M	I've Never Been to Me	Charlene	3/82
6010M	Trust Me	Jean Carn	5/82
6011M	Li'l Suzy	Ozone	7/82
6012G	All This Love	DeBarge	7/82
6013	—	—	—
6014M	Strung Out on Motown	Regal Funkharmonic Orchestra	7/82
6015T	What's Your Pleasure	Gene Van Buren	1/83
6016	—	—	—
6017M	Let Me Tickle Your Fancy	Jermaine Jackson	7/82
6018ML	Escenas de Amor	Jose Feliciano	7/82
6019M	Love Changes	O. C. Smith	5/82
6020M	Pressin' On	Billy Preston	8/82
6021ML	Amor Secreto	Pedro Montero	8/82
6022M	Second to Nunn	Bobby Nunn	8/82
6023G	Blow	Bobby Militello	'82
6024M	The Sky Is the Limit	Charlene	1/83
6025	—	—	—
6026M	Himself	Bill Cosby	'82
6027M	Used to Be	Charlene	'82
6028M	All the Great Hits	Commodores	'82
6029M	Knife	Monalisa Young	—
6030T	Touch the Sky	Smokey Robinson	1/83
6031M	On the One	Dazz Band	1/83
6032G	Surface Thrills	Temptations	2/83
6033M	Love Has Lifted Me	Stephanie Mills	'83
6034M	Reachin' All Around	Thelma Houston	'83
6035M	Romance in the Night	Jose Feliciano	3/83
6036M	Finis	Finis Henderson	4/83
6037M	Glasses	Ozone	3/83
6038M	Kagny and Dirty Rats	Kagny and the Dirty Rats	3/83
6039T	The Spell	Syreeta	4/83
6040G	Mary Jane Girls	Mary Jane Girls	4/83
6041G	Groove Patrol	High Inergy	4/83
6042G	Out from the Shadow	Stone City Band	7/83
6043G	Cold Blooded	Rick James	8/83
6044M	Anthology (2-LP set)	Commodores	5/83
6045M	I Can Make It Happen	Michael Lovesmith	6/83
6046MR	Wolf and Wolf	Wolf and Wolf	5/84
6047	—	—	—
6048M	The Motown Story: The First 25 Years (5-LP set)	Various Artists	5/83
6049M	Anthology (2-LP set)	Diana Ross	5/83
6050	—	—	—
6051M	Private Party	Bobby Nunn	9/83
6052M	Somebody's Watching Me	Rockwell	1/84
6053M	Blow the House Down	Junior Walker	8/83
6054M	"13"	Commodores	9/83
6055	—	—	—
6056MR	Kidd Glove	Kidd Glove	2/84
6057G	Don't Look Any Further	Dennis Edwards	1/84
6058M	Every Great Motown Hit	Marvin Gaye	9/83
6059M	Can't Slow Down	Lionel Richie	10/83
6060MR	Light the Night	Jakata	8/84
6061G	In a Special Way	DeBarge	9/83
6062M	The Big Chill (Soundtrack)	Various Artists	9/83
6063MR	The Coyote Sisters	Coyote Sisters	7/84
6064T	Blame It on Love and All the Great Hits	Smokey Robinson	8/83
6065MR	Get Crazy (Soundtrack)	Various Artists	8/83
6066M	Back Where I Belong	Four Tops	10/83

6067MR	Tiggi Clay	Tiggi Clay	1/84
6068			
6069			
6070			
6071			
6072			
6073			
6074			
6075	Numbers 6068–6083 assigned to Twin-Pak cassettes of previously		
6076	issued LPs.		
6077			
6078			
6079			
6080			
6081			
6082			
6083			
6084M	Joystick	Dazz Band	11/83
6085G	Back to Basics	Temptations	10/83
6086M	Christine (Soundtrack)	Various Artists	11/83
6087	—	—	—
6088M	Love in the Fire	Bobby King	2/84
6089	—	—	—
6090M	Hit and Run Lover	Charlene	7/84
6091M	Making Trax (The Great Instrumentals)	Various Artists	3/84
6092	—	—	—
6093M	Diamond in the Raw	Michael Lovesmith	4/84
6094M	More Songs from the Original Soundtrack of "The Big Chill"	Various Artists	4/84
6095G	Reflections	Rick James	8/84
6096M	KoKo-Pop	KoKo-Pop	5/84
6097MR	White Knuckle Ride	Duke Jupiter	4/84
6098T	Essar	Smokey Robinson	5/84
6099M	14 Greatest Hits	Michael Jackson and the Jackson 5	5/84
6100M	16 Greatest Hits (cassette)	Michael Jackson and the Jackson 5	5/84
6101M	Farewell My Summer Love	Michael Jackson	5/84
6102M	Wild Animal	Vanity	8/84
6103M	Sam Harris	Sam Harris	8/84
6104			
6105	Numbers 6104–6107 and 6109–6111 assigned to compact discs of		
6106	previously issued Motown LPs.		
6107			
6108M	The Woman in Red (Soundtrack)	Stevie Wonder	8/84
6109			
6110			
6111			
6112M	Ain't No Turnin' Back	Phyllis St. James	8/84
6113	—	—	—
6114	—	—	—
6115	—	—	—
6116	—	—	—
6117M	Jukebox	Dazz Band	9/84
6118	—	—	—
6119G	Truly for You	Temptations	10/84
6120	—	—	—
6121M	Thomas McClary	Thomas McClary	11/84

NATURAL RESOURCES

101	Two Friends	Two Friends	5/72
102	Heart	Heart[32]	5/72
103	Corliss	Corliss	5/72
104	Pass the Butter	Gotham	7/72
105	Road	Road	7/72
106	Earthquire	Earthquire	1/73
107	Vancouver Dreaming	Northern Lights	1/73
108	Wine, Women and Song	Gaylord and Holiday	10/76
4001	Motown's Great Interpretations	Various Artists	3/78
4002	Motown Instrumentals	Various Artists	3/78
4003	Motown Show Tunes	Various Artists	3/78

[32] Not the group led by the Wilson sisters

4004	Silk 'n Soul	Gladys Knight and the Pips	9/78
4005	In a Mellow Mood	Temptations	9/78
4006	Where Did Our Love Go	Diana Ross and the Supremes	9/78
4007	The Soulful Moods of Marvin Gaye	Marvin Gaye	9/78
4008	Reach Out	Four Tops	9/78
4009	I'll Try Something New	Smokey Robinson and the Miracles	9/78
4010	Merry Christmas	Diana Ross and the Supremes	10/78
4011	We Wish You a Merry Christmas	Various Artists	10/78
4012	It Takes Two (duets)	Various Artists	1/79
4013[33]	Boogie	Jackson 5	NR
4014	From the Vaults	Various Artists	1/79
4015	Mighty Motown	Various Artists	5/79
4016	Disco Party	Various Artists	5/79
4017	Motown Parade of Song Hits	Various Artists	5/79
4018	In Love	Various Artists	8/79
4019	Brokenhearted	Various Artists	8/79
4020	T.C.B.	Diana Ross and the Supremes with the Temptations	8/79

END OF LABEL

PRODIGAL

10007	Ronnie McNeir	Ronnie McNeir	'75
10008	With a Little Help from My Friends	Shirley Alston	'75
10009	Second Generation	Gaylord and Holiday	'75
10010	Dancers, Romancers, Dreamers and Schemers	Michael Quatro	6/76
10011	Kathe Green	Kathe Green	8/76
10012	Fantacy Hill	Fantacy Hill	8/76
10013	Diggin' It	Dunn and Rubini	9/76
10014	Tattoo	Tattoo	9/76
10015	Charlene	Charlene	11/76
10016	Gettin' Ready	Michael Quatro	1/77
10017	Delaney and Friends—Class Reunion	Delaney Bramlett	2/77
10018	Songs of Love	Charlene	5/77
10019	Rarearth	Rare Earth	7/77
10020	I Sing My Songs for You	Phillip Jarrell	9/77
10021	—	—	—
10022	First Step	Fantacy Hill	1/78
10023	Born Again	Phil Cordell	NR
10024	Feelin' Fresh	Fresh	1/78
10025	Band Together	Rare Earth	4/78
10026	Round One	Friendly Enemies	4/78
10027	Grand Slam	Rare Earth	9/78
10028	Omniverse	Fresh	10/78
10029	Featuring Stoney and Meatloaf	Meatloaf	10/78
10030	Stylus	Stylus	10/78

END OF LABEL

RARE EARTH

505[34]	Blues Helping	Love Sculpture	6/69
506	S.F. Sorrow	Pretty Things	6/69
507	Get Ready	Rare Earth	9/69
508	Bedlam	Rustix	9/69
509	Messengers	Messengers	9/69
510	Generation (film soundtrack)	Rare Earth	NR
511	Toe Fat	Toe Fat	7/70
512	Love at First Sight	Sounds Nice	9/70
513	Come on People	Rustix	7/70
514	Ecology	Rare Earth	6/70
515	Parachute	Pretty Things	9/70
516	The Gospel According to Zeus	Power of Zeus	9/70
517[35]	Easy Ridin'	Easybeats	—
518	Paradise Lost	Lost Nation	9/70
519	Ain't Nothin' in Our Pocket but Love	Poor Boys	5/70
520	One World	Rare Earth	6/71
521	45 Lives	Cats	9/70
522	I Think Therefore I Am	R. Dean Taylor	12/70
523	Brass Monkey	Brass Monkey	4/71

[33] Only promotional copies of this album were released.

[34] Rare Earth albums 505–509 were originally released with die-cut, round-top covers.

[35] Motown claims to have issued this album, but no collector has yet been able to find it.

524	U.F.O. 1	U.F.O.	4/71
525	Toe Fat Two	Toe Fat	3/71
526	Sunday Funnies	Sunday Funnies	5/71
527	Magic	Magic	9/71
528	Stoney and Meatloaf	Stoney and Meatloaf	9/71
529	Down at the Brassworks	Impact of Brass	9/71
530	Dennis Stoner	Dennis Stoner	11/71
531	Jesus Christ's Greatest Hits	God Squad featuring Leonard Caston	1/72
532	Already a Household Word	Repairs	11/71
533	Head to Head	Other People	—
534	In Concert (2-LP set)	Rare Earth	12/71
535	—	—	—
536	Plight of the Redman	Xit	2/72
537	Howl the Good	Howl the Good	2/72
538	Benediction	Sunday Funnies	5/72
539	One Tree or Another	Keef James	5/72
540	The Crystal Mansion	Crystal Mansion	4/72
541	Wolfe	Wolfe	7/72
542	Matrix	Matrix	10/72
543	Willie Remembers	Rare Earth	10/72
544	Puzzle	Puzzle	NR
545	Silent Warrior	Xit	4/73
546	Ma	Rare Earth	5/73
547	—	—	—
548	Back to Earth	Rare Earth	6/75
549	Real Pretty (2-LP set)	Pretty Things	2/76
550	Midnight Lady	Rare Earth	3/76

END OF LABEL

SOUL

701	Shotgun	Jr. Walker and the All Stars	5/65
702	Soul Session	Jr. Walker and the All Stars	2/66
703	Road Runner	Jr. Walker and the All Stars	7/66
704	Sings Top Ten	Jimmy Ruffin	1/67
705	Live!	Jr. Walker and the All Stars	8/67
706	Everybody Needs Love	Gladys Knight and the Pips	8/67
707	Feelin' Bluesy	Gladys Knight and the Pips	4/68
708	Ruff 'n' Ready	Jimmy Ruffin	2/69
709	Here Comes the Judge	Shorty Long	8/68
710	Home Cookin'	Jr. Walker and the All Stars	1/69
711	Silk 'n' Soul	Gladys Knight and the Pips	12/68
712	—	—	—
713	Nitty Gritty	Gladys Knight and the Pips	9/69
714	Greetings! We're the Monitors	Monitors	11/68
715	The Earl of Funk	Earl Van Dyke	9/70
716	Green Grow the Lilacs (Baby I'm for Real)[36]	Originals	7/69
717	The Best of the Fantastic Four	Fantastic Four	2/69
718	Greatest Hits	Jr. Walker and the All Stars	5/69
719	The Prime of Shorty Long	Shorty Long	11/69
720	Switched on Blues	Various Artists	11/69
721	What Does It Take to Win Your Love (Gotta Hold on to This Feeling)[36]	Jr. Walker and the All Stars	11/69
722	How Sweet He Is	Fantastic Four	NR
723	Greatest Hits	Gladys Knight and the Pips	3/70
724	Portrait of the Originals	Originals	5/70
725	Live!	Jr. Walker and the All Stars	4/70
726	A Gasssss	Jr. Walker and the All Stars	9/70
727	The Groove Governor	Jimmy Ruffin	9/70
728	I Am My Brother's Keeper	David and Jimmy Ruffin	9/70
729	Naturally Together	Originals	9/70
730	All in a Knights Work	Gladys Knight and the Pips	9/70
731	If I Were Your Woman	Gladys Knight and the Pips	4/71
732	Rainbow Funk	Jr. Walker and the All Stars	6/71
733	Moody Jr.	Jr. Walker and the All Stars	12/71
734	Definitions	Originals	1/72
735	Soft and Warm	Blinky	NR
736	Standing Ovation	Gladys Knight and the Pips	12/71
737	Neither One of Us	Gladys Knight and the Pips	2/73
738	Peace and Understanding Is Hard to Find	Jr. Walker and the All Stars	4/73
739	All I Need Is Time	Gladys Knight and the Pips	6/73
740	Game Called Love	Originals	5/74

[36] Both albums were originally released under the title in parentheses, then reissued with the title of the hit single from the album.

741	Knight Time	Gladys Knight and the Pips	2/74
742	Jr. Walker and the All Stars	Jr. Walker and the All Stars	NR
743	California Sunset	Originals	NR
744	A Little Knight Music	Gladys Knight and the Pips	3/75
745	Hot Shot	Jr. Walker and the All Stars	1/76
746	Communique	Originals	5/76
747	Sax Appeal	Jr. Walker	6/76
748	Whopper Bopper Show Stopper	Jr. Walker	10/76
749	Down to Love Town	Originals	1/77
750	Smooth	Jr. Walker	4/78
751	Now Arriving	Major Lance	7/78

END OF LABEL

TAMLA[37]

220	Hi! We're the Miracles	Miracles	6/61
221	The Soulful Moods of Marvin Gaye	Marvin Gaye	6/61
222	The Great Gospel Stars	Gospel Stars	11/61
223	Cookin' with the Miracles	Miracles	11/62
224	Tamla Special No. 1	Various Artists	6/61
225	—	—	—
226	—	—	—
227	They Shall Be Mine	Rev. Columbus Mann	12/62
228	Please Mr. Postman	Marvelettes	11/61
229	Sing . . .	Marvelettes	4/62
230	I'll Try Something New	Miracles	7/62
231	Playboy	Marvelettes	7/62
232	Tribute to Uncle Ray	Little Stevie Wonder	10/62
233	The Jazz Soul of Little Stevie	Little Stevie Wonder	9/62
234	—	—	—
235	—	—	—
236	Christmas with the Miracles	Miracles	10/63
237	The Marvelous Marvelettes	Marvelettes	2/63
238	You've Really Got A Hold On Me[38]—The Fabulous Miracles	Miracles	2/63
239	That Stubborn Kind of Fellow	Marvin Gaye	1/63
240	Recorded Live! The 12 Year Old Genius	Little Stevie Wonder	6/63
241	On Stage, Recorded Live!	Miracles	6/63
242	On Stage, Recorded Live!	Marvin Gaye	9/63
243	On Stage, Recorded Live!	Marvelettes	6/63
244	Recorded Live at the Regal	Various Artists	NR
245	Doin' Mickey's Monkey	Miracles	11/63
246	—	—	—
247	—	—	—
248	Workout Stevie Workout	Stevie Wonder	NR
249	—	—	—
250	With a Song in My Heart	Stevie Wonder	12/63
251	When I'm Alone I Cry	Marvin Gaye	6/64
252	Greatest Hits	Marvin Gaye	4/64
253	Greatest Hits	Marvelettes	2/66
254	The Greatest Hits/From the Beginning (2-LP set)	Miracles	3/65
255	Stevie at the Beach	Stevie Wonder	6/64
256	16 Big Hits Vol. 2	Various Artists	6/64
257	Every Little Bit Hurts	Brenda Holloway	5/64
258	How Sweet It Is to Be Loved by You	Marvin Gaye	1/65
259	Gemini	Miracles	'64
260	Side by Side	Marvin Gaye and Kim Weston	NR
261	Tribute to the Great Nat King Cole	Marvin Gaye	11/65
262	—	—	—
263	—	—	—
264	Motortown Revue Recorded Live! In Paris	Various Artists	11/65
265	Hello Dummy	Willie Tyler and Lester	11/65
266	Moods of Marvin Gaye	Marvin Gaye	5/66
267	Going to a Go-Go	Smokey Robinson and the Miracles	11/65
268	Uptight	Stevie Wonder	5/66
269	This Old Heart of Mine	Isley Brothers	5/66
270	Take Two	Marvin Gaye and Kim Weston	8/66
271	Away We a Go-Go	Smokey Robinson and the Miracles	11/66
272	Down to Earth	Stevie Wonder	12/66
273	—	—	—
274	Marvelettes	Marvelettes	3/67
275	Soul on the Rocks	Isley Brothers	8/67

[37]Gordy, Tamla, and Motown labels were consolidated in December 1981.
[38]Originally titled the *Fabulous Miracles*, re-released with the title of the hit single

276	The Tears of a Clown (Make It Happen)[39]	Smokey Robinson and the Miracles	8/67
277	United	Marvin Gaye and Tammi Terrell	8/67
278	Greatest Hits Vol. 2	Marvin Gaye	8/67
279	I Was Made to Love Her	Stevie Wonder	1/68
280	Greatest Hits Vol. 2	Smokey Robinson & Miracles	1/68
281	Someday at Christmas	Stevie Wonder	11/67
282	Greatest Hits	Stevie Wonder	3/68
283	—	—	—
284	You're All I Need	Marvin Gaye and Tammi Terrell	8/68
285	In the Groove (I Heard It Through the Grapevine)	Marvin Gaye	8/68
286	Sophisticated Soul	Marvelettes	8/68
287	Doin' Their Thing	Isley Brothers	4/69
288	In Full Bloom	Marvelettes	9/69
289	Live!	Smokey Robinson and the Miracles	'69
290	Special Occasion	Smokey Robinson and the Miracles	8/68
291	For Once in My Life	Stevie Wonder	11/68
292	M.P.G.	Marvin Gaye	5/69
293	Marvin Gaye and His Girls	Marvin Gaye and His Girls	5/69
294	Easy	Marvin Gaye and Tammi Terrell	9/69
295	Time Out for Smokey Robinson and the Miracles	Smokey Robinson and Miracles	7/69
296	My Cherie Amour	Stevie Wonder	8/69
297	Four in Blue	Smokey Robinson and the Miracles	11/69
298	Live!	Stevie Wonder	3/70
299	That's the Way Love Is	Marvin Gaye	1/70
300	Super Hits	Marvin Gaye	9/70
301	What Love Has Joined Together	Smokey Robinson and the Miracles	4/70
302	Greatest Hits	Marvin Gaye and Tammi Terrell	5/70
303	Great Expectations	Kiki Dee	7/70
304	Signed Sealed Delivered	Stevie Wonder	8/70
305	Return of the Marvelettes	Marvelettes	9/70
306	Pocketful of Miracles	Smokey Robinson and the Miracles	8/70
307	The Season for Miracles	Smokey Robinson and the Miracles	11/70
308	Where I'm Coming From	Stevie Wonder	4/71
309	All by Myself	Eddie Kendricks	4/71
310	What's Going On	Marvin Gaye	5/71
311	Exposed	Valerie Simpson	5/71
312	One Dozen Roses	Smokey Robinson and the Miracles	8/71
313	Greatest Hits Vol. 2	Stevie Wonder	10/71
314	Music of My Mind	Stevie Wonder	3/72
315	People . . . Hold On	Eddie Kendricks	5/72
316	—	—	—
317	Valerie Simpson	Valerie Simpson	7/72
318	Flying High Together	Smokey Robinson and the Miracles	8/72
319	Talking Book	Stevie Wonder	11/72
320	1957–1972 (2-LP set)	Smokey Robinson and the Miracles	12/72
321[40]	—		
322	Trouble Man	Marvin Gaye	12/72
323	Nick and Val	Nickolas Ashford and Valerie Simpson	NR
324	—	—	—
325	Renaissance	Miracles	4/73
326	Innervisions	Stevie Wonder	8/73
327	Eddie Kendricks	Eddie Kendricks	5/73
328	Smokey	Smokey Robinson	6/73
329	Let's Get It On	Marvin Gaye	8/73
330	Boogie Down	Eddie Kendricks	2/74
331	Pure Smokey	Smokey Robinson	3/74
332	Fulfillingness' First Finale	Stevie Wonder	7/74
333	Live!	Marvin Gaye	6/74
334	Do It Baby	Miracles	8/74
335	For You	Eddie Kendricks	11/74
336	Don't Cha Love It	Miracles	1/75
337	A Quiet Storm	Smokey Robinson	3/75
338	The Hit Man	Eddie Kendricks	6/75
339	City of Angels	Miracles	9/75
340	Songs in the Key of Life (2-LP set + EP)	Stevie Wonder	9/76
341	Smokey's Family Robinson	Smokey Robinson	2/76
342	I Want You	Marvin Gaye	3/76
343	He's a Friend	Eddie Kendricks	1/76
344	The Power of Music	Miracles	9/76
345	Anyway You Like It	Thelma Houston	10/76

[39] Re-released with the title of the hit single
[40] The Tamla 321 number was assigned to the 8-track and cassette versions of Tamla 320 (a double LP), most likely to reflect the need for two tapes to handle the extra length.

346	Goin' Up in Smoke	Eddie Kendricks	9/76
347	Full Speed Ahead	Tata Vega	8/76
348	Greatest Hits	Marvin Gaye	9/76
349	One to One	Syreeta	1/77
350	Deep in My Soul	Smokey Robinson	1/77
351	Keep It Coming	Valerie Simpson	1/77
352	Live! At the London Palladium	Marvin Gaye	3/77
353	Totally Tata	Tata Vega	2/77
354	At His Best	Eddie Kendricks	1/78
355	Big Time	Smokey Robinson	6/77
356	Slick	Eddie Kendricks	8/77
357	Greatest Hits	Miracles	7/77
358	The Devil in Me	Thelma Houston	10/77
359	Love Breeze	Smokey Robinson	2/78
360	Try My Love	Tata Vega	2/79
361	Ready to Roll	Thelma Houston	10/78
362	Someday at Christmas	Stevie Wonder	10/78
363	Smokin' (2-LP set)	Smokey Robinson	10/78
364	Here My Dear (2-LP set)	Marvin Gaye	12/78
365	Ride to the Rainbow	Thelma Houston	5/79
366	Where There's Smoke	Smokey Robinson	5/79
367	Warm Thoughts	Smokey Robinson	2/80
368	I Just Need More Money	Shadee	7/79
369	—	—	—
370	—	—	—
371	Stevie Wonder's Journey Through the Secret Life of Plants (2-LP set)	Stevie Wonder	10/79
372	Here's My Love	Syreeta	4/80
373	Hotter Than July	Stevie Wonder	9/80
374	In Our Lifetime	Marvin Gaye	1/81
375	Being With You	Smokey Robinson	2/81
376	Set My Love in Motion	Syreeta	10/81

V.I.P.

400	Darling Baby	Elgins	8/66
401	Greetings! We're the Monitors	Monitors	NR
402	We're Off to Dublin in the Green	Abbey Tavern Singers	2/67
403	Teardrops Keep Falling on My Heart	Chuck Jackson	9/70
404	Stop the World—We Wanna Get On	Hearts of Stone	9/70
405	Second Time Around	Spinners	9/70
406	Ivy Jo Is in This Bag	Ivy Jo	'70
407	Heart of the Matter	King Floyd	4/71

END OF LABEL

WORKSHOP JAZZ

202	All Star Jazz	Earl Washington	11/63
203	Introducing Paula Greer	Paula Greer	2/63
204	Detroit Jazz	Paula Greer and Johnny Griffith Trio	—
205	Jazz	Johnny Griffith Trio	2/63
206	Blue Vibrations	Dave Hamilton	3/63
207	Boss Bossa Nova	George Bohannon Quartet	2/63
208	—	—	—
209	—	—	—
210	—	—	—
211	—	—	—
212	The Right Side of Lefty Edwards	Lefty Edwards	6/64
213	Reflections	Earl Washington	6/64
214	Bold Bohannon	George Bohannon Quartet	
215	—	—	—
216	The Soul and Sound of Herbie Williams	Herbie Williams	—
217	Breaking Through	Four Tops	NR
218	—	—	—
219	Compositions of Charlie Mingus	Pepper Adams	8/64
220	Beat	Roy Brooks	8/64

END OF LABEL

WEED

Gone in a wink, this particular subsidiary's claim to fame was its slogan: "All your favorite stars are on Weed." (LPs)

801	CC Rides Again	Chris Clark	11/69

END OF LABEL

ANSWERS TO TRIVIA QUESTIONS

1. Claudette Rogers
2. Stevland Morris
3. The Four Tops
4. Four
5. Hazel *Joy, Berry,* and *Terry Gordy* are the names of Berry's first three children.
6. "Funny" b/w "The Stretch" by the Contours (Motown 1012)
7. "Please Mr. Postman," first by the Marvelettes and the second time by the Carpenters
8. Shorty Long
9. The Pirates
10. Mary Wells
11. Thomas Chong of Cheech and Chong
12. Brenda Holloway
13. Marvin Gaye
14. The Monitors
15. The Valadiers
16. Autry DeWalt, Jr.
17. Tammy Montgomery
18. Gladys Knight
19. The Undisputed Truth
20. 1972
21. Eddie Holland, Lamont Dozier, and Brian Holland
22. The Marvelettes
23. From Detroit's *Van Dyke Avenue* and Motor City singer *Della* Reese
24. Kim Weston
25. Charles Hatcher
26. "For Once in My Life"
27. The Mynah Birds
28. Mowest Records
29. Berry Gordy, Freddie Perren, Fonzie Mizell, and Deke Richards
30. Tenor saxophone
31. G. C. Cameron
32. Freddie Gorman
33. The Elgins
34. Jimmy Ruffin and David Ruffin
35. The Contours and the Originals
36. Kennedy Gordy
37. Johnny Bristol
38. "Money"
39. Brian Holland
40. Smokey Robinson
41. Cholly Atkins
42. "My Beloved" b/w "Sugar Daddy" by the Satintones (Motown 1000)
43. Robert Gordy, Berry's brother, under the pseudonym Robert Kayli
44. The Isley Brothers
45. Barrett Strong
46. Jermaine Jackson
47. The Moonglows
48. A loose-knit collection of background singers named after *Raynoma Liles* and *Berry Gordy*
49. Eleven
50. James Jamerson (bass) and Benny Benjamin (drums)
51. The Reverend Dr. Martin Luther King
52. "Heat Wave"
53. "The Love I Saw in You Was Just a Mirage"
54. Billy Griffin
55. 1962
56. The Supremes
57. Billie Jean Brown
58. The Jacksons, Diana Ross, Smokey Robinson, and the Spinners
59. Six
60. "Cloud Nine" by the Temptations (1968)
61. The Jackson 5
62. "Merrily We Roll Along"
63. Chris Clark
64. "Motown 25: Yesterday, Today, Forever" in 1983
65. R. Dean Taylor, Deke Richards, Frank Wilson, Hank Cosby, and Berry Gordy
66. The 3-D Record Mart
67. "Let's Go Get Stoned"
68. Because Berry Gordy's first hit as a songwriter, Jackie Wilson's "Reet Petite," was numbered Brunswick 55024
69. So racist white record store owners would carry the albums
70. Flo Ballard
71. Joe Frazier
72. None
73. Twelve
74. Diane Ross
75. Willie Woods (guitar), Vic Thomas (organ), Junior Walker (tenor sax/vocals), and James Graves (drums)
76. Betty Kelly and Sandra Tilley
77. *The Wiz*
78. Jean Terrell
79. Dennis Edwards
80. Anna Gordy (Berry's sister)

81. Paul Williams, Eddie Kendricks, Otis Williams, Melvin Franklin, and Elbridge Bryant
82. Edwin Starr, using his real name of Charles Hatcher
83. *Little Stevie Wonder, the 12-Year-Old Genius* in 1963
84. *Mahogany*
85. "Please Mr. Postman" by the Marvelettes in 1961
86. Invictus Records and Hot Wax Records
87. "I Heard It through the Grapevine" by Marvin Gaye in 1968
88. *Talking Book* by Stevie Wonder in 1972
89. "Big Boy" b/w "You've Changed" on the Steel-town label in 1968
90. "Shop Around" by the Miracles in 1960
91. In order, they were: Mary Wells, Kim Weston, Tammi Terrell, and Diana Ross
92. Smokey Robinson
93. Diana Ross
94. "It" by Ron (nie White) and Bill (William "Smokey" Robinson) on Tamla Records in 1959
95. Johnny (Bristol) and Jackie (Beavers) on Tri-Phi Records in 1961
96. Katherine Anderson, Wanda Young, and Gladys Horton
97. "I've Never Been to Me" by Charlene
98. Eddie Kendricks
99. *Muscle Beach Party* and *Bikini Beach*
100. Levi Stubbs, Renaldo "Obie" Benson, Lawrence Payton, and Abdul "Duke" Fakir

Index

Abbey Tavern Singers, 200
ABC Records, 15, 45, 95, 145, 149, 198
Abdullah, 200
Abner, Ewart, 46
"Abraham, Martin and John," 175
Abrams, Al, 47
Ace, Johnny, 153
"Action Speaks Louder Than Words," 109
Adams, Pepper, 166
A.F.O. (All for One) Records, 45
Agent Double-O Soul, 18, 92, 165
"Ain't No Mountain High Enough," 15, 66, 97, 126, 136, 150 163, 192
"Ain't Nothing Like the Real Thing," 15, 98, 150, 163
"Ain't No Woman (Like the One I've Got)," 78
"Ain't That Love," 76
"Ain't That Loving You," 174
"Ain't That Peculiar," 79
"Ain't Too Proud to Beg," 119, 142
Ales, Barney, 47, 63, 65
Ales, Steve, 48
Alexander, George, Inc. Records, 96
Alexander, J. W., 45
Allen, Johhny, 121, 167
Allen, Richard "Pistol," 160
Allison, Luther, 200
"All Night Long (All Night)," 182
"All Right," 105
All-Stars, 99–100
Almost Summer, 172
Alpert, Herb, 145
Alto Records, 101
"Always," 105
American Gigolo, 88
American Graffiti, 173
A&M Records, 12, 176, 187
Andantes, 143
Anderson, Katherine, 38, 52, 54, 87, 125
"Angel," 40
Animal House, 172
Animals, 55
Anna Records, 27, 28, 34, 36, 71, 84, 109, 115, 138, 156
Anthony, Lamont, 34, 36, 42, 138
Argo Records, 32
Arista Records, 12, 187, 190
Armstrong, Louis, 22
Ashford, Jack, 157, 161, 166
Ashford, Nick, 15, 135, 136, 150–51, 161, 192, 193
Ashford, Rosalind, 41, 85, 86
Askey, Gil, 143, 170
"Ask the Lonely," 77, 149
Astral Weeks, 36
Atkins, Cholly, 50, 52, 121
Atlantic Records, 46, 92, 122, 150, 176, 190
Australian Jazz Quintet, 161
Avalon, Frankie, 48

"Baby Come Close," 191
"Baby Don't You Do It," 79
"Baby I'm for Real," 90
"Baby I Need Your Loving," 14, 76, 128, 140, 143, 161
"Baby Love," 22, 44, 94
"Back in My Arms Again," 94
"Bad Girl," 30, 31, 37
Baker, Chet, 177
Baker, LaVern, 70
Baker's Wife, 173
Ballard, Flo, 34, 35, 93–96, 137
Ballard, Hank, 70
"Ball of Confusion," 14, 119
Bananarama, 14
"Band of Gold," 144
Baraka, Imamu Amiri, 175
Barnes, J. J., 71, 85
Barnes, Ken, 205
Barret, Rona, 201
Barrow, Marlene, 143
Barry, Jeff, 94
Basic Black, 146
Bateman, Robert, 33, 40, 125, 138
Bat Out of Hell, 174
Beach Ball, 48
Beach Blanket Bingo, 172
"Beat It," 187
Beatles, 34, 45–46, 127, 129, 173
"Beauty Is Only Skin Deep," 64, 119, 130, 142
Beavers, 95
Be-Bop A-Lula, 18
Beck, Bogert and Appice, 198
Beck, Joe, 177
"Beechwood 4–5789," 87
B.E.F., 14
"Behind a Painted Smile," 81
"Being with You," 192
"Bells, The," 90
Bell, Thom, 92, 152
"Ben," 187
Benjamin, William "Benny," 75, 154, 156, 158, 159, 160, 161, 164, 167
Bennett, Cliff, 174
Bennett, Tony, 129
"Benny the Skinny Man," 36
Benson, George, 176
Benson, Renaldo "Obie," 75, 76, 77
Benton, Brook, 39
"Bernadette," 44, 131
Berry, Chuck, 134
Biegel, Irv, 65
"Big Bad John," 26
"Big Boy," 185
Big Chill, 173
Bigger Than Life, 146
Big Time, 172
Bikini Beach, 48
BillBoard, 22
"Billie Jean," 188
Billingslea, Billy, 74
Billingslea, Joe, 52, 54, 72, 73, 109, 135
Bingo Long and the Traveling All-Stars and Motor Kings, 171
Birdsong, Cindy, 95, 194, 195

Blackberries, 175
Black Fighting Men, 175
Black Forum Records, 58, 175, 207, 233
"Black Is Black," 152
"Blame It on the Boogie," 187
Bland, Bobby "Blue," 45
Blasters, 16
Blaze Records, 207
Blendells, 42
Blon, Jolé, 18
Bloodstone, 200
Blood, Sweat and Tears, 20, 128
Bloomfield, Mike, 79
"Blow' in the Wind," 151
Bluebelles, 95
Bluenotes, 168
Blue Scepter, 174
Blues Image, 176
Bogan, Anne, 87
Bohannon, George, 166
Bolan, Marc, 200
Bonnie and Friends, 177
"Bony Moronie," 30
"Boogie Down," 151, 190
"Boogie on Reggae Woman," 198
Boom, Taka, 195
Boone, Pat, 178
Bracken, James, 45
Braden, Michie, 155
Bradford, Berry, 27
Bradford, Janie, 27, 66
"Brainwasher, Pt. 2," 99
Bramlett, Delaney, 177
Brashler, William, 171
"Breathtaking Guy," 93
Breen, Bobby, 167
"Brick House," 180
Bridges, Beau, 201
Bristol, Johnny, 20, 40, 95, 135, 136, 150, 157, 164
Brokenshaw, Jack, 161
Brooks, Roy, 166
Brown, Arthur, 177
Brown, Billie Jean, 59–61, 63, 64, 65, 66–69, 124, 140, 147, 153, 158
Brown, Eddie "Bongo," 161, 166
Brown, Elaine, 175
Browne, Severin, 200
Brown, James, 97, 172
Brown, Jim, 201
"Brown Sugar," 198
Brunswick Records, 19, 31, 40, 83
Bryant, Elbridge "Al," 105, 107, 108, 109, 111, 114
Bryant, Willie, 70
Bryson, Wally, 177
Bucker, Teddy, 166
Buddah Records, 84, 144
Bullock, Robert, 63
Bunch, Jimmy Castor, 105
Burnette, Dorsey, 178
Burrell, Kenny, 166, 176
Bush, Eddie, 115
"Bustin' Out," 189
Butler, Billy, 165
Butler, Jerry, 45, 200
"Buttered Popcorn," 93
"Bye Bye Baby," 37, 102

"Call My Name," 176
Calvin, Billie, 196
Cameo-Parkway Records, 31
Cameron, G. C., 67, 92, 175
Campbell, Choker, 167, 200
"Can I Get a Witness," 58, 78
"Can't You See (I'm in Love with You)," 28
"Can You Do It," 74
Capitol-EMI Records, 12
Capitol Records, 15, 46, 144, 151
Captain and Tennille, 128
Carlo, Tyran, 19, 27, 28
Carlton, Carl, 14
Carlton Records, 26
Carmichael, James, 181
Carmichael, Stokley, 175
Carnes, Kim, 128
Carney, Art, 171
Carpenters, 128
Carroll, Diahann, 56, 167
Carter, Ron, 177
Carter, Vivian, 45
"Car Wash," 148
Casablanca Records, 78
Case, Scott Richards, 174–75
Casingettes, 87
Caston, Leonard, 151, 175, 190, 200
Caviar, 146
CBS Records, 12
Chairmen of the Board, 144
Chambers Brothers, 147
Chandler, Gene, 45
Chantays, 32
"Chapel of Love," 22
Charles, Joe, 40
Charles, Ray, 150
Checker Records, 97
Check-Mate Records, 27, 42, 85, 109, 138
"Check Yourself," 108
Cheech and Chong, 96
Chess Records, 27, 31, 32, 34, 37, 40, 41, 76
Chisa Records, 174, 175, 207, 234
Chong, Tommy, 96
Christie, Lou, 101, 178
Christman, Keith, 176
"Church of the Poison Mind," 15
Circle Jerks, 203
Clark, Chris, 170
Clay, Tom, 175
"Cleo's Mood," 99
Cliftons, 193
Clinton, George, 43, 158
"Cloud Nine," 119
Clowns, 74, 200
Coffey, Dennis, 161–62
"Cold Blooded," 189
Coles, Honi, 50
Collins, Phil, 14
Collins, Roger, 16
Colombo, Chris, 154
Columbia Records, 14, 76, 84, 148, 184
"Come and Get These Memories," 86, 137, 138, 152
"Come On and Be Mine," 73
"Come See about Me," 44, 94, 143

"Come to Me," 29, 30, 156
Commodores, 172, 175, 178, 179–82
Cone, Honey, 144
Congressional Black Caucus, 175
Conn, Didi, 172
Conners, Chuck, 201
"Contact," 93
Contours, 17, 38, 41, 54, 70, 72–74, 89, 109, 116, 117, 134, 135, 148, 149, 163
Cooke, Sam, 33, 45, 78, 115
Cooley High, 173
Corporation, 149
Cortez, Dave "Baby," 70
Cosby, Bill, 175
Cosby, Hank, 63, 95, 135, 141, 149, 151–53, 166, 167
Cosby, Pat, 63
Cotillion Records, 176
Country Music Holiday, 27
Covay, Don, 78
Cowart, Juanita, 87
Cox, Taylor, 65
Crawford, Carolyn, 134
Crawford, Hank, 177
Crawford, James, 105, 106
Creations, 41
Creedence Clearwater Revival, 129
Crothers, Scatman, 56
"Cruisin'," 191
Crusaders, 129
"Cry Baby Heart," 27
Crystals, 87, 152
C.T.I. Records, 176, 177, 204
Culture Club, 15
Curtis, King, 45, 166

"Daddy Could Swear, I Declare," 84
"Daddy's Home," 187
Dale, Dick, and His Del-Tones, 32
"Dance to the Music," 119
"Dancing in the Street," 14, 86, 142–43, 149, 173
"Dancing Machine," 151,185
"Danger Heartbreak Dead Ahead," 87, 149
Darin, Bobby, 200
"Darling Baby," 34, 74, 75, 144
Darnells, 87
Davis, Billy (Roquel), 19, 27, 28
Davis, Hal, 135, 151–53, 168
Davis, Hugh, 73,116
Davis, Ossie, 201
Davis, Sammy, Jr., 65, 66, 114, 200
Dawson, Johnny, 74
Day, Bobby, 29, 187
"Day Will Come," 39
Dazz Band, 12, 199
Dean, Debbie, 39
Dean, Jimmy, 26
"Dearest One," 41, 42
DeBarge, 199
Dee, Kiki, 174
Dell-Fi's, 42, 85, 86
Dells, 45
Del-Tones, 32
Demps, Louvain, 143
DeNiro, Robert, 172
Dennis, Bob, 62
de Passe, Suzanne, 63, 170
DePierro, Tom, 205
Desmond, Paul, 177
Detroit Emeralds, 71
Detroit Wheels, 129
"Devil with the Blue Dress," 55, 84, 128, 149

DeWalt, Autry, Jr. *See* Walker, Junior
Diablos, 71
Diana, 192
Diana Ross, 192
Dibango, Manu, 187
Diddley, Bo, 79
Disciples of Soul, 15
Distants, 34, 36, 105, 117, 123
Divinity Records, 58, 207
Dixie Cups, 22
Dixie Hummingbirds, 45, 109
Dixon, George W., 91, 92
Dixon, Hank, 89
Dixon, Herb, 90
Dobbins, Georgeanna, 38, 87
Doctor John, 18
Dodds, Malcom, 28
"Does Your Mama Know about Me," 96
"Do I Do," 15
"Do It Baby," 191
Dominos, 123
Donna Records, 80
"Don't Cha Love It," 191
"Don't Cost You Nothing," 151
"Don't Feel Sorry for Me," 39
"Don't Go Breaking My Heart," 174
"Don't Leave Me Starvin' for Your Love," 145
"Don't Leave Me This Way," 151, 168, 199
"Don't Let Him Shop Around," 39
"Don't Look Back," 119
"Don't Mess With Bill," 87, 134, 146
"Don't Stop the Music," 15
"Don't Stop 'Til You Get Enough," 187
Doobie Brothers, 82
Dorsey, Lee, 45
"Double Shot (Of My Baby's Love)," 179
Dove, Ronnie, 178
Downbeats, 75
"Do You Believe in Magic," 16
"Do You Love Me," 41, 72, 73, 109, 148, 149
"Do You Move Me," 17
Dozier, Lamont, 13, 20, 27, 28, 34, 41, 42, 44, 57, 63, 76, 77, 94, 95, 102, 109, 129, 131, 135, 136, 137, 138, 140, 141, 143, 144, 145, 146, 147, 149, 152, 153, 164
Dramatics, 71
"Dream Come True," 108
Drifters, 36, 39, 123
"Driving Wheel," 16
D-Town Records, 28
Duffy, William, 170
Duke Records, 45
Dunbar, Ronnie, 144, 145
Duncan, Charlene, 177
Dunhill Records, 78
Dylan, Bob, 132, 133, 192
Dynamics, 71
Dynamo Records, 185

Earl of Funk Album, 166
Earl Van Dyke Plays that Mo-town Sound, 166
Earl Van Dyke Trio, 155
"Easy," 181
Easybeats, 58, 174
"Ebony Eyes," 189
Eckstine, Billy, 56, 167
Ecology Records, 207
Edmunds, Dave, 58
Edwards, Bernard, 14, 192

Edwards, Charles "Lefty," 166
Edwards, Chico, 92
Edwards, Dennis, 72, 115, 116, 117, 120
Edwards, Esther Gordy, 19, 53, 58, 63, 65
Edwards, John, 92
Edwards, Sandra, 74
Edwards, Tommy, 78
Elaine Brown, 175
El Dorados, 45
Elgins, 34, 74–75, 108, 127, 144
Ellis, James, 33, 40
Emerson, Lake, and Palmer, 176
Endless Love, 181
End Records, 25, 28
English, David. *See* Franklin, Melvin
Enjoy Records, 45
"Enjoy Yourself," 187
Ensley Jubilees, 114
"Enter Through Any Door," 108
Epic Records, 187, 191
Equadors, 39
E Street Band, 15
Evans, Bill, 177
Everett, Betty, 45
Everlast Records, 45
"Every Beat of My Heart," 45, 83
"Everyday I Have the Blues," 203
"Every Day I More Inclined to Find My Baby," 133
"Every Little Bit Hurts," 65, 80
"Everyone Was There," 26

Fagin, John "Maurice," 89, 117
Fagin, Sandra, 89, 117
Fair, Yvonne, 200
Fakir, Abdul "Duke," 75, 76, 77
Falcons, 27, 71
Fambrough, Henry, 91
Family Stone, 119
Fantastic Four, 71, 200
Fantasy Records, 150
Farrell, Joe, 177
Fastbreak, 173
"Feeling Is So Fine," 36, 37
Ferry, Bryan, 192
5th Dimension, 129, 200
"Fingertips," 15, 103, 148
Finney, Albert, 200
"Fire," 177
Fire Records, 45
"First I Look at the Purse," 74, 134
"Fish Ain't Bitin'," 145
Fitzgerald, Ella, 117
Five Blind Boys, 45
Five Keys, 146
Five Royals, 123
Five Stars, 24
"Fix It," 191
Flamingos, 114, 123
Flanagan, Tommy, 166
Fleming, Robert, 75
Fleshtones, 16
Floyd, Eddie, 71
Floyd, King, 200
"Floy Joy," 195
Fontaine, Lon, 121
Fontana Records, 55
"Forever," 138
"For Once in My Life," 104, 129, 135, 151
Fortune Records, 71
"Found a Cure," 151
Four Aims, 75
Four Seasons, 45, 176
Four Tops, 13, 14, 42, 55, 75–78, 122, 131, 140, 143, 145, 149, 163, 164

Franklin, Aretha, 71, 129, 154
Franklin, Carolyn, 71
Franklin, C. L., 71
Franklin, Erma 71
Franklin, Melvin, 105, 106, 108, 110, 111, 114, 117, 118, 120, 122, 123, 156
Frazier, Joe, 177
Free Huey, 175
"From Me to You," 46
Fulson, Lowell, 203
"Function at the Junction," 85, 142
Funicello, Annette, 48
Funk Brothers, 154–67
"Funny," 73
Fuqua, Harvey, 20, 40, 41, 121, 135, 136, 150, 164
Furie, Sidney, 170
Fury Records, 45, 83

Gaiee Records, 178–79, 207
Gaines, Walter, 24, 27, 89, 90
Galaxy Records, 16
Gamble, Kenny, 152, 168
Garnes, Sherman, 117
Garrett, Kelly, 154
Gay, Council, 70, 72, 74, 116
Gaye, Marvin, 11, 12, 14, 15, 38, 41, 50, 58, 62, 78–80, 86, 89, 90, 97, 101, 102, 104, 125, 126, 136, 143, 147, 149, 150, 151, 152, 158, 161, 163, 172, 178, 183–85, 193, 201
Gaynor, Gloria, 128, 185
GeGe Records, 71
Gere, Richard, 88
"Get a Job," 25
"Get Ready," 119, 134, 146, 163, 166
"Get the Cream Off the Top," 145
"Getting Together on Broadway," 95
Gilbert, Cary, 168
Gill, Carolyn, 98
"Girl's Alright with Me," 142
"Girl (Why You Wanna Make Me Blue)," 105, 142
Gittens, James, 157
"Give It to Me Baby," 189
"Give Me a Kiss," 200
"Give Me Just a Little More Time," 144
Glass House, 194
Glick, Sammy, 26
Glover Records, 150
"God Save the Queen," 179
"Going to a Go-Go," 14, 88, 134, 146
"Going to the Hop," 33
"Goin' out of My Head," 97
Golden Boy, 66
Golden World Records, 40, 55, 139, 165
Goldner, George, 24, 25, 28
Gooding, Cuba, 200
"Good Morning Heartache," 193
"Good Night, Irene," 89
Gordon, Billy, 17, 52, 72, 73, 74, 109
Gordy, Anna, 19, 30, 41, 184
Gordy, Berry, Sr. (Pops), 19, 50, 161, 201
Gordy, Berry, Jr., 11, 16, 18, 19, 20, 21, 24, 26, 27, 28, 29, 30, 31, 32, 34, 38, 40, 41, 43, 46, 47, 48, 53, 54, 55, 56, 58, 59–69, 71, 73, 76, 87, 89, 93, 95, 103, 104, 107, 108, 109, 125, 126, 127, 129, 132, 134, 135,

137, 139, 148–49, 155, 156, 163, 164, 165, 166, 167, 169, 170, 171, 172, 189, 192, 201, 202
Gordy, Berry IV, 19, 48
Gordy, Bertha, 19
Gordy-Bristol, Iris, 63
Gordy, Fuller, 19
Gordy, George, 19, 164
Gordy, Gwen, 19, 27, 28, 40, 92
Gordy, Kennedy, 48–49, 50
Gordy, Kerry, 48–49
Gordy, Raynoma Liles, 28, 48
Gordy Records, 31, 39, 41, 55, 86, 87, 93, 96, 102, 108, 113, 178, 189, 190, 196, 199, 207–10, 234–35
Gordy, Robert, 19, 26
Gordy, Terry, 19
Gordy, Thelma Coleman, 19, 28, 71
Gore, Lesley, 176
Gorman, Freddie, 39, 49, 89, 90, 138, 139
"Got a Job," 25
"Got to be There," 187
"Got to Give It Up," 14, 184
Grand Funk Railroad, 129
"Grapevine," 80
Graves, James, 99, 100
Greatest Hits, Volumes 1–2 (Supremes), 13
Green, Al, 129
Greene, Susaye, 194, 195
Green, Jerry, 72, 116
Greenwich, Ellie, 94
"Greetings (This Is Uncle Sam)," 39, 89
Griffin, Billy, 89, 191
Griffin, Herman, 28
Griffith, Johnny, 157, 162–63, 166
Guest, William, 83
Gull Records, 174, 177, 204
Guys and Dolls, 173

Hale, Faye, 50, 65
Halen, Van, 14
Hamilton, Dave, 166
Hamlinson, Barry, 84
Hammer, Jack, 200
Handshake Records, 150
"Hang on in There Baby," 150
Hanks, Mike, 28
Hanna, Sir Roland, 166
"Happening, The," 95
"Happy People," 122
Hardin, Rim, 77
Harmonizing Four, 109
Harris, Barry, 166
Harris, Calvin, 63
Harris, Damon, 118
Harris, Joe, 195–96, 196
Harrison, Wilbert, 45
Harris, Warren, 89, 117
Harvey and the Moonglows, 78, 123
Harvey Records, 40, 84, 99, 156
Hatcher, Charles. *See* Starr, Edwin
Heard-Maclin, Fran, 63
"Heart of Glass," 193
"Heat Wave," 44, 86, 128, 143, 152
"Heaven Must've Sent You," 74, 75, 126, 144
"Hello Dolly," 22
Hell up in Harlem, 172
Henderson, Billy, 91
Henderson, Wes, 96, 175
Hendrix, Jimi, 82

"Here Comes the Judge," 65, 69, 84
Here, My Dear, 184
"He Was Really Sayin' Somethin'," 14, 99, 147
Hicks, Jackie, 143
"Higher Ground," 198
High Inergy, 199
Hill, Jessie, 45
Hinton, Joe, 200
"Hitch Hike," 78, 86, 149
Hitsville Records, 178, 211, 235
H.O.B. Records, 28
Hoggs, Billy, 72, 73
Holiday, Billie, 170, 193
Holland, Brian, 13, 20, 27, 28, 41, 44, 57, 62, 63, 65, 76, 77, 94, 95, 102, 125, 131, 135, 136, 137, 138, 140, 141, 143, 144, 145, 146, 147, 149, 152, 153, 164
Holland, Eddie, 13, 20, 27, 28, 30, 31, 41, 44, 57, 63, 76, 77, 94, 95, 102, 131, 133, 135, 136, 137, 138, 139, 140, 141, 142, 143, 144, 145, 146, 147, 149, 152, 153, 164
Holloway, Brenda, 20, 46, 49, 65, 80–81, 134, 146
Hollywood Fats, 18
"Hollywood Swinging," 179
"Honey Chile," 86
Hooker, John Lee, 34, 45, 70
"Hope and Pray," 27, 109
Horace Silver Quintet, 166
Hornets, 200
Horton, Gladys, 38, 87, 125
Hot Wax Records, 144
Houston, Tate, 166
Houston, Thelma, 151, 168, 169, 175, 199
"How Sweet It Is," 78, 128, 132, 143, 163
Hubbard, Freddie, 177
Huff, Leon, 152, 168
Hughes, Langston, 175
Hull, Ted, 161
Humble Pie, 129
Hungry Arms, 102
"Hungry for Love," 165
"Hunter Gets Captured by the Game," 13, 87
Hunter, Ivy Jo, 20, 63, 66, 77, 135, 142, 149, 156, 157, 164
Hunter, Janie, 184
Hunter, Ty, 27, 109
Huntom Records, 83
Hutch, Willie, 172

"I Call It Pretty Music but the Old People Call It the Blues," 103
"I Can't Believe You Love Me," 97
"I Can't Concentrate," 33
"I Can't Get Next to You," 118, 119
"I Can't Give Back the Love I Feel for You," 200
"I Can't Help Myself," 77, 136, 152, 163
"Ich-I-Bon #1," 32
"I Comma Zimba Zio," 200
"I Cry," 25
Ideals, 16
"I Didn't Know," 42
"I Don't Want to Do Wrong," 84, 150
"I Feel for You," 15
"I Feel Sanctified," 180
"If I Could Build My Whole

World Around You," 98, 150
"If I Were a Carpenter," 77
"If I Were Your Woman," 84, 135
"If You Can Want," 134
"I Gotta Dance to Keep from Crying," 88
"I Have a Dream," 48
"I Hear a Symphony," 94
"I Heard It through the Grapevine," 79, 84, 126, 147
"(I know) I'm Losing You," 119, 142, 163
"I Laid Such a Tender Trap/Hoping You Would Fall Into It," 133
"I'll Always Love You," 91, 92
"I'll Be Around," 92
"I'll Be Doggone," 79
"I'll Be Satisfied," 31
"I'll Be There," 151, 185
"I'll Cry Tomorrow," 55
"I'll Find You," 150
"I'll Have to Let Him Go," 86
"I'll Keep Holding On," 87, 149
"I'll Never Love Again," 32
"(I'm a) Roadrunner," 99, 143
"I'm a Sucker for Your Love," 190
"I'm Coming Out," 14, 192
"I'm in Love," 109
"I'm Ready for Love," 143
Impact Records, 92
"Indiana Wants Me," 57
"I Need a Change," 37
"I Need You," 28
"I Need Your Lovin'," 190
Inferno Records, 174, 211
"Inner City Blues (Make Me Wanna Holler)," 183
Invictus Records, 144
I.P.G. Records, 99
Isabell, Clarence, 156
"I Second That Emotion," 124
Isley Brothers, 14–15, 72, 81–82, 144
Isley, Ernie, 82
Isley, Marvin, 82
Isley, O'Kelly, 81
Isley, Ronald, 81
Isley, Rudolph, 81
"I Spy (for the F.B.I.)," 93
"It," 32
"It's All in the Game," 78
"It's a Shame," 13, 92
"It Seems to Hang On," 151
"It's Gonna Be Hard Times," 74
"It's Growing," 119
"It's My House," 193
It's Nation Time, 175
"It's the Same Old Song," 131
"It's What's Happening, Baby!" 203
"It's Your Thing," 15, 82
"It Takes Two," 80, 102, 135, 149
"It Will Stand," 45, 144
"I've Gotten Over You," 147
"I've Got the Music in Me," 174
"I've Never Been to Me," 177
Ivy Jo Is in the Bag, 149
"I Wanna Be Where You Are," 187
"I Want a Guy," 93
"I Want a Love I Can See," 105, 108
"I Want You," 184
"I Want You Back," 47, 149, 185
"I Was Born This Way," 178
"I Was Made to Love Her," 104, 135, 151
"I Wish," 198
"I Wish It Would Rain," 119

Jackson 5, 12, 14, 96, 128, 144, 149, 151, 172, 173, 178, 179, 180, 185–88, 201
Jackson, Chuck, 66, 109, 200
Jackson, Hazel Joy Gordy, 19, 187, 201
Jackson, Jackie, 179, 185, 186
Jackson, Janet, 55, 187
Jackson, Jermaine, 47, 185, 186, 187, 201
Jackson, Marlon, 179, 185, 186
Jackson, McKinley, 145
Jackson, Michael, 14, 145, 172, 179, 185–88, 193
Jackson, Milt, 177
Jackson, Pervis, 91
Jackson, Randy, 187
Jacksons, 72, 91, 187
Jackson, Tito, 179, 185, 186
Jagger, Mick, 89
Jaguars, 32
Jamal, Ahmad, 200
Jamerson, James, 154, 156, 157, 158, 164, 166
Jamerson, James, Jr., 157
James, Bob, 177
James, Elmore, 45
James, Rick, 12, 15, 57, 123, 178, 188–89, 190
"Jamie," 139, 149
Jams, 14
Jasper, Chris, 82
Jay and the Techniques, 200
Jazz Crusaders, 175–76
Jeles, Rebecca, 50
Jennings, Maurice, 165
Jiles, Rebecca, 63, 160
"Jimmy Mack," 86, 143
Jobete Publishing, 12, 26, 28, 30, 125, 127, 128–29, 133
John, Elton, 174
John, Little Willie, 70
John, Mable, 37
Johnny and Jackie, 95
Johnson, General, 145
Johnson, Hubert, 72, 73
Johnson, James. *See* James, Rick
Johnson, Marv, 19, 27, 29, 30, 31, 156
Johnson, Norman "General," 144
Jones, Floyd, 166
Jones, Gloria, 200
Jones, Hank, 166
Jones, James Earl, 171
Jones, Jonah, 200
Jones, Leroi, 175
Jones, Phil, 47, 63
Jones, Quincy, 188
Jones, Tony, 63
Jones, Uriel, 156, 160
Jones, Wade, 33
Joplin, Scott, 171
Journey through the Secret Life of Plants, 198
Jubilee Records, 102
Junior, 15
Ju-Par Records, 211, 235
"Just Ain't Enough Love," 81
"Just a Little Bit of You," 145
"Just a Little Misunderstanding," 72, 149, 163
"Just like Marvin [Gaye]," 16
"Just Like Romeo and Juliet," 139
"Just My Imagination (Running Away with Me)," 118, 120, 132, 190
"Just to Be Close to You," 181

Kable Records, 85
Kagny and the Dirty Rats, 49
"Kansas City," 45

Kaplan, Gabe, 173
Kayli, Robert, 19, 26
K-Doe, Ernie, 45
"Keep Holding On," 145
"Keep on Truckin'," 151, 190
Keith and Darell, 199
Kelly, Betty, 85, 86, 98
Kendricks, Eddie, 105, 106, 107, 108, 109, 112, 114, 117, 118, 119, 123, 145, 151, 190
Khan, Chaka, 15, 195, 198
"Kind of Boy You Can't Forget," 94
King, Ben E., 39
King, Martin Luther, Jr., 48, 175, 197
King, Maurice, 121, 167
King, Robbie, 96
Kingsmen, 34
King, William, 179, 180
Kinks, 87
"Kiss Me Baby," 76
Klein, Al, 63
Knight, Gladys and the Pips, 45, 66, 72, 79, 82–84, 127, 147, 150, 172
Knight, Merald "Bubba," 83
Knockouts, 194
Kool and the Gang, 16, 179
K.O. Records, 147
Kudu Records, 27, 174, 176, 177, 204

Labelle, Patti, 95
Lady Sings the Blues (album), 11, 193; (movie), 170
"La La La La La," 42
Lamont, 140, 144
Lance, Major, 199
Lanier, Patrick, 166
LePread, Ronald, 179, 180
Lasker, Jay, 46
Lateef, Yusef, 166
LaToya, Sisters, 187
Lavaille, Martha, 85
Lavette, Betty, 200
Lawrence, Lynda, 194
Leather Tuscadero, 177
"Leaving Here," 139
Lee, Laura, 144
Left Banke, 77
Legge, Wade, 166
Lennon, John, 34
Leonard, Glenn Carl, 118
"Let It Whip," 12
"Let Me Carry Your School-books," 185
"Let Me Go the Right Way," 93
"Let's Get It On," 184
"Let's Get Serious," 187
"Let's Go Get Stoned," 150
"Let's Pretend," 16
"Let's Talk It Over," 34, 36
"Letter Full of Tears," 84
"Let Your Conscience Be Your Guide," 78
"Let Your Hair Down," 122
Leverett, Chico, 32, 40
Lewis, Ramsey, 129
Lewis, Ted, 96
"Like a Rolling Stone," 132
Limeys, 73
"Linda Sue Dixon," 174
Little Anthony and the Imperials, 97
"Little Miss Ruby," 27
"Little Ol' Boy, Little Ol' Girl," 40
Little Richard, 132, 176
Little Steven, 15
Little Stevie Wonder, the 12-Year-Old Genius, 103

"Living for the City," 198
Lo and Joe, 40
"Locking Up My Heart," 152, 153
"Lonely Teardrops," 19, 26, 27
Long Ding Dong from Burma, 18
Long, Frederick "Shorty," 40, 55, 65, 66, 84–85, 89, 128, 142, 149, 154, 157, 164
Longhair, Professor, 44
Los Bravos, 152
Lost Chord, 27
"Love Child," 46, 95, 135, 149
"Love Don't Make It Right," 151
"Love Hangover," 151, 192
"Love I'm So Glad I Found You," 40
"Love I Saw in You Was Just a Mirage," 88
"Love Is Here and Now You're Gone," 95
"Love Is Like an Itching in My Heart," 95
"Love Machine," 191
"Love Me All the Way," 102
Love Sculpture, 58, 174
"Love's Gone Bad," 57
"Love You Save," 149, 185
"Loving You Is Sweeter Than Ever," 77, 149, 163
Lupine Records, 34
Lymon, Frankie, 117, 123, 193

Mabley, Moms, 66
"Machine Gun," 180
Mack, Sammy, 33, 40
Mack, The, 172
Mafie, Kasuku, 166
Mahogany, 170, 172
Mallett, Sandra, 74, 86
"Mama Loocie," 41
"Mama Used to Say," 15
Manticore Records, 174, 176, 204
Marchan, Bobby, 200
Mark-X Records, 24
Marquees, 78
Martha and the Vandellas, 12, 14, 41, 42, 44, 53, 58, 74, 78, 85–86, 94, 121, 138, 143, 149, 173
Martin, Barbara, 34, 35, 93
Martin, Tony, 167
Marvelettes, 13, 20, 38, 40, 41, 52, 53, 54, 86–87, 125, 127, 128, 133, 134, 138, 141, 142, 143, 146, 147, 149, 153, 173
Marvin Records, 66
"Mary Jane," 189
Masekela, Hugh, 175
Mason, Dave, 84
"Master Blaster Jammin'," 198
"Masterpiece," 122
Matheson, Tim, 172
Mathews, Johnnie Mae, 107
Maxwell, Larry, 63
Maxx Records, 84
Mayfield, Curtis, 147
MCA Records, 12, 148
McClary, Thomas, 179, 180
McCloy, Terence, 170
McCoy, Van, 193
McCracklin, Jimmy, 165
McJohn, Goldie, 57
McLain, Michael, 61
McNair, Barbara, 56, 167
M.C. Records, 211, 236
Mean Street, 172–73
Megaphone Records, 146
Melodyland Records, 177–78, 212, 236

Mel-O-Dy Records, 41, 86, 108, 138, 211–12
Melvin, Harold, 168
"Memo from Turner," 89
Merced Blue Notes, 56–57
Mercury Records, 27, 139
"Mercy Mercy Me," 183
Merrick, David, 173
"Merrily We Roll Along," 103
"Merry Go Round," 30
Messengers, 200
Messina, Joe, 157, 162, 165
MGM Records, 102, 149, 150, 185
"Miami Vice," 18
Michelle, 196
"Mickey's Monkey," 88, 129, 143, 172
Midnighters, 70, 123
"Midnight Train to Georgia," 84
Milburn, Amos, 200
Miles, Larry, 62
Miles, Otis. *See* Williams, Otis
Miller, Cleo "Duke," 74–75
Miller, Ron, 135
Mills, Stephanie, 202
"Mind Over Matter," 41, 108
Minit Records, 45
Minor, Raynard, 165
Miracle Records, 39, 108, 212–13
Miracles, 11, 12, 14, 15, 24–25, 30, 31, 32, 33, 36, 37, 41, 49, 53, 58, 63, 66, 74, 79, 87–89, 102, 106, 109, 110, 127, 133, 134, 143, 146, 148, 164, 172, 187, 191
"Miserlou," 32
Mitchell, Blue, 166
Mitchell, McKinley, 16
Mitchell, Willie, 165
Mizell, Fonce, 47, 149
Mohammad Ali, 54, 103
"Money," 34, 126, 127, 148
Monitors, 39, 89, 117
Montgomery, Monk, 175
Montgomery, Tammy. *See* Terrell, Tammi
Moody Blues, 27
Moody, Doug, 205
Moonglows, 41
Moore, Pete, 134, 146, 164
Moore, Warren "Pete," 25, 87–88, 191
"More Love," 128
Morris, Keith, 203
Morrison, Van, 36
Morris, Steveland, 102. *See* Wonder, Stevie
"Mother-in-Law," 45
"Motor City," 33
Motorhead, 129
Motortown Revues, 53
"Motown 25," TV 168, 203
Motown Records, 28, 33, 36, 37, 39, 40, 41, 42, 43–44, 46, 47, 48–50, 52–58, 59–69, 72, 78, 80–81, 82, 84, 85, 86, 92, 93, 95, 99, 100, 102, 104, 119, 122, 123, 126, 127, 135, 144, 150, 151, 152, 156, 168, 170, 171, 213–23, 236–41, 242–43
Mowest Records, 223–24, 241
Moy, Sylvia, 135
"Mr. Bus Driver, Hurry," 109
MRC Records, 28
Muhammed, Idris, 177
Murphy, Carla, 28, 29
Murphy, Eddie, 197
Murray, Bill, 71
Murray, Juggy, 45

Muscle Beach Party, 48
"Muscles," 193
Musical Youth, 145
"My Baby-O," 27
"My Beloved," 36
"My Girl," 118, 146, 162
"My Guy," 14, 22, 100, 101, 146
"My Heart Can't Take It Anymore," 93
"My Mistake," 151, 193
Mynah Birds, 57, 189
"My Smile Is Just a Frown Turned Upside Down," 134
"My Whole World Ended the Moment You Left Me," 135, 150, 193
"My World Is Empty Without You," 94–95

"Nathan Jones," 151, 195
Natural Resources Records, 176, 224, 243–44
Naylor, Jerry, 178
Nebraska, 57
"Needle in a Haystack," 99
"Need Your Loving," 30, 89
"Neither One of Us (Wants to Be the First to Say Goodbye)," 84
"Never Can Say Goodbye," 128, 185
"New Kind of Woman," 145
Nick and the Jaguars, 32
Noonan, Tom, 63
Northern Records, 105, 106, 107
Norton, Margaret, 48
"Nothing But Heartaches," 94
"Nowhere to Run," 86, 143

Ocha, Betty, 63
Off the Wall, 14, 187
"Oh How Happy," 92
"Oh, Mother o Mine," 108
OKeh Records, 78
Oldham, Andrew Loog, 175
"Once Upon a Time," 80, 101
100 Proof Aged in Soul, 89, 144
One-der-ful Records, 16
"One Fine Day," 193
"One More Heartache," 79
"One Who Really Loves You," 41, 93, 100, 134, 146
"Only Time I'm Happy," 95
"Ooh Baby Baby," 88, 128
"Ooh Poo Pah Doo," 45
"Ooh Shucks," 24
"Oops, I'm Sorry," 27
Orange, Walter, 179, 180
Originals, 24, 27, 39, 89–90, 139
Oriole Records, 55
Orioles, 146
Orlando, Tony, and Dawn, 129
Osmond, Donny and Marie, 129
Ossman, Mike 63
Otis, Johnny, 176
Our Lifetime, 184
Ousley, Curtis, 45, 166

Palmer, Bruce, 57
"Papa Was a Rollin' Stone," 14, 118, 120, 196
"Paradise," 105, 108
Parker, Charlie, 162
Parker, Little Junior, 16, 45
Parliaments, 71, 144
Patten, Edward, 83
Patterson, Eddie, 96
Patterson, Norris, 166
Paul, Clarence, 63, 135, 149, 151–53, 157, 161, 163
Payne, Freda, 144, 154, 166
Payne, Scherrie, 194, 195

Payton, Lawrence, 75, 76, 77
Peacock Records, 45
"Pecos Kid," 105
"Pennies from Heaven," 42
Peoples, 15
Performance, 89
Perkins, Anthony, 170
Perkins, Bobby, 145
Perren, Freddie, 47, 149
Perry, Greg, 145
Peters, Nancy, 27
Peterson, Paul, 56
"Pet Names," 134
P.F.M. and Banco, 176
Pharoahs, 179
Philadelphia International Records, 168
Phillips, Esther, 176
Pickett, Wilson, 16, 71, 72
Pipe Dreams, 84
"Pipeline," 32
Pippin, 173
Pips, 45, 66, 72, 79, 82–84, 127, 150, 172
Pirates, 41, 108
Platters, 27, 123
"Playboy," 40, 41, 87, 138
"Please Mr. Postman," 38, 40, 87, 127, 128, 138, 173
Poets, 44
Pointer, Bonnie, 199
Poitier, Sidney, 22
Pollack, Ed, 165
Polydor Records, 187
PolyGram Records, 12
"Popeye," 36
"Pops, We Love You," 201
Poree, Anita, 190
Porter, Cole, 134
Potts, Sylvester, 72, 73, 116
Preston, Billy, 173, 200
Pretty Things, 174
Price, Diana, 18
"Pride and Joy," 78, 86, 149
Primes, 106
Primettes, 34, 93, 106
Prince, 16
Prodigal Records, 177, 224–25, 244
Pryor, Richard, 56, 171
"Psychedelic Shack," 163
"Purple Raindrops," 104

Quatro, Michael, 177
Quatro, Suzie, 177
"Quicksand," 143
"Quiet Storm," 191

Raglin, Melvin, 161
Rainbows, 78
Rare Earth Records, 57, 174, 225, 244–45
Raspberries, 16, 177
Rationals, 140
Rawls, Lou, 45, 129
Rayber Records, 32–33
Rayber Voices, 28
Ray, Johnny, 70
RCA Records, 12, 14, 193
"Reach Out and Touch (Somebody's Hand)," 151
"Reach Out, I'll Be There," 13, 44, 77, 131, 136
Reddick, James, 145
Redding, Otis, 16, 129
Rednow, Eivets, 200
Red Robin Records, 45, 78
Reed, Jimmy, 45
Reese, Della, 70, 86
"Reet Petite," 19, 20, 24, 32
Reeves, Lois, 86

Reeves, Martha. *See* Martha and the Vandellas
"Reflections," 69, 71, 95, 139
"Remember Me," 151
Rhodes, Todd, 70
Richards, Deke, 47, 95, 149
Richie, Lionel, 12, 179–80, 181, 182
Ric-Tic Records, 40, 44, 55, 92, 93, 165
"Ride Captain Ride," 176
Righteous Brothers, 152
Ripples and Waves, 185
Riser, Paul, 143, 166, 167
Riverside Records, 42
Rivers, Johnny, 128
Robey, Don, 45
Robin Records, 45
Robinson, Bobby, 45, 83
Robinson, Claudette Rogers, 24–25, 60, 63, 88
Robinson, William "Smokey," 12, 13, 15, 20, 25, 29, 32–33, 37, 42, 60, 63, 65, 67, 68, 74, 78, 80, 87–89, 91, 93, 108, 110, 120, 121, 124, 129, 132, 133, 134, 135, 136, 146, 149, 156, 172, 189, 191, 195, 201
Rock-A-Teens, 32
"Rockin' Behind the Iron Curtain," 200
"Rockin' Robin," 29, 187
Rockwell, 48, 49, 50
"Rock with You," 187
Rodgers, Nile, 14, 192
Rogers, Bobby, 25, 87, 135, 164, 191
Rogers, Lee, 71
Rolling Stones, 14, 34, 129, 140, 172, 175, 198
Romeos, 138
Ronettes, 54, 152
Ronstadt, Linda, 12, 128
Ross, 192
Ross, Diana, 11, 12, 14, 15, 34, 35, 68–69, 91, 93–96, 126, 136, 137, 141, 142, 150, 151, 169, 170, 172, 173, 178, 181, 185, 188, 192–93, 194, 201
Ross, T-Boy, 184, 200
Roxy Music, 16, 192
Royals, 70, 83
Royce, Rose, 148
Ruffin, David, 27, 39, 90, 105, 106, 109, 111, 114–15, 116, 117, 118, 119, 123, 147, 150, 193–94
Ruffin, Jimmy, 38, 39, 89, 90–91, 149
Rufus, 198
"Run Run Run," 94
Ryan, Irene, 56
Ryder, Mitch, 129

Saleem, Abdul, 167
Sales, Soupy, 56, 154, 162
"Sally, Go 'round the Roses," 195
Sam and Dave, 16
Sam Remo Golden Strings, 165
Sam the Sham, 18, 179
Sanders, Sonny, 33, 40, 165
Santamaria, Mongo, 129
Sar Records, 45
Satellite Records, 16
Satintones, 33, 36, 39–40, 138
"Save the Overtime for Me," 84
Sawyer, Pam, 95, 135
Scott Joplin, 171

Sebastian, John, 16
Seltzer, Ralph, 58, 63, 165
Serenaders, 55
Sex Pistols, 179
"Sexual Healing," 14, 184
Seymour, Robin, 58
Shades of Blue, 93
"Shake Sherrie," 74
"Shakey Ground," 119, 122
"Shake Your Body Down to the Ground," 187
Shannon, Scott, 177
"She Blew a Good Thing," 44
Shep and the Limelites, 66, 187
Sheppard, Wyatt "Big Boy," 30
"She's Loving Good," 16
Shields, Brooke, 181
Shirelles, 39, 41, 66, 93
"Shock," 27
"Shoeshine Boy," 190
"Shoo-Be-Doo-Be-Doo-Dah-Day," 104, 151
"Shop Around," 11, 37, 88, 128, 138, 146, 148, 149
Shorter, Willie, 167
"Shotgun," 12, 99, 148, 149
"Shout," 14, 81
Showmen, 45, 144
"Signed, Sealed, Delivered I'm Yours," 104
Silhouettes, 25
"Silly Wasn't I," 151
Silverstein, Robert Ellis, 193
Simpson, Valerie, 15, 135, 136, 150–51, 163, 192, 193
"Since I Don't Have You," 36
"Since I Lost My Baby," 14, 119
Singleton, Raynoma, 63
"Sir Duke," 198
Skyliners, 36
Sledge, Sister, 14
"Sleepin'," 193
"Slippery When Wet," 180
"Slipping Away," 145
Small Faces, 16
"Small Sad Sam," 26
"Smiling Faces Sometimes," 147, 196
Smith, Bobbie, 91
Smith, Huey "Piano," 74
Smith, Winston, 49
"Snake Walk," 31
"Society's Child," 96
"Solid Sender," 32
"Somebody's Been Sleeping," 144
"Somebody's Watching Me," 49
"Someday We'll Be Together," 95, 150
"Someone to Call My Own," 39
Sonnettes, 147
"Soul Makossa," 187
Soul Records, 55, 84, 90, 99, 178, 199–200, 226–27, 245–46
"Soul Stomp," 166
"Soul Twist," 45
Spaniels, 45, 123
Spector, Phil, 46, 152
Spector, Ronnie, 54
Spencer, C. P., 24, 27, 89, 90, 92
Spinners, 13, 40, 67, 72, 91–92
"Splitsville," 144
Springfield, Buffalo, 57
Springsteen, Bruce, 15, 57
"Square Biz," 190
"Standing in the Shadows of Love," 44, 77, 131
"Standing on the Top," 15, 123
Stark, John, 171
Starr, Edwin, 14, 44, 47, 52, 56, 71, 92–93, 132, 147, 150, 165, 172

Stateside Records, 55
Stax-Volt, 16
"Stay," 93
Steeltown Records, 185
Stein and Van Stock, 129
Steppenwolf, 57
Sterling, Annette, 41, 85
Stevenson, Mickey, 20, 42, 63, 65, 77, 85, 86, 99, 102, 125, 135, 141, 142–43, 149, 160, 163, 164, 166
Stewart, Billy, 78
Stewart, Rod, 129
"Still," 181
"Still Water (Love)," 78
"Stoned Love," 151, 195
Stone, Sly, 119
Stoney and Meatloaf, 174
"Stop Her on Sight," 44, 92
"Stop! In the Name of Love," 94
"Strange I Know," 138
Stray Dog, 176
"Street Corner," 151
Street, Richard, 89, 105, 106, 111, 116, 117
Street Songs, 189
"Stretch, The," 73
Strong, Barrett, 20, 33, 34, 126, 127, 132, 133, 135, 146, 148, 196
Strong, Nolan, 70, 108
Strunk, Joe, 178
"Stubborn Kind of Fellow," 11, 12, 78, 149
Stubbs, Joe, 71, 72, 89, 90, 144
Stubbs, Levi, 13, 75, 76, 77, 78, 131
Sue Records, 45
Summer, Donna, 172
"Summertime," 132
Sunday Funnies, 175
"Super Freak," 189
"Superstition," 130, 197
Supremes, 13, 14, 17, 22, 34, 38, 41, 44, 46, 47, 48, 53, 55, 58, 78, 93–96, 121, 137, 140, 143, 149, 150, 151, 155, 172, 173, 194–95
Swan Silvertones, 109
"Sweet Love," 180
Swingin' Medallions, 179
Swingin' Tigers, 31
Swing Time Records, 203
Switch, 199
Symbol Records, 44
Szabo, Gabor, 177

"Take Me in Your Arms (Rock Me a Little While)," 81, 102, 143–44
"Take My Heart," 16
Talking Book, 104
Talking Heads, 16
"Talk That Talk," 31
T.A.M.I. Show, 172
Tamla Records, 11, 26, 28, 29, 30, 31, 32, 33, 34, 36, 37, 38, 41, 55, 71, 74, 75, 78, 80, 81, 87, 88, 93, 97, 102, 103, 168, 178, 190, 199, 227–32, 246–48
Tarplin, Marv, 15, 79, 135
Tattoo, 177
Taylor, Bobby, 58, 96, 175
Taylor, Creed, 176
Taylor, D. Dean, 95
Taylor, James, 16, 128
Taylor, Johnnie, 45
Taylor, R. Dean, 57, 174
"Tears of a Clown," 88, 134
"Tears of Sorrow," 34
techniques, 200

Teenagers, 117, 123, 193
Teena Marie, 190–91
"Tell Me Something Good," 198
"Tell Me Tomorrow," 15
Temptations, 14, 15, 27, 34, 38, 39, 41, 53, 65, 74, 90, 105–23, 134, 136, 142, 145, 146, 147, 162, 163, 166, 172, 173, 190
Terrell, Ernie, 194
Terrell, Jean, 194, 195
Terrell, Tammi, 15, 62, 66, 80, 97–98, 126–27, 136, 150, 151, 163
"Terrible," 183
Terry, Mike, 166
Thank God It's Friday, 172
"That Girl," 15, 198
"That's the Reason Why," 99
"That Sucks," 183
"That's What Girls Are Made For," 40, 92
"That's Why," 31
Thee Image, 176
Thelma Records, 71
"Theme from Mahogany (Do You Know Where You're Going To)," 192
"There Goes My Baby," 36
"There He Goes," 99
"There He Is (at My Door)," 41, 86
"There She Goes Again," 78
"These Things Will Keep Me Loving You," 99
"Think," 174
"39–21–46," 144
"This Heart of Mine," 27
"This Is Our Night," 41
"This Old Heart of Mine," 15, 81, 144
Thomas, Jamo, 93
Thomas, Vic, 99, 100
"Three Times a Lady," 181
Thriller, 14, 187, 188
Tilley, Sandra, 86, 98
Tinpanalli, Tony, 104
"Tisket, A Tisket, A," 116–17
T-Neck Records, 15, 82
"To Be Loved," 26
"Tomorrow and Always," 40
"Too Busy Thinking About My Baby," 79–80
"Too Hurt to Cry," 87
"Too Many Fish in the Sea," 87, 142, 147
"Touch Me in the Morning," 135, 192
Toussaint, Allen, 45
"Town I Live In," 16
"Tracks of My Tears," 88, 128, 133, 146
T. Rex, 200
Tri-Phi Records, 40, 84, 92, 95, 156
Trouble Man, 172
Trudeau, John, 167
"Trying to Hold on to My Woman," 145
Try Me Records, 97
Tunedrops, 28
Turbans, 123
Turner, Dan, 156
Turner, Ike, 45
Turner, Tina, 14, 45
Turrentine, Stanley, 177
"Tutti Frutti," 132
20th Century-Fox Records, 28, 101

20th Century Records, 93
"Twenty-five Miles," 47, 93, 150
"Twist and Shout," 14, 81, 109
"Twistin' Postman," 138
"Twistlackawanna," 99
"Two Faces Have I," 101, 178
"Two Lovers," 41, 100, 101
Tyler, Willie and Lester, 56
Tyson, Ron, 118

Uggams, Leslie, 56, 201
Underdogs, 57
Undisputed Truth, 147, 195–96
United Artists Records, 19, 30, 31, 139
Upchurch, Phil, 165
"Upside Down," 14, 192
"Up the Ladder to the Roof," 151, 195
"Uptight," 13, 15, 103, 135, 149
"Urgent," 100

Valadiers, 39, 89
Valentinos, 45, 178
Valli, Frankie, 175
Vancouvers, 96, 175
Vanda, Harry, 58
Vandellas, 12, 14, 41, 42, 53, 58, 74, 78, 85–86, 94, 121, 138, 143, 149, 173
Van de Pitte, Dave, 167
Vandross, Luther, 14
Van Dyke, Earl, 154, 155, 156, 157, 160, 161, 162, 165, 166–67
Van Halen, Eddie, 188
Vanilla Fudge, 128
Vee-Jay Records, 45, 83
Vells, 41, 42, 86
Velvelettes, 14, 86, 98–99, 142, 147
Velvet Underground, 78
Venture Records, 149
V.I.P. Records, 55, 75, 89, 92, 99, 149, 176, 195, 199, 200, 232–33
Vita, Larry, 156
Vocaleers, 45
Voice Masters, 27, 28, 109, 138
Volumes, 71

Wakefield, Loucye Gordy, 19, 53
"Walk Away from Love," 193
"Walk Away Renee," 77
Walker, Junior, 12, 40, 55, 99–100, 135, 143, 148, 150
"Walk in the Night," 99
Wand Records, 15, 97
"Wanna Be Startin' Somethin'," 187
"Want Ads," 144
"War," 14, 93, 147
Ware, Leon, 184, 200
Warner Bros. Records, 15, 145, 148, 151, 194
Warwick, Dee Dee, 54
Warwick, Dionne, 54, 175, 201
Warwick Records, 105
Washington, Dinah, 70, 176
Washington, Grover, 176
Washington, Tom-Tom, 165
Watson, Wah-Wah, 161
Wayne, Edith, 144
"Way over There," 36, 37, 108
"Way You Do the Things You Do, The," 109, 110

WEA Records, 12
Weatherspoon, William, 149
Webb, Jimmy, 195
Wells, Mary, 14, 20, 22, 28, 37, 40, 41, 49, 54, 67, 68, 80, 86, 93, 100–2, 134, 146
"We're Almost There," 145
Weston, Kim, 80, 81, 102, 121, 143, 149, 164
"What a Difference a Day Makes," 176
"What Becomes of the Broken-hearted," 90, 149
"What Does It Take (to Win Your Love)," 99, 150
"Whatever Happened To," 175
What's Going On, 80, 183
"What's So Good About Good-bye," 133
"What's the Matter with You Baby," 80, 101
"What the World Needs Now," 175
Wheelsville Records, 28
"When I'm Gone," 80, 134, 146
"When She Was My Girl," 78
"When the Lovelight Starts Shining through His Eyes," 94
"Where Did Our Love Go," 22, 44, 94, 136, 140, 141, 163
White, Robert, 154, 156, 161, 162, 166
White, Ronnie, 24–25, 32, 58, 87, 102, 134–35, 146, 191
Whitfield, Norman, 20, 63, 119, 120, 121, 135, 136, 142, 146–47, 149, 157, 162, 163–64, 196
Whitfield Records, 147–48, 196
"Whole Lotta Woman," 73
"Who Wouldn't Love a Man Like That," 37
"Why Can't We Be Lovers," 145
"Why Do Fools Fall in Love," 193
Why I Oppose the War in Vietnam, 175
Wiggins, Jay, 71
Wiliams, Paul, 70
Wilkins, Jimmy, 167
Williams, Andre, 70
Williams, Billy Dee, 170, 171
Williams, Gloria, 42, 85, 86
Williams, Herbie, 166
Williams, Larry, 30, 200
Williams, Maurice, 39, 93
Williams, Milan, 179, 180
Williams, Otis, 105, 106, 107, 108, 111, 112, 114, 117, 118
Williams, Paul, 106, 107, 114, 117, 118
Williams, Tony, 27
Williams, Vernon, 33, 40
Willis, Eddie, 157, 162
"Will You Still Love Me Tomorrow," 39, 40
Wilson, Frank, 63, 95, 135, 151–53, 190, 200
Wilson, Jackie, 19, 23, 24, 26, 27, 28, 29, 31, 32, 37, 39, 42, 70, 73, 114, 115, 139, 154
Wilson, Leonard, 151
Wilson, Mary, 34, 35, 93–96, 94, 137, 194, 195
Wingate, Eddie, 55, 165
"With You I'm Born Again," 173
Wiz, The, 172

Womack, Bobby, 45
Womack, Cecil, 45
Wonder, Stevie, 12, 13, 15, 26, 42, 46, 48, 53, 54, 55, 58, 61, 77, 89, 102–4, 121, 130, 148, 149, 151, 152, 154, 161, 163, 178, 187, 195, 197–99, 201
"Won't You Let Me Know," 85
Wood, Ronnie, 140
Woodson, Ollie, 118
Woods, Willie, 99, 100
"Woo-Hoo," 32
"Wooly Bully," 179
Workshop Jazz Records, 166, 233, 248
Workshop Records, 58, 76
Wright, Art, 168
Wright, Rita, 200
Wright, Syreeta, 173, 175, 199, 200
Writers of the Revolution, 175
Wylie, Popcorn, 164
Wynne, Phillippe, 92

X, 16
XIT, 175

Yarbrough, 15
"Ya-Ya," 45
"Yester-Me, Yester-You, Yesterday," 135
"You," 27
"You and I," 189
"You Are," 181
"You Are the Sunshine of My Life," 198
"You Beat Me to the Punch," 41, 101, 133
"You Can't Hurry Love," 14, 95, 136
"You Don't Have to Be Twenty-one to Fall in Love," 185
"You Got What It Takes," 19, 31, 37
"You Haven't Done Nothin'," 198
"You Keep Me Hangin' On," 95, 128
"You Lost and I Won," 16
"You Make Your Own Heaven and Hell Right Here on Earth," 196
Young, George, 58
Young, Neil, 57
Young, Wanda, 38, 87, 153
"Your Baby's Back," 75
"You're All I Need to Get By," 98, 150
"You Really Got Me," 87
"You're a Special Part of Me," 193
"You're My Desire," 39
"You're My Everything," 119
"Your Heart Belongs to Me," 93
"Your Precious Love," 62, 98
"You've Made Me So Very Happy," 20, 80, 128
"You've Really Got a Hold on Me," 41, 88, 127, 133

Zadora, Pia, 153
Zandy, Miami Steve Van, 15
Zappa, Frank, 74
Zimmerman, Robert, 192
Zodiacs, 39, 93
Zombies, 55